Angel of Apocalypse
BLAKE'S IDEA OF MILTON

Angel of Apocalypse

BLAKE'S IDEA OF MILTON

JOSEPH ANTHONY WITTREICH, JR.

THE UNIVERSITY OF WISCONSIN PRESS

Published 1975
The University of Wisconsin Press
Box 1379, Madison, Wisconsin 53701

The University of Wisconsin Press, Ltd.
70 Great Russell Street, London

Printed in the United States of America

For LC CIP information see the colophon

ISBN 0-299-06800-5

Publication of this book has been made possible in part
by a grant from the Andrew W. Mellon Foundation

for Carol Sue Wittreich

> . . . men may arise
> Pure from fire to join the angelic race.
>
> —Lord Byron, *The Prophecy of Dante*

Contents

Preface   xiii
Citations   xxiii

Chapter 1:   "HIS LINEAMENTS DIVINE":
BLAKE'S PORTRAIT AND PORTRAYALS
OF MILTON   3
"Divine Countenance"   4
"The Immortal Man"   13
"Albion Agonistes"   48

Chapter 2:   "THE HOUSE OF THE INTERPRETER":
BLAKE'S MILTON ILLUSTRATIONS   75
Techniques and Strategies   78
Tradition and Blake's Talent   103
Milton's "Autumnal" Vision   129

Chapter 3:   "MENTAL PRINCE":
MILTON AS A REVOLUTIONARY   147
Revolutionary Art   151
The Tradition of Revolution   171
Blake's Milton   188

Epilogue: "FORWARD THRO' ETERNITY"   221
A Theory of Influence   223
Hayley's Milton   229
The Milton of *Milton*   236

Notes   253
Index   319

List of Illustrations

following page 136

1. Blake's *Head of Milton*
2. Faithorne's Crayon Portrait
3. Milton Portrait Engraved by Marshall
4. Richardson's Frontispiece-Portrait
5. DeLaunay's Frontispiece-Portrait
6. Plate 1 of Blake's *Milton*, Copy B
7. Plate 1 of Blake's *Milton*, Copy C
8. Plate 1 of Blake's *Milton*, Copy D
9. The Book of Revelation as a Picture-Prophecy
10. Plate 13 of Blake's *Milton*, Copy B [Plate 16 in Copy D]
11. Plate 16 of Blake's *Milton*, Copy D
12. Plate 15 of Blake's *Milton*, Copy A [Plate 18 in Copy D]
13. Plate 18 of Blake's *Milton*, Copy D
14. Plate 29 of Blake's *Milton*, Copy B [Plate 32 in Copy D]
15. Plate 38 of Blake's *Milton*, Copy A [Plate 42 in Copy D]
16. Plate 38 of Blake's *Milton*, Copy B [Plate 42 in Copy D]
17. Plate 42 of Blake's *Milton*, Copy D
18. Plate 1 of *Jerusalem*, Copy E
19. The Vision of the Candlesticks (Illustration for the Book of Revelation)
20. A. Balestra's Frontispiece, *Milton's Apotheosis*
21. *Milton Triumphing Over Salmasius*
22. Illustration for Young's *Night Thoughts*, no. 537
23. *Albion Rose* (line engraving)
24. *Albion Rose* (color print)
25. *Albion Rose* (color print)
26. Plate 76 of *Jerusalem*, Copy E
27. Plate 2 of *Jerusalem*, Copy E
28. Illustration for the Book of Job, no. 3
29. Illustration for the Book of Job, no. 6

30. For *Comus* (water color, no. 7, early version): [Sabrina Disenchants the Lady]

31. For *Comus* (water color, no. 7, late version): [Sabrina Disenchants the Lady]

32. For *Paradise Lost* (water color, no. 12, early version): [The Expulsion]

33. For *Paradise Lost* (water color, no. 9, late version): [The Expulsion]

34. For *Paradise Regained* (water color, no. 1): [The Baptism of Jesus]

35. For *Paradise Regained* (water color, no. 2): [The First Temptation]

36. For *Paradise Regained* (water color, no. 3): [Andrew and Simon Peter]

37. For *Paradise Regained* (water color, no. 4): [Mary Meditating]

38. For *Paradise Regained* (water color, no. 5): [Satan in Council]

39. For *Paradise Regained* (water color, no. 6): [The Banquet Temptation]

40. For *Paradise Regained* (water color, no. 7): [The Second Temptation]

41. For *Paradise Regained* (water color, no. 8): [Satan Inspiring Jesus' Ugly Dreams]

42. For *Paradise Regained* (water color, no. 9): [Morning Chasing Away the Spectres of the Night]

43. For *Paradise Regained* (water color, no. 10): [The Third Temptation]

44. For *Paradise Regained* (water color, no. 11): [Jesus Ministered to by Angels]

45. For *Paradise Regained* (water color, no. 12): [Jesus Returning to Mary]

Preface

> ...the arts mirror the greatest single cultural prob-
> lem we face ... how to use a heritage, when we know
> and admire so much about it, how to grow by means
> of it, how to acquire our own "identities," how to be
> ourselves.
>
> —Walter Jackson Bate

THE INTERPRETATION OF LITERATURE depends upon the
determination of its contexts; and, as Earl Wasserman observes
while relating such a principle to the poetry of Shelley, our
interpretative disagreements arise from our differences over "what
the relevant context is, over whether we have the right framework
for putting the work together organically." Blake's poems are
enclosed within enlarging circles for interpretation: the circle of
the Blake canon, which provides a context for any individual
poem contained within it, and the multiple circles of tradition,
which meet within Blake's canon and which may have a common
point of intersection within any individual poem. Blake creates a
poetry of contexts, and thus his poetry remains sealed until the
contexts around it are penetrated. Robert Gleckner comprehends
this fact of criticism, explaining that the reader of Blake's poetry
"must be constantly aware of the context or state in which each
individual poem appears"; and so does Hazard Adams, who contends that Blake "consciously attempted traditional utterance,"
that "all his work" possesses a strong attachment "to the tradition
of symbolic utterance" which is finally "the tradition of the
Bible." However, the premises of Gleckner and Adams have not
always been welcomed by critics who, succeeding them, have more
commonly agreed with Arthur Symons that Blake "enters into no
tradition." Recent students of Blake tend to argue as T. S. Eliot
did, that Blake was not disposed "to imitation of himself or of
anyone else," or as F. R. Leavis had done, that Blake was "com-

pletely and uncompromisingly individual [in] idiom and technique." Indeed, Leavis has recently taken his own proposition to the extreme position of chiding Eliot for wanting Blake to be, in any sense, a traditionalist and of accosting Kathleen Raine ("the recognized high-priestess in our time," Leavis calls her) for being "Blind to Blake's genius," assuring us that "Blake's own success had *no* influence," that, when all is said and done, "Shakespeare counts for essentially more in it than Milton does." New Criticism, not only at its inception but now, is impervious to Blake's genius—not because its methodology is without merit but because its biases, ideological and aesthetic, are limiting to Blake's vision. New criticism (to turn Leavis's own words against him) has generated blindness, and "perpetuate[d] a cult that, whatever it serves, doesn't serve Blake or humanity." Blake's work invites not *a* criticism but *criticisms* that can be joined together to surpass the boundaries to vision as they are so narrowly set by Leavis.

When he wrote *Jerusalem,* Blake distinguished between the "sheep" and the "goats" who made up his "Public." Had he lived into this century to witness his rise to fame and fortune, we might very well have expected him to pen a lethal epigram or two, applying the same distinction to his critics; for they would do to him what some of Milton's critics, in the eighteenth century and since, have done to Blake's favorite poet: they would "tame [his] mind down from its own infinity—/To live in narrow ways with little men." The critical perspective of Leavis, which would tame us by protecting us from Blake's prophecies and by isolating us from the very contexts that illuminate his work, gets us nowhere; but the principle of criticism articulated by Earl Wasserman, though it does not involve all poetry, is indispensable when it comes to reading not only Shelley, but also Blake and Milton. It also provides a convenient way of settling upon a problem of criticism that W. B. Yeats and T. S. Eliot gather into focus. Yeats was deeply committed to the notion that the great artists "look backward to a long tradition, for being without fear, they have held to whatever pleased them." The great artists have also discarded whatever did not please them; and they have taken liberties in altering tradition and have altered it so frequently and so completely that the very artists "who have been freed by the traditions of art" have been regarded as having "something terrible about them, a light that is unendurable to eyesight." Were it not that "Poetry and Tradition" (the essay from which I am quoting) was written in 1907, one might reasonably suppose that it was written as a response to Eliot with Eliot's pronouncements on Blake foremost in Yeats's mind.

When Eliot wrote about Blake in *The Sacred Wood* (1920), he denied the poet precisely what Yeats on so many occasions attributed to him—a profound sense of tradition. Blake not only has *"something terrible"* about him from Eliot's point of view, but he is *"peculiarly terrifying"*; Blake's "light . . . unendurable to eyesight" is to Eliot's mind the light of "honesty against which the whole world conspires, because it is unpleasant."Many critics may be said to have conspired against Blake—for various reasons and in different ways. The "many" includes Eliot himself, his dissatisfaction with Blake's poetry being evident in even his favorable remarks: Blake, until the age of twenty, is "decidedly a traditional"; but in maturity he steps beyond the confines of tradition, surrendering a "framework of accepted and traditional ideas." Tradition "would have prevented him from indulging in a philosophy of his own" and, by concentrating his attention upon the problems of art, would have bestowed upon him the "gift of form which knows how to borrow."

Yeats and Eliot may agree about what poetry is, but they disagree (and disagree profoundly) when it comes to explaining what tradition is. Yeats's tradition is inclusive: it encompasses poets—revolutionary poets—like Milton and Blake and Shelley, the very poets who by Eliot are relegated, usually with deprecation, to the margins of tradition or, in the case of Blake, are situated outside its boundaries. Eliot celebrates what Yeats once called "changeless tradition," while Yeats, acknowledging the efficacy of tradition, ascribes to it the qualities of mutability and flexibility. Eliot would consign Blake to a splendid isolation from which Yeats sought to rescue him, an effort that has been continued most recently by Kathleen Raine's *Blake and Tradition* (1968) and by a special issue of *Blake Studies* (1972) which takes Raine's subject as its theme without adopting her conclusions.

Yeats would have expected Blake to agree with his own sentiment: "I condemn all that is not tradition"; for, according to Yeats, his own subjects, themes, and even poetical forms are, like those of Blake, elements "received from the generations." Yeats could not break from tradition, and neither could Blake. An artist of the first order and an iconoclast with a revolutionary temperament, Blake did not, indeed could not, always encompass tradition in a loving embrace; he understood that tradition was a burden upon him and that it could be encumbering to his art. But Blake, instead of crumpling under the anxiety of influence and casting it off, learned to use tradition both creatively and subversively, abhorring, as Yeats was later to do, a "changeless tradition." We will not progress very far in our understanding of Blake, therefore, without a knowledge of tradition, but neither will we progress very far until we achieve an understanding of the transformations of tradition that occur in his art.

The chapters that compose this book share a common premise and a common purpose. All of them relate Blake to central traditions of western culture, its literature and its art; all of them recognize the value to be found in attending to Blake's dialogue with those traditions; and all of them use tradition as a way of defining more exactly than has previously been done the revolutionary character of Blake's genius. Whether employing the traditional techniques of eighteenth-century illustrators or the common themes with which they worked, whether developing his subjects from a biblical or a Miltonic context (and it is often difficult to separate the two), Blake invokes tradition only to subject it to radical transformation. Without tradition Blake would have been speechless; and without a knowledge of multiple traditions and of the ways Blake altered them we, too, are speechless, especially when it comes to defining the nature of his artistic statement and the breadth and subtlety with which it is invested.

One hopes that a book's achievements are as many as its various purposes. One purpose of this book is to clarify a reigning motif in Yeats's criticism: the dichotomy, implied by critics like T. S. Eliot, between tradition and revolution is a false dichotomy. All art, even Blake's, is traditional; but some art, like Blake's, is mounted upon a radical rather than a conservative aesthetic. The question to pursue, then, is not so much whether Blake's poetry is informed by tradition but rather, assuming that it is, what it is he makes of the various traditions he invokes. That question is paramount in the chapters that follow. Another related, and already evident, purpose of this book is to rescue Blake from those who believe with F. R. Leavis that he was "isolated enough to be without influence" and even from those who believe with Harold Bloom that he "read little with any care besides the Bible and Milton." Bloom provides a focus for my own book, but not a point of view; for it is not just the Bible and Milton that elicit Blake's admiration and attention, but the traditions deriving from the one and converging upon the other. In his poetry and in his art, Blake displays an extraordinary knowledge of traditions, both biblical and Miltonic; yet before any study of Blake and tradition can be undertaken, the relationship of Blake and Milton must be explored. This exploration is the immediate concern of the following chapters.

Milton was not only an heir to the biblical tradition but, from Blake's point of view, its best knower, its most distinguished purveyor. Indeed, what may strike us as two discrete traditions are, in Blake's mind, one tradition—a Milton tradition, which is also a tradition of revolution. The potential illumination of Blake's poetry and art that a study of the Milton tradition can provide is considerable, but such a study must also heed A. L. Morton's cautionary words: " . . . Blake is a difficult poet, and no good is done by pretending that he is not. But I think that part of the difficulty has been created by ourselves, through forgetting the tradition in which he wrote. By rediscovering this tradition, and seeing him in relation to it, we do not remove the difficulties, but we do begin to equip ourselves to grapple with them." The difficulty of Blake's poetry is compounded by the difficulty of Milton's: if the contention that Milton provides the most important context for reading Blake has any merit, then we cannot pursue Blake with full comprehension until we examine the Miltonic contexts he invokes; and we cannot do that until we have determined what Blake's attitude toward Milton really was. This book investigates Blake's *idea* of Milton, for the most part leaving the considerable task of exploring Miltonic contexts for another study.

Many critics have pondered the Blake-Milton affiliation; but few have been able to define it, chiefly because their knowledge of Milton does not match their knowledge of Blake, and because, in consequence, they associate Blake quite mistakenly with a level of perception represented by the most banal criticism of this century and of the last decades of the antecedent one. Moreover, anatomizing Blake's idea of Milton, not to mention building a theory of poetic influence upon it, requires consideration of all the evidence—Blake's portrait and portrayals of Milton, his illustrations for Milton's poetry, his critique of the poet in *The Marriage of Heaven and Hell,* and his celebration of him in *Milton.* The following three chapters and their epilogue scrutinize these matters in that sequence.

An awareness of Blake's artistic principles, ones he shares with Milton, helps to define another concern of the following chapters. As a student of Milton, Blake expected and found something akin to what we today call "relevance." Blake was incapable of divorcing the artistry of a poem from its content, of making aesthetic judgments without considering ideological questions. A criticism that separates such matters in order to attend to the one while ignoring the other abandons its purpose of improving literary understanding. It is not the "perishable elements" of art, lost by "time's transhifting," that Blake attends to; and thus Blake's purpose in invoking Miltonic contexts, in illuminating Milton's poems, is not to dismiss the poet's theology (the religious content of his verse) as obsolete (this was a Victorian pastime, and remains a modern one). His purpose is, instead, to redeem Milton's Christian vision from the encumbering intrusions of orthodoxy. As a critic of Milton, Blake is peerless: his understanding far outruns the understanding of Milton that dominated the nineteenth century; and, though his idea of Milton resembles the current idea of him, it is still, in many ways, as much in advance of our time as it was of his own. The complexity of Blake's Milton and the compass of his comprehension may be suggested best by turning to one recent poetical interpreter and by then holding his Milton in mind as we explore Blake's. In a collection of poems called *History,* Robert Lowell portrays Blake's "immortal Man" as "the cool and Christian Homer" who "only cared for life in the straits":

> free to serve what wooed him most, his writing,
> the overobsessiveness posterity must pay
> on the great day when the eyelids of life lift
> and blind eyes shiver in the draft of heaven . . .

Blake's idea of Milton comprehends Lowell's idea of him, but is also infinitely more varied: though a "Christian," Blake's Milton is not "cool," and though oppressed by orthodoxies he was finally freed from them.

No work is written without sources. This is true of Blake and doubly true of this book about him. Here I acknowledge Miltonists and Blakeans alike—*all of them, all their books*—for what I have been able to learn from them. Not everything I have read is acknowledged in the notes to individual chapters, and what is acknowledged in notes sometimes appears in a context of contention that may register disagreement with a critic to whom my debts are countless. One of the ironies of literary criticism is that what is "right" is frequently inconsequentially "right" and what is "wrong" is often provocatively "wrong." The books from which I have learned most are the ones with which I have, on occasion, disagreed. My own book probably would never have been written—it certainly would not have been written as this one is—without the work of Northrop Frye, Harold Bloom, David Erdman, Hazard Adams, Jean Hagstrum, John Grant, and Edward J. Rose. Nor could it have been written without the brilliantly incisive work on Milton by John Steadman, C. A. Patrides, Irene Samuel, Angus Fletcher, and Stanley Fish. My preface may acknowledge a universe of scholarship, but that universe has been guided by these stars.

There are others to whom this book is more personally indebted. Were it not for several tedious assignments in connection with the *Milton Encyclopedia* (John Shawcross is responsible for them and will understand the spirit of this citation), much of the material included in this book would not be here because I would have known nothing about it. Conversations with my students, especially Leslie Tannenbaum, Stephen Behrendt, and Jackie DiSalvo, have been stimulating; and each of their dissertations has proved rewarding and helpful. So have some hard discussions with my colleague Stuart Curran, who has read this book in manuscript and offered valuable criticism of it. J. Max Patrick, Edward J. Rose, and Merton Sealts have done the same, while Karl Kroeber, Edward Tayler, and Joan Webber have read individual sections of it. To them, and also to those who produced the memorable

dialogue on Blake in *Blake's Sublime Allegory,* I extend very
special thanks. Finally, I must acknowledge Jan Wilson and Doris
Stude for the care they have displayed in preparing this manuscript
for the Press, and also those at the Press, especially Joan Krager
and Elizabeth Steinberg, for the expertise they have shown in
preparing the manuscript for the printer.

The following have generously extended their permission to
reproduce the illustrations that appear in this volume: The City of
Manchester Art Galleries, The Princeton University Library, The
Henry E. Huntington Library and Art Gallery, The Folger Shakespeare Library, The British Museum, The New York Public Library, Lessing J. Rosenwald and The Library of Congress, The
Houghton Library (Harvard University), The Fitzwilliam Museum,
The Boston Museum of Fine Arts, The Metropolitan Museum of
Art, and Mr. and Mrs. Paul Mellon. And the following have in
various ways supported me during the period when I was contem-
plating this book: The Henry E. Huntington Library and Art
Gallery, The Folger Shakespeare Library, The Newberry Library,
and The University of Wisconsin Graduate School. This book was
begun—my interest in Blake and Milton fired—at the Huntington
Library, whose director, James Thorpe, and whose staff, especially
Mary Isabel Fry, Mary Wright, G. William Stuart, and John Steadman, were a constant source of help and inspiration, as was
Kathleen Williams, who, when not at the Huntington, was unfail-
ingly at poolside, charming, gracious, and inspiring. Much of this
book was written at the Folger Library, whose proximity to the
Library of Congress made tedious work tolerable and whose direc-
tor, O. B. Hardison, and staff, especially Sandy Powers and Esther
Washington, made hectic days less wearying.

A portion of the first chapter, here revised, first appeared under
the title, " 'Divine Countenance': Blake's Portrait and Portrayals
of Milton," *Huntington Library Quarterly,* 38 (1975), 125–60.
The second chapter is a greatly expanded version of "William
Blake: Illustrator-Interpreter of *Paradise Regained,*" published in
*Calm of Mind: Tercentenary Essays on "Paradise Regained" and
"Samson Agonistes,"* ed. Joseph Anthony Wittreich, Jr. (Cleveland:
Press of Case Western Reserve University, 1971), pp. 93–132. In
the third chapter and in the book's epilogue, I have developed

positions first formulated in " 'Sublime Allegory': Blake's Epic Manifesto and the Milton Tradition," *Blake Studies,* 4, ii (1972), 15–44, in "Milton's 'Virtuoso' Forms: A Review Article," *Genre,* 5 (1972), 307–25, and in "Domes of Mental Pleasure: Blake's Epics and Hayley's Epic Theory," *Studies in Philology,* 69 (1971), 201–29. When I have assimilated material from this previously published work into my book, I have done so with the permission of the editor and publisher. More often I have simply repeated arguments from these essays so as to build upon them; and thus I mention them not to suggest that what is here is a recapitulation of them, but to identify what the prospective reader may find as a series of useful essays, offering an expansive introduction to this book. Another essay, "Opening the Seals: Blake's Epics and the Milton Tradition," in *Blake's Sublime Allegory: Essays on "The Four Zoas," "Milton," and "Jerusalem,"* ed. Stuart Curran and Joseph Anthony Wittreich, Jr. (Madison: University of Wisconsin Press, 1973), pp. 23–58, may be read as epilogue to the epilogue.

J. A. W.

Cape Cod, Massachusetts
23 July 1973

Note on Citations

Quotations of Blake's works, unless otherwise indicated, are from *The Poetry and Prose of William Blake*, ed. David V. Erdman, rev. ed. (New York: Doubleday, 1970), and citations to that edition are given in parentheses in the text. Poems are generally cited by line and/or plate number; other works, simply by the page number in the Erdman edition. When this volume is referred to for Erdman's notes, I have abbreviated its title to *Poetry and Prose*.

Quotations of Milton's poetry are from *The Works of John Milton*, ed. Frank Allen Patterson et al., 18 vols. (New York: Columbia University Press, 1931–38), and those of Milton's prose are from *Complete Prose Works of John Milton*, ed. Don M. Wolfe et al., 8 vols. (New Haven: Yale University Press, 1953–). When quoting poetry, I have given line and, where appropriate, book numbers; in citations, I have often used the abbreviation *Yale Milton*, and sometimes the abbreviation *Columbia Milton*. Whenever possible I have imbedded references, both to Milton's prose and poetry, within the text of individual chapters.

Angel of Apocalypse
BLAKE'S IDEA OF MILTON

CHAPTER ONE

"His Lineaments Divine"

BLAKE'S PORTRAIT AND PORTRAYALS OF MILTON

> An attempt . . . can be made to distinguish two paths
> open to the portraitist, namely, on the one hand the
> unbiased re-creation of the physical phenomenon
> and, on the other, feeling one's way into the psychol-
> ogy of the model, so that in effect, the actual appear-
> ance is subordinated to an "idea."
>
> —Max J. Friedländer

> Then shall they know me, travelling in the Greatness
> of my strength; cloathed with Majesty. Then will I be
> known, by the Colour of my Garment . . . For, I say,
> my Garment shall be stained with their Blood: It
> shall.
>
> —J. Potter

IN THE LAST DECADE, three different critical activities have
been prominent in Blake studies. There has been a continuing
interest in the important and complicated relationship between
Blake and Milton; considerable attention has been paid to Blake
and his ties with a variety of poetical and intellectual traditions;
and most recently there has been a surge of interest in Blake the
illustrator. These three interests should, but do not always, intersect in the study of Blake's Milton illustrations and of his portrayals of Milton. Only such a study can provide a reliable guide to
one of the great poetic alliances in the history of English literature. The relationship Blake entered into with Milton, when pursued through its complexities, yields a theory of poetic influence
different from the theories currently fashionable, but nonetheless
archetypal for the relationship between Milton and the major
poets of the Romantic period.

3

Not looking at illustrations to Milton's poetry, except for *Albion Rose,* which in its different versions relates in an important way to *Samson Agonistes,* this chapter is concerned with Blake's portrait of, and portrayals of, Milton; it also outlines the context in which Blake's Milton illustrations may be profitably studied. The context developed here invites commentary on Blake's use and abuse of a variety of traditions, and such commentary develops into a statement on the kind of relationship that exists between Blake and tradition, especially between Blake and what he would have acknowledged to be the Milton tradition.

"DIVINE COUNTENANCE"

Students of illustration, through their disagreements, have isolated the problem necessarily confronted in any exploration of Blake in relation to tradition. On the one hand, there are those who insist that "the illustrative genius of William Blake stands independent of tradition,"[1] and on the other, those who contend that the very nature of the tradition of illustration in which Blake was working "provided a place for 'imitation,' copying, using other men's ideas."[2] Both perceptions distort rather than illuminate Blake's achievement. To divorce Blake from tradition results in an exaggeration of his originality; and, at the same time, such a separation conceals the very contexts that illuminate his genius, that give it the hardness of definition. To define tradition too narrowly, to comprehend it only as ground for source-hunting, involves other confusions that result in the assignment of debts where there are none and in the failure to acknowledge debts that are outstanding. These tendencies are clearly evident in studies of Blake and Milton, especially in studies of Blake's designs for Milton's poetry, which show that it is finally not very helpful to talk about what Blake derived from the designs of a particular artist. What we should talk about instead is how Blake expanded upon the whole tradition of Milton illustration, how, even when his designs abandon established iconography, they continue to have important conceptual ties with the tradition of which they are a part. This premise involves the rejection of a more common one, which would have us believe that Blake knew very little, that he created *ex nihilo*. The more popular thesis may have the weight of critical tradition on its side, but there is evidence to the contrary provided by Blake's art, which shows that he possessed an impressive knowledge of the arts—of painting, illustration, and engraving—and subdued their traditions to his own purposes.

Blake's *Head of Milton,* done as part of a frieze for William Hayley's library, is a convenient starting point for a discussion of Blake's *idea* of Milton and the use Blake made of tradition (see fig. 1). Blake's *Head,* however, does not represent his first attempt to portray Milton. Among the designs for the poems of Gray are two different portrayals of Milton, one showing him composing on his harp, with Newton above him nodding his hoary head, and the other showing him deep in contemplation, with Cambridge University in the background.[3] Moreover, Blake's *Head* is just a starting point, and consideration of it can yield only tentative conclusions. The *Head* was commissioned by Hayley; and judging from Blake's correspondence with his patron, we can conclude that even before moving to Felpham Blake found his work for Hayley being closely supervised. The choice of a portrait may not have been Blake's alone; and Hayley, if not directly, then through his library, probably contributed to Blake's knowledge of Milton iconography. Yet the very fact that the *Head of Milton* is "More than usually worked up"[4] invites the speculation that, while Hayley had something to do with the choice of a portrait, Blake synthesized an iconography around it. In Blake's *Head of Milton* (and this observation holds true for the other heads of poets Blake painted[5]), the iconography is masterfully chosen to project an *idea* of the poet; it carries the burden of the portrait's meaning—a meaning that conforms to Blake's idea of Milton, yet is still compatible with Hayley's. Both men's views are integrated here and remain so even later; and properly so, for Hayley not only contributed to Blake's knowledge of epic poetry but also honed his comprehension of Milton. Yet Blake's portrait is not a mere echo of Hayley's conception of Milton. To be sure, it represents Hayley's Milton through a traditional, seemingly innocuous, iconography. Yet this iconography, within the context of Blake's own symbolic system, is nicely ambiguous. Without being openly contemptuous of Hayley's bardolatry, Blake introduces iconographic detail that complicates without compromising Hayley's view of the poet.

It is tempting to see in the iconography that surrounds Blake's
Milton portrait, especially in the serpent that holds an apple in its
mouth, an early assertion of the Romantic doctrine of Satanism.
Blake's iconography, however, derives not from his imagination
but from the collective imagination of the tradition in which he
was working. Recently linked to the portraiture of William Faithorne, George Vertue, and G. B. Cipriani, the head of Milton in
Blake's portrait is enwreathed by "bay and oak leaves inter-
twined"[6]; below the head there is a serpent holding an apple in its
mouth. At the viewer's left is a harp leaning against a palm tree;
and at his right, under a frond of palm, are the pipes of Pan. The
portrait derives ultimately from Faithorne's seventeenth-century
depiction—not his line engraving but his crayon portrait (see fig.
2).[7]

The appropriateness of Blake's deriving his portrait from Faithorne's cannot be exaggerated: Faithorne's portrait is "a docu-
mented likeness of Milton at the height of his powers"; and "taken
by a competent artist with the sitter's consent, and published
during his lifetime, it had some claim to be regarded as the 'official
image' of the poet."[8] Yet it is not the "published" portrait but
rather the crayon portrait that seems most prominent in Blake's
own depiction. The two portraits are markedly different from one
another, the chief difference between them being visible in the
face of the crayon portrait, which, calm and impassive, "is the
image of one who, though touched by suffering, is now beyond
suffering. And this serenity, together with the arrangement of the
hair, parted in the middle and falling in long waves to the shoulders, gives to the pastel portrait an almost Christlike quality that is
wholly lacking in the engraving."[9] The fact that Blake preserves
the facial characteristics of the Faithorne portrait, even while
rejecting many distinctive features of Milton's costume, underlines
his effort to simplify traditional themes and motifs. The black
garments of conventional portraiture are gone; but the collar,
stiffened, is boldly delineated. Such details alert us to the fact that
Blake's *Head* is not a mere copy of Faithorne. To the characteristic features of the Faithorne physiognomy, Blake adds that of
Milton's blindness, freezing his image into a stony bust and recalling his wish that after his death someone "might fashion [his] features from marble" (*Manso*, l. 91).

Gathered around Blake's *Head* is an array of iconography that is doubly significant: most of it derives from the images that Milton portraiture accumulated during the eighteenth century; but this tradition, along with Blake's portrait, which is a culmination of it, finds its inception in the William Marshall portrait, commissioned by Humphrey Moseley for the 1645 edition of Milton's poems (see fig. 3). The Marshall portrait serves as a prototype for the many eighteenth-century depictions that develop an iconographic meaning (see figs. 4 and 5). Blake does not, like Marshall, obliterate physical likeness; but he does take Marshall's objective as his own: the transmission of an idea of a poet through the attributes assigned to him and through the details that surround him. There is also an important analogy between Marshall's conception and Blake's own. In the background of the 1645 frontispiece-portrait there is a pastoral scene visible through the window behind the poet—a scene which recalls the lines from *L'Allegro* that tell of "many a youth, and many a maid,/Dancing in the chequer'd shade" to the music of a piper (ll. 95–96). The portrait itself depicts an aged Milton, the bard of experience, who in *Il Penseroso* achieves the prophetic strain. By juxtaposing the piper of innocence and the bard of experience, Marshall's frontispiece suggests the progress from pastoral to prophecy that is the subject of the two poems. In conception, Milton may have approved the portrait; but his epigram, which chides Marshall for the poor likeness, indicates that he did not admire the execution. Blake doubtless knew the circumstances under which the Marshall portrait was made and knew, too, of Milton's disappointment with it, not only because of its poor execution but because of its extravagant praise. Marshall's portrait is the referent of both Milton's epigram and his Vergilean epigraph to the 1645 edition—an epigraph which implies that unqualified praise is "evil," for it excites the envy of the gods and causes the poet to relax in his struggle for perfection. Blake's *Head of Milton* avoids all the inadequacies of Marshall's; it employs an iconography of praise through which it presents a judiciously balanced estimate of Milton.

Some of Blake's iconography was introduced by Nicholas Pigne and some of it by Louis Cheron. The serpent with an apple in its mouth is, of course, conventional in depictions of the fall and thus becomes a leitmotif in Milton illustration and portraiture, appear-

ing first in Pigne's 1713 frontispiece to *Paradise Regained*. Moreover, a design on the title page to the first volume of the 1720
Tonson edition, illustrated by Thornhill and Cheron, depicts Milton with his muse, who holds a harp; two branches with apples
extend over the top of the portrait, and two serpents extend
across the bottom. Jonathan Richardson, Sr., adds further to this
iconography in a depiction that shows the poet wearing a crown of
laurel and in still another that displays, below the portrait, a
serpent with an apple in its mouth (see fig. 4). Ten years later
there appeared a frontispiece-portrait recapitulating many of these
earlier motifs and contributing to them the figure of the trumpet.[10] The tradition is expanded still further by a Milton portrait,
engraved by Nicholas DeLaunay, which is partially encircled by a
wreath of laurel and which is ornamented by a serpent, wound
around a disk, preparing to strike a pomegranate that lies before it.
Shooting up from behind the apple are the flames of hell, and
bound to the oval frame is the trumpet of prophecy (see fig. 5).
The motif of the striking serpent had been used previously by
Cheron in his letter ornament to Book I of *Paradise Lost,* but the
other details may be claimed by DeLaunay as his invention.

Blake's *Head of Milton* owes much to this alphabet of imagery;
yet it copies no one of these earlier depictions but instead assem-
bles a variety of motifs previously used at the same time that it
introduces two new ones, the palm tree and the pipes of Pan,
which invoke the image of paradise informing Milton's epics and
the pastoral image dominating his early lyrics. Given the long
tradition of associating the harp with epic and the pipes with
pastoral, one should, in this context, recall the popular legend that
gathered around the palm tree. Not only is it said to have bent its
branches at Christ's command to shade his mother; but, with each
bending of its branches, it is supposed to have broken another
idol.[11] A symbol of iconoclasm and thus an appropriate emblem
for Milton's achievement as a polemicist, this image combines with
the earlier two to portray Milton against the backdrop of his total
poetic achievement, while marking his progress from pastoral to
prophecy.

Like Blake's other Heads, the *Head of Milton* employs "acces-
sories" that can be said to illustrate the poet's genius or works;[12]
yet the iconographic meaning of this portrait, whose oval wreath is

interestingly elucidated by Stephen Behrendt,[13] is much richer, and more complicated than has thus far been acknowledged. The images of bay and oak leaves may, in fact, derive from *Lycidas,* where Milton begins with an apostrophe to the bay (or laurel), whose leaves he is about to shatter, and continues by singing "to th' Okes" (see ll. 1–5, 186). Blake's images identify Milton as the poet-prophet of *Lycidas* whose words burst forth apocalyptically (see Hebrews 12:26–27); but they are also invested, as Behrendt suggests, with Blake's own symbolic meaning. Like Milton himself, Blake fashions a garland of laurel leaves for a dead poet: *they* testify to Milton's poetic achievement. But the oak leaves—Blake's usual symbol for stubborn, rooted error—introduce an element of criticism, enabling Blake, through the image of the garland, to represent Milton's achievement as being inextricably involved with error. A similar point is made by Irene Tayler when, referring to the coiled serpent below the portrait, she explains that "the allusion is to *Paradise Lost,* of course, . . . to the whole complex of human error resting in our mistaken notions about the nature of the generative life."[14] This observation and Behrendt's are complementary; and both are corroborated by the detail of the collar— a traditional image for order and constraint and one that, as E. H. Gombrich explains, can lend meaning to any portrait, especially when it is used as a device for caricaturing, thus substituting "significance" for "the likeness" of the man. The artist, compensating for the absence of movement in portraiture, "first of all mobilise[s] our projection" and then "exploit[s] the ambiguities of the arrested face" along with the ambiguities inherent in the images surrounding it.[15] The mobilized, sculpturesque face of Blake's portrait is thrown into relief by the stiff collar that rings Milton's neck; and in this image, particularly, we see Blake exploiting the "ambiguities" that Gombrich finds so essential to the art of portraiture.

Often identified specifically with the restraints imposed by the conscience, the collar is an image of what Blake would call the "mind-forged manacles" that impeded the full expression of Milton's vision in poems like *Comus* and *Paradise Lost.* But the collar also reinforces the posture of radicalism, political and theological, that Blake attributes to Milton, this reinforcement coming from the association of the collar with the rebellious soul and defiant imagination.[16] The iconographic meaning of Blake's portrait is further expanded by the images of the pipes, the harp, and the palms.

Of special importance is the image of the harp, used often by Blake and very notably in the design accompanying the Ancient Bard poem in *Songs of Innocence and of Experience* and in plate 18 of *Milton* (see figs. 12 and 13), where it symbolizes not only the Bard's song to which Milton responds but the prophecy that, in responding to it, he fulfills. The classical association of the harp is with Orpheus, who produced a sweet harmony that soothed the savage beasts, that drew after him not only the beasts of the wild but rocks and trees, thus symbolizing the concord of discordant elements in society. When the Orpheus myth and harp image are Christianized, Orpheus is usually seen as a type of the minister-orator; his instrument, associated with both the harp of David and the harp of the Book of Revelation (5:8), is "the Harp of God's Word." "By *Orpheus* charming of stones, trees, birds, and beasts with his musick, is meant," says Alexander Ross, that poets and orators "by their wisdom and eloquence did bring rude and ignorant people ... to Civility, and Religion";[17] or as John Rainolds puts it:

Do not think, that ... Orpheus by his tuneful playing on the lyre moved mountains, held rivers, softened rocks, charmed deserts, tamed savage beasts, and made trees follow him; but believe that by the sweetness of the poet's song he soothed men more wrathful than mountains, restrained men more changeable than rivers, softened men harder than stone, civilized men ruder than forests, mastered men fiercer than wild beasts, and delighted men more senseless than blocks of wood.[18]

There is a special propriety in Blake's choosing to portray Milton through the image that Milton used to portray himself on the title page of *Pro Populo Anglicano Defensio,* for the harp is the instrument used by orator and prophet alike to dispel the evil spirit within and to remove the corrupting principle from society (see 1 Samuel 16:13).[19] In its context in Revelation, the harp signifies those who overcome tyranny, oppression, Antichrist.

It has been said that Blake is England's "first great exponent" for combining the roles of poet and prophet, that Blake is there-fore "the archetype of prophetic poets" for the modern age.[20] This is not a claim that Blake would have made for himself. The

harp, in conjunction with the pipes, confirms Blake's identification of Milton as England's great prophet, even as it suggests the
relationship the artist perceives between himself and his subject, a
point underscored by the scriptural passage the portrait unmistakably invokes: " . . . thou shalt meet a company of prophets
coming down from the high place with . . . a pipe, and a harp,
before them; and they shall prophesy: And the Spirit of the Lord
will come upon thee, and thou shalt prophesy with them, and
shalt be turned into another man" (1 Samuel 10:5–6). This
passage is important not only for the context it provides for
Blake's portrait but for the meaning that was customarily assigned
to it. Around this passage John Smith, widely read by Blake's
contemporaries, turns his entire discussion of sonship, discipleship,
in prophetic tradition, explaining that every prophet has his "emanation." Christ has his Apostles and Elijah had his Elisha—just as
Milton, we may be led to infer, has his Blake. "All the prophets,"
Smith explains, "prophesied by virtue of some influence
raying forth from the spirit of some other prophet into them";[21]
each prophet has his disciple whose function it is, even as he
assumes a mantle and prepares himself for vision, to be a student—
a scholar and an interpreter—of his precursor's vision. Or, as
Richard Brothers suggests, every prophet communicates through a
precursor prophet, the precursor providing the key that unlocks
the vision of his successor, holding up the lamp without which the
new prophecy receives no illumination.[22]

If the harp of David identifies Milton as a prophet, the palms
identify him as a pilgrim—as the wayfaring, warfaring hero of
Areopagitica already celebrated by Hayley when he wrote, "Had
the author of the *Paradise Lost* left us no composition but his
Areopagitica, he would still be entitled to the affectionate venera-
tion of every Englishman."[23] Besides remembering the association
of the palm with iconoclasm, one should recall with Arnold
Whittick that during the Middle Ages the palm was the usual
accouterment of the pilgrim journeying toward Jerusalem, an
association that harkens back to Matthew's description of Christ's
triumphant entry into Jerusalem (21:8) and to the victorious
heroes of the Book of Revelation (7:9), who, clothed in white,
stand with the palm of victory before the throne of God.[24]
Similar associations accompany Blake's occasional use of the

image. In both *The Four Zoas* and *Jerusalem,* the palm tree and the oak—images of suffering and weeping—stand upon the edge of Beulah (see I, p. 18, ll. 11–13, and 18:19–20, 23:24–25). It is here that Albion falls into his death sleep and here, between the two trees, that in *Jerusalem* Los builds the Mundane Shell, which is "the Place/Of Redemption & of awaking again into Eternity" (59:8–9). One is the tree of life, the other the tree of death; the world of error, of deathlike sleep, associated with the oak, may be transcended by the act of self-annihilation symbolized by the palm. The bearer of the palm is, like the Christian martyrs, victorious over death and like the prophets, victorious over the enemies of true religion. He is also, as Emanuel Swedenborg explains, in possession of the divine vision; but, what is more important, he is distinguished for his capacity to translate vision into action. To be a bearer of the palm, to be in touch with "the divine wisdom of the Lord," is not enough, however; "for only to think good, and not to wish to do it," says Swedenborg, "does not constitute good in any one."[25] Milton, then, is marked as the true visionary, who like Christ, depicted in the last design of the *Paradise Regained* series against a background of palms (see fig. 45), is also a man of action. Blake's *Head of Milton* may, therefore, serve as a pictorial epigraph to *Milton*: it points to Milton's errors that have spread like a dark cloud over Europe, even as it identifies Milton as a prophet intent upon opening the gates of perception, an aim realized only when Milton, a pilgrim of eternity, goes to Eternal Death, annihilating selfhood and thereby achieving the vision through which he, as the Awakener, can transform all the Lord's people into prophets.

Above all, Blake's *Head of Milton* exhibits the fundamental conflict that involves any portrait artist: "The job of painting a portrait entails something akin to obsequiousness, against which the creative power puts up a fight"[26] —in this case obsequiousness to the Faithorne model and, beyond that, obsequiousness perhaps even to the wishes of Hayley, whose library the portrait was to decorate. Like many of his contemporaries, Blake remained faithful to the physical features of his model; but at the same time he used iconographic details to reveal the subject's chief attributes. The real point of Blake's portrait is less to depict Milton as he actually was than to portray him in terms of what surrounded him.

"THE IMMORTAL MAN"

Blake's desire to express attributes of personality, to portray the mental life of his subject, manifests itself most fully in his portrayals of Milton in *Milton* (see figs. 6–8, 10–17). In them Blake abandons all obligations, all servitude, and engages in willful deviation from his subject as he is customarily represented. The consequences of such an approach are suggested by Max Friedländer, when he writes that "the more resolutely painters begin with ideas the more thoroughly they destroy the individual, stylizing and caricaturing it, above all the human face."[27] To realize the uniqueness of Blake's portrayals, one needs only to juxtapose the stern, sometimes cantankerous, face and heavily garmented figure of tradition and the nude figure of Blake's designs, which represent Milton from a variety of perspectives and in a multiplicity of postures—even in a state of high sexual excitement (see fig. 15).[28] Putting a portrait head on an ideal nude body had long been an artistic device used to mythologize historical figures; it was a particularly effective way of pointing to the divine nature of one's subject, of justifying the epithet "heroic" and at the same time, by conveying ideas of energy and imagination, suggesting the artist's and his subject's triumph over rules and authority, over institutions, aesthetic and moral, that oppressed man.[29] These implications all lie behind Blake's portrayals of Milton.

Blake himself provides the best key to what he is doing in these representations when he explains, in *A Descriptive Catalogue,* that he wishes to portray the "spiritual form" of figures, some of them historical, who are presented, in a "mythological cast" and with a visionary grandeur, in designs that carry "recondite meaning, where more is meant than meets the eye" (pp. 521–22). In the eleven portrayals of Milton in *Milton,* Blake departs from the usual iconography that shrouds the poet and instead depicts him, ungarmented, pushing through dark clouds, then going through the fires of purgation (plate 1; see figs. 6–8) as prologue to his transfiguration (plate 16; see fig. 11). Blake also depicts Milton as a star (plate 2)[30] about to enter William's foot (plates 17 and 32; see fig. 14) and his brother Robert's (plate 37), Milton triumphing over his spectre Satan (plate 18; see figs. 12 and 13), and Milton, with his three wives and three daughters looking on, being opposed by the vegetating Los (plate 19). Finally, at the end of the poem, Milton, in accordance with one possible interpretation of this plate, joins with his emanation Ololon in the moment of poetic inspiration (plate 42; see figs. 15–17), then struggles through the cave of error (plate 46), having assumed an attitude of forgiveness (plate 45).[31] Whatever their individual purposes, these designs all participate in Blake's ultimate object, which is to portray the apotheosis of Milton.

Blake's *Milton* designs require another study which will examine each of them in detail and in relation to the other illuminations they accompany. Here my intention is only to lay down some considerations that may provide a point of departure for such an undertaking. Three of these portrayals (plates 1, 18, and 42), Florence Sandler has observed, "mark the moments of dramatic climax—Milton the Christian Agonist, undertaking the Hero Journey into the black cloud of Time and Space; Milton the Iconoclast confronting and overcoming Urizen, the Spectre of the Law, with the stone tablets in his hand; and, finally, Milton the Creative Spirit lying upon the Marriage-bed with his Bride, the Emanation, while St. John's Eagle of Inspiration hovers above him."[32] Sandler's perception should be extended to all these designs: together they present pictorially the dramatic moments in *Milton,* and they all convey the intimations of apocalypse that Sandler senses in three of them. This is true both of the seven illustrations that portray Milton formally (as a human figure) and of the four that portray him emblematically (as a falling star).

Blake's emblematic portrayals are doubly significant; for even as they emphasize the apocalyptic thrust of all these designs they capture their ambiguity, alluding simultaneously to Prometheus, who brought fire down from heaven, thereby enlightening the human race, and to the falling Lucifer, who is regarded by commentators on Revelation as representative of any one of the great religious heretics or as an emblem for all of them collectively. The image of the star trailing light as a comet, a leitmotif in illustration for the Book of Revelation and a recurrent theme in commentary on Saint John's prophecy,[33] punctuates Blake's theme, which involves a theological criticism of the very poet whom *Milton* is meant to celebrate. Highly allusive, the image recalls Milton's Satan, who in *Paradise Lost* burns like a comet (II. 708), as well as Homer's "red Comet from Saturnus sent/To fright the nations with a dire portent" and Shakespeare's comet which, like some malignant planet that lowers upon the world, "impart[s] change to times *and states*"; the image, perhaps even more pointedly, recalls the prophetic words of Christopher Love: "Out of thee, O England, shall a bright star arise, whose light and voice shall make the heathen quake, and bow with submission to the Gospel of Jesus"—words containing a promise, says Love, that is not yet fulfilled.[34] Yet it is the Apocalypse which seems to provide the most immediate referents for Blake's image, one of them suggested by the following verses: "there fell a great star from heaven, burning as it were a lamp, and it fell upon the third part of the rivers, and upon the fountains of waters; And the name of the star is called Wormwood: and the third part of the waters became wormwood; and many men died of the waters, because they were made bitter" (8:10–11). The star falling from heaven, signifying man's falling away from true religion, from the divine vision, is a "great" star because of the tremendous intellectual and religious eminence of the "heretic"; and it is called *Wormwood* because the star is known by its effects, by the "pestilent institutions" it created through the perversities of its doctrines.[35]

Swedenborg's commentary confirms such a reading but also particularizes it in a way that is especially appropriate to *Milton*. The falling star signifies the falsification of truth, the obscuring of light; it is, says Swedenborg, the emblem of "all those who are in the love of self" and who thus "falsify the Word, not as to the sense of the letter, but as to the understanding of the truth therein contained." The star is called *Wormwood* to indicate "truth mixed with . . . falsity . . . the truth of the Word falsified by self-love." [36] These implications of the star image convey the gist of Blake's criticism of Milton: his predecessor has clouded the divine vision with error, with error that derives from the selfhood that, in Blake's poem, Milton is poised to destroy. In an important sense, however, these emblematic portrayals recall conventional interpretations only to invert them: Milton, though once in error, comes not as the purveyor of error but as its destroyer; his doctrines have had a perverting effect on religion, but his descent promises that he will annihilate the part of his religion that in the eighteenth century manifested itself as Deism. The idea of Milton's being the destroyer of error is, of course, not unique to Blake. James Thomson had already celebrated Milton as a great proponent of liberty, explaining that, as a libertarian, Milton was involved "in correcting and refuting errors" and in "undeceiving Mankind." [37] Blake simply amplifies this perception and, in the process, attributes to Milton himself at least a modicum of the error from which mankind is being "undeceived."

Yet another star in the Book of Revelation emphasizes the positive elements in Blake's image: "I saw a star fall from heaven unto the earth: and to him was given the key of the bottomless pit" (9:1). This star, the primary referent of Blake's image, relates Milton to the angel who appears as a star, a connection Blake reinforces by having Los and Enitharmon, beholding Milton's descent, perceive that Milton performs an errand comparable to the one performed by the fifth angel in Revelation: "Surely to unloose my bond/Is this Man come! Satan shall be unloosd upon Albion" (17 [19]:32–33). Again the star signifies the divine vision that, because it is falling, symbolizes those who pervert truth, those who, though they may acknowledge the Word, distort it to serve their own purposes. But here the meaning of the image is complicated, for the star is identified with an angel who, given the keys to the bottomless pit—"the hells where and whence falsities are"[38] —is about to explore and expose a universe of error. Those errors are specifically identified by Swedenborg as "dense falsities . . . originating in the evils of earthly and corporeal loves";[39] and the pit—a place of fire, throwing off clouds of smoke—is explained by him as having its reference point not in the external world but in "the interiors of the mind," the world within that is being opened, that is ready to be explored.[40] The very act of entering this universe of error promises the exposure of falsities, and that exposure may culminate in their annihilation. This angel of the Apocalypse, like Milton, descends into error in order to confront and consolidate it, in order finally to cast it off. In the light of these interpretations, the image of the falling star represents both the embodiment of error and the source of its exposure. It fuses

Blake's themes of Milton's error and self-redemption with his themes of self-redemption and the redemption of a whole society, which Milton is ready to accomplish. Besides functioning thematically, the star image serves as an associative link between portrayals of Milton on plates 2, 17, 32, and 37 (see fig. 14) and the depictions of him on plates 1, 16, and 42 (see figs. 6–8, 11, 15–17). These designs remind us of still another angel in the Apocalypse—the "mighty Angel" who, as the morning star, is the source of true light and of John's divine vision.

In Chapter 10 of the Book of Revelation, John writes: "And I saw another angel come down from heaven, clothed with a cloud: and a rainbow *was* upon his head, and his face *was* as it were the sun, and his feet as pillars of fire: . . . and he set his right foot upon the sea, and *his* left *foot* on the earth . . . and lifted up his hand to heaven" (10:1–2, 5). This is John's description of the Angel Christ, who gives him the book and tells him to eat; and that Angel is linked by a visionary line to another angel who flies "in the midst of heaven, having the everlasting gospel to preach" (14:6) and to yet another angel who, "standing in the sun," calls "all the fowls that fly in the midst of heaven" to the marriage feast (19:17). Both these angels, though not explicitly called eagles, are, because they are associated, the one with the sun, the other with fowls flying in the midst of heaven, often portrayed as eagles. Moreover, this "mighty Angel" is the figure who appears on a horse, his "vesture dipped in blood," his name being "The Word of God" (19:11–13).

In these passages, pointed to by the star image, we find a major source for the iconography that surrounds Blake's Awakener in plates 1, 16, and 42. In plate 1, we see Milton—one foot firmly planted, the other about to enter the Sea of Time and Space—lifting up his hand to heaven; in at least one copy his right foot has a line of fire seeming to extend from it (see fig. 7). In all copies his hand is lifted, to dispel the cloud of "erroneous doctrine"[41] that hides his glory and majesty, attributes which become manifested as Milton, casting off one set of garments, assumes another in the final version of plate 16 (see figs. 10 and 11). The new garments, white and stained with blood, symbolize the man who "overcometh" now wrapping himself in "The Word of God" (Revelation 3:5, 19:13). In this plate, the clouds surrounding Milton in early versions of plate 1 have been purged by the flames of fire that envelop the poet in the final version; the poet's head, circled by a darkened halo in early versions of plate 16, shines like the sun dawning behind it. The translation of Milton into the God-Man is deliberate,[42] Blake, through this device, reaffirming the father-son, mentor-disciple relationship that is fundamental to the prophetic tradition in which Blake, joined by Milton, participates. Later, from the double perspective of plate 42, we see Milton awakening and Milton as the Awakener, the poet emblematized here by the eagle who inspires Albion-England (see figs. 15–17).

Before examining these designs, and related ones, any further, we should make some observations about how they may be profitably studied. An artist committed to the minute particulars of others' visions surely expected an audience who would attend to the minute particulars of his own vision, both in pictures and in poems. Anyone familiar with the different copies of *Milton* will be aware of both textual and iconographic variation separating one version of the prophecy from another; yet he will doubtless recognize that there is a "deep-structure"—a form common to all versions of a single plate. In the initial plate of *Milton,* for instance, the nude poet, back turned toward the viewer, has his right hand raised, extending into his own name and over the world he is now entering. All versions of the plate employ, through an iconography of gesture, a language universally understood by writers of and commentators on prophecy. If God's power is signified by his right hand raised over the world, Milton's power over England, over the world which he now enters, is signified analogously by his raised hand, a symbol of both his "influence" over the nation and his "favour" among its prophets.[43] The nature of Milton's power (pernicious if we are looking at the ominous clouds in Copy A, purgative if at the shooting flames in Copy D) is defined differently by an iconography that shifts both subtly and meaningfully from copy to copy. Such iconographic differences should cause us to resist those who would, like the Milton of *Paradise Lost,* reduce a figure, or an entire plate, to a "ratio"; and the realization that the plates composing any one copy are carefully integrated should dissuade us from accepting, for interpretative purposes, a composite *Milton,* which draws one plate from this copy, another from that. Such a *Milton* exists only in the imagination of its compiler;[44] it cannot be said to be an accurate representation of Blake's *Milton,* of any existing version of it, of which there are four we know about and thus four with which we must eventually contend.

In most cases, the subjects of Blake's *Milton* designs may be quickly identified and verified by taking account of Blake's text.[45] For instance, plates 2, 17, 32, and 37 clearly reiterate the passage that describes Milton, like a star, "Descending perpendicular" (15 [17]:47–48); and each of these plates depicts Milton as he is seen from "the shades/Of Hell": "in a trail of light as of a comet/That travels into Chaos" (15 [17]:18–21). Plate 19, in its upper design, draws upon the textual allusion to Milton abusing his wives and dictating to his daughters (17 [19]:10–14) and, in its lower design, pictorializes the passage describing Los's "fibrous" limbs shooting forth "like roots of trees against the forward path/Of Miltons journey" as the head of Urizen, seeming to emerge from the ground, beholds "the immortal Man" (ll. 34–36).[46] Plate 18 shows Urizen rising and confronting Milton, then fainting "in terror" as he strives "With Miltons Spirit" (see 19 [21]:1–6; 39 [44]:53–56), while plate 45 recalls the same moment. Here the stooped figure is Ololon, before whom Milton stands as he perceives "the Eternal Form/Of that mild Vision" (40 [46]:1–2) and from whose perspective we see him, in plate 46, laboring "in Chasms of the Mundane Shell" (39 [44]:57), opposing the "awful Man," "striving/In Self annihilation giving [his] life to [his] enemies" (40 [46]:4–8). The text may not always accompany the design, or even be in close proximity to it; but in every instance there is agreement between text and design, however much distance may separate them.

In plates 1 and 16, however, precision of description becomes problematical, especially when it comes to looking at corresponding plates in different copies of *Milton.*[47] Though it may be desirable to establish an ultimate version of *Milton,* it is more productive, at this juncture, to acknowledge that corresponding plates in the different copies of the poem make their own separate statement and that each copy of the poem provides its own distinctive perspective on the poet who is Blake's hero. In his initial portrayal of Milton, Blake draws his poet-hero as Milton had depicted his political hero Cromwell, moving "through a cloud,"

guided by "matchless Fortitude," ploughing his "glorious way" to
"truth" (see Sonnet 16, ll. 1–4). Yet the different versions of
plate 1, united by this shared idea, display variations. This plate in
Copies A and B, for example, shows Milton, with long flowing
hair, the traditional symbol of repentance,[48] pushing through the
black cloud of Time and Space (see fig. 6), having "turned [his]
back upon these Heavens builded on cruelty" (32 [35]:3). In
Copy C, a new detail is added (see fig. 7): a row of sulphureous
flames, on a plane with Milton's feet, throws off clouds of smoke,
which Milton is rolling back. In Copy D (see fig. 8), the clouds are
replaced by flames that envelop the front portion of Milton's
body. In Copies A, B, and C, then, the design accentuates the
process of annihilating error; but in Copy D, it dramatizes the
theme of purgation. Early versions of the design show Milton,
from Los's perspective, as a "Cloud . . . stretching over Europe"
(21 [23]:36) but also, from the Assembly's perspective, with
"lineaments divine" obscured by "the shades of Death & Ulro"
that are represented in Copies A and B (see fig. 6) by the net of
crosshatching that covers Milton's body as he goes "down to self
annihilation and eternal death" (14 [15]:12, 22).[49] Not only is
Milton depicted here from Los's perspective, but he is shown
making Los-like gestures, dispersing the clouds (cf. 23 [25]:31).
In the last version of this design, most of the crosshatching is lifted
as Milton is seen, having annihilated error, stepping into the fires
of purgation.

   Blake's designs, then, are no mere excrescences; they are something more than decoration. The text of Blake's poem binds the
illuminations to it, and the text and the designs together bind the
poem inextricably to the Book of Revelation. Throughout the
Renaissance and into Blake's own time, it was understood that the
prophet offered both a vision and a commentary on it. One way of
pursuing the illuminated books is to apprehend the text, written in
Blake's native idiom, as the vision that the pictures themselves,
composed from the universal language of prophecy, are designed
to elucidate. Encouragement for such an understanding comes
both from the fact that the Book of Revelation had come to be
regarded as the prototype of picture-prophecy (see fig. 9) and
from the literature on prophecy that flooded the 1780's and 90's.
First of all, pictorial prophecy was an accepted visionary mode.

William Lilly, for instance, had set forth his seventeenth-century prophecies in words *and in pictures,* in a system of "Hieroglyphics." Quoting Lucian ("Memphis yet knew not how with Reeds to frame/Her books, but Birds and Beasts Letters became"), Lilly's commentator explains that pictures, or "witty *Hieroglyphic*[s]," are an ideal medium for prophecy, especially for prophetic commentary on the verbalized vision; and for just this purpose, he says, they are used by Lilly.[50] Employing a pictorial language, the prophet, knowing what his images mean, arranges them, builds a context for them, to create a vision to which they provide the quickest access. Thus, to ignore Blake's pictures is, in a very real sense, to close off access to his poems.

If picture and poem collaborate to yield meaning, it is pointless to isolate the one from the other, and downright foolish to elevate the auditory over the visual (as Thomas Frosch would do) or vice versa (as students of Blake's art are increasingly prone to do).[51] It is a commonplace of literary criticism that Blake's largest aim was the expansion of man's consciousness. Yet commonplaces too often conceal their predications and corollaries. Poetry and painting, for instance, do not, says Roland Barthes, call for the same type of consciousness; and pictures themselves involve varying levels of consciousness and thus submit to many kinds of reading: "a diagram lends itself to signification more than a drawing, a copy more than an original, and a caricature more than a portrait." But even so, pictures "are more imperative than writing, they impose meaning at one stroke, without analysing or diluting it." "Pictures," Barthes concludes, "become a kind of writing as soon as they are meaningful: like writing, they call for a *lexis*."[52] The best *lexis* for Blake's illustrations to *Milton* is provided by the Book of Revelation—the prophecy itself and the tradition of illustration it inspired.

In this regard, two facts of literary history should be remembered: first of all, Blake was "that rarest of phenomena in English art, a Christian painter";[53] and secondly, in Blake's time the Book of Revelation had achieved the status of a handbook for prophets, the best reader of prophecy being "a subtile excercised Interpreter of the *Revelation* of St. *John*," composed, it was understood, of "a number of scenic pictures."[54] According to James Bicheno, Saint John's Revelation, employing a "hieroglyphic" language, involves a form of "picture-writing"[55] (see fig. 9). Its iconic character, together with the fact that it is composed of what Bicheno calls "visions" and "explanatory visions," invited illustration, especially illustration designed to elucidate verbalized visions and verbalized commentary on them. Fundamental to the interpretation of Blake's *Milton,* the Book of Revelation, providing the immediate context for Blake's designs, contributing a richly suggestive iconography to them, is an indispensable guide to understanding the statement about Milton that Blake's prophecy makes.

The Milton of the early versions of plate 1 recalls the fifth angel of the Apocalypse, who enters the bottomless pit, the world within, to expose and extirpate error. The accompanying iconography, especially in Copy C (see fig. 7), confirms this identification. The flames of fire, the clouds of smoke, remind us that when this angel of the Apocalypse entered the world within "there arose a smoke . . . as the smoke of a great furnace" (9:2), the smoke signifying the intellectual failings of those who would pervert the divine vision, as well as the hitherto unrecognized evils that derive from the pride of selfhood and from one's attendant failings in "earthly and corporeal loves."[56] The effect of the rising smoke is to darken the air and the sun, isolating the erring figure from the divine vision. The purpose of entering the pit is to bring the misguided figure to an awareness of his failings, effecting his regeneration by exposing him to the fires of purgation, as Milton is exposed to them in plate 1 of Copy D (see fig. 8).[57] Appropriately, the first design, in all copies of the poem, takes its place within the tradition of baroque title pages, having been conceived, like them, "as a gateway leading into the text."[58]

Blake's *Milton* is the story of a poet's journey, of his pilgrimage; and thus whatever the stage of Milton's journey may be—the moment of its undertaking or the purgation it involves—plate 1 always depicts the journey, showing Milton in the moment following the one in which he casts off his garments. This earlier moment is the subject of the designs corresponding with plate 16 in Copies A, B, and C of *Milton* but not of plate 16 in Copy D (see figs. 10 and 11). The early versions of the plate depict the moment recorded on plate 41 [43], when "the Sexual Garments . . . /Hiding the Human Lineaments" are "rent" and "wholly purge[d] away with Fire/Till Generation is swallowd up in Regeneration" (ll. 25–28). In these designs, Milton is shown as he takes off "the robe of the promise," ungirds himself "from the oath of God" (14 [15]:13) and, "Tho darkend," walks "above in power and majesty" while his "Mortal Part" sits "frozen in the rock of Horeb" (20 [22]:10–11, 13–14). The last version of the plate, that in Copy D, differing from earlier ones in the coloration of the poet's garments, shows Milton about to don the clothes of redemption. The early plates recall Milton "clothed in black, severe & silent . . . descend[ing]" (38 [43]:8) and "put[ting] off/In Self annihilation all that is not of God alone" (38 [43]:47–48).[59] On this plate, the garments signify the "false body: an Incrustation" over Milton's "immortal Spirit"—they are "the rotten rags . . . his filthy garments," which are cast off as a prelude to the moment depicted in the final version of plate 16, when Milton assumes the clothes of redemption (see 40 [46]:35–36 and 41 [48]:4–6). This act is symbolized by the girdle in the poet's right hand, which can be identified by the buckle visible on the lower left panel of the garment. Now greatly transformed from the stiff, icy object that protrudes from Milton's right hand in Copies A and B, the girdle reinforces the biblical allusion to Christ, who appears in the vision of the candlesticks with "a golden girdle" (Revelation 1:13)–a symbol of his "majesty" but also of his determination and diligence, inasmuch as the purpose of the girdle is to prevent Christ's garments from hindering him in travail.[60] "The 'new' Milton," it is here implied, "is a type of the Christ of the Apocalypse," of Christ as the true visionary.[61] If any line associated with *Milton* glosses the last version of plate 16, it is the one inscribed on the back of plate 43 [50]: " . . . I return from flames of fire tried & pure & white."[62]

The meaning of the garment image in different versions of plate 16 is illuminated by verses from Hebrews:

. . . Thou, Lord, in the beginning hast laid the foundation of the earth; and heavens are the works of thine hands:
They shall perish; but thou remainest; and they all shall wax old as doth a garment;
And as a vesture shalt thou fold them up, and they shall be changed . . .
(1:10–12; see also 2 Kings 2:12)

As early as *The Marriage of Heaven and Hell* Blake used the figure of the garment as a symbol of intellectual error: Swedenborg's writings, says Blake, "are the linen clothes folded up" (plate 3). Moreover, as Morton D. Paley suggests, the garment is a major figure in Blake's final prophecies, its ambiguity pointed to by Blake himself when, in *The Four Zoas,* he distinguishes between the "mantles of life & death" (VIII, p. 115, l. 41), the latter being the "death clothes" he associates with the web of Urizen (VI, p. 71 [second portion], l. 37, and VI, p. 73, l. 35).[63] The same ambiguity is brought into focus in *Milton* when he distinguishes between the "Clothing" of "Cruelty" and the "Garment of Pity & Compassion like the Garment of God" (18 [20]:20, 35), and later in that work when he draws a contrast between souls descending to the body and souls delivered from it (26 [28]: 16–17).

The web of crosshatching that envelops, or that partially envelops, Milton on plate 1 may have only negative implications; but the garment imagery on plate 16 has both negative and positive implications. Again Paley is helpful, observing that "it is ... possible to view the garment from two perspectives at once, as 'fallen' and as resurrected," this double perspective being established when plate 16 of Copy D is set alongside the corresponding plates in Copies A, B, and C.[64] Not only are the black garments of the early versions of this plate transformed into white ones; what is more, in Copy D the white garments are unmistakably stained with blood. This detail should remind us that when Ololon, in the climactic moments of *Milton,* "descended to Felphams Vale/In clouds of blood, in streams of gore," the Starry Eight, the last of whom is Milton, "became/One Man Jesus the Saviour" and "round his limbs/The Clouds of Ololon folded as a Garment dipped in blood." This image, Blake emphasizes, "Is the Divine Revelation in the Litteral expression" (42 [49]:7–8, 10–12, 14).

The distinction made here also finds corroboration in the Book of Revelation, especially in Swedenborg's commentary on it. The "rotten rags," the black garments of plate 16 in Copies A, B, and C, recall the same image in Jeremiah (38:11–13), which, like the clouds of smoke in Revelation, signifies truth perverted. The act of casting off the rags is thus interpreted by Swedenborg as a vindication and restitution of truth; and, accordingly, the white garments of the Apocalypse are taken to signify the divine truth unobstructed by error and protected against falsification.[65] In the

verse, "He that overcometh shall be clothed in white raiment," the
garment signifies the divine vision possessed by the mental soldiers
who "enter into warfare for divine truth,"[66] as Milton claimed to
do in prose tract after prose tract, nowhere more eloquently than
in *Areopagitica* and in his two Defenses of the English people.
Moreover, the ambiguity that Paley assigns to the garment image
finds confirmation in Swedenborg's commentary; he explains that
customarily robes, gowns, and cloaks signify received opinion but
that in the Apocalypse the image is used to represent the divine
vision, the color of the raiment being white because "white is
predicated of truths": "whiteness is from Light, and the light
proceeding from the Lord as a sun is in its essence divine truth." [67]
The heroes of Revelation, garbed in white, are thus in possession
of the divine vision, their raiment identifying them as true visionaries living in the presence of prophecy. Appropriately, then, the
regenerate Milton, though nude, holds white garments, a symbol
of his transfiguration just as they are a symbol of Christ's.[68] Old
garments are cast off, as in Canticles 3:3, so that new ones, white
in color, may be put on; and these new garments, not a literal
covering, are a figure for "Christ himself": man rejects error only
to put on—to become one with—Christ, who, for Blake, is all
vision, all imagination.[69] Moreover, in accordance with Ecclesi-
astes ("Let thy garments be always white" [9:8]), the donning of
the new garment involves not a rejection of, but a rejoicing, a
taking pleasure, in the things of this life[70] —in Milton's case, an
acceptance of the sexual freedom without which both his life and
his vision were restricted.

Nowhere in the *Milton* designs is the poet more like Jesus than
here. The clouds of plate 1 have disappeared, the sun rises behind
Milton, and a sun circles the poet's head, seeming to radiate from
it: Milton's head, like Christ's both in the vision of the candlesticks and in his appearance as a mighty angel, shows as a sun. In
these corresponding moments between Blake's poem and Saint
John's prophecy, "the Divine Humanity . . . [is] seen."[71] Christ,
who appears in white, with hair that is white, is the conspicuous
reference of plate 16, where Milton, hair streaked with white,
holds in each hand white raiments, which signify, as they do in the
Apocalypse, "the divine proceeding, which is divine truth, united
with divine goods, which fills the universal heaven, and enters into

the interior of the mind." "This," says Swedenborg, "is what is understood by being clothed with white garments."[72] This is also a part of the meaning of Blake's design, another part of which is invested in the image of the sun, its function being both to dispel darkness, to enlighten the world, and "to warm and comfort dead ... bodies, ... to revive them."[73] Not only does the sun radiate upon Milton; but in Copy D it radiates from him, suggesting that one aspect of the poet's struggle involves reception of the divine vision, while another involves its extension. Only in the act of transmitting the vision—making the Word into flesh, hammering it into form—does the poet become the Awakener. Only through this act can the apocalyptic moment, involving the renovation of history, occur.

This interpretation of plate 16 finds separate corroborations in the text of *Milton* and in the iconographic tradition from which Blake's design, as well as the glosses cited from the Book of Revelation, derives. That early versions of this plate differ sequentially from the last one is substantiated by the fact that when Milton goes "guarded within," passing through his own "Vortex," it "roll[s] backward behind/His path, into a globe itself infolding; like a sun" (15 [17]:20–24). Aside from the nude Milton, the sun is the most conspicuous feature in all versions of the plate; what, in this context, distinguishes the different versions of the plate is the fact that in Copy D the rising sun in the distance is replicated by the fiery sun that surrounds—that seems to be emanating from—the poet's head. This detail invokes the iconography of transfiguration. Milton, who went down "to the sepulcher to see if morning breaks" (14 [15]:21), becomes himself an image of dawn, the rising sun.

The alterations of this plate, as we move from Copy A to Copy D, turn us from a darkened to a transfigured Milton, to a Milton who has undergone the metamorphosis into glory. The Christian theme of transfiguration, as Gertrud Schiller observes, has its basis in the apocryphal Revelation of Peter: "when I come in my glory ... I shall shine seven times brighter than the sun."[74] Iconographically, then, depictions of transfiguration deliberately develop the comparison between the apotheosized figure and the sun;[75] at the same time, they often introduce the figures of Moses and Elijah, who represent law and prophecy respectively. Those figures do not themselves appear in any version of plate 16, though this design does portray imagistically the concepts the figures supposedly represent: the girdle of convention, of the law, is in Milton's right hand; the mantle of prophecy, of vision, is in his left. Blake's implication is clear: the journey Milton makes through the wilderness of the self enables him to transcend the law and to embrace the spirit of prophecy. The garments that figure in early versions of the design identify the darkened poet as one who, having "entered into the Covering Cherub," is "one with/Albions dread Sons." Hand, Hyle, and Coban are represented as a girdle; "Gwendolen & Conweena as a garment woven/Of War & Religion" (23 [25]:15–17). The effect of Milton's journey is to move him to cast off false prophecy and the Mosaic law (one set of garments) as he assumes the garments of the new law (those of love and forgiveness) and the mantle of true prophecy that, as an Elijah, he can pass on to Blake, who is his Elisha. Blake's portrayal of Milton transfigured not only develops the comparison of the poet with the sun but incorporates all the supporting motifs from conventional portrayals of the transfiguration. The white raiments, the upward gaze, the sun that has broken through the clouds of plate 1, the golden rays streaming both from it and from the sun-like mandorla circling Milton's head—all testify to the divinity of Milton's form, to his personal regeneration, and to the collective resurrection it presages. What Jean Hagstrum says of Blake's relationship to Christ has some bearing here on Milton's relationship to Christ and on Blake's identification with both of them. "When in the moment of great artistic and prophetic inspiration Blake says that he became 'One Man' with Los, he is virtually saying," according to Hagstrum, "that he became Christ, who is often called One Man, the authenticator and supporter of all artistic form, the breath and finer spirit of all prophecy."[76] This proposition has its corollary: it is only because Milton becomes Christ that Blake is able to identify with him. Milton, awakened in the last version of plate 16, achieving oneness with Christ and with Blake, becomes the Awakener of Albion, giant man and nation; and this double vision issues as the subject of plate 42.

In plate 42 (see figs. 15–17), description becomes more problematical still, owing largely to calculated ambiguities that cause the figures portrayed to resist identification and owing also to deliberate alterations of the design that make it impossible to believe that separate versions of it are intended to make the same statement. This design, which relates to those on plates 1, 16, and 18 (see figs. 6, 8, 10–13), should be seen in the light of the following lines from Blake's poem, lines portraying Milton from three distinct perspectives:

> . . . his [Milton's] Mortal part
> Sat frozen in the rock of Horeb: and his Redeemed portion,
> Thus form'd the Clay of Urizen; but within that portion
> His real Human walkd above in power and majesty
> Tho darkend . . .
>
> (20 [22]:10–14)

It has been said that the poem *Milton* is "a brilliant experiment in the shifting of visionary perspectives";[77] it should be added that this array of perspectives is also evident in the illuminations that accompany the poem, Blake's strategy here finding succinct formulation in the words of Henri Bergson: "We set our states of consciousness side by side in such a way as to perceive their simultaneity, no longer in one another, but alongside one another . . ."[78]

In all versions of plate 1 and in the early versions of plate 16, Blake portrays the "real Human" part of Milton walking "above in power and majesty/Tho darkend"; in the final version of plate 16, he shows Milton's "Redeemed portion" about to form "the Clay of Urizen" (plate 18; see figs. 12 and 13); finally in plate 42, we see, at least from one perspective, the "Mortal part" of Milton "frozen in the rock of Horeb," his emanation embracing him protectively. Interestingly, when Milton begins his descent he is seen from two different perspectives. One is his own (and ours) on plate 1: "*to himself* he seemd a wanderer lost in dreary night" (15 [17]:16; my italics). The other is that of the Eternals (and of us) on plate 42: here Milton is seen in his "cold and dim repose," appearing to those "*Who dwell in immortality*" as "One sleeping on a couch" (15 [17]:10–15; my italics). But then Milton is not the only character seen in the posture of death, sleeping on a couch. Early in the poem we hear of "Albions/Death Couch" (9:2–3); and Leutha, some lines later, says that her "Sick Couch bears the dark shades of Eternal Death infolding/The Spectre of

Satan" (13 [14]:1–2). Repeatedly, Milton himself sees "Albion upon the Rock of Ages":

> Deadly pale outstretchd and snow cold, storm coverd;
> A Giant form of perfect beauty outstretchd on the rock
> In solemn death: the Sea of Time & Space thunderd aloud
> Against the rock, which was inwrapped with the weeds of death
> Hovering over the cold bosom, in its vortex Milton bent down
> To the bosom of death, what was underneath soon seemed above.
> A cloudy heaven mingled with stormy seas in loudest ruin . . .
>   (15 [17]:36–43; cf. 18 [20]:2–3; 19 [21]:57; and 34 [38]:44–46)

And when the Shadowy Female sees Milton, she howls "in her lamentation/Over the Deeps outstretching her Twenty seven Heavens over Albion" (18 [20]:2–3). Even Satan sinks down in "a dreadful Death" and is seen "repos'd on his Couch/Beneath the Couch of Albion" (9:48–50).

If we look outside of *Milton,* back to *The Four Zoas* or forward to *Jerusalem,* we find an accumulation of passages that encourage us to identify the male figure in plate 42 as Albion, especially the passage in which Blake speaks of "Man who lays upon the shores leaning his faded head/Upon the Oozy rock inwrapped with the weeds of death/His eyes sink hollow in his head his flesh coverd with slime/And shrunk up to the bones alas that Man should come to this" (VII, p. 108, ll. 29–32; but see also *Jerusalem,* plate 94). Beating the heavy air with its enormous wings is "the Strong Eagle" who watches "with Eager Eye/Till Man shall leave a corruptible body" (VII, p. 109, ll. 1–6). But this passage also serves to remind us that Blake uses the image of the death couch less to depict individuals than to depict states in which individuals find themselves. Later in *Milton* it becomes evident that the death couch represents the state from which Milton is rising:

> And Milton oft sat up on the Couch of Death & oft conversed
> In vision & dream beatific with the Seven Angels of the Presence[.]
>   (32 [35]:1–2)

But the death couch also emblematizes a state that all the other characters at one time or another inhabit:

> And Ololon examined all the Couches of the Dead.
> Even of Los & Enitharmon & all the Sons of Albion

> And his Four Zoas terrified & on the verge of Death
> *In midst of these was Miltons Couch . . .*
>
> (35 [39]:26–29; my italics)

In Copies A, B, and C (see figs. 15 and 16), the figures on the couch may be differently construed, though in Copy C the fact that the male body has the same rainbow coloration as Milton's has on plate 15 [18] at least hints that the sleeping male in plate 38 [42] is Milton. In Copy D (see fig. 17), however, a detail is added that specifically invites us to see the death couch as Milton's. In all the early versions of the plate, in which the male and female figures are enveloped in a system of lines, the couch itself is colored in dark tones. This is true even of Copy C, though here some yellow is apparent on the face of the rock. In Copy D, however, the system of lines is lifted, and at the same time, both the bed of the couch and its face are painted gold. This detail establishes the Eternals' perspective from which we see the vegetating Milton—"his Shadow"—"as One sleeping on a couch/Of *gold* (15 [17]:8–13; my italics). Only Milton is represented in the poem as inhabiting a golden couch; and in the instant he is so perceived, "those in immortality gave forth their Emanations/Like Females of sweet beauty, to guard round him & to feed/His lips with food of Eden" (ll. 13–15). The detail of the golden bed forces upon us a perspective from which we may view Milton; however, it does not prevent us from seeing in the design other figures who have fallen into the sleep of death, Albion among them.

Plate 42, then, is deliberately ambiguous, Blake wishing to emphasize a state rather than the individuals who occupy that state. It is one of those pictures that, in the words of David Erdman, present "a wealth of . . . contrary or ambivalent visionary forms"[79] or that, in the words of Janet Warner, portray "the potential for regeneration" without itself being a portrayal of regeneration.[80] Yet the plate is not so ambiguous that identifications are impossible: it draws into one image both Milton and Albion. Doubtless, Blake wishes us to remember that the state depicted here is the one from which Milton is rising and the one from which Albion is awakening (the one which in *Jerusalem* he will transcend). The eagle of genius, through the Bard's Song, inspired Milton's awakening; and Milton, in turn, becomes the eagle of genius who awakens Albion:

> Now Albions sleeping Humanity began to turn upon his Couch;
> Feeling the electric flame of Miltons awful precipitate descent.
>
> (20 [22] :25–26)

This is not the first time that the eagle, a traditional symbol of the prophet, appears in Blake's work as an awakener: in *Visions of the Daughters of Albion,* "the Eagle returns/ . . . and lifts his golden beak . . . /Shaking the dust from his immortal pinions to awake/The sun that sleeps too long" (2:25–28). Even so, this design resists the easy interpretation that John Grant would place upon it, when he says, uncompromisingly, that Blake depicts the male and female figures "being awakened rather than tormented by an eagle."[81]   The fact is that all versions of the design are ambiguous and that, in the last version of it, the ambiguity is centered in the image of the eagle, which, though it may promise the resurrection and the new life, is very like the "screaming eagle" of *America* and the devouring eagle of *The Four Zoas.* But these negative implications of the image are mitigated by the streaks of sunlight that reflect off the eagle's head and wings, a conjunction of imagery that recalls the eagle who flies into the sun to refurbish itself. With the male figure still in a death sleep, one cannot really argue that he is "awakened" by the eagle; and with an eagle, beak open and fierce in aspect (details alluding conspicuously to the Promethean myth), one cannot argue that the figures below are not "tormented." The process of awaking, after all, is painful, even torturous. But given the conjunction of eagle and sunlight, together with the sun's breaking through the dark sky (and this is true *only* of the version of plate 42 in Copy D), one can argue that the design promises an awakening even if it does not formally portray it.

The ambiguity of Blake's eagle image has illuminating analogues in Christian literature and art, and these analogues reinforce the interpretation of plate 42 given here. Blake's eagle calls to mind the devouring bird of Deuteronomy and Ezekiel referred to in the Book of Revelation (18:1–2). It also reminds us, especially as it is colored in Copy D, of the "great eagle with great wings . . . full of feathers, which had *divers colours*" (Ezekiel 17:3; my italics)–a passage foreshadowing the flying eagle who is "full of eyes within" in the Book of Revelation, but is also the harbinger of woe, who in the authorized version of the Apocalypse is represented as an angel but who in biblical illustration is often portrayed as an eagle (see 4:7–8, 8:13).[82] Swedenborg comments illuminatingly when, after associating Ezekiel's eagle with its wings of many colors and two eagles of Revelation (4:7; 18:2), he explains that the eagle represents "the divine intelligence . . . and providence of the Lord"; as symbol it points to the divine vision whose emanation is "the light of heaven." Emblematized as an eagle, Milton or the Bard, depending upon the perspective from which we view plate 42, is like the Revelation angel (eagle) "flying in the midst of heaven" (8:13), representing the divine vision proceeding from the Lord.[83] Further observations by Swedenborg confirm the identification of Milton with the eagle at the same time that they underscore the regenerative aspects of this design. Ezekiel's eagle with its many-colored wings (like Milton in plate 19) is confronted by a vine (like Los in the same plate) that bent its roots and shot forth branches toward him. In this context, the eagle is not only a symbol of regeneration but a figure for *the process* that regenerates "the spiritual or internal man," especially his "intelligence."[84]

When Blake called Milton the Awakener, he did so with great care, aware that an "awakener" is both one in the process of waking up himself and one who would awaken others. The eagle image captures the nuances implicit in Blake's epithet. The eagle in Copy D has presumably flown into the sun, but the eagle's flight into the sun was generally understood as merely a stage in the regenerative process:

The nature of the eagle is such that in old age its beak and claws grow so large that it is unable to refresh itself with food. And indeed it then ascends toward the sun, until its feathers are burned away by the heat, and thence it falls into living water. . . . it pares down its beak and claws on a rock and, afterward taking food, renews its youth.[85]

The sinister beak of the eagle in Blake's design, especially in Copies C and D, and the presence of rock and water constitute a significant conjunction of imagery. The point of the Christian allegory is that, like the eagle, we draw near, become one with,

Christ, the true sun, and are thus able to dash to pieces our curved beaks, our evil habits of mind, after which we accomplish our transfiguration. This is precisely the process under way in Blake's poem: Milton, as he draws near Christ, sheds his erroneous doctrines, becoming like Christ so that we may become like him. Not until his awakening is fully achieved can he accomplish the awakening of Albion-England.

The initially sinister quality of the eagle is mitigated by these associations and by the fact that the sunlight thrown off the eagle's wings is the radiance that transforms the fallen world into the heavenly Jerusalem. The eagle is the bird of apocalypse, not only because it is Saint John's symbol and a prominent image in all apocalyptic literature, but also because it is the bird that, with plumes of gold and wings outspread, intent to swoop, startled Dante from his sleep in the *Purgatorio* (IX. 19–21, 28–33). The eagle is the visionary power that awakens the poet, awakening Dante and Milton and now, through Milton, about to awaken Albion; and in Dante's poem, as well as in Blake's, through the frantic pattern of its flight, the eagle emblematizes the psychic turmoil of the struggling hero.[86] Moreover, nearly any bestiary that tells the story of the eagle flying into the sun allegorizes it, enabling Blake to recall in plate 42 the garment motif of plate 16:

Do the same thing, O Man, you who are clothed in the old garment and have the eyes of your heart growing foggy.... and then your youth will be renewed like the eagle's.[87]

No design accompanying *Milton* is so ambiguous as this one, nor is any design so fully enmeshed in a system of lines, a device used here, along with the enveloping female, to symbolize the weeds of repression and death. At least this observation is true of the renderings of this plate in Copies A, B, and C (see figs. 15 and 16). But in Copy D (see fig. 17), significant alterations occur: the screaming, devouring eagle becomes also an eagle of inspiration, the system of lines is lifted from the design, and the eyes of the female figure are opened. With these alterations, the theme of awakening into a new life—a life of continuous vision—is heightened. The cycles of history are broken by Milton, and the Last Harvest of the Apocalypse is ready to begin.

This discussion, if it has penetrated the subjects of Blake's designs, has also revealed something of their artistry. Concerned with man's awakening into eternal life through the agency of imagination represented by Milton, these designs establish the multiplicity of perspectives within Blake's epic; and they also illuminate the various perspectives that Blake, at different times, took on his subject. Moreover, they show that, however far he may stray from the usual Milton iconography, Blake still remains within the venerable tradition of portraiture that is concerned not with "the unbiased re-creation of the physical phenomenon" but with "the psychology of the model." Struggling "to avoid reportage" by employing the devices of "periphrasis or aphoristic exaggeration of characteristic features,"[88] Blake embraced this tradition, not because he mindlessly submitted to its force but because he felt a genuine affinity with it. The play of this tradition upon Blake's illuminations had the effect of subordinating the actual appearance of Milton to an *idea* of him as the hero of political radicalism, as awakener and deliverer of his nation; and in the process Blake liberated himself from a tradition of art and of criticism that had repeatedly misrepresented and misconstrued his subject.

Yet even as Blake reverted to this older tradition, he retained important ties with more conventional eighteenth-century Milton portraiture. Marcia Pointon has separated "anecdotal portraits" of Milton into three groups, "each symptomatic of one particular aspect of the Milton cult."[89] First, there are a number of pictures portraying Milton, with his daughters, composing; second, there are those with a particularly romantic appeal, many of which depict Milton inspired; finally, there are those in which the interest is political and historical. Blake's designs for *Milton* participate in this tradition of "anecdotal" portraiture, but they are not themselves "anecdotal portraits."

Plate 19 of *Milton* and also plates 42 and 45 owe something to the tradition of portraiture that depicts Milton with his wives and daughters, the great examples of which are George Romney's *Milton Dictating to His Daughters* and Richard Westall's *Milton's Apparition.*[90] So does plate 18 (see fig. 13; cf. fig. 12), which through the six dancing figures implies that Ololon is looking on, beholding Milton's victory, even as those figures, which hold the instruments of prophecy, suggest that Milton, responding to, in-

spired by prophecy, is in this moment fulfilling it. Here, as in
plates 2, 17, 32, and 37 (see fig. 14), Blake is playing variations
upon the Milton portraiture described in Pointon's second category: instead of portraying Milton inspired, these latter designs
show him inspiring both William Blake and his brother Robert.
The double theme of Milton inspired and inspiring is gathered into
the deliberate ambiguity of plate 42 (see figs. 15–17), which,
viewed one way, shows Milton inspired by the eagle (the Bard's
Song) to undertake his descent and which, viewed another way,
shows Milton, emblematically, as the inspiring eagle awakening
Albion, both giant man and nation, from his couch of slumber—an
act that presages the apocalyptic moment alluded to on plate 50
and so fully anatomized in *Jerusalem*. Plates 1 and 16 (see figs.
6–8, 10 and 11), which show the Milton who has been inspired by
the Bard's song, also fit into Pointon's second category, though
these designs, along with plates 18, 19, 42, 45, and 46, may be
considered with equal profit as representatives of her last category.
Each of these designs points to moments in Milton's own life—his
struggle, in the prose tracts and epics, for liberty and against
orthodoxy, his reconciliation with Mary Powell and his other
marriages, his recovery, when he composed *Paradise Regained*, of
the God whom he had lost in childhood. All these historical,
biographical, and political moments are being mythologized in
Milton. But however efficacious Pointon's categories may prove,
they should not be allowed to blur the purpose that all these
Milton designs serve: each of them contributes to the theme of
Milton's apotheosis. Nor should any of these designs be reduced to
the status of mere "anecdotal" portraits. That is where Blake
began, of course, portraying the Milton of Gray's *Ode to Music*
with his harp composing and then Milton in the groves of Cambridge University contemplating; but this is not where Blake's
interest finally rests. Depictions of Milton's apotheosis are more
properly seen in relation to his poetry, especially in relation to the
poet who lays claim to divine inspiration, who repeatedly dons the
mantle of the prophet, and who soars on extended wings.[91]

When Blake, in *A Descriptive Catalogue*, described his portrayals
of Nelson and Pitt, he set them within the apotheosis tradition,
which he traced to classical antiquity. To this tradition Blake's
portrayals of Milton belong. They are a supreme example of

Blake's effort "to emulate the grandeur" of classical and Christian heroes "seen in his vision, and to apply it to modern Heroes" (pp. 522–23); yet once the apotheosis tradition is noted, it should be acknowledged that Blake's portrayals of Milton, though they possess important ties with that tradition, involve a radical reassessment of it. Not the first visionary to attempt a portrayal of Milton's apotheosis, Blake, intentionally or not, takes up where one popular rendering of Milton's apotheosis terminated. An earlier recording of this moment describes the appearance of a figure "girded with white," arm raised, who causes the visionary, William Gutherie, to fall to his feet, after which, in resistless motion, he flies with the figure through air. They come upon a great hall, with a great assembly, on the night Milton is to be admitted to the pantheon of poets; however, what Gutherie witnesses is not Milton's apotheosis but the assembly's denial of apotheosis to the poet, who is judged defective in character for having been the architect of "black Designs" against the King and State and for having then "varnish[ed] and defend[ed] the most inhuman Action."[92] Blake's *Milton* begins with a judgment of Milton that is no less harsh, Blake scoring him, not for being a revolutionary, but for allowing contradictions in his ideology to impede the revolutionary cause. In plate 1 of *Milton,* the poet walks naked, Blake exhibiting Milton's shame, exposing his faults, so that in overcoming them Milton can be clothed in white raiment (see Revelation 3:5 and 16:15). The apotheosis tradition is thus invoked, but at the same time that Blake observes its literary and artistic conventions he provides a critique of the philosophy, the morality, that the tradition usually enshrined.

The apotheosis of the hero, as John M. Steadman explains, is a conventional motif whose purpose is to trace a figure's progress toward heroic knowledge, a knowledge that has the status of a divine orthodoxy. The apotheosis tradition, signaled by a flight or by an ascent, depicts the hero, literally or fictively, in a period after his death; the hero is shown in a region of dark clouds, cleansing himself of error, "of the contagion of earthly sins," and inuring himself "to withstand the pure flames of heaven."[93] This tradition, with its strong apocalyptic overtones, is generally confined "to a handful of verses"—it constitutes "a brief episode" in a long poem.[94] Connections between this tradition and Blake's poem should be obvious: *Milton* is about an epiphany that, bringing Milton to illumination, causes him to cast off his previous errors, represented by the dark clouds rolled back in early versions of plate 1, as, in the final version of this plate, he steps into the fires of purgation.

Besides these parallels between the apotheosis tradition and *Milton,* there are also important deviations from the tradition that are integral to the poem's meaning. The hero's journey is neither a flight nor an ascent; it is a descent into the self and into the world of generation. The apotheosis motif, rather than being relegated to a brief episode, is expanded into the central episode of a brief epic poem. These inversions of tradition point to Blake's radical reassessment of it: his purpose is not playful perversity; it is to rid a literary and artistic tradition of its usual philosophical underpinnings. Ordinarily the hero's apotheosis is the result of his adopting an attitude of contempt for this world; only by divorcing his soul from his body, only by freeing himself of worldly concerns by taking on the cloak of chastity, is he able to achieve his apotheosis. Blake's point is otherwise. Precisely because Milton exhibited contempt for this world, precisely because he donned the robes of chastity, holding his soul distinct from his body, he remained isolated, for most of his life, from the divine vision, from the fiery city of Jerusalem. Milton's errors, then, are the errors of the philosophical tradition behind the apotheosis motif; and so, fittingly, Milton undertakes a descent into this world, not a flight from it, which begins with his re-entering his body and which culminates in his union with Ololon, who is "a Virgin of twelve years" (36 [40] :17).

Blake employs the apotheosis tradition as his precursors did, to focus sharply on "the hero's intellectual development";[95] and, as he does so, a comic vision overcomes the initially tragic implications of his theme. Milton, for most of his life, was like Chaucer's Troilus, who asked "the right questions" but did not always "find the right answers"; and, as in Chaucer's poem, the result of this questioning "is to enhance the irony ... of the *condition humaine.* "[96] Yet Milton is, from Blake's point of view, more than an idiot questioner: the questions he asked, though for a time unanswered or wrongly answered, involved him in a mental journey that turned secular tragedy into divine comedy where finally answers are found as errors are purged. Milton justifies the ways of God not in *Paradise Lost* but in the act of asking in that poem the questions which led to the vision of *Paradise Regained.* That is why Milton's famous proclamation, "To Justify the Ways of God to Men," appears on the title page of *Milton.* Ultimately, Milton rose higher than other poets because he penetrated and unveiled the errors with which other poets tried to wing their way to Jerusalem. The act of annihilating error, depicted in early versions of plate 16, and the subsequent transfiguration, in the last version of the same plate, are made possible only through Milton's decision to scrutinize his intellectual system and to purge from it all that taints his vision. The decisive "action" in *Milton* occurs in a moment of silence, when the poet stands quietly before "The darkend Urizen; as the sculptor silent stands before/His forming image; he walks round it patient labouring/ . . . forming bright Urizen" (20 [22]:7–10)—an image that on plate 18 is broken (see figs. 12 and 13). No one now needs to call on Milton for atonement: he here comprehends the difference between a destructive act and a creative one, between putting to death a king and tearing asunder what the king signifies. In the spirit of at least one treatise on prophecy, belonging to his own time and place, Milton Agonistes has now become Milton Eikonoklastes, here engaging in the very activity that signals individual redemption and that presages the deliverance of a nation.[97] The story of one epic hero concluded with the death and burial of "a breaker of horses"; the story of this epic hero cannot even begin until he determines to engage in the iconoclastic enterprise, to become a breaker of images. Blake's *Milton* designs are a vital part of his poem and of the mythology that informs it, but they are equally important as illuminations of Milton's life and art as Blake understood them.

In this regard, Robert N. Essick provides us with an important comment as he asserts the significance of "the linear net" in the designs that accompany Blake's illuminated books:

A system of crosshatching . . . completely covers the nude male pictured on the title-page of *Milton.* . . . If this is a portrait of Milton, then it is surely the poet bound to conventions as potentially misleading as those dominating the representation of his body.[98]

There is no reason to doubt that this is a portrait of Milton nor any reason to question the accuracy of Essick's description of this frontispiece. What Essick says by way of annotation is equally suggestive: the crosshatching that completely covers the nude in Copy B of *Milton* "is partly painted out in Census copy D" (see figs. 6 and 8).[99] Furthermore, and this point Essick does not make, the crosshatching is nowhere evident in the corresponding plate for Copy C (see fig. 7). To assign symbolic meaning to an artistic technique may indeed be justified; but what this particular device testifies to is Blake's continually shifting view of his mentor.

It is significant that just as Blake mitigates the criticism of Milton made by his pictorial statement so, too, does he eliminate the accusatory Preface that chastizes the poet for being "curbd by the general malady & infection from the silly Greek & Latin slaves of the Sword" (plate 2).[100] Once the symbolic significance of "the linear net" is established—and this device has its counterpart in the system of lines in plate 42 (see figs. 15 and 16)—the portrayal of the regenerate Milton becomes all the more poignant as the crosshatching is eliminated and the oppressive garments of convention are cast off. Early versions of plate 16 (see fig. 10) brilliantly dramatize the identity between Milton's experience within the poem and Blake's experience in writing and illuminating it: Milton now casts off the garment of error, the garment of convention symbolized by the black swatch of material held in his left hand—a swatch resembling the drapery that envelops the poet in numerous eighteenth-century depictions of him (see, e.g., figs. 2–4). Blake, himself undergoing the experience of purgation and purification, also casts off the errors of convention represented in plate 1 (see fig. 6) by the visual syntax of crosshatching—errors that involve not only artistic techniques he is ready to reject because they are disfiguring to imaginative vision (both his own and Milton's) but also misreadings and misinterpretations of Milton generated by eighteenth-century commentary, both verbal and pictorial.

It has long been acknowledged that Blake is intent upon correcting Milton's mistaken vision, but it needs to be made clear that there are two distinct kinds of error for which Milton is being held accountable. There are Milton's own mental failings that infect his vision and, besides, the inadequacies of vision deriving from his artistic techniques that constricted and confused the visionary dimensions of his poetry. There is, over and against these errors attributable to Milton, the obstacle to vision created by Milton's eighteenth-century commentators. Blake's task, therefore, involves both correction and clarification—correction of Milton's vision but also clarification of it, especially that part of it which was hidden by repressive artistic techniques and concealed under layers of mistaken criticism that proliferated during the eighteenth century. Blake's insistence that Milton be interpreted anew, that there are elements in his poetry that have been lost in misunderstanding, was not without precedent. Dr. Johnson's *Milton,* written in 1779, summarized a whole century of criticism that not only Blake but also Thomas Hollis, Philip Neve, and William Hayley were ready to reject; and their "new" criticism was mounted upon a fresh appreciation not of Milton's poetry only, but also of the experiences Milton underwent and the profound alterations in his thought that those experiences induced.[101]

The pattern of experience represented in *Milton* is a pattern derived from Milton's own life—a life replete with "signs of pattern," to use the words of Milton's most recent biographer.[102] The poet who lost God in his childhood returned to him in old age. This observation Blake makes to Henry Crabb Robinson, but it is also implicit in Blake's reference to Milton's "bright pilgrimage of sixty years" (*Milton* 15 [17]:52).[103] Milton, born in 1608, had reached "sixty years" in 1668, the year after *Paradise Lost* was first published and the year in which he was contemplating, if not writing, *Paradise Regained.* In his brief epic, Milton breaks away from the terrifying theology that clouded the vision of his earlier epic; he returns to the Christocentric theology of his early poems, especially the *Nativity Ode* and *Lycidas,* and to the radicalism of his early prose tracts. He returns to the theology that prevented him, at an early point in his poetic career, from completing *The Passion.* That return was made possible by an understanding he acquired while living and writing under the stress of revolution and, in a very real sense, experiencing that revolution in his own mind: in prose work after prose work, Milton associated custom with tyranny, and both with error. Interestingly, Blake confided to Samuel Palmer that his sympathies were with Milton's political ideology, not with the theology of a poem like *Paradise Lost.*[104]

In this context, it is useful to recall the Preface to *Milton,* especially its prose section, which presents a harsh criticism of Blake's hero, though that criticism, ironically, recalls the criticism that Milton, through Christ, levels against the classics in *Paradise Regained* (IV. 285–364). Moreover, this Preface, present in Copies A and B, is dropped from Copies C and D. Its omission is no less significant than its inclusion; and if Essick is right about the negative implications of the device of crosshatching, then it is significant that the Preface is withdrawn from *Milton* at the same time that the crosshatching is lifted from plate 1. The Preface itself combined a prose statement with a lyric poem; it set Blake's critique of Milton the artist against a brief poem constructed out of imagery, out of phrases, lifted from Milton's prose works. Blake's attitude toward Milton, expressed by the Preface, was ambiguous; but when the Preface was discarded and the crosshatching removed, that ambiguity was removed from Blake's epic. Milton, Blake came to understand, accomplished his own redemption; and the pattern set down for it in Milton's own lifetime and preserved in his art became the pattern by which Blake and his contemporaries could achieve their redemption. In that sense, Milton might be called England's awakener and redeemer; and in that sense, Milton might be seen within the lineage of Christ, who created a similar pattern for man's redemption out of his experience in the wilderness.

The primary analogues for Blake's Milton myth are provided, then, by Milton's own life and by the resemblances Blake observed between it and Christ's experience in the wilderness. Yet one suspects that Blake perceived still other analogues that lent support to the correspondences he had already drawn between Milton and Christ. The Milton myth, like the Christ myth, involves a pattern of descent, which may be comprehended metaphorically (as a descent into the self) but which is portrayed literally (as a descent into the world of generation). Not only does Christ descend into this world for the Incarnation, but he undertakes another descent, after his death, just before his resurrection, which is motivated, just as Milton's is motivated, by the desire to rescue Adam *and his sons* from hell, from their death sleep. The source for this tradition, as it involves Milton, we can trace to eighteenth-century poetry and commentary; the source for the tradition, as it involves Christ, derives from the Gospel of Nicodemus. In each case, the tradition exists in order to accentuate its protagonist's commitment to the human race, his determination to return it to paradise.

There is, moreover, a native tradition of prophecy, which yields a configuration like the one Blake associates with Milton. The prophecy, attributed to Mr. Truswell, is a variation on one with roots in both religious and secular mythology, many men, all in a different idiom, prophesying the coming of a virgin king who will appear in brightness like an angel. That king, it is promised, will correct the errors of an impoverished kingdom, exposing the false prophets, destroying their falsehoods; he will subvert both institutionalized religion and monarchical government, the two being manifestations of a corrupt nation. Both Mr. Truswell and Mother Shipton centered their version of this prophecy in the image of an eagle, Truswell promising that "there shall come an eagle out of the East, and his wings spread with the beames of the son of man." [105]   William Lilly, two years later, proclaimed the prophecy of the eagle to be fulfilled by King Charles, observing that he alone, of all the monarchs, *"was crowned in white saten, all his clothes that day being white, his Ancestors ever wearing purple."* [106]   Lilly's own formulation of this prophecy contains several relevant particulars: the white king, appearing with a young eagle, "obtaine[s] the Kingdome of Brittaine . . . not with the sword, but by . . . love of the British"; yet he allegedly loses the affections of his people, departing this life, but leaving the young eagle behind to restore harmony and then to rule. [107]   Lilly's suggestion is that the white king, falling into error, purges it, being reborn as an eagle into true kingship. Furthermore, this prophecy is conjoined by Lilly with one that tells of a "Deadman" who will "set England on the right way, and put out all Heresies." [108]   The white-king/dead-man prophecy was given new currency at the end of the eighteenth century by Richard Brothers; and whether or not Blake took iconographic hints from this prophecy, the white garments of plate 16 and the eagle of plate 42 find striking analogues within it. Beside them are the coincidences of this prophecy, and Blake's, beginning with the admonition, "Mark well" what is said, their proceeding with the idea of death as the annihilation of error, and their concluding with a transfigured hero poised to set England back on the right track.

Of greatest importance, these analogues help to clarify the

meaning of Blake's most enigmatic prophecy. For a long time, it has been acknowledged that *Milton* is a "criticism" of Blake's favorite poet; but this perspective on the poem should be complemented with another. The motive of criticism is far more prominent in Copy A than in Copy D; to move from the one copy to the other is to lay down one perspective on Milton and adopt another, to progress from criticism to celebration. All copies of the poem may have the same title, but that title does not in every instance head the same poem.

There is no wonderful consistency that we can attribute to Blake's idea of Milton as it unfolds in the various copies of *Milton*. From those copies, we can only conclude that, as Blake's understanding of the poet—both his life and works—advanced, Blake became less and less intent upon rebuking Milton and, simultaneously, much more cognizant of the visionary dimensions of Milton's art. The same shifts in attitude and motive, evident in the different copies of *Milton,* also emerge when we turn to different sets of designs that Blake prepared for Milton's poetry. Initially Blake might have confused Dante and Milton, thinking that both espoused the "gospel of punishment"; but he quickly comprehended that whatever Milton's errors were in *Paradise Lost* they were repudiated when he composed *Paradise Regained,* the poem in which Milton embraces unequivocally "the gospel of forgiveness," thus providing Blake with the pattern of conversion that became the informing mythology in *Milton*.[109] That Dante and Milton do not have the same status in Blake's pantheon of poets Blake emphasizes repeatedly. Dante had taken Vergil as his guide in the *Commedia;* by taking Milton as his own guide in *Milton,* Blake introduces an analogy only to explode it. As a guide, Vergil had to be abandoned—abandoned at precisely the moment when Dante comes to the threshold of Paradise. In contrast, it is at exactly the moment when Blake is ready to enter Eternity that Milton joins with him: grasping Milton, in the form of "a bright sandal" that he binds on, Blake proceeds "to walk forward thro' Eternity" (21 [23]:13–14). The contrasting status that Blake assigns to Dante and Milton is further indicated by the image of the eagle in plate 42: it had awakened Dante in the *Purgatorio;* now, as Milton, it is poised to awaken Albion, to prepare England for apocalypse.

The idea of Milton's returning as England's saviour, dramatized on plates 1, 16, and 42, yet woven through the entire poem, finds analogues in Cowper and Hayley, in Wordsworth and Coleridge. But the idea extends further back into the eighteenth century than these analogues might suggest. It informs the poetry of Collins and Gray; and in the 1738 stage adaptation of *Comus* the following prefatory lines appear:

> Like some bless'd spirit he [Milton] to-night descends,
> Mankind he visits, and their steps befriends;
> Thro' mazy error's dark perplexing wood,
> Points out the path of true and real good . . .[110]

These lines take on a very special interest when we recall, with Irene Tayler, that Blake's *Comus* designs, besides constituting an important gloss on Milton's poem, provide a rich commentary on *Milton*. [111]   And predictably, these lines have not an easy, but an ironic, relationship to the poem Blake has written. They depict "Mankind" wandering "Thro' mazy error's dark perplexing wood," which is where mankind still is when Blake writes his epic, partly because Milton himself is shown, through the fiction of Blake's poem, still lost in error. Thus, it is Milton who is depicted as "a wanderer lost in dreary night" (15 [17]:16); and yet it is also Milton who, as a redeemed prophet, finally leads mankind back to the path. Connections of this sort between Milton commentary and Blake's poem proliferate and, in their proliferation, emphasize that *Milton* is the culmination of a tradition of eighteenth-century criticism that is still too little known, as well as the culmination of a tradition of illustration that depicts "episodes of national history, especially those concerning a struggle for liberty," many of which are "based on scenes from Milton's life." Those traditions of criticism and illustration result in "the crystallization of the concept of Milton the man as a great revolutionary, nonconformist protagonist of liberty which, current in the early nineteenth century," was espoused by Blake in his poem.[112]

   One depiction of Milton, belonging to this tradition of portraiture, requires special notice: the emblematic print called *Milton Triumphing over Salmasius* (see fig. 21), which, engraved by Cipriani, was initially intended for Thomas Hollis's projected edition of Milton's prose works but was then included in his *Memoirs*. This portrait becomes a prototype—not in details but in conception—for Blake's depiction of Milton triumphing over Satan-Urizen (see figs. 12 and 13). Blake has taken a well-known and much celebrated historical situation and then has mythologized it; or, as Robert Rosenblum explains by way of articulating a general principle that governs Blake's art, he has taken a "compositional type and further and further abstract[ed] it in terms of both subject and form."[113]

What is true of this design is true of many other Blake designs: however remote Blake's depictions may seem from tradition, especially if their viewer is looking for pictorial quotation and iconographic repetition, they remain, conceptually at least, within the margins of tradition. None of Blake's portrayals of Milton's apotheosis, for instance, resembles earlier ones of Milton or even of other apotheosized poets (see, e.g., fig. 20); and yet in Blake's portrayals this whole tradition reverberates. So too here. To set Blake's design against Cipriani's engraving is to be struck, especially as one observes visual details, by dissimilitude: in the engraving Milton is above Salmasius, whereas, in Blake's design, Milton's spectre is above him. In the first instance, Milton's earthly enemy has been defeated, but that is not really Blake's point, which is that the poet has not yet overcome the Urizenic figure, the enemy within, who is responsible for the sterilities of his vision and also for the sterilities of mind in the eighteenth century that had prevented the strength of his vision from being penetrated and disclosed. Having now consolidated his own errors in the figure of a law-giving God, Milton is ready to stamp out those errors, an act which will have the effect of liberating his own vision and, beyond that, of liberating a whole culture so that it may penetrate his vision and be roused to action by it. There is also the suggestion, mentioned to me by Jean Hagstrum and brought into focus by setting Cipriani's engraving and Blake's design side by side, that the extraordinary pride manifested in Milton's triumph over Salmasius and in his identification with Samson in *Pro Populo Anglicano Defensio* is what Milton is now poised to overcome. Thus Milton, the awakener and liberator, is shown triumphing over error, over law, over Satan—over the pride of his own selfhood. Moreover, the mythologizing that occurs in Blake's design is suggested by Milton himself. Responding to Salmasius, who had identified Milton with the devil's party, the polemicist represents himself as Satan's (Salmasius's) adversary and pursues the fiction that he is engaged in a mental fight with the devil.[114]

Such a fiction, Blake understood, was in keeping with the general drift of Revelation commentary both in Milton's time and in Blake's own. The devil (Antichrist), a principle rather than a person, invades God's temple, the human mind, and there establishes his throne:

> The nature of the Christian war is divers from other warre. In other fields the enemie is without, here the strongest enemie is within: there the enemie is another person from the souldier, here the enemie is the same person with the Christian souldier . . . : the Christian souldier hath more adoo to conquer himself . . . and is then the greatest conqueror.[115]

To topple Antichrist (Blake's Satan-Urizen) from his throne involves the angels of apocalypse in a battle whose theater is the human mind and whose spoils are won by those who triumph through the might not of the sword but of the Word. The prototypes of the fallen hero are the various angels of the Apocalypse who contrast with the Mighty Angel, the conquering hero, who is Christ. He, and those who follow him, extirpate the beast from within and thereupon become ready to destroy his manifestations in the world. Milton's action here, as Blake understands and portrays it, is a fulfillment of the apostrophe that concludes the last of the seventeeth-century commentaries on the Book of Revelation: "O England, England!"—the time has come for the destruction of Antichrist—an "Antichrist in the midst of thee."[116] Christ is the pattern Milton adopts and Milton the pattern that England must now follow.

It has often been argued that Milton, disenchanted by the failure of the Puritan Revolution, gave up his hopes for cultural renovation, expressed in his prose, and confined himself, in his epics, to exploring the possibilities for man's individual redemption. This argument is then deployed against Milton in order to distinguish him from Blake. One cannot, of course, extend such a pattern of experience to Blake; but neither can one assume that this pattern of experience was seen by Blake as integral to Milton's life as he understood it. Blake is concerned, finally, not with individual redemption alone, but with individual redemption as it may effect the transfiguration of an entire culture. Milton may recall Samson, but insofar as Blake invokes such an analogy he uses it not to force identity but to focus on distinction. Samson, awakened, at most redeemed himself. Milton, awakened, becomes "the Awakener" (*Milton* 21 [23]:33) of an entire civilization, of Albion. As he performs the work of his own redemption, he becomes the instrument of Albion's redemption as well: by bursting through the cycles of history, Milton leads a whole nation toward apocalypse.

Blake's portrayal of Milton triumphing over Satan-Urizen recalls Milton's portrayal of himself (see *Paradise Lost,* I. 6–12) as a second and greater Moses leading a second and greater Chosen People out of the wilderness into the promised land. Moreover, Blake's withholding of the Samson analogy from his hero recalls Andrew Marvell's withholding of the same analogy from Milton in his lines on *Paradise Lost,* first printed as a poem prefatory to Milton's epic when, in 1674, the poem went into a second edition. Both Marvell and Blake resist the Milton-Samson analogy for much the same reason: Samson is a type of the false revolutionary who, in Marvell's words, "groap'd the Temples Posts in spight/The World o'rewhelming to revenge his sight"; but Milton is a type of the true revolutionary who precipitates the apocalypse that Moses and, after Moses, Samson promised. Perceiving a comparable relationship between Milton and his "types," Harold Bloom writes that Milton and Urizen "meet and wrestle, two silent and mighty champions, on the shores of Arnon, the body of law striving with the human form divine. Their struggle," says Bloom, "is like the wrestling of Jehovah and Jacob, except that Milton will not repeat Israel's mistake; he wants to re-form God, and not merely to extract a blessing from him." [117] This re-forming of God occurs in *Paradise Regained* and is emphasized by Milton himself through the coupling of this poem with *Samson Agonistes.* In his brief epic, Milton accomplishes the fulfillment of the history that he charted in the final books of his first epic, a fulfillment he could not achieve until he liberated himself from the value system that led the Puritan revolutionaries to accept Samson as their hero. [118] Blake, in turn, abstracts from Milton's life a pattern that he fictionalizes, that he mythologizes, in his own epic.

The portrayals of Milton in *Milton* not only recall the Samson story but also exhibit, in doing so, a debt to the tradition of illustration that surrounds *Samson Agonistes.* Milton, tearing down the tablets of Urizenic law (see figs. 12 and 13), recalls Samson the revolutionary, the tyrant-queller, hurling the temple down on the Philistines (see fig. 22).[119] If Swedenborg is a type of Samson shorn by the churches, Milton is a type of Samson feeling a rousing motion within and going forth to defeat those who have oppressed him. But Milton is *only* a type. Blake emphasizes the fact by portraying Milton with long, flowing locks (see, e.g., figs. 8, 11, and 17); but in plate 18 (see figs. 12 and 13), the plate in which the Samson analogy is invoked, the poet's hair is cropped short, suggesting that Milton is impelled not by physical strength, but by wisdom, to accomplish his triumph and suggesting, too, that Milton is less like Samson than like Job, who rending his mantle (as Milton does in early versions of plate 16) appears with shorn hair (as Milton does on plate 18).[120] The Milton-Samson equation lurks behind the depictions of Milton in *Milton.* It is never made explicit, however, for reasons best explained by turning to Blake's *Glad Day,* dated 1780, which in its different versions explores the nature of revolution, as well as the states in which the revolutionist may find himself. Gathering into focus Blake's different attitudes toward revolution, presented throughout his poem in a series of shifting and subtle pictorial statements, this design contributes in an important way to an understanding of Blake's idea of Milton as a revolutionary.

"ALBION AGONISTES"

The *Glad Day* design, more properly called *Albion Rose,* is among the most enigmatic of Blake's creations. It is also among the most complicated and profound of his pictorial statements. Like plate 42 of *Milton,* this design—at least the engraved version of it—belongs to that category of pictures which present "alternative or simultaneous visionary forms of one form that hint a metamorphosis to tease us *into* thought."[121] To enter into the images of Blake's line engraving and color print (see figs. 23–25) is to recognize in a moment that the engraving, showing the fallen Albion, only alludes, through its ambiguous iconographic detail, to man's potential for regeneration; the color print portrays the truly redeemed man.

Anthony Blunt has shown that *Albion Rose* is not "a pure piece of invention" but rather "a curious instance of Blake's direct method of borrowing from other artists" and an amalgam of "hidden symbolism, of allusion to the work of predecessors, of philosophical ideas." [122] Like other commentators on the design, Blunt directs attention toward the color print, usually dated about 1795, but makes no effort to discriminate between it and the line engraving, other than to say that the moth and chrysalis between the feet of Albion are not evident in the color print. The main purpose of both these designs, says Blunt, is to show man "rising again to spiritual life," triumphant "over his reason and selfishness." [123]

Blunt is not alone in confusing Blake's line engraving with his color print (George Wingfield Digby makes the same mistake [124]); but he does help to harden this tradition into an orthodoxy that should be mocked by Blake's statement in *A Descriptive Catalogue,* "the clearer the organ the more distinct the object" (p. 532). Blunt, like Kathleen Raine and W. J. T. Mitchell, [125] contributes to "the process of romanticizing" Blake's subject, a process Geoffrey Keynes traces to Alexander Gilchrist's uninformed observation:

> The subject is evidently a personification of Morning or Glad Day: a nude male figure, with one foot on earth, just alighted from above; a flood of radiance still encircling his head; his arms outspread—as exaltingly bringing joy and solace to the lower world—not with classic Apollo-like indifference, but with the divine chastened fervour of an angelic minister. [126]

"This interpretation," says Keynes, "was pure conjecture on Gilchrist's part," for probably "he had never seen an impression with the inscription." [127] One cannot say that Gilchrist's successors have labored under the same handicap: the line engraving has been as easily accessible to them as the color print. But one must observe that recent commentators have not, in a Blakean sense, *seen* the line engraving, chiefly because they have ignored the artist's own counsel from *Vision of the Last Judgment,* where he insists that all art is "founded" on "discrimination":

> I intreat ... that the Spectator will attend to the Hands & Feet to the Lineaments of the Countenances they are all descriptive of Character & not a line is drawn without intention & that most discriminate & particular <as Poetry admits not a Letter that is Insignificant so Painting admits not a Grain

of Sand or a Blade of Grass <Insignificant> much less an Insignificant Blur or
Mark>[.]

(p. 550)

Of the many commentators on *Albion Rose,* David Erdman is
the most comprehensive and the most exacting. "A companion
picture" for *Our End is Come* (1793), *Albion Rose* is "a startling
example of how Blake's 'sublime allegory' can be missed and
misread," says Erdman; it is "a terrific social utterance" related to
both the American Revolution and Gordon Riots—a view that
Erdman substantiates by finding in the inscription, belonging to
the line engraving, echoes of the *Declaration of Independence:*

> Albion rose from where he labourd at the Mill with slaves
> Giving himself for the Nations he danc'd the dance of Eternal Death[.] [128]

Erdman's discussion of that inscription dispels the usual association of the drawing with lines from *Romeo and Juliet:*

> Night's candles are burnt out, and jocund Day
> Stands tiptoe on the misty mountain-tops.

(III. v. 9—10)

And it discourages identification of Blake's engraving with lines
from his *King Edward the Third:*

> . . . the bright morn
> Smiles on our army, and the gallant sun
> Springs from the hills like a young hero
> Into the battle, shaking his golden locks
> Exultingly[.]

(iii. 1—5)

But Erdman's discussion also fails to account for the primary
literary association in Blake's design, which is underscored by the
inscription; and thus his interpretation, though penetrating, is
incomplete.

Blake's inscription, "Albion rose from where he labourd at the
Mill with slaves," recalls the lines from Milton's tragedy that
describe Samson "Eyeless in *Gaza* at the Mill with slaves,/Himself
in bonds under *Philistian* yoke" (*Samson Agonistes,* ll. 41—42);
and Blake's design itself calls to mind the opening lines of the
drama that predict the regeneration of Samson, which allegedly
occurs at the end of the play:

> I feel amends,
> The breath of Heav'n fresh-blowing, pure and sweet,
> With day-spring born . . .

(ll. 9–10)

Given the great sunburst that dominates the drawing, Blake probably intends to invoke not only the Samson of Milton's tragedy but the Samson of *Areopagitica* as well:

> Methinks I see in my mind a noble and puissant Nation rousing herself like a strong man after sleep, and shaking her invincible locks: Methinks I see her . . . kindling her undazl'd eyes at the full midday beam; purging and unscaling her long abused sight at the fountain it self of heav'nly radiance . . .
>
> (*Yale Milton*, II, 557–58)

Milton's oration, together with his *History of Britain,* provides Blake with a precedent for identifying Samson with England and both with Albion; and Thomas Hollis, William Hayley, and others offer a precedent for associating Samson and Milton, an identification that Milton himself encouraged in *Pro Populo Anglicano Defensio.* [129] Blake's employment of these precedents, however, is ironic; and through this irony Blake reveals a keen sense of Milton's shifting understanding of the Samson story. Blake did not need modern commentators to tell him that *Samson Agonistes* probably antedates Milton's epics; he had Hayley to tell him this, and he had his own critical intelligence to tell him that, even if *Samson* was initially written as a drama of regeneration, its message was decidedly altered by Milton's decision to publish his tragedy with his brief epic, which, coming first in the volume, established a qualifying context for the poem that succeeded it.

Whether we are contemplating Milton's rendering of the Samson story in his tragedy or Blake's version of it depicted by the Orc cycle, Samson is at most an ambiguous figure. That is why he lent himself so well to Milton's tragedy mounted on Aristotelian theory and why, through the character of Orc, he figures so prominently in the despairing vision of Blake's early prophecies. Even if one reads Milton's poem as a drama of regeneration and regards Samson as a hero of faith (and recent criticism seems less and less inclined to read *Samson Agonistes* in this fashion [130]), the play still culminates in a mighty (but unstaged) scene of destruction and carnage; and subsequent history testifies that even if Samson achieves spiritual salvation (the point is disputable, however) he does not liberate his people from the cycles of history. The pattern of oppression culminating in holocaust continues. This is surely the awareness achieved by Blake and imposed on us as we contrast the Orc of *America* with the same figure in *The Four Zoas.* In the interval between these poems, Blake shifts his emphasis from energy to imagination, from political revolution to mental apocalypse, and begins to "revile the heralds of peace-through-revolution as having been false prophets."[131] In the process, the revolutionary Orc is "transformed in a way that strikingly suggests the metamorphosis of Milton's Satan from the brightest angel to the grovelling serpent."[132]

As Irene Samuel observes, the Samson story has multiple associations, most of which are alluded to by Milton at one time or another: "He can be an emblem for the dependence of strength on wisdom ... the strong man 'shorn of his strength' by the harlot ... a figure of the tyrant-queller." But the closest approximation of Milton's "tragic" meaning can be found in *The Reason of Church-Government,* where "the golden beams" of Samson's hair are likened to the "law," which even when imposed "justly" causes *"great affliction,"* both for the Philistines and for Samson himself.[133] Milton's own words here and his later tragedy sanction the idea that Samson is by no means a wholly regenerate figure. Samson the liberator, instead of releasing mankind from bondage, unleashes destruction; instead of being an awakener and a redeemer, he is a destroyer and a perverter.

Blake's own representations of Samson reveal a similar understanding (see fig. 22). As Northrop Frye observes, Samson is "one of the many Biblical Orcs"; and his story is just "another version of the Orc cycle" that in Blake's mythology receives fullest expression in the vision of the fallen Albion. Orc, says Frye, is "the equivalent of Albion in his fallen aspect" in much the same way that Samson in *Paradise Lost* is depicted as the equivalent of the fallen Adam.[134] Blake's own identification of Samson-Orc-Albion is affirmed by the echo of *Samson Agonistes* in the inscription for *Albion Rose* and by three later designs as well, two of which depict Samson pulling down the pillars and one which shows Samson bursting his bonds.[135] When the literary echoes of Blake's design and inscription are perceived, it becomes evident that the artist is juxtaposing the defeated Samson of the inscription with the seemingly triumphant Samson of Milton's tragedy and of his own design, or so it would appear until we take account of one fact: Blake is not content with simple juxtaposition and thus insists that we scrutinize the nature of the triumph that Samson-Albion achieves.

Blake's own scrutiny of that triumph may be studied through the figure of Orc, who represents a state, a condition, that is "essentially ambiguous" and dramatizes, in the words of Edward Rose, "frustrated desire" and "misdirected energy." [136] The state of Orc is a *universal* condition; for as Blake explains in *Milton,* " . . . every Man born is joined/Within into One mighty Polypus, and this Polypus is Orc" (29:30–31). Like the Samson of Milton's tragedy, who inhabits his state, and the Albion of Blake's line engraving, who is passing through it, Orc symbolizes "the defeated, fallen, or damned hero who as victim foreshadows the victorious, unfallen, or apocalyptic hero," [137] the "hero" of Blake's *Milton* designs and of the color print of *Albion Rose.* The fallen hero, like Orc, is not Elijah or Los; he contrasts with them, for "in times that tried men's souls he was not 'Enough!' And although he appeared 'Too much' to the establishment, he was only ironically so." [138]

One must acknowledge that Blake's attitude toward Orc becomes increasingly more critical; but one should not concede to David Erdman that the Orc of *America* is an unambiguous, heroic figure, who is not yet connected with the cyclical process of the later historical prophecies. [139] W. J. T. Mitchell shows otherwise by attending to the depictions on plates 8 and 10 of *America,* through which Blake points to the identity of Orc and Urizen, thereby confirming "the cyclical repetition of tyrannic repression and rebellious reaction"; [140] and Mitchell's argument is corroborated by Robert Simmons as he shows that, already in *America,* Urizen and Orc are "inextricably linked" in a poem that presents yet "another version of the fall"—"a false dawn, a spring that must turn to winter." [141] However muted Blake's criticism of Orc may be in *America,* and my point here is only that it is less muted than Erdman believes, that criticism quickly becomes conspicuous as we move into the harsher tones of *Europe, The Book of Urizen,* and *The Four Zoas;* and it is to this later period that Blake's line engraving of *Albion Rose* belongs. The design gathers into itself the full ambiguities of the Orc cycle, which are suggested by the forward thrust of the nude male that is countered by the contrary direction in which the moth flies; and, when set alongside Blake's color print of the same subject, it confirms Erdman's admonition that "our imagination must have . . . two eyes." [142] It has been said of plates 8 and 10 of *America* that they represent "two aspects of the same psyche . . . the demonic and the regenerative impulses of fallen man"; [143] the same point should be made about the major versions of *Albion Rose:* the line engraving portrays Albion in his fallen aspect; the color print depicts him as the redeemed man.

There are six different versions of *Albion Rose:* two pencil sketches probably dating from 1780; two different states of the line engraving belonging, according to most speculation, to the 1790's, the second state carrying the inscription (see fig. 23) that is cropped away from the first state; and finally two similar, but not identical, versions of the color print dating from about 1795 (see figs. 24 and 25). [144] It has been suggested that the 1780 pencil sketch, now in the Victoria and Albert Museum, is the "direct preliminary" for the line engraving. [145] Inasmuch as the pencil sketches contain only the figure of Albion without background and iconographic detail, one may conjecture that there was another pencil sketch dating from 1780 that, carrying the full design, accounts for Blake's wish to identify his engraving of the 1790's with a conception he had arrived at a full decade before; or one may argue, much more cogently, that the pencil drawings, having more in common with the color print than with the richly iconographic detail of the line engraving, contrast with rather than replicate a conception arrived at much later, when the figure of Albion became fixed in Blake's mythological system. The latter view, though it does not really dispel our curiosity about the 1780 date, accords with the few facts that can be deciphered from the designs themselves.

The pencil sketches are indisputably early; the line engravings and color prints, when it comes to dating them, are problematical. Keynes, like Erdman, assigns the pencil drawings to 1780; but he differs from Erdman in his suggestion that the engravings precede the color prints, which were made, he says, about 1794. One of these color prints (see fig. 24) is bound with the copy of *The Song of Los* now in the Huntington Library, though this binding cannot be attributed to Blake since it occurred, we are told, sometime after the volume "was sold with the Crewe collection at Sotheby's in 1903." [146] The other (see fig. 25) is included in the *Large Book of Designs* assembled by Blake about 1795. Arguing that the engraving and the color print are done from the same plate in successive order, Keynes says that by 1794 "the idea of Albion, embodying the people and personality of England, was established in Blake's mind, and his revolutionary tendencies might well have found their expression in the symbolism of the inscription. Passages in his later writings," Keynes concludes, "particularly in *Milton* and *Jerusalem* throw much light on the meaning of these lines." [147] Erdman employs the same argument and uses it, rather more convincingly, to assign a much later dating to the line engraving. The color print clearly requires "a very flexible date beyond 1794," belonging to sometime between 1794 and 1797. The line engraving, with its "apocalyptic irony of 'Eternal Death,'" belongs to the *Vala* period": in technique it "is close to . . . the 1796 engravings for Young's *Night Thoughts*"; and in theme— " 'dancing the dance of Eternal Death and giving oneself for the Nations'—it belongs to the period of *Milton*." "The concept of Albion as a person," Erdman concludes, "does not otherwise precede *Milton* [see especially 14:14]. Up through the works of 1795 Albion is a *land;* only in additions to the manuscript of *Vala* does the 'Eternal Man' change to 'Albion'." [148] On the basis of this evidence, Erdman postulates a date about 1800 for the line engraving. [149] It is possible, of course, that Blake pictorialized a concept long before he verbalized it; but it is probable that its pictorialization and verbalization occur about the same time; and it is useful, in any case, to invoke the poetic line to explain the pictorial concept. That concept, in the engraved design, includes an *apparently* regenerate figure, whose hair is twisted into flame-like points and whose facial expression is rather more "sober than glad." [150] It includes, besides, a great burst of sunlight that may be penetrating black clouds or that may be about to be obscured by them, as well as a sandy mountain top and, what neither Blunt nor Erdman really takes into account, a bat-winged moth that has emerged from the chrysalis beneath Albion's left foot. Whether the human figure is identified with the spiritual life (see Blunt) or with revolutionary energy (see Erdman), the design continues to be interpreted as Laurence Binyon interpreted it—a portrayal of "Light as the disperser of Error and Evil, and, perhaps unconsciously, himself [Blake] as the herald of the Light."[151]

This wave of interpretation crests in the essay by Robert Essick where it is argued that, in the background of the line engraving, an "almost pure syntax without image" emphasizes the theme of "power liberated rather than power controlled." In this reading, the line engraving is made into an allegory of Blake the artist who, having slaved at the mill of James Basire's shop, now rejoices in his liberation as he prepares to transform "mortal life into the redemptive energies of eternal art." For Essick, we must assume, the reign of eternal art is announced by "clouds in the form of parallel lines and rain in the form of grossly enlarged crosshatching," with the result that in this allegory Blake, rather curiously, employs images of destruction to relate an allegory of creation—images typically associated with Urizenic oppression rather than artistic creation. [152] What Essick and his predecessors do not recognize is that the iconography of Blake's engraving, including its "syntax," tends to diminish the sense of triumph. This perception is approached by Keynes when he observes that "bat wings . . . always symbolized for Blake the power of evil" but is then obfuscated in his contention that "the worm at Albion's feet and the moth flying away from his radiant figure represent his victory over the 'dark Satanic Mills' of reason."[153]

What Keynes calls a "worm" is a deliberately ambiguous image that gathers into a single figure chrysalis, caterpillar, worm, and serpent. When seen as a worm, the icon serves as a reminder of the Orc state in which Albion is depicted, especially when we remember Orc's own words in *The Four Zoas:* "Like a worm I rise . . . unbound/From wrath Now When I rage my fetters bind me more" (VIIA, p. 80, ll. 29–30). When seen as a caterpillar, the image recalls the priests who blight "the fairest joys" in *The Marriage of Heaven and Hell* (plate 9), as well as the creatures who feed on the pages in *Europe;* it also reminds us of the caterpillar "Who creeps into State Government . . . to destroy" in *Milton* (41:11) and of the metamorphosis from worm to serpent in *The Four Zoas* (II, p. 26, ll. 7–14). When seen as a serpent, Blake's image acquires another dimension of meaning. The Orc state is like the state of Satan associated by Blake with "the blood of War" and the "Chains of imprisonment" (*Milton* 32:16–17). Albion (as Samson-Orc, not as their antitypes, Blake and Milton) seems to stand on the worm-like, snake-like chrysalis as if to bruise the head of a serpent, while the moth escapes, unleashing the rain of destruction upon the world. The picture, which seems to promise apocalypse, actually portrays a false apocalypse. Within this context, it is worth recalling Blake's depiction of the crucifixion in his designs for *Paradise Lost:* the nail that pierces Christ's foot also pierces the head of the serpent. [154] But in this line engraving, the bat-winged moth, instead of being thwarted, is freed; and with that a new cycle of destruction is born. If Albion's left foot is with the serpent-like chrysalis, his right foot, rather than simply resting on an angle of rock, appears to have radial lines extending from it; and these lines constitute, if not an image of imprisonment, at least a suggestion of it. These images, together with the dark clouds and pouring rain, indicate that Blake's line engraving is less a celebration of revolution than a critique of it; and that critique, through Blake's inscription, is tied closely to *Samson Agonistes,* which dramatizes the irony of Albion "Giving himself for the Nations" and dancing "the dance of Eternal Death."

The irony of Blake's inscription manifests itself in the realization that "revolution" had for Blake a negative meaning and that, during the 1790's, the word took on a generally sinister cast, as indicated by Edmund Burke, who "in 1796 speaks of 'the death-like dance of . . . revolution'." [155] The irony is even more sharply defined when we recall that "in the late eighteenth and early nineteenth centuries . . . the turmoil of the French Revolution and the succeeding Napoleonic Wars" stimulated considerable interest in the traditional theme of the dance of death—a theme often pictorialized by representing Death in a dance to which he is leading his human companions and invoked by Blake when, in *Milton,* he refers to the "Loud sport" of "the dancers in the dance of death, rejoicing in carnage" (24:62). [156] Blake's inscription, then, connects *Albion Rose* with a long and popular tradition of art, whose grotesqueness Blake translates into the sublime at the same time that, by alluding to the Samson story, it "underlines the theme of liberation through revolutionary violence"; [157] it re-

minds us that in Milton's tragedy Samson dances a "dance of
Eternal Death" that concludes not in self-annihilation but in
self-destruction.

Blake's point is not, as Blunt would have it, that the Samson-
Albion of the line engraving is like the Christ-Albion in plate 76 of
Jerusalem (see fig. 26). His visionary forms, with outstretched
arms suggesting the traditional image of the cross, are no less
ambivalent than his icons: the gesture can represent "man's essential divinity and capacity for regeneration—or from the aspect of
fallen vision, man's own error of turning that divine creativity into
mental tyranny or spiritual death." [158] Like Blunt, Janet Warner
would identify the Albion of Blake's line engraving with the
Albion of *Jerusalem,* plate 76, but her essay points to another
conclusion, counseling that the demonic aspects of a form are
signaled by the presence of sinister imagery and that any one of
Blake's forms may connote "the benevolent or malevolent aspects
of the divine creative impulse" depending upon the iconographic
details that "contextualize the forms." [159] If, in fact, the position
of the hands is a crucial detail—if the hands turned upward in plate
76 of *Jerusalem* and downward in plate 6 of the *Job* series (see
figs. 26 and 29) connote the creative and destructive impulses
respectively—then Blake's line engraving, which has the hands in a
medial position, must be distinguished from both. More than
either of these related designs, Blake's line engraving is lodged in
ambiguity. To be sure, the theme of crucifixion is invoked by
Blake's inscription and by the outstretched arms in the picture
itself; and this theme, as Blunt suggests, generally signifies "the
sacrifice which man makes of himself in imitation of the sacrifice
of Christ." [160] The sacrifice that Samson makes when he hurls
down the temple, killing not only the Philistines but himself, and
that Christ makes when he submits to death on the cross is the
same sacrifice that Albion of the line engraving is prepared to
undergo. However, it is not Christ's sacrifice understood literally—
it is his sacrifice understood metaphorically—that Albion should
make, that Albion does make in the color print and in plate 76 of
Jerusalem. In *Samson Agonistes,* Milton presents the tragedy that
accompanies energy divorced from prophecy and that marks the
failure to distinguish corporeal from mental warfare. The same
tragedy is the subject of Blake's line engraving.

Other details qualify the sense of triumph that has so often been inferred from Blake's line engraving. There is, first of all, the flame-like hair that identifies Albion with Samson and Orc and both Albion and Orc with Satan, who, though once for Blake a symbol of heroic energy and eternal delight, has by 1800 lost his original brightness.[161] In *Paradise Lost,* Satan stands "Unterrifi'd, and like a Comet burn'd," shaking "from his horrid hair/ . . . Pestilence and Warr" (II. 707–11); and Sin recalls the time when Satan's head "flames thick and fast/Threw forth" (II. 754–55). The sinister quality of Blake's image is pointed out with further emphasis by Elizabeth Luther Carey, who observes that one page of the British Museum copy of *Europe* carries four separate quotations relating to comets, one of which I have just quoted and two others that are pertinent here:[162]

> "As the red Comet from Saturnus sent
> To fright the nations with a dire portent,
> With sweeping lows glides along in air
> And shakes the sparkles from his *blazing hair*."
>
> —Homer

> "Comets imparting change to times and states
> Brandish your *golden tresses* in the skies."
>
> —Shakespeare

The *bat-winged* moth also qualifies the sense of triumph the engraving initially conveys. Repeatedly, Blake associates the moth with apocalypse. In *Auguries of Innocence,* he writes, "Kill not the Moth nor Butterfly/For the Last Judgment draweth nigh" (ll. 39–40); in both *The Four Zoas* and *Jerusalem,* he speaks of "the golden moth" of dawn (V, p. 61, l. 31, and 91:49) and, in the former poem, has Enion say that, like "a Golden Moth," she will "cast off [her] death clothes & Embrace Tharmas again" (IX, p. 132, ll. 21–22). Moth imagery also figures prominently in plate 2 of *Jerusalem* (see fig. 27), where the moth is seen in both its regenerate and demonic aspects: there are those who escape the prison of the chrysalis (the golden moths), and there is the bat-winged insect that lies paralyzed, perhaps dead, at the bottom of the plate.

This complex of insect imagery has an important place in Blake's art, with the result that "the life of man is continually compared to the chrysalis and winged lives of the worm-fly or caterpillar-moth."[163]   These images, says Edward J. Rose, identify "the condition of man with the condition of the insect"; they associate "*metamorphic* developments in insect life . . . with [man's] spiritual or mental life."[164]   When these images appear, then, both on plate 2 of *Jerusalem* and on Blake's line engraving, they at once imply a metamorphosis and force a question about it. The worm-man is being born into winged life; but what, Blake makes us ponder, is the condition of that life: Is the figure born into a higher spiritual condition; or is he, to use Rose's words, "born from the larval state" into "a perverted monstrosity"? What is being portrayed—"another cycle in the fallen cycle ruled by the Female Will or the liberation of the psyche"? [165] Does the figure—in the case of Blake's line engraving—create Jerusalem or breed pestilence; does he instigate mental fight or man-slaughter? Iconographically, all these questions are answered. David Erdman, noting the connection between bat wings and Satan-Urizen, associates the bat symbol with the spectral self; and Janet Warner, noting that "the bat is the demonic aspect of the eagle," a negative image for the creative act, reiterates what Geoffrey Keynes has already observed, that the "demonic aspect" of a form "is made obvious when it appears as a bat-winged creature." Bat wings, Warner tells us, emblematize the "ultimate Satanic form." [166] The bat symbol recurs often in Blake's art, always with negative, never with positive, connotations.

Blake's iconography illuminates the design, then, but again so do the traditions of Milton portraiture and illustration. Marcia Pointon reminds us that although "*Samson Agonistes* was seldom illustrated, . . . when it was, the artist generally showed Samson sitting alone, a tragic, blind figure." [167] The first illustrator of the poem set the pattern for others. Louis Cheron depicted three subjects—Samson eyeless in Gaza, Samson spurning Dalila, and Samson pulling down the pillars of the temple—subjects treated by later illustrators like Hayman (1752), Metz (1791), Burney, Stothard, and Graham (1796), Westall (1797), and Rigaud (1801). [168] The only illustrator before Blake to deviate from this pattern was John Hamilton Mortimer, and his design exhibits the closest ties with *Albion Rose*. In a frontispiece illustration, engraved by Hall and dated 1778, Mortimer depicts, not Samson despairing, but Samson feeling "The breath of Heav'n fresh-blowing, pure and sweet,/With day-spring born" (ll. 10–11).[169] The very lines used as an inscription for Mortimer's design are the ones invoked by Blake's line engraving and set in bold relief by the irony of its inscription.

The words appended to Blake's engraving recall Milton's tragedy, as well as the traditions of illustration and criticism it had accumulated. Apparently Blake's intention was to set his own conceptions against a critical tradition that comprehended Milton's play as both biographical and historical allegory. When read in the one way, *Samson Agonistes* identifies Samson and Milton; but when read the other way, it identifies Samson, England, and Albion. Both readings treat the play as a celebration of Samson the liberator and his drama as a drama of regeneration. Considering the 1780 date on the line engraving and the fact that Blake may have worked on Thomas Hollis's *Memoirs* published during the same year, it is worth quoting the following remark:

Let us consider his [Samson's] tragedy in this allegorical view. Samson imprisoned and blind, and the captive state of Israel, lively represents our blind poet, with the republican party after the Restoration, afflicted and persecuted. But these revelling idolaters will soon pull an old house on their heads; and GOD will send his people a deliverer. How would it have rejoiced the heart of the blind seer, had he lived to have seen with his mind's eye the accomplishment of his prophetic prediction! when a deliverer came and rescued us from the Philistine oppressors.

It is also worth recalling here Hollis's final note: "these mystical and allegorical reveries have more amusement in them, than solid truth, and savour but little of cool criticism . . ."[170]

The important point is that for Blake, as for his best interpreter, "the link between Samson and Milton does not mean that *Samson Agonistes* is an autobiographical poem: it simply means that Milton is the only man who could have written it."[171] Milton, of course, through conspicuous allusion, both autobiographical and historical, draws the parallels between himself and Samson that have preoccupied his commentators; but from Milton's perspective, and from Blake's own, parallels may suggest either true or false similitude. One suspects that Milton might have come to see the "heroism" of his early years, his defense of regicide, as a parody of the heroism he achieved in his later years—a heroism modeled on that wrought on the pinnacle not at the pillars. If

Samson was written early (and I suspect it was), it may very well have been intended to celebrate the figure whom John Lilburne urged the revolutionaries to follow even unto death, resolving that either he would be delivered "from his causelesse and illegall imprisonment" or he would "by his death . . . doe them [his oppressors] (*Samson* like) more mischiefe, then he did them all his life."[172] But whenever the play was written, it was not published until late, and then in the setting of *Paradise Regained,* which projects a vision that *Samson Agonistes* parodies and a scheme of values to which the play is an affront. *Samson* may, then, reflect Milton's experiences, his once-held attitudes; but the play is also a critique of them.

Milton, had he lived to read his commentators on *Samson Agonistes,* might have accused them, as Blake apparently does, of having mistaken a false similitude for a true one, false similitude being "one kind of blockage in the doors of perception."[173] Samson was often identified with Christ through a system of typology—a system of typology that Milton nowhere in his play employs, his point being, like William Perkins's, that if Samson "slue more by his death, then by his life," Christ "saved more by death then by . . . life."[174] To argue from the basis of typology may, indeed, yield the conclusion that "The tragedies of the Philistines and of Samson are, respectively, the elements of demonic parody and of analogy in the tragic action."[175] But whether such an argument is tenable at all is called into question by the fact that, brilliant exploiter of typology that he was, Milton does not mention Samson in *Paradise Regained* and Christ in *Samson Agonistes.*[176] Whereas a typological reading recognizes agreement between Samson and Christ, a nontypological one recognizes difference. Whereas Samson hurled down the pillars to destroy his enemies, Christ submitted to the crucifixion to save them; similarly, if Samson is, as much as Satan, "the prototype of apocalyptic haste," Christ is "the model of the prophet."[177]

For Milton, as for Blake, "the most excellent and worthy part of divine wisedome [is] to know Christ crucified";[178] and to know Christ crucified means, as William Perkins explains, that all of us must submit to Christ's passion, enter into his crucifixion, follow him into the grave, there burying ourselves with him so that we may then be resurrected with him. The crucifixion is not, therefore, an experience belonging to Christ only: it is the central event—a perpetually recurring event—in the life of every Christian, and so Blake portrays it on plate 76 of *Jerusalem* (see fig. 26). Through this event, we cease to be a member of the first Adam and become a member of the second Adam. This metamorphosis into glory is the subject of plate 16 of Blake's *Milton* as well (see fig. 11) and of the color print, *Albion Rose* (see fig. 25). In these plates, Milton and Albion respectively cease to be "types" of Christ, their relationship with him here being founded upon identity, not, like Adam's and Samson's, upon distinction. As a prophetic commentator, Blake intends, not to bind Milton's art down to a critical tradition, but rather to expose a false similitude; in the process, he shows Milton not confined to one state but passing from one into another; and unlocking the doors of critical perception by revealing false similitude, he lifts the meaning of *Samson Agonistes* from the poet's own personal history to the level of understanding world history as a drama of redemption. That drama, in its tragic dimensions, is recorded in Milton's tragedy and in Blake's line engraving, both artists proclaiming, as Milton does in Sonnet 15, " . . . what can War, but endless war still breed," both prognosticating a time when "Truth and Right from Violence [will] be freed" (ll. 10–11).

Blake is more in tune with *Samson Agonistes* than Milton's eighteenth-century commentators were, and thus it is no less an error to identify Samson and Milton than it is to identify Milton with the Samson-Albion of Blake's line engraving. One should not dispute Michael Phillips's contention that as early as the "Samson" piece, written for *Poetical Sketches,* Blake "indicates his acceptance and willingness to take up the mantle of [Milton] the last poet-prophet of England."[179] Indeed, it is at least retrospectively interesting that Blake addresses his muse as "white-robed Angel" (p. 434) and that an angel concludes this sketch with the admonition, " . . . offer an offering unto the Lord" (p. 436). Presumably the offering is to be one of self-sacrifice, not blood-sacrifice, not the sacrifice of Samson that occurs when the "sword was bright" and "the plow-share rusted," when the "country is plowed with swords, and reaped in blood," and that reverses nothing: "The echoes of slaughter reach from hill to hill! Instead of peaceful pipe, the shepherd bears a sword; the ox goad is turned into a spear" (p. 436). The "warfare" with which the angel is identified is not the carnal warfare of Samson but the mental warfare of Blake and Milton. Samson cannot so easily be associated with Blake's "deliverer-revolutionary figure";[180] nor can Blake be represented as acquiescing in the "commonplaces" of a critical tradition that time after time he is bent on subverting. Blake has not, as Phillips would have it, "transformed the hour of Samson's fall into one of promise and wonder," but he has let the one fall presage the greater one, which will involve not Samson alone but his people who, though not destroyed by Samson's folly, are not released from their misery either.[181] The prophecy of Blake's "Samson" piece is grimmer than usually thought; yet it is still compatible with his line engraving. In it, Blake is willing to read *Samson Agonistes* as a tragedy but not strictly as an autobiographical statement. Milton the revolutionary, from Blake's point of view, comprehended the futility of the energy embodied in Samson—an energy that precipitated a holocaust rather than an apocalypse, that instead of liberating a nation hurled it into ruins. Grasping the demonic aspect of energy, Blake dissociates both himself and Milton from Samson, insisting that the apocalypse, if it is to occur, must occur within before it can occur without.

This reading of Blake's line engraving should not obscure the fact that the subject of Blake's color print (see figs. 24 and 25) is regeneration, which is to say that the line engraving makes one statement and the color print quite another. Its theme is liberty in all its aspects, and that theme is underscored by what is omitted from the line engraving and by what is substituted in place of those omissions. The color print carries no inscription, an omission that should discourage any identification of it with *Samson Agonistes*. The moth and the chrysalis are gone; so are the clouds and the sandy mountain top. In their place is a field of flowers, suggested by the array of variegated colors. There is an obvious connection between the mountain here and the rocks on which Newton sits in Blake's famous portrayal of him. There is also an obvious difference: Newton is seen on the hills "Now barr'd out by the Atlantic sea"—he is enveloped by the Sea of Time and Space; but Albion, having transcended the fallen world, is shown on the "Atlantean hills," "those vast shady hills" that once stood, that now stand again, between "America and Albions shore" and that represent the "bright summits" from which man "may pass to the Golden world" (*America* 10:5–7). Not in the line engraving but in the color print the "prophecy" of *America* is fulfilled: "The morning comes . . . /The grave is burst"; and "the slave grinding at the mill," now loosed from his chains, "run[s] out into the field" (6:1–2, 6). The same prophecy is reiterated in *The Four Zoas* (IX, p. 134, ll. 18–19) immediately after we behold the risen Albion, stooping his head over the universe, and just before we are reminded that "The Pangs of Eternal birth are better than the Pangs of Eternal Death" (IX, p. 136, l. 15).

David Erdman's notion of "companion" designs is pertinent here: the engraved design depicts Albion in his fallen condition, in the world of *The Four Zoas,* where "all is Rock & Sand" (I, p. 16, l. 5); it shows Albion rising but "Turning his Eyes outward to Self" and thus bringing "Jerusalem . . . down in a dire ruin over all the Earth" (II, p. 23, ll. 1–3, and p. 25, l. 13). Here Albion stands "in pomp/Of warlike selfhood" (*Milton* 14:15–16); and losing the Divine Vision, he "frown[s] over the Nations in glory & war" (*Milton* 6:24). In the color print, Albion is shown entering the Divine Vision he has lost. The line engraving, then, represents Albion in the posture of error; the color print shows Albion transfigured, Albion redeemed. The line engraving depicts a figure like Jeremiah's mighty man who, though expending great energy, cannot save; the color print figures not energy alone, but energy drawn to prophecy, energy transformed into a vehicle for redemption.

Blake doubtless discerned some similarities between Samson and Milton; but he seems to have chosen, especially in *Milton,* to emphasize their differences. It has often been suggested that *Albion Rose* is a self-portrait; and Blake himself provides some evidence for arguing that he saw himself, on occasion, as a Samson-like figure. His letter to Thomas Butts, where he writes that "I have traveld thro Perils & Darkness not unlike a Champion" (p. 691), recalls lines from *Samson Agonistes* that describe Milton's hero as a "glorious Champion" (ll. 705, 1751); yet epithets like these belong to Milton's notoriously unreliable Chorus, not to Milton himself. There is also a passage in *Milton* that invites us to see in the so-called *Glad Day* design another portrayal of Milton, for Blake's Shadowy Female implies that Milton is "The Prisoner in the stone Dungeon & the Slave at the Mill" (18:11). Yet Blake, student of prophecy that he was, knew that true and false prophets alike claim divine inspiration and that the test employed to determine the credibility of the prophet is whether his inspiration comes at night or at noon. The latter is the time of false prophecy, the hour when Samson proclaims, "I begin to feel/Some rouzing motions in me which dispose/To something extraordinary my thoughts" (ll. 1381–83). And there were other tests besides—tests nicely summarized by Richard Bernard in his commentary on the Book of Revelation, [182] all of which point to the kind of discrimination that should be observed as one sets the Samson story and Blake's story of Milton side by side. The true prophet has his wife, the false prophet only his whore; the true prophet, living by the waters of the Gospel, rises into new life; but the false prophet, drunk with the blood of murder and sacrifice, goes down to destruction. The true prophet, committed to mental fight, contrasts with the false prophet who engages in carnal warfare: the former triumphs through the sword that comes out of his mouth, whereas the latter, whose instrument is the carnal sword, pursues a course that through force and violence culminates in self-destruction and slaughter. The "extraordinary" act undertaken by Samson commits him once again to "mortal fight" (l. 1175), not to the mental warfare that Milton embraced in his epics and that Blake, in turn, celebrated him for in the epic poem to which the name of Milton is given. The true prophet goes to death, experiences self-annihilation, so that his enemies may be saved; the false prophet and those who follow him, in accordance with Deuteronomy, "grope at noonday, as the Blind gropeth in darkness" (28:29). From Blake's perspective, shared with some of his contemporaries, Samson was a prince of this world; Milton, a mental prince, who strove for and finally achieved the divine vision. Because Milton separated himself from Samson he was able to symbolize, for Blake, the true revolutionary, whose prototype is the figure in the color print—a figure who, by liberating a nation from the cycles of destruction, became its Awakener. And because Samson, a type of Orc and of the fallen Albion, precipitates destruction, he, in contrast to Milton, can represent the false apocalypse of Blake's line engraving. Samson is a part of England's tragic history; Milton, a part of her triumph and thus an appropriate figure on whom to center an epic poem. Nor is Blake alone in celebrating Milton in this way: in 1799 Mrs. West had published a poem, reprinted in 1810, that acknowledged Milton as the great force behind the modern epic because he pushed into "realms unknown to pagan lays:/He sings no mortal war."[183]

Samson may also be seen in conjunction with the tragic Job, whose God is one of vengeance and wrath and whose own mental attitudes, symbolized by a bat-winged Satan, with hair curled into flame-like points, bring on the havoc and destruction both experience. This equation is not mine, but Blake's; and it is articulated through pictorial quotation, through the falling pillars on plate 3 of Blake's *Job* series (see fig. 28 and cf. fig. 22), a representation that irrevocably involves the supposed triumph of Samson and the temporary defeat of Job. Interestingly, Blake's depiction of Satan in the Book of Job is not unlike his portrayal of the fallen Albion in his line engraving, though Satan, with scaled loins and without genitals, presents an image much less ambiguous than the one conveyed by Albion. Plate 6 (see fig. 29) portrays Satan as a "strong . . . and even graceful youth"; standing in "joyful triumph," his arms are "extended in the crucifixion position, and a halo is formed behind his head."[184] The very mental attitudes that Samson was unable to cast off are the ones that Job, Milton, and Blake, in their respective periods of spiritual development, came to transcend; and it is in this moment of transcendence that each experiences his apotheosis, figured by the act of turning inward and upward.[185] These three heroes go to a death that, unlike Samson's, culminates in the annihilation of selfhood and in the resurrection of the spirit. The Samson story is, from this point of view, a grotesque parody of the profound metaphorical significance that both Milton and Blake assign to the idea of crucifixion.

What is true of all Blake's designs for Milton is true of *Albion Rose:* in its different versions, it looks back upon the Milton tradition, not just the poems Milton wrote but the commentary they elicited; it is interpretive, not of Milton's poems only but of the critical traditions that surround them, and those traditions are composed of both verbal and pictorial criticism. All these traditions stand behind *Albion Rose,* which simultaneously draws upon and illuminates them and which thereby exemplifies the way that Blake integrated "strangely different strands . . . picked—here, there and everywhere—to weave ... the complex fabrics of his utterance."[186]

My purpose in invoking this Miltonic context for Blake's line engraving is not to discredit the historical connections Erdman perceives, but to supplement those connections with literary ones and to adjust the interpretations, especially of Erdman and Blunt, by attending more sharply to the iconography of Blake's drawing. This iconography, together with the inscription of Blake's line engraving, invites our viewing this picture within the perspective of other depictions, not only those from the *Job* series but also those portraying Pitt and Nelson, which, like Blake's line engraving, express enormous power. Such a context points to agreement rather than disparity in the ideational content of these designs. Blake's depictions of Pitt and Nelson do not parody the vision of his *Albion Rose* line engraving: [187] they echo and extend its vision by turning careful insinuation into bold declaration. These three designs, along with the water-color version of *Albion Rose,* exhibit power liberated, energy expended: the line engraving, together with the depictions of Pitt and Nelson, points to the consequences of uncontrolled power and undirected energy that erupt in violence and presage destruction; but the color print figures the creative redemption that accompanies power and energy which, when joined to prophecy, are harbingers of apocalypse. Both Morton Paley and John Grant are right to insist upon minute discrimination once the correspondence is observed between Blake's line engraving of Albion and his depictions of Pitt and Nelson; however, the discriminations required are subtler than those either critic provides. The difference between the representations of Pitt and Nelson and the Albion of the line engraving is not the difference between black and white: Pitt and Nelson are portrayed as "heroic villains"; Albion is not. They are to Samson-Albion what Satan is to Adam, what the demonic man is to the tragic hero. The former are the purveyors of evil, while the latter are mistakenly and momentarily involved in it. Blake did not confuse Satan and Milton, but his critics often have; we should not here submit to a comparable confusion: we should not equate the erring figure of Blake's line engraving with the redeemed man of the color print, nor should we let it blur into the demonic figures it resembles in the *Job* series or in the drawings of Pitt and Nelson.

The "dancing" Albion of the line engraving *resembles* the "Ugly Man" of *A Descriptive Catalogue,* whose archetype is Satan and whose historical manifestations were Pitt and Nelson; like them, he "acts from love of carnage, and delight in the savage barbarities of war" (pp. 534, 535). Albion, however, is not Satan or Pitt or Nelson—he is merely passing through the state they epitomize; and with the capacities of the "Beautiful Man" who "acts from duty" and of the "strong Man" who rages "with the inspirations of a prophetic mind" (p. 535), he achieves the state of redemption portrayed in the color print. The Albion of the line engraving holds the empire of the world in the dark age; the Albion of the color print releases man from it.

My own observations on *Albion Rose* confirm Blunt's emphasis upon its allusive quality and Erdman's upon its political character, even while confirming what is true of all the other designs discussed in this chapter: they cannot be fully comprehended apart from the traditions of Milton illustration and commentary, but neither can they be understood without taking into account Blake's deviations from both these traditions. In the act of employing traditions, Blake has radically altered them; yet instead of spurning traditions, he has harnessed them to a chariot of creativity that goes forth, in mighty intellectual warfare, to hurl down the very orthodoxies that those traditions were customarily used to support. What we learn, then, by exploring Blake's achievement within the context of tradition is not how a recalcitrant poet withdrew from his cultural heritage but how a revolutionary artist learned to use his heritage both creatively and subversively.

Blake's various portrayals of Milton, along with *Albion Rose,* point to conclusions relating to both his knowledge of Milton and his *idea* of the poet. The emphasis given here to Blake's deviations from the Milton tradition, especially that part of the tradition which he conspicuously invokes, should not hide his remarkable knowledge of Milton and of the commentary that Milton elicited. Nor should this emphasis conceal the fact that Blake's knowledge of Milton derives chiefly from critics from whom he sought to differentiate his own views. Only where there was the "knit of identity" did Blake think it useful to belabor distinctions.

Petronius once said that the imagination will not act until it has been flooded by a vast torrent of reading. Blake's imagination was constantly and vitally active, and it was activated not only by his reading of Milton but by his reading of commentary on Milton, whether it took the form of an essay or a pictorial design. Blake's Milton portraits and illustrations give important clues to what he read and to what his intentions were in preparing those designs. The only verbal clue to Blake's reading of Milton comes in a reported conversation with Henry Crabb Robinson; Blake was asked which of the many portraits in Hollis's *Memoirs* Milton most closely resembled and his response indicated familiarity with the volume, which presents a view of Milton that, however partial, was congenial with Blake's own—a view that celebrates Milton as polemicist and politician, while leaving "the poet Milton to the vindication of some future Addison" and "some yet unknown Edwards." [188]   Samuel Palmer's recollection that Blake's sympathies were with Milton, especially with his "grand ideal scheme of republicanism," corroborates the similarity between Hollis's view of Milton and Blake's; [189] but the point to emphasize is that Blake takes up where Hollis leaves off, becoming the "future Addison" and the "yet unknown Edwards."

The view of Milton sketched by Hollis is, of course, the view of the poet amplified by William Hayley in *The Life of Milton,* a work that Blake never mentions but one that he assuredly read. [190]   The Blake-Hayley relationship thickened and thinned during the Felpham years, while Blake was, among other things, working on illustrations to accompany Hayley's *Life of Cowper;* and one suspects that Blake had the opportunity to peruse Cowper's notes on *Paradise Lost* during this time. [191] Moreover, Blake's knowledge of Milton's prose is so thorough, so exacting, that he could not have gotten it second hand. Assuming that he read what prose works were available, he probably read them in one of Thomas Birch's editions. [192] Finally, to turn from these designs to Blake's Milton illustrations is to confront evidence suggesting that, besides being familiar with the Warton and Todd editions of Milton's poetry, Blake knew countless other illustrated editions and illustrators of Milton, none more intimately than Fuseli, whose illustrations he discussed with Thomas Dibdin. [193] The best guides to understanding Blake's *idea* of Milton, then, are Hollis, Hayley, and Cowper, plus Birch, Warton, Todd, and Fuseli. These minds shaped an understanding of Milton that Blake was to refine and to amplify.

We shall come to the fullest understanding of Blake's Milton illustrations when we have comprehended the motives behind them, when we can answer the question: Why did Blake, a poet and painter in his own right, illustrate so many poems by Milton, on so many different occasions, in so many versions?[194] This question we have begun to answer by focusing on Blake's desire to portray Milton as a way of rescuing him from eighteenth-century misunderstandings. Related to Blake's effort to wrest Milton from the perversions of eighteenth-century aesthetics and interpretations is the complementary goal of placing Milton's poetry within a perspective that insists upon the revolutionary character of his art and thought and that represents the principles of art and the systems of value that will bring about a total revolution in England. Milton was an appropriate model for those who wished to undermine the old orthodoxies; and for this reason Blake was moved to portray the poet and to illustrate his works in designs that present, in glowing outline, the imperishable value of Milton's thought, the minute particulars of Milton's vision. Often when Blake illustrated another poet's work (and this observation is especially pertinent when it comes to talking about his illustrations for Dante, Young, and Gray) there is an "ensuing warfare of design against text,"[195] which leads to the conclusion that Blake's illustrations are alterations, not recapitulations or unfoldings, of other poets' visions. This spirit of contention is evident in both Blake's illustrations for Milton and his portrayals of him, but it is not the hinge on which either turns. To move through Blake's illustrations for Milton's poetry—from those for *Comus* to those for *Paradise Regained*—or even through the various copies of *Milton*—from A to D—is to discover contention subsiding as Blake's comprehension of Milton and his art heightens.

Between the motives that spurred Blake to illustrate Milton's poetry and those that spurred him to illustrate his own we may acknowledge a correspondence. Blake was not the first writer of illustrated epics, nor even the first writer of epics to participate in the illustration of his own poems. There is a long tradition of illustration accompanying the poems of Homer and Vergil, Tasso conferred with the illustrator of *Gerusalemme Liberata,* and Milton's epics accumulated a vast number of illustrations during the eighteenth century. Blake's uniqueness lies not in having written epics that are illustrated but in doing all the illustrations for the poems himself and in steadfastly refusing to have those poems published and those illustrations independently engraved. Blake learned, through his study of Milton, a great deal about illustration. Among other things, he learned that illustration is interpretive; yet he must have recognized at the same time that it was not always representative of the illustrator's idea of what a poem means. More usually, the illustrator, especially of Milton's poetry, was held in servitude by a publisher and an editor who were intent upon having designs that supported a single corporate image of the poet—an image determined by Addison, Newton, and Dr. Johnson rather than by Hollis, Hayley, or Mr. Blake. The illustrator was bound down to his age and to its tastes in still another sense: if his designs were to be published, they were also to be engraved by a sculptor, probably of the publisher's choosing; and the engraver of the illustrations was apt to intrude his conceptions upon the artist's designs, significantly altering their statement.[196] Blake clearly did not want to run the risks that had so badly perverted Milton's vision; he did not want his own poetry to come under the tyranny of the sort of misguided commentary from which he spent the better part of his life liberating Milton's writings.

Recently, Harold Bloom has asserted that "if one examines the dozen or so major poetic influences, before this century's, one discovers quickly who among them ranks as the great Inhibitor, the Sphinx who strangles even strong imaginations in their cradle"—it was Milton. Ironically, according to Bloom's argument, the very poet who was himself "incapable of suffering the anxiety of influence" held most of his successors in bondage. Most of his successors, says Bloom, but not Blake: *he* broke away from Milton's influence by radically and deliberately misrepresenting and misinterpreting his poetry.[197] This is one assessment of the Blake-Milton relationship, but it is not mine, and I do not think it was Blake's.

Behind Bloom's argument is a recognition that one cannot pursue a study of Blake and tradition without discussing the *psychology* of influence. Establishing this principle, Bloom's essay becomes a starting point for any study of Blake and tradition; but, pursuing this principle perversely, Bloom also rolls back—he does not advance—our understanding of the Blake-Milton relationship. Years ago, S. Foster Damon formulated a premise that should now be accepted as a fundamental principle of Blake studies: Blake deliberately set his own poems within the context of Milton's. [198] There is not, perhaps, the simple one-to-one correspondence between Blake's poems and Milton's writings that Damon suggests; but there is clearly an attempt on Blake's part to invoke a Miltonic context for his poetry. It should be said, therefore, that Blake moves decidedly beyond a poetry of allusion, creating instead a poetry of contexts; and thus the principles governing Blake criticism should be precisely those formulated for Shelley criticism by Earl Wasserman. [199] Blake may be less subtle than Shelley in invoking his contexts (he often etches them into his plates); but then he is superbly subtle in working those contexts into the fabric of his vision. Reading Shelley, we may have to ponder just what context he means to invoke; reading Blake, we must ponder instead just how an openly acknowledged context figures in his art—what elements of tradition are being retained? what elements are being discarded? The traditions Blake invokes belong invariably to the mainstream of western art, which reached its greatest flowering during the Renaissance, especially in the poetry of Milton.

As Blake looked back upon the Milton tradition, upon what Milton wrote and what subsequent generations made of it, he saw a poet who, rather than escaping the anxiety of influence, was doubly afflicted by it. Milton had spent an entire career breaking loose from convention, undermining orthodoxy, and revolutionizing forms to encompass his radically new vision. Now that vision had become bound down by the very system of aesthetics from which he tried to liberate the poet and by the very orthodoxies, political and religious, that he tried to subvert. If there is egregious misunderstanding, it is to be located not in Blake's "criticism" but in that of his predecessors. From Blake's point of view, no English poet felt the burden of the past, the anxiety of influence, more acutely than John Milton; and no English poet made a bolder attempt to cast off that burden, to free himself from its bondage. This is the understanding that moved Blake to portray Milton and to illuminate his works; and this *idea* of Milton as revolutionary artist, as radical thinker, informs Blake's portrait and portrayals of him. Both, however, are part of a larger goal, which is to enable Milton to rise again "with all the energy of a giant refreshed by slumber" so that he may take his "proper place of pre-eminence among the few names of universal celebrity, that are privileged to sleep no more." [200] This purpose is pursued relentlessly not only in Blake's portrayals of Milton but in his illustrations to Milton's poetry, especially those for *Paradise Regained.*

CHAPTER TWO

"The House of the Interpreter"

BLAKE'S MILTON ILLUSTRATIONS

> When ... one speaks of a man illustrating a poem,
> one must surely mean that he has done more than
> paint a pretty picture to accompany it. He has pre-
> sumably succeeded in translating something of that
> poem into his own plastic medium.
>
> —Guy Eglington

> ... shall Painting be confined to the sordid drudgery
> of fac-simile representations of merely mortal and
> perishing substances, and not be as poetry and music
> are, elevated into its own proper sphere of invention
> and visionary conception? No, it shall not be so!
> Painting, as well as poetry and music, exists and
> exults in immortal thoughts.
>
> —William Blake

FOR ALL THAT twentieth-century criticism has taught us about
Blake as a poet-painter, it has done little, until very recently, to
enhance our understanding and appreciation of Blake as an illus-
trator-critic.[1] An evaluation of Blake as a critic depends on our
establishing his canon of criticism, but this we can do only after
we have explored the nature of literary criticism; and as we begin
such an undertaking it is better to acquire a sense of how criticism
was categorized and defined in the late eighteenth and early
nineteenth centuries than to detail and elaborate what it means
today. In the process, we are likely to discover that Blake advances
beyond "the cultured gardens of conventional criticism" and "demands that we surrender much of our usual operational gear."[2]

That Blake understood the interpretive function of illustration is
made apparent by the illustrations he painted for poems that he

himself composed, and his assertion in *Annotations to Reynolds* that "Imitation is Criticism" (p. 632) indicates his adherence to the idea of the imitative or parodic poem as interpretation and elucidation of the work it assumes as context. Neither attitude is eccentric in an age that regarded imitation and illustration as legitimate, indeed valuable, modes of illumination and elucidation. The eighteenth century took it for granted that an illustration should not only explain a passage but, because of its special quality, should focus upon the poem's subject matter and unity. The illustration, therefore, was expected to be more than decorative; it was a mode of explanation and enlightenment intended "to create a coherent imaginative entity of the poem."[3] This perception points to the interpretive function of Blake's illustrations, enabling us to establish a canon of Blake's criticism, one that includes not only his written commentaries but his illustrations to an array of poets—the most important of the illustrations being the designs for Milton's poetry. When his canon of criticism is assembled, both his verbal and his illustrative criticism, we are confronted with a body of material surpassed in quantity by very few critics of the Romantic era and in quality by fewer yet.

The subject of Blake's Milton designs requires a book by itself; thus this chapter focuses on just one set of designs (those for *Paradise Regained*), though illustrations made for Milton's poetry before that set are alluded to (some of them prominently), not because they submit to quick, definitive interpretation but because, shedding light on Blake's method of illustrating, they yield a set of premises on which an interpretation of the *Paradise Regained* series may be mounted. That series is especially suited to the larger concerns of this book, for it is the last set of illustrations to Milton that Blake completed and, thus, may be supposed to contain his final crystallization of the Miltonic vision. Moreover, inasmuch as Blake did multiple sets of illustrations to *Comus, Paradise Lost,* and the *Nativity Ode*—each new set differing significantly in detail and sometimes in subject matter from the one it superseded—the problems of interpretation are minimized by concentrating on the illustrations to *Paradise Regained*.

Whatever their relationship to Blake's poetry, these designs are inextricably involved with Milton's text; they have an *interpretive* function, apart from a *corrective* one, forming a series of important and original perceptions into the poems they accompany. These suppositions predicate, in the words of Max J. Friedländer, that "to ignore the content of a work of art" is to be like someone "who doesn't know Latin enjoying Latin verse for the sound of it";[4] they also attribute to Blake a comprehensive knowledge of the poems he illustrates and to the illustrations themselves the formidable achievement of having effected a truly collaborative relationship between design and text. At the very moment when illustration was becoming mere decoration, when the intimate relationship between text and design was being broken, Blake was asserting the integrity of that relationship. Instead of ushering in the new era of decorative design, Blake stands as the culmination of the great tradition of interpretive illustration that flowered during the Renaissance. Neither mere ornament nor simply pictorial quotations of poetic lines, Blake's designs impress a whole complex of images upon the mind so as to reveal the higher conceptions and deeper meanings of the texts they illuminate.

By 1801, the time at which Blake seriously committed himself to Milton illustration and about the time when he conceived of *Milton,* one poet-interpreter of Milton, William Cowper, was already dead, and one artist-interpreter, Henry Fuseli, was being applauded. Before Fuseli's Milton Gallery even opened, Mr. Seward was praising Milton for his "uncommon and heterodox opinions" and Fuseli for exhibiting them: "Mr. Fuseli's pencil," says Seward, "is the only true translator this great poet has ever possessed"; Fuseli is a "commentator" for Milton just as Michelangelo was for Dante.[5] The praise once heaped on Cowper and subsequently delivered to Fuseli is the praise that Blake, through his Milton illustrations, was ready to claim for himself.

The illustrations to Milton enable us to wind our way through the inner recesses of his poetry, and they introduce the paradox that involves all the illustrations Blake did for the works of other authors. Those illustrations are too laden with symbolism to allow the designs to be dismissed simply as literal renderings; yet the symbolism is so completely entangled with the poems that Blake finally comes closer to the text of his author than a literal illustrator could. When Blake illustrated the Book of Job, he stated at the lower center of his first design the principle that underlies all his illustrations, "The Letter Killeth/The Spirit giveth Life" (2 Corinthians 3:6), suggesting that he is never concerned with detail for its own sake, but only insofar as it enables him to focus upon those parts of a poem where its spiritual significance is most completely manifested. Blake's illustrations "are present-ments of the spiritual essence."[6] In his designs to Milton's poetry in general and in the illustrations to *Paradise Regained* in particu-lar, Blake lifts us to his own level of perception, abstracts the "spiritual essence" of the poem, and lays bare its metaphorical and mythic structures in designs that probe the central issues of Milton's art and resolve those issues in interpretations with which Milton's critics are just now becoming familiar.

TECHNIQUES AND STRATEGIES

By 1816 Blake had failed magnificently in his effort to compose a diffuse epic under the title first of *Vala* and then of *The Four Zoas,* but he had also succeeded brilliantly in writing a brief epic called *Milton* and was nearly finished with another entitled *Jeru-salem.* Still before him were a set of twenty-one illustrations to the Book of Job, a third but unfinished set of illustrations to *Paradise Lost,* a series of twenty-eight illustrations to Bunyan's *Pilgrim's Progress,* and the designs to Dante's *Commedia.* Like Milton, Blake moved from the lyric to the epic mode as his poetical powers developed; and thus *Paradise Regained* was illustrated, as it was written, in the maturity of genius with the intent of presenting a final epitome of Milton's vision. It was probably in 1816 that Blake illustrated *L'Allegro* and *Il Penseroso* and *Paradise Regained,* presumably in that order.[7] In Milton's twin lyrics Blake found a total pattern of human experience defined in terms of contrary states and progression. In *Paradise Regained* he found more. Mil-ton's brief epic laid down for him not only the main lines of his conception of epic poetry but the very basis of "the Romantic myth"[8] of which he, under the guidance of Milton, was a primary shaper.

Commenting on Blake's *Tiriel* designs, Robert Essick has sug-gested that in them Blake "set for himself an extremely difficult task—to portray and comment upon fallen vision without placing his own style and point of view beyond the artistic limitations imposed by that vision. It was not until years later, in the Job engravings, that Blake created a form of illustration at once both conventional in its medium and expansive in its imaginative perceptions."[9] The claim made here for the Job engravings can more appropriately be made for Blake's Milton illustrations. That Blake had found his medium by the time he executed the designs for *L'Allegro* and *Il Penseroso* is indicated by the fact that he no longer felt compelled to prepare multiple sets of designs. In the *Paradise Regained* series, Blake's talent as a critic—the expansiveness of his insight, the originality of his perception—is powerfully evident. In the earlier designs (those for *Comus, Paradise Lost,* and the *Nativity Ode*), one can trace Blake's struggle, on the one hand, to overcome the limitations, artistic and otherwise, of another poet's vision and, on the other, to deliver the vision that is there in his predecessor's achievement. Initially, Blake burst beyond the boundaries of Milton's vision, which he did not always rightly or fully understand, by violating Milton's text through pictorial deviation from it. Later, as his own comprehension of Milton developed, Blake delivered that poet's vision in designs that faithfully delineate it even as they suggest its failings or, more often, the failings of others who either wrote about it or rendered it pictorially.

The accent Geoffrey Keynes has placed on the literal character of Blake's designs implies an attitude toward them that runs counter to what more recent students of Blake's art have been telling us. Other critics stress the discontinuity between design and poem, thereby emphasizing Blake's departures from the text to direct attention to his own mythology, whereas Keynes, underscoring "the literal character of the [Milton] illustrations," concludes that they require "little 'interpretation.' "[10] Both positions oversimplify at the expense of accuracy. What we discover is that the early sets of illustrations possess an immediately apparent literal character, even while displaying imagistic transformations that lend to them a symbolic quality; the later ones, however, move conspicuously into the realm of symbolism—a symbolism that grasps the spiritual content and aesthetic unity of the poem Blake is illustrating. The point is demonstrated easily by turning to the designs for *Comus,* then to those for the *Nativity Ode,* or by turning to the first set of illustrations to *Paradise Lost* and considering it in relation to the second set.

Blake made two sets of illustrations for *Comus,* one in 1801, the other in 1809. Each set contains eight designs that are the same in subject but different in detail. These illustrations are characterized by their literal quality; and, significantly, where Blake has deviated from Milton's text in the first set, he generally returns to it in the second. The initial illustration is a case in point. In the first set, Blake depicts Comus and his revellers, headed like sundry sorts of wild beasts, with the Lady seated in the foreground and the Attendant Spirit descending from the sky. The illustration draws upon the first 243 lines for its details and, in fact, conflates three separate episodes from that part of the poem within a single design—the descent of the Attendant Spirit, the rout of the monsters, and the Lady's entrance into the woods. This illustration departs from the text in two significant details. The Attendant Spirit, who descends and enters the woods, concludes his prologue with the words, "I must be viewles now" (l. 92); and the Lady appears to be observing a scene that in the poem she does not see. If the Attendant Spirit is not "viewles" in the illustration to the first set he is made so in the same design for the second set; and the Lady, who in the first set has her head bent toward the scene, has it turned away in the second set, making clear that her experience of the scene is imaginary rather than actual, that the entire drama, in the words of Irene Tayler, is "played in the theater of her own mind."[11] Similarly, in the illustration to the first set, the reveller on the far left of the drawing is carrying the cup, Blake apparently forgetting Milton's direction, "Comus *enters with a Charming Rod in one hand, his Glass in the other.*" This departure from the text, too, is corrected when Blake illustrates the poem a second time.

Despite the impression of literalness given by these designs, they suggest, as Irene Tayler demonstrates, various "images familiar from Blake's other art."[12] However, the purpose of the Blakean detail is not to reshape Milton's poem into a work that bears no meaningful relationship to its original. Distortion of that kind had already occurred in various stage adaptations, irrelevant illustrations, and obfuscating textual annotations. Rather than pushing

Milton's poem still further away from his intention, Blake attempts to rescue it; and his pictorial vocabulary, however distinctly his own, contributes to, rather than impedes, this purpose. Blake's designs spring from the understanding that Milton's vision has been darkened not only by his commentators but by his own spectral self, which by revising the masque inaugurated the critical tradition that served to "complicate and confuse the whole question of its moral message."[13] The early version of *Comus,* as it was presented at Ludlow Castle, did not overplay the theme of sexuality. The masque, as it was revised for publication, restored passages deleted from the original manuscript—passages emphasizing the sexual nature of the encounter—and added the famous speech wherein the Lady unfolds the sage and serious doctrine of virginity. Blake could not have known the full dimensions of the occasion for Milton's masque, nor the extreme decorum that it demanded;[14] but, sensitive critic that he was, he would certainly have intuitively understood the seriousness of Milton's intention, as well as the mental failings that eventually led Milton to adopt the stinging repudiation of sexuality as the moral resolution for his poem. Even so, in the very act of revising *Comus,* Milton, in Blake's view, was not simply falling into error but was consolidating the errors that, proving disruptive to his friendship with Charles Diodati and to his marriage with Mary Powell, also created the tensions so debilitating to *Paradise Lost.*[15] The first set of designs for *Comus,* therefore, takes *correction* as its principal motive; but that motive should not obscure the fact that the *Comus* designs reveal a remarkable attention to the details of Milton's poem, even if a few details seem unauthorized by it.

Blake's first set of designs has been judiciously commented on by Irene Tayler; but her essay ignores an aspect of illustration, pointed to by Kurt Weitzmann, that should not be blocked from the reader's attention: "Not every deviation of a picture from a text is a pictorial corruption resulting from a misunderstanding of the model"[16] —or even from a desire to correct the model. Often an artist, often Blake, assumes the writer's competence to narrate a scene and thus proceeds, through his own idiom and pictorial language, to interpret it. In poetry, meaning is frequently conveyed in a moment of silence or in a moment about which the poet is silent, thus providing an illustrator with considerable latitude in his representation of it. This is not to say that there are not conscious deviations in Blake's illustrations, only that any effort to explain an intentional alteration should be "supported by convincing suggestions as to the reasons which might have induced the artist to make his alterations"[17] and should flow from an awareness of both the text and the tradition of illustration surrounding it. What appears to be a bold departure from a poem may, in fact, be an iconographic cliché; and when this is the case, the meaning of a deviation may be decipherable not from the text itself but from the tradition of significance assigned to it. Again Weitzmann offers wise counsel: explaining that pictorial criticism works off two discrete traditions—one of verbal criticism, the other of pictorial art—he observes that "a decrease in iconographic agreement with the archetype may be countered by a new inventive spirit of the copyist, who by following less literally an earlier text-bound illustration, may, by changing it, even intensify its meaning."[18]   As an engraver, Blake had been faced with the task of copying the designs of another artist; but as an illustrator, he *copies* nothing, though the illustrations themselves have, in a very special sense, the status of a picture copy of a text and they have, too, a pattern of association with previous illustration that a text has accrued. Within the context of pictorial tradition, the literalistic character of Blake's illustrations is most emphatically evident; within the context of the poetic text, their symbolic quality is most fully manifested, along with the paradox that iconographic corruption and critical perception can coincide.

The astonishing precision with which Blake illustrates *Comus* is confirmed by a detail in the fourth design for the first set—a detail that Irene Tayler finds baffling. The "oddity" of this design, she contends, is in the way the figures are enclosed by the trees, then by the "draped female overhead, guiding her chariot of fiery dragons. This strange figure is not in Milton's masque."[19] It is true that the details in the upper portion of the design are not in the masque as we know it today, but they can be accounted for in terms of the masque as it was originally written. Charles Lamb reminds us that the following lines, "not printed in the common editions of Milton" and not "generally known to belong to that divine 'Masque'," were printed in both the 1801 and 1809 editions by Henry John Todd, having first been published in Todd's 1798

edition of *Comus.*[20] The Attendant Spirit, descending and entering, explains that his mansion is *"Amidst th' Hesperian gardens
. . ./. . . on whose faire tree/The scalie-harnest dragon ever keeps/
His uninchanted eye."* A few lines later we read of the "jealous
ocean" winding his "farre extended armes, till with steepe fall/
Halfe his wast flood the wild Atlantique fills."[21] The scaly dragon
derives from these lines, and so does the figure of jealousy, which
is transformed by Blake into the "female" riding the dragon. The
arching trees, creating a den-like place, may also be explained by
turning to the cancelled lines that speak of "this *arched* wood"
and its *"yawning dens."*[22]

The point of Blake's designs is not to rewrite *Comus* but to
return to the poem as it was originally written, to rescue the
visionary drama from the moral allegory subsequently imposed
upon it, not only by Milton but by his later commentators. Just as
Blake takes details from the cancelled lines, consolidating them
into a single pictorial image, he transforms the haemony root into
a golden flower, thereby recalling the "Golden Key" through
which one may "by due steps aspire" and eventually attain "the
Palace of Eternity" (ll. 12–14). For Blake, key and root alike
symbolize the world of error and, ironically, the error of Milton,
who, protecting the children from sexuality rather than exposing
them to it, would harness them within the world of innocence
rather than usher them into the world of experience, whose
trodden paths lead to eternity. The whole purpose of taking
imagistic details from Milton's cancelled lines and using them in
this illustration is not to distort Milton's vision but to purify and
clarify it: the scaled dragon hovering above a fair tree in the
Gardens of Hesperides (in Blake's Beulah) is deliberately trans-
ferred to the forest, the world of experience, both to define the
mental state the children inhabit and to emphasize that those
making this incursion into the world of experience do not necessarily embrace it. The Lady does. Her brothers do not. To be in
this world is not always to be of it, and to be of it should mean
that one is passing through it. The point is emphasized by the fact
that the image derived from the cancelled lines and belonging
originally to the Attendant Spirit is altered and assimilated into a
speech by the Second Brother, who speaks of "the guard/Of
dragon watch with uninchanted eye" (ll. 394–95). Though in the

world of experience, the Brothers, never entering it psychologically, are still of the world of innocence, figured by the
Hesperides, where nymphs are protected from the dragon that
hovers over their world.

Those entering experience should be consigned not to Comus
but to the Attendant Spirit, who will guide them through it. Each
step into that world may be a step further into the prison of the
self or, as with the Lady, may be a step closer to the world of
higher innocence promised but not achieved in the eighth design
of the series, where the Attendant Spirit is shown in the posture of
resurrection with dawn breaking in the distance. Though this final
design depicts no public display of celebration, it has a celebrative
character to it, especially the version of it included in the second
set of designs. The Brothers turn toward the Attendant Spirit, one
in a gesture of admiration, the other in a gesture of thanksgiving;
and the Attendant Spirit turns toward the Lady, about to be
embraced by her parents, making a gesture of applause. It may be
that the final design seems curiously remote from Milton's text
and "the very public celebration" it implies;[23] but Blake is, after
all, illustrating a poem, not a production of it, and to that poem
he is faithful even as he registers disdain for the ideology which, as
poem, Comus has accrued. That ideology, taking the form of
puritanical morality, is an obstruction to Milton's vision, which
Blake's designs are meant to retrieve.

The fact that Blake's second set of designs is significantly different from the first is unacknowledged by Tayler's essay. Working
with only the first set of illustrations, Tayler calls attention to the
seventh design (see figs. 30 and 31), which includes "none of the
gestures described by Milton" and which refocuses Comus so that
"the attention of the group . . . [is] centered on the brothers"
rather than on the Lady herself.[24] The latter observation is
questionable: the Lady is in the center of the design; and while she
does not heed Sabrina's words, "Brightest Lady look on me" (l.
909), Sabrina, her nymphs, and the Lady's brothers all have their
eyes fixed on the Lady. The impression of refocusing (and I think
it is only an impression) is created by Sabrina, whose enormous
height dwarfs the figure of the Lady. Indisputably, "none of the
gestures described by Milton" is pictured. Indeed, the two versions of this design, when viewed together, raise a real question

about whether details are mindlessly ignored or mindfully omitted, especially when we discover that in its final version the forest of error is replaced by rich foliage, the dawn just beginning to break has become a day flooded with golden sunlight, and the blue mist initially whirling through the design has become a rainbow arching over Sabrina and her nymphs. The Lady's head is not turned toward Sabrina, it is true; and none of the gestures attributed to Sabrina are portrayed. This is not because Blake is inattentive to Milton's poem but because the moment in it he is depicting is not the one that Tayler assumes it to be. The illustration portrays not the gestures that contribute to the Lady's release, but the release itself—the moment when the Lady rises and presumably turns to her brothers, observing the Attendant Spirit's gesture for departure as Sabrina and her nymphs descend. The second version of Blake's design confirms this interpretation, and it suggests that Blake is repairing a design that he had not effectively executed. Even so, not all alterations of detail can be explained so easily; and those that cannot invite the observation that, just as different copies of *Milton* make different statements, so too do different sets of illustrations.

We observed earlier that as Blake's attitude toward Milton changes so do his portrayals of him. Dates now become particularly important. Apparently *Milton* was already begun in 1803, perhaps the writing of it finished; but it was not printed until 1809. The *Comus* designs, then, precede and succeed the writing of *Milton,* the two sets dating from 1801 and 1809 respectively. In the interim, Blake's attitude toward Milton shifted as his knowledge and comprehension of him heightened. By the time that Blake undertook a second set of illustrations for *Comus,* he had completed two decidedly different sets of illustrations for *Paradise Lost;* and in the process, he had come to see that Milton's poetry requires from the illustrator not so much correction as exposure. This is not to say that Milton's vision has no limitations (if it had none, Blake would have no reason to write poems of his own); but it is to suggest that sets of illustrations are altered as the motive for doing them changes. Initially intent upon the correction of Milton's poetry by locating and exposing its ideological failings, Blake is now bent upon abstracting the visionary dimensions that have been concealed under layers of misinterpretation and mistaken strategies of interpretation—Milton's own, *and Blake's,* as well as those of eighteenth-century commentators.

Blake's *Comus* designs exhibit a spirit of contention—the first set, contention with Milton's poem, the second, contention with the tradition of commentary, verbal and pictorial, that developed around the poem in the eighteenth century. Besides the designs by Francis Hayman (1752), Robert Smirke (ca. 1780), Joseph Wright (1785), Elias Martin (1788), Conrad Metz (1791), Richard Westall (1794–97), and Henry Fuseli (1799)—all catalogued by Marcia Pointon—there were seven others by the time that Blake set out to illustrate the poem. Three of them, dating from 1777, depict Miss Catley as Euphrosyne. One was designed by Alexander Dighton, the other by J. Roberts, and the last anonymously. Another by S. Shelley, dated 1789, also portrays Euphrosyne. Two others, dating from 1791 and designed by Edward Burney and Samuel DeWilde, depict Comus offering his cup and Miss Storace as Euphrosyne; a final one, published in 1801 by Stephen Rigaud, takes as its subject Sabrina rising.[25] Despite the number of illustrators of *Comus,* relatively few subjects were being illustrated. Many designs simply portray the Lady, more exactly the actress performing her role, while others fasten attention to the Lady in Comus's chair, depicting either the moment of bondage, her temptation, the Brothers' routing of Comus, or Sabrina's rising and releasing her. Of Blake's eight designs, five portray new subjects: Comus with his revellers, Comus disguised, the Brothers plucking grapes, the Brothers in the wood, and the Lady restored to her parents.

Even though *Comus* was often adapted to the stage, it was, during the eighteenth century, generally denied dramatic quality. The headnote to the adaptation printed in Bell's edition says, "it was the most felicitous circumstance of his life" that Milton abandoned drama; for the poem, though exhibiting a "florid imagination and elegant expression, is nonetheless remote from modern sentiment and modern language."[26] Blake's designs are corrective not only of Milton's poem but of criticism that failed to grasp its interiority—its mental landscape and action. The point is emphasized, in Blake's designs, by the Lady, who is present in all but one of them. She is not, every time, the dominant presence in the illustration; but when she is not, as in the third design, she is there in the distance, sitting upon the roots of error ("Root-bound," Milton says in line 661), having assumed an attitude of contemplation. Analogously, the Lady is not present in the sixth design; but in both versions of it the mist or clouds that swirl around her—the images of horror protruding from them—objectify her mental state. The detail of the rising mist is not so "curious" as Tayler believes. After all, in *Paradise Lost,* as Adam and Eve are being exiled from Eden into the world of Satan, the simile employed is of "Ev'ning Mist/Ris'n from a River o're the marish glides" (XII. 629–30); and in the same poem Satan is repeatedly associated with the mist, in Book IX "involv'd in rising Mist" (l. 75) in order to evade detection by the angelic guard, then preparing to incarnate a serpent who, "Like a black mist," is "low creeping" (l. 180). It is appropriate, therefore, that Milton should have employed the same image in *Comus,* thereby associating the tempter of the Lady with Satan, with the serpent: the world of Comus is, of course, described as a world of black mists (l. 336). Moreover, the rout of Comus is not formally described in Milton's poem but simply directed in a note, giving both the producer of the masque and its illustrators considerable license. Finally, the image of the cloud is not Blake's pictorial device, but Hayman's.[27] In Hayman's design, Comus is releasing clouds of smoke that the Brothers dispel as he flees from them. By associating the clouds with the Lady, by giving to them a nightmare quality very much like that in the eighth design for *Paradise Regained* (see fig. 41), Blake reinforces the idea that the real drama is not in the confrontation between the Brothers and Comus but in that confrontation as it is experienced within the mind of the Lady. By insisting, through his designs, on the interiority of *Comus,* emphasizing sexual and psychological dimensions of the poem, Blake adds a new perspective to commentary on Milton's masque.

Blake furnishes yet another perspective for *Comus* criticism—a perspective most clearly seen by setting Blake's illustrations against the whole tradition that stands behind them. Previous illustrators and editors had been concerned with the historical aspects of the poem—with the identity of the original participants and of those who performed in subsequent stage adaptations of the masque. The accepted understanding of the poem acknowledged a dramatic intent without crediting *Comus* as a dramatic success. The poem's achievement was located elsewhere—in its moral allegory, which celebrated the triumph of virtue over vice. Unlike previous commentators, Blake looked not at the historical and moralistic elements in the masque but at its mythic and visionary dimensions. Viewed together, his designs define the mythic pattern at the heart of Milton's poem—a pattern of temptation and return, of evil confronted and overcome; and they internalize that pattern as it is internalized in the later designs for *Paradise Regained*, drawing from the poem not allegory but vision, thereby insisting that its true meaning inheres within the visionary forms dramatic that are the real subject of Milton's poem and consequently the subject of Blake's designs for it.

If there is any precedent for Blake's undertaking in these designs, it is to be found not in formal commentary but in the prologue affixed to a popular eighteenth-century adaptation of the masque. This prologue, admitting that Milton has been sadly neglected, announces that the function of the new generation is to assert a true understanding of Milton's masque, to bring Milton forth and spread his vision "thro' the nation." The author of this prologue, seeing in *Comus* "the flame divine," emphasizes its visionary and apocalyptic dimensions: its purpose, as explained by the first of the two Attendant Spirits, is "to guide/An old and haughty nation, proud in arms" toward the Jerusalem Milton hoped to establish in England's green and pleasant land. Lines like these are, however, an aberration in this adaptation; and its prologue has little relation to the production that follows, contrasting with its epilogue, spoken by Euphrosyne, that asks, "What means this wild, this allegorick masque," only to answer it with banality: "All vice is folly, and makes man a beast."[28] Blake, too, was concerned with the poem's meaning—not its "allegorick" but its apocalyptic meaning. In the words of the prologue, Milton's masque confirmed in Blake's mind that "Not art nor nature his genius bound"[29] —all that Milton beheld was transmuted into poetry distinctly his own.

To turn from the *Comus* illustrations to those for the *Nativity Ode* is to turn from a relatively literal to an openly symbolic mode of interpretation. As with *Comus*, Blake made two separate sets of illustrations for the poem, both probably in 1809; and both those sets deviate from Milton's text. Again the subjects are the same, but in detail the illustrations differ decidedly. The first illustration may serve as an example. In both sets the first design presents in tableau the Nativity scene with Peace descending and Nature, having shed her gaudy trim, reclining below. The central episode in both is the birth of Christ. In the first design the stable scene is bisected, with oxen eating from the manger on the viewer's left and Mary cradling Jesus in her arms, Joseph standing beside her, on the right. In the same illustration to the second set, the manger has disappeared altogether, the oxen are only dimly visible, Mary is slouched over with astonishment in Joseph's arms; and the child, springing from the lap of Mary into a blaze of light, dominates the center. Both designs are interesting interpretively, but both also depart conspicuously from the poem Milton has written and from the usual iconography of Nativity paintings. Milton's poem, of course, departs radically from both poetic and pictorial treatments of this subject; and Blake uses Milton's departures from tradition as precedent for his own, thereby calling attention to the innovative character of Milton's poem.[30]

Only in the first and last stanzas of his "Hymn" does Milton allude to the Nativity scene; and only in those stanzas does he undertake a description of it, a description remarkable for its brevity and for its want of usual detail. In the visual arts, the Nativity scene itself generally occupies our attention, as it usually does in poetic treatments of this subject. Related figures and episodes may be introduced, but ordinarily they are represented marginally or else assimilated into the Nativity image itself. The two constants in the Nativity scene are the ox and the ass: they "are present ... even when neither Mary nor the shepherd is depicted," giving "visual expression to the manifestation of God in the world."[31] These icons point both to Christ's humanity and to man's burden, from which Christ liberates him. Milton casts aside that formula, inverting that whole tradition, his motives being different from those of other artists. They wished to focus on the event and to celebrate it; he wishes to concentrate not so much on the event as on its immediate historical consequences and to celebrate them. Acutely aware of Milton's innovation, Blake invokes the usual iconographic tradition only to show pictorially how Milton, by telescoping the Nativity scene within a more encompassing vision, shifts its accents.

Although nowhere before the last stanza of his poem does

Milton really describe the Nativity scene, Blake makes it central to the first three of his six illustrations for the poem. Yet this scene, as we move from the first to the third design, diminishes in importance. The absolute focus of the first illustration, the Nativity scene is obscured in the second by the marginal clutter and, in the third, recedes into the background as our attention is attracted to the heavenly choirs above and the shepherds in adoration below. By giving central importance to the Nativity scene, Blake reveals the celebrative rather than descriptive character of Milton's poem. By depicting the infant springing miraculously from his mother's arms, and also from the furnace of Moloch, Blake suggests even further that the poem is a celebration not of the Nativity *per se* but of the Incarnation, an event that for Blake signifies God's becoming as we are so that we may become as he is. By relating the Nativity scene to both the descent of Peace and the purification of Nature, and particularly by pushing the Nativity scene farther and farther into the distance with each successive illustration, Blake implies that the poem's subject is not primarily the Incarnation but its effects upon human history. This theme all his illustrations share; and this theme, as Michael Tolley observes, had already provided Blake "with a framework and a stimulus" for his prophecy called *Europe,* where "the beautiful meditation of Milton becomes Blake's terrifying prophecy."[32] *Europe* is described by Tolley as a reworking of Milton's *Nativity Ode;* but judging from Milton's poem and Blake's illustrations for it, Blake's early prophecy may more aptly be regarded as a focusing and an extension of the vision beneath Milton's poem, which though a "hymn" is also a "prophecy": it celebrates the peace that attends Christ's birth but also acknowledges, more quietly than Blake's prophecy, that the newly arrived peace will be disrupted, that disorder again will reign until the Apocalypse. Just as Milton altered the accents of the tradition he inherited, so Blake altered the stresses of the tradition that Milton's poem had come to represent—the very ones that Blake studiously observed in his later illustrations for it.

Unlike the designs for *Comus,* those for the *Nativity Ode* have no real tradition of illustration standing behind them. Only one illustration for the *Nativity Ode* had been done before Blake's two sets of designs; and that illustration, by Richard Westall, depicts the routing of the pagan deities, corresponding with the last design in Blake's series.[33] Westall's design shares with Blake's the motif of a triumphant infant, in a miraculous stance, watching the pagan deities flee. Yet Blake's design, coming as it does within the context of a highly symbolic statement, is remarkable for its fidelity to the subtleties of Milton's text—subtleties elucidated for us, and probably elucidated for Blake, by a gloss to the poem provided by Thomas Warton:

A book, popular in Milton's time, thus describes the dreadful sacrifices of the worship of the idol Moloch. "Wherein [the valley of Tophet] the Hebrews sacrificed their children to Moloch; an idol of brass, having the head of a calf, the rest of a kingly figure with arms extended to receive the miserable sacrifice, seared to death with his burning embracements. For the idol was hollow within, and filled with fire. And lest their lamentable shrieks should sad the hearts of their parents, the priests of Moloch did deaf their ears with the continual clangs of trumpets and timbrels."[34]

Warton's description, quoted from George Sandys's *Travels,* not only sheds light on Milton's poem but provides a precise description of Blake's design for it. Milton, as Warton observes, infuses these images "with life and action," making them "subservient to a new purpose . . . by the superinduction of a poetical fiction, to which they give occasion":

"The sullen spirit is fled of a sudden, and has left his black burning image in darkness and solitude. The priests, dancing in horrid gesticulations about the blue furnace from which his idol was fed with fire, in vain attempt to call back their grisly king with the din of cymbals, with which they once used to overwhelm the shrieks of the sacrificed infants." A new use is made of the cymbals of the disappointed priests. He does not say, "Moloch's idol *was* removed, to which infants *were* sacrificed; *while* their cries *were* suppressed by the sound of cymbals." In Burnet's treatise DE STATU MORTUORUM ET RESURGENTIUM, there is a fine picture of the rites of Moloch.

Milton, like a true poet, . . . selects [subjects] such as were most susceptible of poetic enlargment; and which, from the wildness of their ceremonies, were most interesting to the fancy.[35]

Milton's own "poetic fiction" focuses, through irony, on the discrepancy between Moloch's triumph over the children sacrificed to him and the triumph of Christ, as child, over Moloch, who now flees the scene. Blake's own comprehension of the Moloch story is revealed in *Songs of Experience* where, in "A Little Boy Lost," he writes of the weeping child whose weeping parents "strip'd him to his little shirt./And bound him in an iron chain./And burn'd him in a holy place,/Where many had been burn'd before" (ll. 17–22). In the song, Blake imposes his own allegory on the Moloch story; but in his Milton design, he observes, in all its details, the new fiction Milton has created, one of the ironies of which it brilliantly renders. In Milton's poem the fleeing Moloch does not have bat wings; but the detail is true in spirit if not in letter to Milton's notion that Moloch is one with Satan, that he is one of the devil's many manifestations. This observation leads into the conclusion that, when Blake deviates from traditional representations, he does so in order to move closer to the meaning of a poetic text; when he observes the particulars of a conventional representation, as he does with the Warton note, he does so because the tradition observes the subtleties of meaning that, through the medium of illustration, he wishes to reveal. Thus even within the context of symbolic illustration Blake finds a place, occasionally, for literal observance of his text.

Blake's movement from literal to symbolic interpretation is complicated but nonetheless apparent when we turn to the two sets of illustrations to *Paradise Lost.* These sets differ in detail and, unlike the previous series of designs, in subject matter as well. The Huntington set is composed of twelve subjects; the Boston set, as it now exists, of only nine. Whereas the former group of designs commences with *Satan Calling His Legions* and *Satan Coming to the Gates of Hell,* the latter begins with *Christ Offers to Redeem Man.* And whereas the second group omits the subjects of *Satan's and Raphael's Entries into Paradise* and *Judgment of Adam and Eve,* it contains a new design, *Adam and Eve Sleeping.* The matter is more complicated than it seems, however.[36]

Martin Butlin, who once asserted the merest suggestion by Alexander Gilchrist as hard fact, has now laid out all the evidence that verifies Gilchrist's conjecture: indisputably, the nine designs that now constitute the Boston set, along with the three designs later separated from it, are from the Butts collection.[37] Of these three designs—the larger of the two Huntington depictions of Satan, Sin, and Death, the Victoria and Albert Museum's Satan calling his legions, and the judgment of Adam and Eve, in the Harvard College Library—the first two, highly conventional in subject, would probably have been desired by Butts, along with the other nine. This much of his argument should be conceded to Butlin, though other elements in it require further attention.

"The common-sense solution" does not force us to accept the conclusion, as Butlin would have it, that Blake "with one change" simply repeated the first set, now in the Huntington Library, "for his most important patron Thomas Butts."[38] Understandably, Butts would have wanted these very conventional designs; and understandably, too, Blake might have acquiesced to his wishes. But there is the additional fact, that these three designs were sold separately, and the hint, that though prepared at the same time as the other nine designs, and for the same patron, they were not a part of Blake's conception for the second set. This hint accompanies the realization that, when reproducing a set of illustrations for Milton's poetry, Blake always altered individual designs, always the most conventional of them. This is true of the illustrations for *Comus* and the *Nativity Ode* and also true, emphatically so, of those for *L'Allegro* and *Il Penseroso* and *Paradise Regained,* where *Mirth* and *The First Temptation* are subjected to new scrutiny and then to alteration. In each instance, the design is strengthened, even while its conventionality is maintained. This habit of illustration, however, is curiously broken when Blake undertook to illustrate *Paradise Lost* a third time. It is not the most conventional designs that Blake now turned to but those depictions of Adam and Eve in the garden, of God creating Eve, and of Michael foretelling the Crucifixion that elicited Blake's attention. These new designs, if nothing else, should point us in the direction that Blake's own critical interest moved him; they indicate where that interest finally came to rest—in the world of Eden and in the figure of Christ who came to restore what by Adam and Eve was lost.

The motives that inspired Blake's illustrations to *Paradise Lost* contrast strikingly with those that produced the designs to Dante's *Commedia.* From Blake's point of view, Dante's entire vision was built upon the fundamental error of punishing sins rather than forgiving them. Blake's illustrations to Dante, therefore, are largely concerned with *correcting* the poet's vision. Blake's principal objection to Milton was somewhat different. *Paradise Lost,* Blake understood, was written in part to criticize the very theology it postulated; Milton's difficulty lay not so much in what he said but in how he said it. Blake, believing that epic poetry had both a narrative and a visionary dimension, came to see that in *Paradise Lost* the narrative interfered with Milton's vision. With this in mind, Blake set out to illustrate Milton's epic and, in those illustrations, to illuminate the visionary experience that Milton's poem afforded—an experience that Milton's own narrative and the eighteenth-century commentaries obscured. One may reasonably conjecture that, being dissatisfied with his first set of illustrations, Blake felt compelled to try again. With the aim of retrieving the visionary poem Milton had written, Blake very possibly eliminated three designs from his conception, as represented by the Huntington set, in order to deflect attention from the first two books of *Paradise Lost* to Christ who is at its center, to Christ who in Milton's epic is an instrument of mercy rather than of justice. In the act of apprehending the Christocentric character of Milton's diffuse epic, Blake, by making Christ the focus of the second set of designs, acknowledges Christ as Milton's hero, as the ethical nucleus of the poem. These changes in subject matter do not support an *a priori* thesis about the meaning of Blake's illustrations; they simply show Blake bringing his second set of designs into closer alignment with the poem Milton wrote.

Both sets of designs reveal Blake's close adherence to Milton's text. From the initial designs for the first set to the last design for the second set, that concern is paramount. With customary accuracy, Samuel Taylor Coleridge has observed that "sundry painters have attempted pictures of the meeting between Satan and Death at the gates of Hell; and how was Death represented? Not as Milton has described him," says Coleridge, "but by the most defined thing that can be imagined—a skeleton, the dryest and hardest image that it is possible to discover; which, instead of keeping the mind in a state of activity, reduces it to the merest passivity."[39] The exception, of course, is Blake. His depiction of Satan, Sin, and Death reveals how scrupulously he, unlike his predecessors, followed Milton's text. Alone among eighteenth- and early nineteenth-century illustrators of Milton, Blake preserved Milton's conception of Death as a shadow. He could not have known Coleridge's feelings, but he doubtless shared with his contemporaries an admiration for the sublimity of Milton's allegory—a quality that some eighteenth-century commentators denied it.

Indeed, Blake may owe something to Hogarth and Gillray; but his most important debt in this illustration is probably to Cowper, for whose edition of Milton he began illustrating Milton's poetry.[40] In his notes for a commentary on *Paradise Lost,* later published by William Hayley, Cowper observes that Milton's Death is "a decided shadow . . . a kind of intermediate form between matter and spirit, partaking of both, and consisting of neither. The idea of its substance," continues Cowper, "is lost in its tenuity, and yet, contemplated awhile as a shadow, it becomes a substance. The dimness of this vague and fleeting outline is infinitely more terrible than exact description, because it leaves the imagination at full liberty to see for itself, and to suppose the worst."[41] Under the influence of Cowper, Blake translated the amusingly grotesque representations of Hogarth and Gillray back into the sublime of Milton.

The succeeding designs, presumably belonging to a later date, are more symbolic and seemingly less precise renderings of Milton's text, as the final illustration to both sets may suggest. In the last lines of Milton's poem, there are no horsemen, no stems of thorns, no thunderbolts; there is no coiled serpent. Yet all these images figure in Blake's concluding illustration (see figs. 32 and 33). Blake's depiction of the expulsion, of course, is more than another design; it constitutes an epilogue to Milton's poem and is, therefore, an epitome of its action. The serpent recalls the fall (its cause), the thunderbolt the action that immediately ensues (the judgment); and the fall and judgment together point to the ultimate consequence of transgression (man's expulsion from Eden). Moreover, the four horsemen and the stems of thorns are faithful in spirit, if not in letter, to the poem Milton wrote. The thorns at once symbolize the world of experience—its misery, fever, and fret—that Milton so vividly portrayed in the biblical visions of Book XI and that man now enters;[42] and they anticipate the coming of Christ, who, through his passion and death, will restore man to a paradise happier far than the one from which he was exiled. Correspondingly, Milton makes no reference to the four horsemen of the Apocalypse[43] as he draws his poem to its period; but he does allude to the Book of Revelation, saying of Adam and Eve, "Som natural tears they drop'd, but wip'd them soon" (XII. 645), and thus looking forward to the time when "God shall wipe away all tears from their eyes; and there shall be no more death, neither sorrow, nor crying" (Revelation 21:4). What Milton does verbally Blake does visually: both dramatically juxtapose the worlds of experience and higher innocence, the worlds of tragic defeat and spiritual triumph.

Even so, certain details in the final illustration to the first set seem to contradict both the letter and the spirit of the poem's ending. Speaking of "Blake's resistance to Milton and 'reformation' of him," Kester Svendsen says that Blake's expulsion scene is as "faithful in fact (the clasped hands) as it is creatively free." Whereas Milton's emphasis is on fallen humanity moving into an alien and hostile world, Blake's is on the "hope" in expulsion. Blake misses, says Svendsen, the "paradox of banishment."[44] Reaching conclusions about Blake's illustrations on the basis of Svendsen's article and thus the first set of designs to *Paradise Lost,* Merritt Hughes believes that Blake distinguishes himself from Milton's other illustrators by "interpreting the Expulsion in terms of redemption and possible joy." Blake's illustration, "solemnly symbolic of redemptive joy," presents "hope and love in the faces of Adam and Eve."[45] Two details in this illustration support the conclusions of Svendsen and Hughes: Adam and Eve seem to be moving swiftly (Milton says they leave Paradise "with wandring steps and slow" [XII. 648]); and they seem, with heads turned upward, replete with joy.

With these interpretations in mind, it is instructive to consider the final illustration to the second group of designs. The subject is the same, but the details are altered. The heads of Adam and Eve are bent downward; motion is arrested as a thorn punctures the left foot of Adam. The first depiction of the expulsion may seem joyful, but details in the design mute the apparent joy, anticipating the second design which is more in keeping with the sense of sorrow that pervades the closing lines of Milton's poem. In the first instance, Adam and Eve, their expressions incredulous, look up like cowed children; their steps are short, unlike those of Michael, who seems to be on a forced march. In the second instance, the steps of Adam and Eve are slow and wandering, just as Milton describes them, having little to do here with nostalgia and a great deal to do with the dangers they confront on the ground before them: Adam, though stepping on a thorn, seems less worried about that than the serpent lying before him. If the movement of the first version is upward and outward, the movement of this one is downward and inward. Adam and Eve, like Michael and like the four horsemen in the background, are wholly inside themselves. They are now in the wilderness where salvation is to be found, where a new and happier paradise will be raised. Thus even as Blake pushes relentlessly toward symbolic interpretation by making Christ the focus of the second set of illustrations, his interest is clearly in the poem another poet has written and not in a poem he wishes to rewrite. This "process of revision," evident in the *Paradise Lost* series and in those designs for *Comus* and the *Nativity Ode,* is for Blake, as it was for Wordsworth, a "correction" of perspective, not so much Milton's as Blake's own; it is, for Blake, "a way of writing oneself into the poetic tradition" represented by Milton.[46] Within that tradition, and thus from a Miltonic perspective, Blake was later to illustrate *L'Allegro* and *Il Penseroso,* as well as *Paradise Regained.*

Blake's illustrations, we may conclude, assiduously follow Milton's text, but they are also more than literal renderings of it. Blake evolves a symbolic method of illustrating that forces him beyond the text so as to capture its spiritual content with greater force of imagination and with sharper precision of pictorial language. Blake's illustrations, then, are both intellectual and utilitarian: they are something to be understood in their own right and, once understood, to be used as a gloss on the poem they adorn; they are pictorial criticisms that greatly increase the intelligibility of Milton's poetry. The main thrust of our discussion thus far has been toward this realization, but the discussion yields yet other conclusions.

Before 1800, Blake made individual illustrations for Milton's poetry; afterwards, he made only sets of designs. This shift in mode of illustration is itself significant, especially when we remember that, once the artist forsakes an individual design for "sets and sequences" of them, he "enters into competition with the epic and the drama"[47] —a competition that Blake engages in not only as artist but as poet. The field of endeavor Blake now entered had gained considerable importance through the cycle paintings of the Renaissance that gathered large segments of spiritual history into a single tableau. The Moses or the Christ cycles in the Sistine Chapel provide a magnificent example of the form, each cycle portraying relatively few events, each with its own marginal designs, representing the whole of a figure's life.[48] The traditional cycle painting attempts to create a pictorial narrative, but Blake seems to have understood that the artist-illustrator could embrace a purpose different from that of the poet-narrator.

One perceptive student of book illustration observes that "the essence of good pictorial narrative is not so much the concentration of a single event in a comprehensive picture . . . as to divide an episode into a series of consecutive phases in which the protagonist is repeated again and again. The aim is to have the changes of action represented in such a dense sequence that the beholder can read the pictorial story almost without resorting to the text for supplementary information."[49] The critic is talking about early illustrators of Homer and Vergil; but the essence of what he has to say pertains to Blake's Milton illustrations as well, especially his observation that the process of fragmenting an episode into consecutive phases "introduces into painting the element of moving action which previously had been considered the provenance of the poet. The art of such extensive picture narratives is an invention of the Hellenistic age, and with it began a development which reached its final solution in our day in the motion picture."[50] In this development Blake's Milton illustrations participate in an important way. Rather than representing a series of related episodes that extend over a long period of time, Blake seized upon a crucial moment or two, which he proceeded to anatomize and then explore. As a consequence, his designs, individually and collectively, may provide a gloss on the text just as a medieval or Renaissance commentary provides a gloss on the words of a poem or a scriptural text; but, more important, those designs also comprise a "totality."

The fact that Blake, in most cases, abandoned the practice of binding his illustrations with the text of the poem they illuminate, or even of indicating passages or line references on the illustrations themselves, has caused some confusion. Many critics have concluded that Blake's illustrations, wrenched from the poetic text, illuminate his own poetry rather than that of the poet he is illustrating. Such a conclusion is easily inferred from Irene Tayler's remarks on Blake's "transmutations of Milton's art" and from W.

J. T. Mitchell's observation that "when Blake 'illustrates' a text, he expands and transforms it, and often provides a vision that can operate in complete separation from it."[51] Yet Mitchell's observation also points in another direction, drawing us into the perception of David V. Erdman, who, pondering the relationship of Blake's designs to his poetry, reaches an understanding that illuminates the relationship between Blake's designs and the poetry of other poets. The pictures and the words, says Erdman, "point not at each other . . . but beyond themselves. The artifact only opens the sensory doors to the mental theatre. In other words, the text is not there to help us follow the pictures, nor the pictures to help us visualize the text; both lead us to an imaginative leap in the dark, a leap beyond the dark and fire—from perception to Intellectual Vision."[52] Erdman recognizes with Kurt Weitzmann that the understanding of any illustration "depends on a clear comprehension of . . . [its] relationship to the written word."[53] He is right to emphasize that, as an illustrator, Blake was not immediately concerned with painting pictures that laced into the text but attempted instead to achieve through his designs what a poem could not do, either because its own vision was mistaken or because misguided commentary had confused and concealed its visionary dimensions. Yet Erdman mistakes Blake's means for his end. The artist's ultimate goal is not to divorce illustration from poem but to create, through illustration, a perspective from which a poem can be read—a perspective through which its vision can be penetrated and what Erdman calls its "human, apocalyptic meaning"[54] be revealed. It is worth recalling here the tradition of prophecy, wherein what is written elusively is elucidated pictorially, the prophet's native, even private, verbal language receiving illumination from the universal language of iconography. The pictorial prophecy is thus a key to, a gloss on, the verbal prophecy, the picture pointing *to* the word, not away from it (see fig. 9).

In this capacity, illustration is rhetorical in its function, acting as a kind of punctuational device that restores emphases that have been lost, either because an author obscured them or because subsequent commentators missed or suppressed them. Something of this can be seen in the manner in which Martin Luther's September Bible was illustrated, a Bible containing numerous pictorial initial letters and some full-page designs. All the full-page designs appear in relation to one biblical book—the Apocalypse of Saint John—which seems especially curious, for in this Bible "the Book of Revelation is given what appears to be somewhat of an inferior status." Being relegated to "a sort of appendix position,"[55] it is omitted from the rest of the New Testament and excluded from Luther's enumerations. By reserving the full-page illustrations for the Book of Revelation, the illustrator restores the Apocalypse to a prominence Luther would deny it, correcting the "error" of Luther, compiler and commentator. Analogously, Blake, especially in the designs for Milton's epics, uses his pictures rhetorically, restoring the accents of his original, the accents other commentators had ignored or, in some cases, deliberately misplaced.

Whatever moved Blake to illustrate the works of a poet—and, as we have seen, the motive for illustrating Dante was different from the one that prompted most of the Milton designs—he would have resisted the notion that he was misreading, misinterpreting a text. So should we. When Blake's object was to correct, the illustration was necessitated by contradictions within the fabric of a poet's vision, by contradictions deriving from the poet's own unsuccessful attempt to overcome his Urizenic spectre and release his vision. In such cases, the illustration becomes "a synopsis of vision and error,"[56] Blake's aim being to complete another poet's articulation and to clarify it. When his object is to interpret, the illustration is inspired by generations of misunderstanding that had gathered around a text—misunderstanding from which the illustration was designed to release the poem, unfolding the poet's own apocalyptic meaning. It has been said of the *Job* series that "Blake's diabolical reading with its textual alterations was probably closer to the original intention than most of the translations."[57] A similar observation may be extended to all Blake's illustrations, especially those for Milton. The "devilish" devices of his art are a form of viewer harassment meant to shock us into perceiving what we had not seen before—not something Blake adds to his source but something he draws from it. In the process, Blake asserts a new understanding of the poem he illustrates, and even as he sets himself within the tradition of Milton illustration he strikes a stance that distinguishes him from that tradition.

Blake's fracturing of the customary relationship between text and illumination encourages the beholder to see the illustrations, for the moment at least, as a totality, as a related sequence of perceptions that comment in several consecutive stages on a single momentous event. If turning from Blake's illustrations for *Comus* to those for *Paradise Regained* is, in one sense, moving from a literal into a symbolic mode of illustration, it is, in another sense, moving away from the eighteenth-century habit of illustration, in which various events are condensed within a single picture, toward a mode of illustration in which a great event is fragmented and represented in a series of related designs. Yet even this description of deviation from tradition simplifies what is actually an immensely complicated association with it. At the same time that Blake is simplifying the tradition of the synoptic design he is collapsing into a single illustration devices that, during the eighteenth century, were distinct from one another, thereby creating a new version of synoptic illustration.

James Thorpe notes that "ornamental borders, initials, headpieces and tailpieces are not illustrations but decoration. Like the type and the. cover," he says, "they belong to the production of the book rather than to the author's text. The two processes—decoration and illustration—are quite distinct, although they are often confused."[58] Thorpe is talking about book illustration during the 1890's; but however true his observation may be to the period he is discussing, it just does not have validity for most pre-Blakean illustration and can, in fact, be easily discredited by a great deal of "decorative" design that comes after Blake.[59] David Bland offers the proper historical corrective when he observes that "while illustration came first it was followed . . . by its abstract counterpart, decoration," which, rather than being a mere embellishment, worked in harness with illustration to convey a poem's meaning.[60] The fullness of an illustration makes meaning concrete; the decoration succeeds by presenting meaning abstractly, iconographically. Blake's sets of designs syncretize both devices: any single design may possess the explicitness of a conventional illustration; but its meaning is augmented and extended by decorative, iconographic devices assimilated within it. Often the so-called ornaments for a text develop through repetition, focus through reiteration, the essential motifs of a poem absorbed into a set of illustrations for it. The serpent of *Paradise Lost,* for instance, readily lent itself to letter ornamentation. Severing the ties between illustration and text, in the sense that no text accompanies his illustrations, Blake seems to eliminate the possibility for employing decoration; but in actuality he introduces the device within the illustrations themselves, making the serpent of conventional letter ornaments into what Edward J. Rose calls the "visual melody" that plays throughout the *Paradise Lost* designs.[61]

This important, but neglected, relationship between Blake and the eighteenth-century tradition of Milton illustration should be seen over and against an equally important disjunction between Blake's designs and those of his predecessors. Illustration has been described as the "art of compromise," which requires the artist "to work within the confines of a defined context and to allow his drawings or designs to be prepared for the accidental fortunes of reproduction."[62] Nowhere was the art of compromise more evident than in Milton illustration of the eighteenth-century. From that tradition—and from his own experience as an engraver—Blake had become sensitive to such adaptation. On several occasions, Blake himself submitted his work to the tyranny of engravers and publishers; and on other occasions—for instance, when he engraved John Opie's design to *Romeo and Juliet* for *Boydell's Shakespeare* or when he engraved designs after Fuseli[63] —he himself took considerable liberties with the artist's original. Blake's experience in engraving others' work and his experience in having others engrave his work taught him the extent to which an artist is subject to enslavement by an editor and publisher, and the extent to which a poet is as subject to it as an illustrating artist. In his Milton designs, therefore, he breaks boldly away from two conventions of illustration: not only does he omit references to the lines he is illustrating (the designs for *L'Allegro* and *Il Penseroso* are the exception that confirms the rule); but he prepares designs without making provisions, or even wanting them, for engraving and publication. In the process, Blake rejects the customary notion of illustration defined by Weitzmann when he writes, *"Illustrations are physically bound to the text...."*[64] Blake's Milton illustrations are bound to no text; in consequence they are not a part of the great corporate image of Milton that eighteenth-century editors and publishers were engaged in creating, but instead part of an effort to rescue himself from the tyrannies of art at the same time that he delivers Milton's vision from the darkness in which those tyrannies hid it.

Illustration in Blake's day, as in our own, was regarded as a lesser art, having the same kind of relation to painting that journalism today has to literature. Blake knew that "until the illustrator enjoys complete independence from outside pressure and direction, complete responsibility for his own work, and complete freedom to do whatever he deems fit—all necessaries in the making of art—until then illustration cannot be art but only a branch of advertising."[65] Blake's Milton illustrations—the experiments they involve—constitute an assertion of this understanding: they are remarkable testimony to the fact that an illustrator can circumvent the "corporate editorial image" and advance his own "strong opinions."[66] The art of illustration, as practiced by Blake, reveals the full possibilities of a genre greatly abused in his time and afterwards. Albrecht Dürer has been credited with revolutionizing "the attitude of the Central European artists toward the arts of the books" with his designs for the Apocalypse.[67] Blake should be credited, even if he did not altogether succeed, with revolutionizing the attitude of his own culture not only toward Milton but toward the form in which so much Milton criticism had been advanced. Such a realization leads into yet another matter that should be broached before embarking upon an interpretation of the illustrations to *Paradise Regained*—the contention that Blake works within traditions of Milton interpretation and illustration. Consideration of it, to the extent that such consideration directs attention toward the tradition of Milton illustration, should proceed from the perception that illustrators of Milton were generally much more progressive than, for instance, illustrators of Shakespeare and could therefore be expected to have more appeal for Blake.

TRADITION AND BLAKE'S TALENT

Jean Hagstrum believes that in Blake's illustrations to Milton's poems "Milton is interpreted as the pictorialist school of the Wartons would have wished";[68] that is, Blake interprets Milton as the eighteenth century wanted to interpret Milton, not as Milton would have wanted to be interpreted. The validity of this observation can be tested easily by exploring how the eighteenth century read *Paradise Regained,* both in its commentaries on the poem and in its illustrations for it, and by then considering how Blake read the poem in his designs and in his "imitations" of it, the most important of which is *Milton.*

Paradise Regained, of course, did not attract the same amount of attention or inspire the same volume of commentary that *Paradise Lost* did; but, despite assertions to the contrary, it did not fall into total neglect either. Not only was *Paradise Regained* frequently reprinted in the eighteenth century, and often illustrated, but as early as 1690 it was translated into Latin; in 1740 it inspired a poem entitled *On the Resurrection* and five years later one called *Jesus.*[69] Moreover, *Paradise Regained* was the subject of three separate commentaries before 1750 and later in the century was printed separately on various occasions, in both England and America.[70] And in 1752 Thomas Newton offered a new edition of the poem, which was liberally annotated by various hands. *Paradise Regained,* the initial note to that volume suggests, "has not met with the approbation it deserves," largely because of its narrowness of plan, though of its kind the poem is no less excellent than *Paradise Lost.*[71]

In his edition, Newton himself raises a new issue in the criticism of *Paradise Regained*—the nature of its genre—and allows the commentators he quotes to raise some others. In this respect, the notes by Thyer and Warburton require more attention than they ordinarily receive. Thyer writes,

> It may seem a little odd at first, that Milton should impute the recovery of Paradise to this short scene of our Saviour's life upon earth, and not rather extend it to his agony, crucifixion &c; but the reason no doubt was, that *Paradise regain'd* by our Saviour's resisting the temptations of Satan might be a better contrast to *Paradise lost* by our first parents too easily yielding to the same seducing Spirit. Besides he might very probably, and indeed very reasonably, be apprehensive, that a subject so extensive as well as sublime might be too great a burden for his declining constitution, and a task too long for the short term of years he could then hope for. Even in his Paradise Lost he expresses his fears, lest he had begun too late, and lest *an age too late, or cold climate, or years should have damp'd his intended wing;* and surely he had much greater cause to dread the same now, and be very cautious of launching out too far.

Warburton comments in a similar vein:

It is hard to say whether Milton's wrong notions in divinity led him to this defective plan; or his fondness for the plan influenced those notions. That is whether he indeed supposed the redemption of mankind (as he here represents it) was procured by Christ's triumph over the Devil in the wilderness; or whether he thought that the scene of the desert opposed to that of Paradise, and the action of a temptation withstood to a temptation fall'n under, made *Paradise Regain'd* a more regular sequel to *Paradise Lost*. Or if neither this nor that, whether it was his being tired out with the labor of composing Paradise Lost made him averse to another work of length ... is very uncertain. All that we can be sure of is, that the plan is a very unhappy one, and defective even in that narrow view of a sequel, for it affords the poet no opportunity of driving the Devil back again to Hell from his new conquests in the air. In the mean time nothing was easier than to have invented a good one, which should end with the resurrection, and comprise these four books, somewhat contracted, in an episode, for which only the subject of them is fit.[72]

Newton's edition of *Paradise Regained* opens a new chapter in the history of the criticism of that poem. It raises the whole question of its genre, the matter of its relation to *Paradise Lost,* and the propriety of Milton's complementing the fall with the temptation in the wilderness. These questions lie behind much Romantic criticism of the poem and are deeply involved in the illustrative criticism of William Blake.

Unquestionably Blake and the writers of the Romantic era displayed the greatest sensitivity to and appreciation for *Paradise Regained*.[73] If Newton's edition raised the issues that occupied readers of *Paradise Regained* during the last half of the eighteenth century, William Hayley, together with Charles Dunster, formulated the ones that were to engage students of the poem during the Romantic period. Whereas the eighteenth century stressed the continuity between *Paradise Lost* and *Paradise Regained,* Hayley attempted to dissociate the two poems in order to assert the integrity of the latter. In the first poem, Hayley tells us, Milton "seems to emulate the sublimity of Moses and the prophets"; but in *Paradise Regained* he attempts "to copy the sweetness and simplicity of the milder Evangelists." Not wanting to encroach upon Cowper's critical edition of Milton, Hayley confines himself to biographical details except when he leaps into the province of criticism to formulate an elaborate defense of *Paradise Regained* against its detractors. There is "no poem of epick form," concludes Hayley, "where the sublimest moral instruction is so forcibly and abundantly united to poetic delight: the splendour of the poet does not blaze indeed so intensely as in his larger production"; but despite that, *Paradise Regained* embodies "the truest heroism, and the triumph of Christianity."[74] Hayley is not necessarily dealing with issues different from those that Newton's edition posed, but he does present a new and distinctively Romantic attitude toward them. Hayley, like Newton, recognizes that *Paradise Regained* is different in kind from *Paradise Lost;* but he realizes, too, that its form is not necessarily a constraining influence upon the poet. Hayley asserts the integrity of Milton's brief epic, which is to say that he regards the poem as neither companion nor sequel to *Paradise Lost;* and he sees *Paradise Regained* as the culmination of Milton's genius, the final embodiment of his radically new version of Christianity.

In 1795 a separate edition of *Paradise Regained* appeared with notes by various hands, its editor Charles Dunster explaining in his preface that although *Paradise Regained* has been only "negligently and scantily illustrated," a new appreciation of the poem "begins to prevail." If Newton had tried to assert an understanding of *Paradise Regained,* Dunster was intent upon furnishing new perspectives on the poem, thereby encouraging the kind of critical inquiry from which a new understanding might eventually emerge. And if Hayley had sought to dissociate Milton's two epics, Dunster argued instead that "the Paradise Regained is so necessary a sequel to the Paradise Lost, that we cannot but imagine that Milton, when he wrote the one, was not without an intention . . . of producing something of the kind for the purpose of completing his subject. Accordingly, the two poems mutually coincide with, and admirably illustrate, each other. . . ."[75] But like Hayley, Dunster understands the poem's perfection and unity; like Hayley he insists that failure to appreciate the poem stems from a failure to comprehend the poem's genre.

If Hayley and Dunster managed to present new attitudes toward *Paradise Regained,* they did not succeed in dispelling the old ones. In both his 1801 and 1809 editions of Milton, Henry John Todd, though he praises *Paradise Regained,* finds it lacking when compared to *Paradise Lost:* "The plan," he says, "is faulty: For to attribute the Redemption of Mankind solely to Christ's triumph over the temptations in the wilderness, is a notion not only contracted but untrue.''[76] And Charles Symmons, after asserting that *Paradise Regained* "possessed no charms for the multitude," suggests that "the voice of the public, which on the question of poetic excellence cannot for a long time be erroneous, has irrevocably decided" the fate of *Paradise Regained*.[77] The poem, he concludes, suffers from extreme narrowness of plan, little action, too much disputation and didactic dialogue, paucity of character and poetic imagery. Moreover, the content of the poem does not fulfill the expectations created by the title: *Paradise Regained* should be about the death and resurrection of Christ, not about his temptations.

Like Dr. Johnson in so many of his critical forays, the editors and critics who comprise this conservative tradition of criticism point to the right issues but say the wrong things about them. The main lines of this tradition are firmly drawn by John Aikin in his popular "Critical Essay," appended to so many early nineteenth-century editions. Whether *Paradise Regained* is "ranked among the epic or heroic," he says, it remains "a kind of after-piece, springing rather from the theological than the poetical conception" of *Paradise Lost* and comprehensible only in terms of the diffuse epic. The radical theology of Milton's brief epic continues to dominate the attention of critics, but it does not meet with approval. "The awful words, *It is finished*," concludes Aikin, "will never by a Christian be taken from the solemn catastrophe of the death of his Saviour, and be applied to the completion of his trial."[78] For all their efforts, Hayley and Dunster were unable to put this critical tradition to rest. It persists into the 1820's, reaching its apogee in an unsigned essay called "A Critique on the *Paradise Regain'd*." *Paradise Lost* is here portrayed as the poem of "invention" and "imagination"—as "a new creation"—in a lapse of taste that designates *Paradise Regained* as its "after-birth." This anonymous critic remarks tartly that the defects of Milton's brief epic, "glaring and unpardonable," are of two kinds: one is a defect of action, the other a defect of sentiment. In the first instance, Milton should have called his poem "The Temptation of Christ"; *then,* says the critic, "the action of the poem . . . would have been complete." But Milton unhappily chooses to sing of "Recover'd

Paradise to all mankind," creating expectations that his poem does
not meet:

That Paradise was regained, and human redemption effected, by the single act
of our Saviour's temptation in the wilderness, is an open contradiction to the
sacred Scriptures. They plainly declare that he saved us by *his obedience unto
death;* that his temptation was *initiatory* to his glorious Priesthood. . . .[79]

There are no apologies for Milton here: he steps outside of
Christian orthodoxy; *ergo* he is no Christian.

Even more interesting are this critic's observations on the defect
of sentiment in *Paradise Regained.* Twentieth-century commentators on Milton's brief epic have spent considerable time haggling
over Christ's divinity; but that, for eighteenth- and nineteenth-
century critics, was not the problem. Rather, it is the small
attention given to Christ's divinity that these critics found discon-
certing:

Poetical license does not extend to the violation of divine truth. The *proper
Divinity* of the Eternal Son, so unequivocally revealed in the Holy Scriptures,
is kept entirely out of sight. Thus the Poet has injured himself no less than in
excluding the scene of the crucifixion from the action of his Poem. He has
torn the Son from the firmament . . . [and] the absence of this stupendous
doctrine casts a gloom over his work, and occasions incongruities which
would disgrace an Author far below the rank of Milton.[80]

Ten years later this essay crossed the Atlantic, where its sentiments were handsomely reinforced by two frontispiece illustrations for *Paradise Regained*—one depicting Christ bruising the head
of the serpent, the other displaying him hanging on the cross.[81]

It may be, as one member of the Milton establishment is now
trying to tell us, that *Paradise Regained* is not primarily a "religious" poem—not a "theological" poem.[82] Such a pronouncement, however, is not supported by the critical history of Milton's
poem. For two centuries after its publication, *Paradise Regained*
was regarded quite differently. Historically, criticism of the poem
centered on the poem's theological position and on its hero—a
realization that forces us to dismiss the confident conclusion that
"until the present century, for the most part critics of *Paradise
Regained* and readers generally seem to have found in the person
of Christ little to which they thought it necessary to take exception."[83] Such a conclusion betrays the facts of literary history

and makes it impossible to comprehend the place of Blake's statement within a history that includes not just Newton, Dunster, and Todd, but also, *and equally important,* Richard Meadowcourt, William Hayley, and John Aikin.

This is the shape of the critical tradition with which Blake was probably familiar. Hayley, whom Charles Dunster considered to be the "best critic" of *Paradise Regained,* owned various editions of Newton; he owned an inscribed copy of Dunster's 1795 edition, which included many of the notes used by Newton; his library also contained various copies of his own *Life of Milton.* If Blake did not read these works, he might, nevertheless, have become acquainted with their contents through discussions with Hayley, who did read them.[84] In any event, it is Hayley who seems to have provided the critical perspective that is manifested in Blake's illustrations to *Paradise Regained.*

Illustration, regarded as a form of nonverbal criticism by Blake and his contemporaries, was an essential part of the critical tradition accumulated by *Paradise Regained* during the eighteenth century. With this tradition, too, Blake seems to have had at least nodding familiarity. Just as Jean Hagstrum sees Blake working within the tradition of eighteenth-century criticism of *Paradise Regained,* so Morse Peckham contends that Blake worked within the same tradition of illustration. The nature of that tradition, especially for Blake's illustrative works, says Peckham, "provided a place for . . . copying . . . other men's ideas." Thus Peckham concludes that "when we have resurrected and studied the work of forgotten illustrators and painters of his time . . . we shall be in a position to understand far better both the nature and the quality of Blake's genius."[85] The most recent and, to my mind, the most important general statement about the tradition of Milton illustration is provided by J. B. Trapp, who, though he does not single out Blake by name, argues that from the sixteenth century onward "little that is new and significant is added to the Fall [or the Redemption] in any medium, including book-illustrations." For Trapp, Milton's illustrators—and he does not except Blake—are best viewed in the light of traditional biblical illustration, where any single illustration is laden with typology. In any individual depiction of the fall, Trapp contends, there will be "a more or less explicit proleptic reference to Redemption and/or Judgment"; or conversely, in any depiction of the redemption, there will be reference, direct or oblique, to the fall. Indeed, "the whole drama of Salvation is condensed into a single picture: Salvation, or its means, writ large, but its antecedent crime merely stated, as it were, in the margin."[86] Trapp's conclusions take us a long way toward understanding Milton's eighteenth-century illustrators but not far at all if our intention is to explicate the illustrations by Blake. The aim of Blake's predecessors was to tie Milton's poem firmly to traditional theology. This meant relating *Paradise Regained* not only to the fall but to the drama of the Crucifixion and Resurrection.

One cannot overestimate the importance of subject matter in a consideration of illustration, Blake's or anyone else's. As E. H. Gombrich has reminded us, "the subject of illustration was notoriously more important . . . than what we call the formal treatment."[87] What is depicted should be significant—it should be worthy of memory. The splendor of an illustration is not an end in itself but a rhetorical device through which what is significant is made to impinge upon one's consciousness. A cursory look through the illustrations to *Paradise Regained* that precede Blake's own throws into relief his departures from the tradition of typological illustration described by Trapp. For instance, two of Pigne's five designs deflect attention from the temptation *per se* in order to recall events typologically related to it—the finding of Jesus in the temple and Christ's bruising the head of the serpent by his death on the cross.[88] Two of Cheron's illustrations do the same, namely, his depictions of the Nativity and the crown of thorns. Another noteworthy use of typology occurs in a depiction by an unknown artist in 1779. Upheld by an angel, Christ is shown in mid-air. On the ground below are Adam and Eve applauding. Death, depicted as a skeleton, is, from the viewer's perspective, in the far left corner, hurling his dart; and coiled at the feet of Adam and Eve is a serpent. Three apples lie on the ground. These few but representative examples establish a principle that underlies all illustration: "some amount of telescoping is necessary."[89] An entire poem, along with the context of associations it develops, cannot be pictorialized. Thus the illustrator resorts both to typology and to episodic treatment, often in the form of a "cosmic painting with a main scene in the center and a garland of other incidents arrayed around it."[90] The "cosmic painting" is commonly used by biblical illustrators and illustrators of epic. It is the mode of illustration chosen by Tasso and imposed upon the illustrator of *Gerusalemme Liberata* with whom he worked in consort. It is also the mode of illustration employed by Milton's first illustrator, but not the one used by Blake in illuminating his own epics or those of Milton.

Blake's attitude toward the tradition of typological-episodic illustration has two aspects. The synoptic design, gathering an array of episodes around one of central importance, stresses what happens rather than the significance of what happens. Its concern is with narrative, not with the vision contained in it. Blake shifts these emphases, while making designs that preserve important ties with this tradition. Often Blake reduces a narrative moment to a single icon. A more conventional illustrator, working with Blake's conception for his concluding design in the *Paradise Lost* series, would have presented the expulsion of Adam and Eve and, around it, would have arranged a series of vignettes depicting the temptation of Adam and Eve, probably separately, and God's subsequent judgment of them. Blake reduces both these earlier events, which stand causally behind the one portrayed in his last design, to simple icons. The design is synoptic, to be sure, but not in the usual sense of that term. In the very act of simplifying the tradition of episodic illustration, Blake, instead of representing an event, abstracts from the event its meaning, which he then presents iconographically.

At the same time that Blake revised the tradition of synoptic illustration he eschewed the tradition of typology, except where, wishing to subvert the tradition, he used it against itself. While Blake's predecessors were concerned with conveying, through their illustrations to *Paradise Regained,* the grand lines of scriptural history, whether or not it pertained to the poem, Blake seems to have been intent upon discerning doctrinal subtlety, upon showing through his illustrations the extent to which Milton subdued a Christian theme to unorthodox purposes. His designs, like those for *Paradise Lost,* may be described as "a series of visual notes from underground appearing to illustrate Milton's text in a manner which the Establishment will innocently accept while also portraying the Devil's or Blake's version."[91] But to say this of the

Paradise Regained series requires the acceptance of certain corollaries. *Paradise Regained* is not an "establishment" poem. This
understanding is shared by all parties up to Blake's time; what
distinguishes him from other commentators is his refusal to distort
Milton's poem into an acceptable orthodoxy, his insistence upon
preserving the integrity of Milton's vision. If we are to continue to
talk about "the Devil's or Blake's version" of the poems Blake
illustrates, then we should acknowledge, when we come to the
Paradise Regained series, that here Milton's voice is the voice of a
true poet who read the Bible in its infernal sense. In these designs,
then, Blake's voice is an echo of Milton's: to Milton's commentators Blake might quote himself from *The Everlasting Gospel,*
"thou readst black where I read white" (p. 516); but he would not
have directed the line against the Milton who wrote *Paradise
Regained.*

    If, as Blake says in his *Annotations to Watson,* "Miltons Paradise
Lost is as true as Genesis or Exodus" (p. 607), the vision of
Paradise Regained may be said to go a step beyond the Bible,
adding to it chapters not yet written, then using those chapters to
interpret the meaning of Christ's life anew. What Edward J. Rose
says of Blake's *Milton* may also be said, with equal propriety, of
Paradise Regained: here Milton casts off "all that is not inspiration, such as judgment and punishment and accepts the gospel of
forgiveness." In this poem, Milton steps into the divine vision with
the "full possession of all his prophetic faculties."[92] I use Rose's
words by way of emphasizing that what occurs in Blake's epic *has
already occurred* in Milton's. Myths are born out of history and
relate back to it, so that the Milton myth of Blake's epic at once
derives from the historical moment represented by Milton's poem
and anatomizes the significance of it.

    Conventional typology is invoked on only three occasions in the
Paradise Regained series; first in the opening design (see fig. 34),
where Job, standing to the left of Jesus, behind the woman and
child, is introduced on the authority of Milton's text to recall the
"model" for *Paradise Regained* and the chief biblical prototype of
its hero; second, in the tenth and eleventh designs (see figs. 43 and
44) where, in both instances, Blake's purpose is to assert the
revolutionary character of Milton's poem by rejecting the typology of the Crucifixion so often associated with it. In the tenth

illustration, Christ is shown in the cruciform position as Satan topples from the temple and as an angel, in a hapless gesture, prepares to catch Jesus, should he fall. Two other angels look on in adoration, beholding the spectacle of Christ's standing. Blake's point, like Milton's, is that Christ's resurrection occurs now, paradise is regained now; and it is underscored through the allusion to the Crucifixion story in the next design. This illustration recalls *not* traditional representations of the angels serving Christ a banquet once his temptations are ended *but rather* conventional depictions of him, arms extended on the cross, blood spewing from his stigmata as ministering angels with cups gather the flow of his sacrifice.[93] In Blake's design, the ministering angels offer Christ bread and wine, which, with hands lowered and turned down over the offering, he declines. In parody of the traditional symbol of benediction—the blessing of the bread and wine (his own body and blood)—Christ's gesture implies a rejection of not the offering but the doctrine, the mystery religion, that it signifies. In this design, the figure of Christ may not suggest the Crucifixion, but the angels with their icons do. On them its meaning depends. We should here acknowledge, then, that the device of iconographic repetition is no less important than one poet's quoting another in his poem. Verbal and pictorial quotations alike draw forth a context of meaning that, in Blake's design, is being regarded only to be discarded. This point will draw more of our attention later.

As we turn to the *Paradise Regained* illustrations, we should have in mind what is known about their history, how these designs have been received and interpreted, along with a knowledge of what is conventional, what an innovation, when the designs are viewed in terms of the tradition of illustration that by Blake's time surrounded Milton's poem. Blake's designs for *Paradise Regained,* each measuring 17 X 13 cm, were prepared in 1816 and then purchased nine years later by John Linnell, in whose collection they remained for nearly a century.[94] On March 15, 1918, the series, now in the Fitzwilliam Museum, was sold to Mr. T. H. Riches. The first recorded comment on the *Paradise Regained* illustrations comes in a letter, addressed to Mrs. Gilchrist and dated December 13 [1862], from William Michael Rossetti. Rossetti writes, "I will consider about the Paradise Regained. The designs were shown to me by John Linnell as being more than

usually beautiful, and I do not directly *dissent* from the terms
used in the slip you send me; only my feeling is that Blake has
here been less inspired than usual, and the result comparatively
tame."[95] The "slip" to which Rossetti refers is apparently the
comment on the series published in Gilchrist's *Life of Blake* the
following year. That comment suggests that the illustrations to
Paradise Regained are "a sequel to those from the *Paradise Lost*"
and are "of great beauty, refined in execution, especially tender
and pure in colour, and pervading feeling";[96] and elsewhere in his
Life Gilchrist describes the illustrations as possessing "a remarkable affinity to the character of the poem, which is more distinguished by stately and elaborated method than by inspiration."[97]

In our own time the illustrations to *Paradise Regained* have been
five times reproduced and four times discussed. Darrell Figgis, the
first commentator on this set of illustrations, reaches three conclusions about them: (1) Blake expresses himself more fully in his
illustrations to *Paradise Regained* than in those to *Paradise Lost;*
(2) in execution the illustrations to *Paradise Regained* seem to
stand between the first and second sets to *Paradise Lost;* and
(3) the theme of the illustrations is Christ's initiation. Marcia
Pointon is also highly conscious of the stylistic differences between them and Blake's earlier illustrations, a difference that she
defines in terms of their "symbolic . . . iconic quality." And
Geoffrey Keynes, who stands in the forefront of this tradition of
commentary, says that the task of the editor-commentator is not
great when it comes to the Milton illustrations, since Blake was
content "to illustrate almost literally."[98] With Keynes's remark
our discussion may begin, but to the concerns of Figgis and
Pointon it must eventually return.

In the set of twelve illustrations to *Paradise Regained,* the last
complete set of illustrations to a poem by Milton, there are only
minor departures from Milton's text; but these few alterations are
of real interest. Keynes has drawn our attention to three contradictions of Milton's poem. He properly observes that in the third
illustration (see fig. 36), depicting Andrew and Simon Peter, "the
attendant angels are not mentioned in Milton's text"; nor are they
mentioned—and this point Keynes does not make—in the illustration of Mary meditating that immediately follows (see fig. 37).
Still further, Keynes tells us in his note to the sixth design (see fig.

39) that "the crown held in Satan's left hand has been added by Blake's imagination" and in his note to the last illustration (see fig. 45) that Blake "has added on either side the figures of Andrew and Simon Peter who are not mentioned in the text."[99]

Keynes poses a question regarding the relationship of Blake's illustrations to Milton's text that should not go unanswered. The illustrations to *Paradise Regained* fall into four groups. There are, first, the purely literal renderings. But there are also conflations as well as anticipatory designs. There are, finally, the symbolic interpretations. Most of the designs are literal renderings of symbolic events. But the fourth illustration (see fig. 37), for instance, conflates two episodes through the merest shorthand into a single design. Mary is meditating upon the meaning of the baptism she has just beheld; but, as she does so, her mind wanders back to the Nativity. Jesus, who made one descent in order to become man, is in process of making another descent, this one into himself in order to become God. Through the faintest suggestion, Blake allows two events, typologically related, to conflate within a single design and thereby calls attention to Milton's suggestion that all Christ's descents are implied by his descent into himself. The sixth design (see fig. 39), if not a true conflation of events, is at least an anticipatory design. The banquet serves as a prelude to, may even be regarded as the first stage of, the second temptation. By introducing the image of the crown, Blake allows this design to anticipate the long sequence that immediately follows.[100] The last design (see fig. 45) in the series, on the other hand, requires symbolic interpretation. Blake, as we shall see later, was concerned finally with the Christ myth as it is presented and interpreted by Milton's poem. That myth involves withdrawal, temptation, and return. Through the inclusion of Andrew and Simon Peter in the design Blake allows the beginning and the end of that myth to converge, with the suggestion that the real force of Milton's poem derives from its symbolic structure, that the end of Milton's poem constitutes a new beginning.

Blake uses highly conventionalized designs; he repeats traditional subject matter. More often than not, such designs have been ignored in favor of others that show marks of great originality. But to overvalue originality is quite to miss the mark: conventional designs are there not as artistic embarrassments but as determiners of context; they set Blake's designs firmly within a tradition of illustration, a tradition of interpretation, that, in these designs, he hopes to overturn. Comprehending this point requires our dismissing the notion of Morse Peckham that when Blake "was interested in the subject, he created original symbolic designs; when he was less interested, he took matter and design from another man's work and developed them more or less in the direction of symbolism and symmetry; when he wanted details for things he had no interest in drawing, he took them boldly from another man's work."[101] An investigation of Blake's subject matter in the *Paradise Regained* series proves otherwise: conventional compositions and traditional iconography are no less significant than subjects Blake chooses to illustrate for the first time.

Seven of Blake's subjects for Milton's brief epic are traditional, and five of the subjects he originates—*Andrew and Simon Peter, Satan in Council, The Second Temptation,*[102] *Morning Chasing Away the Spectres of the Night,* and *Jesus Returning to Mary.* Of the traditional subjects, only *Mary Meditating* is first depicted in the nineteenth century. It has been suggested that *Paradise Regained* is inhibiting to the artist who would illustrate it: the paucity of "local colour" and "pictorial variety" in the text force "most illustrations of the poem to be biblical rather than Miltonic."[103] However, Blake does not seem to have been fettered by the poem. He probably knew that one of his "traditional" subjects, *Mary Meditating* (see fig. 37), had just recently been taken as a fit subject for illustration; and this illustration, pointing to the interiority of Milton's poem, suggested to Blake other possibilities for illustrating it. As Blake surveyed the whole tradition of illustration that had gathered around Milton's brief epic, he doubtless perceived that it was greatly inhibited—not by the paucity of detail in Milton's poem, but by the eighteenth-century impulse to bring Milton's poem into line with Christian orthodoxy, an impulse that confined the illustrator at the same time that it divested Milton's epic of its momentous significance. Thus, in the six illustrations with subjects of long-standing tradition, Blake makes no reference to the loss of paradise by Adam and only alludes ironically to the regaining of it on the cross. By omitting any allusion to the fall, Blake stresses the integrity of Milton's poem and fastens attention to the myth of reintegration;

by subverting the tradition that identifies Christ's journey into the wilderness and triumph on the pinnacle with the Passion, Crucifixion, and Resurrection, he remains more faithful than his predecessors to the emphases of Milton's poem.

With the exception of Hayley, Blake is the only critic of *Paradise Regained,* before the twentieth century, to expose the sequel fallacy. The view that Milton's poem is a companion to the diffuse epic, an extension and an epitome of it, was firmly established by the beginning of the Romantic period. But for Hayley and Blake that proposition was also the chief stumbling-block to an appreciation of the poem. In his illustrations to *Paradise Regained,* Blake elects to note differences rather than similarities between the two epics—differences that are both stylistic and thematic. *Paradise Lost* is portrayed as a song of woe, *Paradise Regained* as a song of joy; the first poem is presented in a highly ornamented style, the second in a plain, almost austere, style. In dissociating the two poems Blake also spurns the bounds of the critical tradition that had grown up around them and thus may be identified with a small band of dissenters whose chief spokesman has been Don Cameron Allen. "It is difficult not to read *Paradise Regained* as an immediate poetical continuation of *Paradise Lost,*" says Allen; "but if we indulge in such a reading, if we constantly return to *Paradise Lost* for annotations, we confuse our judgment of the short epic and distort, if we do not destroy, the central issues of the second poem."[104]

Blake's illustrations to *Paradise Regained* are not in any sense a continuation of those to *Paradise Lost.* If these illustrations seem "comparatively tame" in relation to those for the preceding poem, it is because Blake sought to make the same kinds of differentiations visually that Milton made verbally; it is because he knew that "successful interpretation implies a need for a reflection of the author's style."[105] This meant finding a style less luxurious than the one used to illustrate *Paradise Lost*—a style that in its plainness and severity duplicated the one Milton used in writing his brief epic. It meant capturing the sense of joy that pervades *Paradise Regained* and opposing it to the bitter-sweet ending of *Paradise Lost.* It also meant distinguishing between the characters in the two poems: Satan has lost his former glory in the brief epic; and Christ is present in the poem, at least until the moment on the pinnacle, in his human aspect. In this regard, it is interesting to turn to Blake's portrayal of the first temptation (see fig. 35) and especially to his representation of Satan. The subject is extremely popular among biblical illustrators; and Blake's final conception for the design does not differ radically from theirs, except in minute particulars and especially in the depiction of Satan. Most Renaissance portrayals of the first temptation accentuate Satan's physical hideousness. Milton's eighteenth-century illustrators, remaining "true" to Milton's poem but still reluctant to eschew the older tradition, present Satan in his rural weeds but not without some of his attributes—horns, claws, or a tail trailing from under his robes. In Blake's depiction, however, Satan's attributes silently disappear; and the tempter, even if he lacks his former glory, is represented as an attractive, if aged, man.[106]

Like many other students of *Paradise Regained* (most notably Barbara Lewalski [107]), Blake was inclined to see Milton's poem as the fulfillment of his plan to write a brief epic and as the poem in which Milton managed to extend and ennoble the province of epic poetry. Yet Blake's conception of the brief epic surpasses in sophistication any that has recently been advanced. Lewalski has reminded us that the brief epic of the Middle Ages and the Renaissance generally dealt with New Testament subjects while using narrative, structural, and stylistic devices of the classical epic. Primary attention, then, is focused upon the life of Christ, while a complicated typology recalls the whole of biblical history. For Lewalski, and for many of Milton's illustrators before Blake, typology was the chief hallmark of the brief epic. The "epic" dimensions of the brief epic, in other words, were implied rather than clearly articulated; biblical history was gathered together in the typology rather than explicitly recounted as in the diffuse epic.

Though acutely aware of the fact that the brief epic involves drastic reduction and severe compression, Blake realized, too, that the brief epic is not a miniature epic in the strictest sense. It is not for Blake—nor was it for Milton—a scale model of the diffuse epic; but, rather, reduction and compression are accompanied by distortion and exaggeration. Prologues and foreshadowings are abbreviated; epic paraphernalia are held to a bare minimum. Yet the epic action is magnified. Blake recalled, no doubt, that Milton had concentrated the drama of *Paradise Lost* within the ninth book, whereas in *Paradise Regained* he allowed it to extend over all four books. It is the dramatic element that Blake, following Milton, seems to regard as the salient characteristic of the brief epic poem.[108]   One of the new subjects Blake adds, *Satan in Council* (see fig. 38), depicts the one epic convention that Milton utilizes prominently in *Paradise Regained,* but without the same detail and variety that characterize the corresponding scene in *Paradise Lost;* the convention is here, not to be developed but to signal the genre to which the poem belongs, to invite comparison between a tradition and what Milton's talent has made of it. For Blake, it was not enough to say that Milton "displays a singular independence of traditional literary forms" in *Paradise Regained;*[109]   the poem belongs to the genre of epic, to a genre that Milton, in writing his poem, has radically transformed.

In *Paradise Regained,* epic conventions are pared away at the same time that two of them are seized upon, joined together, and then transmuted. There is the descent into the underworld, through which the hero comes to terms with the dark side of human existence; and there is also the descent of the heavenly messenger, who brings divine illumination to the hero. The brief epic, as *Paradise Regained* exemplifies it, is an internalized drama that these epic conventions, transformed, clarify and support. The descent into the underworld is modulated into Christ's descent into himself; the descent of the heavenly messenger is modulated into Christ's willing descent from the pinnacle to begin the work of man's redemption. The first descent brings the hero into the presence of the divine vision; the second effects its extension to mankind. The same conventions, similarly combined and transformed, are incorporated into *Milton,* where the hero, like Christ, descends into himself to annihilate selfhood and, accomplishing that, descends into the world (into Blake's garden) to become its Awakener.

What is but an element in the diffuse epic, the initatory experience, is made absolutely central to the brief epic. The hero and his audience are together brought to the threshold of vision. There is, in this educative process, an analogy between "initiation" and "death" that is perceived by William Warburton. "TO DIE," says Warburton, "is TO BE INITIATED "; and the initiation by death occurs, he argues, in three stages: the hero is filled with uncertainties (Christ in *Paradise Regained*) or with an awareness of his errors (Milton in *Milton*) and "wander[s] . . . through night and darkness" (Christ and Milton); all that the hero confronts "wears a dreadful aspect: it is all horror, trembling . . . affrightment" (Christ confronting the spectres of the night and Milton confronting his own spectre who is Satan); suddenly the divine light displays itself, revealing "holy visions" (the moment on the pinnacle in *Paradise Regained* and the moment of which *Milton* is an anatomy).[110]   For Blake, no poem before his own *Milton* more fully revealed this process than *Paradise Regained*—a process that is rendered by another of his new subjects, *Morning Chasing Away the Spectres of the Night* (see fig. 42), which combines with *Satan's Inspiring Christ's Ugly Dream, Mary Meditating,* and *Andrew and Simon Peter* (see figs. 41, 37, 36) to accentuate the introspective, psychological character of Milton's poem. In this regard, it is important to observe that, through iconographic repetition, Blake identifies Christ's experience in the wilderness with the Lady's experience in the dark woods of Comus. The serpent who is the agent of the Urizenic god, of the Moral Law, in the eighth design for *Paradise Regained* (see fig. 41) is the same serpent who appears in the phantasm of the fifth design for *Comus.* Moreover, one cannot easily ignore the fact that, in illustrating *Paradise Regained,* Blake has collapsed one half of the poem, the kingdoms temptation, into a single design, concentrating instead on those temptations that are contemplative in character, on those that lend themselves to the mental landscape that dominates most of his illustrations. Finally, in recognition of the fact that Milton's drama of the mind gathers intensity as it drives toward the epiphany on the pinnacle, Blake concentrates his designs within the fourth book of *Paradise Regained,* thereby defining the poem's thematic and dramatic center. But Blake also underscores the epiphanic character of *Paradise Regained* through the symbolic "stationing" of Christ in the designs that deal specifically with the temptations. In the second illustration (see fig. 35), Christ, wandering in the wilderness, is seen from the back; only the right half of his face is visible. In the seventh design (see fig. 40), Christ is seen from the side; this time the left half of his face is visible. Then in the tenth illustration (see fig. 43), which depicts the epiphanic moment, Christ is seen as the full man poised triumphantly on the pinnacle as Satan—stripped of his garments, exposed—falls.

Blake's illustrations to *Paradise Regained,* emphasizing the interiority of Milton's poem, deviate conspicuously from the traditions of criticism and illustration that surround it, Blake making no effort to impose the Passion, Crucifixion, or Resurrection upon a poem that underplays those events. For years, James Holly Hanford told his students that Milton was never mature enough to handle the Passion and thus chose a subject within his limited abilities. Elizabeth Pope argues, on the other hand, that Milton simply rejects one tradition in favor of another, pointing out that in some Cluniac art, recently unearthed, the fall and the temptation in the wilderness are paired. [111] Neither explanation is to the point. Hanford disparages the poet by dwarfing the quality of his mind, and Pope unwittingly deprecates the poem. For, admittedly, a poem that makes sense only in terms of an atrophied tradition is severely limited both in its appeal and in its achievement. Two further points complicate the matter: first, Milton always guarded against shifts in scriptural emphasis; and second, in all previous instances, departure from Scripture involved embellishment rather than contradiction of it. Therefore, it would seem that the revision of biblical emphasis in *Paradise Regained* is calculated and meaningful.

Milton avoided the subject of the Passion for aesthetic *and theological* reasons. The aesthetic reasons were grasped by Blake's contemporaries; the theological reasons, understood by Blake alone. Milton avoided the Passion because it is too fully elaborated in Scripture; thus, to choose the subject is to choose the most intractable material imaginable. Besides, the emphasis on the Passion is wrong for Milton's purposes. It illustrates Christ's triumph at the divine rather than the human level. The obvious disadvantages inherent in the story of the Passion and Crucifixion are avoided by dealing with the temptations. There the risk of contradicting Scripture is checked, for the accounts by Matthew, Mark, and Luke are brief, and each contradicts the others. Significantly, however, Milton departs from his sources on four occasions—in three instances by elaborating upon Scripture, in the last by bold contradiction of it. The banquet scene, the storm scene, and

Satan's falling from the pinnacle are Milton's own contributions to the tradition (or so it is assumed), contributions that Blake would have recognized and that he chooses to emphasize in four of his twelve illustrations (see figs. 39, 41, 42, and 43).

One of these departures from tradition, Satan's *falling* from the pinnacle, finds its precedent in biblical illustration, which though deliberately altering the gospel accounts, does so to emphasize the intensely dramatic character of Christ's triumph in the wilderness. [112] Two others, the banquet scene and the storm scene, have an analogous function, both in Milton's poem and in Blake's illustrations for it. These temptations, contemplative in character, center attention in the arena of the mind, where the drama of the poem unfolds. The banquet temptation may have yet another function, however. There are, of course, the literary analogues in Malory and the Renaissance epic; but there is also, more pointedly, the artistic one, represented by Botticelli's depiction of Christ's temptation, which shows the ministering angels preparing a banquet table with food. [113] The detail is theologically an important one, for it firmly ties the temptation in the wilderness to the drama of the Crucifixion, which begins with the Last Supper. Milton does here what he had previously done with the war in heaven: he takes what is epilogue to history and makes it prologue, in the process transforming corporeal warfare into mental fight: "Dream not of thir Fight,/As of a Duel," Michael cautions Adam (XII. 386–87). In taking the banquet and its associations with sacramental, sacrificial religion out of a divine context and putting it into an infernal one, Milton clearly implies a judgment on what the whole tradition signifies. A fourth departure from tradition, also depicted by Blake (see figs. 36 and 45), requires closer attention.

In the prologue to Book II of *Paradise Regained,* Milton introduces the figures of Andrew and Simon Peter who "Began to doubt, and doubted many days" (l. 11). Milton has authority for presenting Andrew and Simon Peter in the context of the Baptism (John 1:40), but it is curious that he should do so. Throughout *Paradise Regained,* Milton has been following the accounts of Matthew, Mark, and Luke; here he turns to John, whose account he contradicts. In the Gospels by Matthew, Mark, and Luke, Andrew and Simon Peter are represented as the first disciples

Christ gathers *after* his ministry begins (see Matthew 4:18, Mark 1:29, Luke 5). In John, Andrew and Simon Peter are portrayed as recognizing Christ's messiahship at the Baptism. John identifies the Lamb as the leader and suggests that spiritual vision is granted to those who follow him. By contradicting Scripture on this one point, by presenting Andrew and Simon Peter in the posture of doubt, Milton calls further attention to the human context in which Jesus appears until the triple epiphany on the pinnacle when Satan, Christ, and the reader simultaneously apprehend Christ's divinity. Blake not only illustrates this seemingly innocuous episode in the second book (one of two episodes, the other being Mary meditating, that the eighteenth century considered to be "little disgressions") but allows Andrew and Simon Peter to figure in his final illustration as well. Jesus returns to Mary *and to Andrew and Simon Peter*. Blake's intention here is twofold: wishing to underscore yet another of Milton's departures from Scripture, he first illustrates the scene for Book II, then recalls it in the final illustration, thereby suggesting that Christ gathers his disciples only after his ministry begins; but Blake wishes also to stress that it is only through repetition of Christ's experience, only through a corresponding journey to the very center of being, that spiritual vision is achieved. *Paradise Regained* involves the gradual awakening of Jesus to his mediatorial offices and culminates in a general acknowledgment of his divinity. Until that acknowledgment, the Lamb cannot lead; and until we, like Andrew and Simon Peter, repeat that experience, we cannot apprehend.

These elaborations of Scripture and this contradiction of it pave the way for Milton's audacious departure from the tradition of complementing the fall and the Crucifixion—a departure from tradition that is announced boldly in the final lines of the second verse paragraph in *Paradise Regained*. Describing his poem not as an "adventrous Song" but as a "prompted Song," Milton says that he will tell of things "unrecorded ... through many an Age,/ Worthy t'have not remain'd so long unsung" (I. 16–17). The Crucifixion is referred to twice in the poem, each time cryptically, both references coming in the first half. Jesus tells Satan that "a Crown, / ... is but a wreath of thorns" (II. 458–59); and he recounts earlier that the scribes in the temple told him, "this chiefly, that my way must lie/Through many a hard assay even to the death,/E're I the promis'd Kingdom can attain" (I. 263–65). Even so, Milton can hardly be referring to the atonement on the cross as Christ's "unrecorded" deed; for it is clearly not in keeping with the main thrust of the poem. The poem asserts that paradise is "Recover'd . . . /By one mans firm obedience fully tri'd/ Through all temptation . . . ," that Eden is "rais'd in the wast Wilderness" (I. 3–5, 7). With similar assertions the poem ends. "By vanquishing/temptation," Milton says, Christ "hast regain'd lost Paradise"–"A fairer Paradise is founded *now*" (IV. 607–8, 613; italics mine). The lines are puzzling, and Walter MacKellar does not help us to read them. The language here surely means more than he attributes to it when he says, "The Gospels . . . give only summary accounts to the temptation. *Paradise Regained* will give a detailed account, telling what Milton believes to be ideally true." [114]   *Unrecorded* cannot be glossed so briskly: it must mean something more, something different, from what MacKellar suggests.

The poem's reference to John's gospel for the purpose of contradicting it helps to explain these assertions in Milton's prologue; indeed, the reference lends credibility to them. Only in John's gospel is the story of Christ's temptation omitted. Thus, when Milton says that he will sing of an event left "unrecorded . . . through many an age," he presumably refers to a story whose full significance is unattended to by Matthew, Mark, and Luke and to one unmentioned by John. *Paradise Regained* is written, then, as an elaborate commentary on one moment in Christ's life, a moment which Milton invests with new significance. In the process, a new story is told—one which should be inserted into the blank space that John leaves between his accounts of the Baptism and the beginning of Christ's ministry. *Paradise Regained* is, after all, a new revelation, one that offers, in the words of Leslie Brisman, "a respectful acknowledgment of, yet independent departure from, scriptural authority." [115]   If the Son, as he stands on the pinnacle, can be said to assert "his continuity in the prophetic line . . . by standing in relation to Mosaic dispensation as commentator to text," then Milton, in process of writing this poem, can be said to stand in a comparable relationship to his "acknowledged" sources, not negating them but "open[ing] a shadowed world into new imaginative space and time, more than on earth was previously understood."[116]

Milton in his poem and Blake in his illustrations for it invoke the tradition of the "Everlasting Gospel"—a tradition associated with three ages of the world: an age of fear and servitude that terminates with the death of Christ; an age of filial obedience and faith; and an age of spiritual liberty and love. The "Everlasting Gospel," as A. L. Morton explains, is not a new book but "a new revelation of the spiritual sense of the Bible":

In this age God will be with man and therefore all existing forms of worship, ceremonies, churches, legal and moral codes will become superfluous. Instead of appearing as a source from without, God will now be within, and the unity of God and man will be fully accomplished.[117]

In *Paradise Regained,* the second of these ages is seen passing imperceptibly into the third: Christ, through an act of obedience, becomes the harbinger of an age of love.

Paradise Regained, then, articulates a vision that may assume its place in the fourth gospel, a vision that bridges the gap between individual redemption and the general redemption of the Apocalypse, one that shows man how, by achieving a paradise within, he may eventually achieve a paradise without. In a very real way, *Paradise Regained* is designed as a gateway into Jerusalem. This is how Blake interprets the poem Milton has written; and this suggests why, during the period when his own poem *Jerusalem* was being engraved, he took the time to illustrate Milton's brief epic. Blake, along with Hayley, is the first critic to share Milton's own enthusiasm for *Paradise Regained,* the first to comprehend the ground on which such enthusiasm was based. Milton's brief epic begins with an allusion to the cancelled lines of Vergil's *Aeneid.* The allusion is important, for in those lines Vergil proclaims the superiority of his new poem to everything else he has written; by invoking these lines, Milton implies the superiority of *Paradise Regained* to his earlier poems, *Paradise Lost* included. His first epic took the main lines of its vision from Christian orthodoxy; his brief epic, projecting a new vision that assigns new meaning and importance to Christ's temptations in the wilderness, subverts the old orthodoxy, putting a new one in its stead. One student of

Milton has recently tried to nudge us into this perception, which is central not only to Milton's poem but to Blake's designs for it.

C. A. Patrides has pointed out, quoting from J. S. Whale, that

"no theological theory is binding upon Christians, no explanation of the Cross is a Christian dogma. We may reject all the theologies of the Atonement . . . on the ground that they are inadequate to the mystery of the Crucifixion of Him who was God as well as man, but the mystery itself is at the heart of the Christian faith." It is a mystery whose capital aim is to uphold the "at-one-ment" of God and man—"the creation of the conditions whereby God and man come together"—through the Christ Jesus.[118]

Blake is almost alone among critics and illustrators of his time in inviting us to consider what Milton's attitude toward the atonement may have been. With the exception of the explanation offered by Bernard of Clairvaux, all previous rationales for the atonement stressed the wrath of God, his dreadful anger, his awful aspect. Blake seems to have understood that the prevailing Protestant sentiment by the mid-seventeenth century was that all theories of the atonement were inadequate to the mystery and that many came to regard the whole notion of the atonement as immoral. What Patrides admits somewhat reluctantly Blake would probably have asserted emphatically:

We cannot be absolutely certain whether some such notion had not occurred to Milton as well; we can only suspect that it might have, principally because nearly every time God appears in *Paradise Lost* the poetry responds adversely, becoming flat, dull, monotonous. Certainly an impressive number of Milton's contemporaries were quite troubled by the "fire and bloud" so often intimated by their God, while even before the middle of the sixteenth century the very word "satisfaction" was . . . "hated to al christen eares." By 1661 finally, only six years before the publication of *Paradise Lost,* George Rust protested that "modern Theology," suffering from "an excess of complement to the Justice of God," had become "as rude and troublesome as the Ass in the Fable, who did not fawn upon, but invade his masters."[119]

Blake grasped that Milton's "prompted Song" was an attempt to reorganize Christian precepts, dispelling the specious orthodoxy of recovering Eden on the cross and presenting in its place the new idea that paradise was regained in the desert.

Erwin Panofsky comments pertinently as he reminds us that in Christian painting and poetry, especially that of Protestant artists, "conspicuous omission" is a significant element of meaning.[120]

The remark has special application to Milton when we recall not only the importance of the Crucifixion to Protestant theology of the Renaissance but also its popularity as a subject for Renaissance artists. For example, Craig Harbison observes that between 1560 and 1600 the Crucifixion, along with the Last Supper, was the most popular subject for artists depicting events from the life of Christ—popular because of its centrality to "Protestant doctrine."[121] The peculiarity of Milton's centering the story of Christ's temptation in a poem on the recovery of paradise is compounded when we remember that "no Early Christian representation of the Temptation is known" ("probably none was executed") and that at no period in the history of Christian art was Christ's temptation "a particularly prominent pictorial theme; indeed *it was strikingly rare,* even among New Testament cycles."[122]   On the few occasions when the subject was depicted, its importance was diminished by its abbreviated, usually marginal, treatment; the subject was seen within the context of the fall, the Baptism, or the Crucifixion, but never was it portrayed as equal in significance to these events. On the one hand, then, we have a singularly unpopular subject; on the other, a tradition of "conspicuous omission" in illustration that enables an artist to assert dogmas and beliefs peculiarly his own. Milton eliminates the Crucifixion from *Paradise Regained,* and in illustrating that poem Blake omits the subject from his designs; in the process, he is faithful to a belief "peculiar" to Milton rather than one "peculiar" to his own understanding of the poet.

Blake's knowledge of Milton was sufficiently deep to suggest to him that Milton's departures from tradition were as significant as his uses of it. By deviating from the tradition of presenting the fall and the Crucifixion together, Milton suggested that *Paradise Regained* was a criticism of the very theology he had postulated in *Paradise Lost.* Blake himself strove to return to a purified version of Christianity based upon the values of love and forgiveness, and he detected in *Paradise Regained* the same impulse. Milton omitted reference to the Passion and Crucifixion not because he lacked the ability to handle the subjects but because he found those subjects uncongenial to him and alien to the spirit of Christianity that his poem enshrined. Not caring for the doctrine of the atonement, Milton deflected interest from it, thereby eradicating the "torture" and "horror" of Christianity. In *Paradise Regained* Milton is not concerned with a God who deserts his champion and allows him to be taunted; he is concerned rather with Christ as Redeemer, not of mankind only but of the Christian religion. Like Hayley, Blake found in Milton's poem a "purer religion" accompanied by "greater force of imagination" than had been presented in *Paradise Lost;*[123] he saw poetic imagination triumphing over popular orthodoxy. Through his illustrations to *Paradise Regained,* Blake was able to bring into sharp focus Milton's radical Christian vision and to proclaim with Shelley that Milton was a bold and inquiring spirit who "shook to dust" repressive orthodoxies.[124]

If Blake insists upon symbolic reading of his illustrations, he also compels us to read Milton's poem in the same fashion. Taken literally, the poem's action may seem trivial; but understood symbolically, that action has momentous significance. As Blake interpreted the temptations in the wilderness, they revealed Christ's "energy of mind" and the "majesty" of his human nature. This Blake makes clear in his *Annotations to Lavater* and in his designs to *Paradise Regained.* In his initial illustration, Blake depicts the baptism of Jesus; in the second, the temptation to turn stone into bread. The third, fourth, and fifth illustrations call attention to the poem's genre, to the human context in which Jesus appears, and to the poem's meditative character; but the sixth illustration, with its depiction of the banquet temptation, returns us to the poem's central event—the temptation. In the seventh illustration, Blake conflates the entire sequence of the kingdom temptations. The eighth and ninth illustrations accentuate the psychological character of the poem's action. The tenth illustration, Christ on the pinnacle, returns us to the temptation sequence; and the final two illustrations deal with the aftermath of temptation—Christ being ministered to by the angels and his return to his mother's house. A rising crescendo until the pinnacle scene, the poem drives unremittingly toward that moment of self-discovery. Not only does the preponderance of illustrations to the fourth book fix our attention to that moment, but the fact that all the designs except the tenth one (see fig. 43) possess a static quality causes that illustration to distinguish itself from the rest. Through the concentration of illustrations within the fourth book, Blake places himself in the company of those who believed that "all the poems ever written must yield, even *Paradise Lost* must yield, to the *Paradise Regained* in the grandeur of its close."[125]

Blake's illustrations to *Paradise Regained*, then, serve various functions. They establish the human context in which Christ moves; they illuminate the poem's genre by pointing to its meditative, psychological character; they give an architectonic clarity and vigor to Milton's verbal expression. But they also bring into focus the three major events of the poem—baptism, temptation, and return. This is the great pattern Blake discerned in Milton's poem and the one to which his illustrations give formal substance. It is the poem's myth that fascinates Blake, and his interpretation of that myth can now elicit our attention.

MILTON'S "AUTUMNAL" VISION

Blake's illustrations to *Paradise Regained* exist, in large part, to express his dissatisfaction with the critical tradition that grew up around the poem, just as Northrop Frye's observations, and Howard Schultz's, exist to express dissatisfaction with the same tradition, not significantly altered, that extends into the twentieth century. [126] Like Frye and Schultz, Blake seems to think that the chief trouble with the criticism of *Paradise Regained* is that those who read the poem do not bring to it sufficient mythic perception. With the mythic aspect of Milton's poem Blake's illustrations are ultimately concerned.

Blake understood that in *Paradise Regained* Milton subscribed to the Hero-Christology of the Bible which yields the tradition of Jesus as the hero of heroes. [127] Milton's descriptive phrases in Book I of *Paradise Regained*—"deeds Above Heroic," "th' exalted man," "man of men," "the perfect Man," and "victorious deeds . . . heroic acts"—and his fierce insistence upon Christ's heroic acts of virtue, heroic capacity for love, heroic magnitude of mind, are calculated to recall this tradition and bring forward the idea that Jesus, enacting his human career, epitomizes the pattern of the "Most perfect *Heroe*" (*The Passion*, l. 13). It is this pattern of perfection and beauty that Blake sees Milton celebrating and exalting in his brief epic.

Blake understood, too, what has eluded many recent critics, namely, that the life of Jesus submits to various interpretations. On the one hand, we may regard Jesus as a man who by virtue of his austerities and meditations attained wisdom. This view implies that we should follow the myth literally, that paradoxically contemplation and abstraction are the way to life and that action and involvement are the way to death. On the other hand, we may regard Jesus as a God descended who took upon himself the enactment of a human career. Such a view suggests that Jesus is a symbol, a revelation of the indwelling life, and invites us to meditate upon our own immanent divinity. This view implies that all men are human forms divine and that retreating into the self culminates not in estrangement but in communion.

Joseph Campbell provides us with at least two observations on the Christ myth that are anticipated, if not clearly articulated, by Blake. Contending that there are essentially two degrees of heroes, those who return to the world as emissaries and those who return with the knowledge that "I and the father are one," Campbell suggests that the heroes of this "second, highest illumination" are the world-redeemers, the incarnations, whose "myths open out to cosmic proportions."[128] And still further, Campbell says that there are three significant ways through which the hero may enact his destiny: he may renounce the world, he may become an emperor in the world, he may redeem the world. Most heroes appear in one of these roles, but Milton's Christ as "Most perfect *Heroe*" appears in all three. He rejects the kingdoms of Satan in order to rule over the Kingdom of God; he returns to the world of civilization in order to become its spiritual leader and redeemer. If *Paradise Lost* recounted the story of loss and fragmentation, *Paradise Regained* countered with one of recovery and reintegration. The finding of a paradise within, Blake understood, preceded the recovery of one without.

This theme, no less prominent in the illustrations to *Paradise Regained* than in Blake's imitations of that poem, is conveyed most forcibly in figures 35, 36, 41, and 42, all of which emphasize the introspective nature of Milton's poem. The one interpretively important subject that was contributed to the tradition of illustrations for *Paradise Regained* during the early nineteenth century was the depiction of Christ with a "swarming multitude of thoughts" wandering into the desert. For Blake's contemporaries, and for Blake himself, the central act in *Paradise Regained* was Christ's "tracing the Desert wild/ . . . with holiest meditations fed" and then "into himself" descending (II. 109–11)—an act that is immediately preceded and thus punctuated by the introspection of Andrew and Simon Peter and the extended meditation of Mary. In Blake's *Milton,* his most exacting imitation of *Paradise Regained,* Milton assumes the role of Jesus, goes "guarded within," and wanders "lost in dreary night" (15:16, 20). One third of the illustrations to Milton's brief epic drive the same theme. Andrew and Simon Peter wandering and doubting, Mary meditating, and Christ dreaming, then awakening "with untroubl'd mind"—all these subjects combine to suggest that the human mind itself is the theater for epic drama. Through these designs, Blake implies that *Paradise Regained* is a poem of definition and discovery: Christ *defines* himself by *discovering* his roles as prophet, king, and priest and by recovering the knowledge of which he has been "emptied."

Like *Milton, Paradise Regained* is the story of "gathering self-awareness."[129] The dramatic center of Blake's epic involves a sudden change in attitude, which enables the hero to come to full self-knowledge. Milton casts off selfhood, goes to Eternal Death, and recovers the values of love and forgiveness. These are the same values that Christ acquires in the desert. In resisting the temptation to turn stones into bread, Christ adheres to the authority of the Law; in rejecting the temptation on the pinnacle, he embraces the power of Love. The ethical nucleus of Milton's poem, as Blake reads it, involves casting aside the primitive ethic of the Old Testament in favor of the more humane ethic of the New Testament. By 1798 Blake had come to believe that the whole purpose of Christ's Incarnation was to "abolish the Jewish Imposture." "Was not Christ murderd," Blake asks in his *Annotations to Watson,* "because he taught that God loved all Men & was their father & forbad all contention for Worldly prosperity . . . [?] Christ died as an Unbeliever [a rejector of the Law and the wickedness attendant to it]. & if the Bishops had their will so would Paine. . . . let the Bishops prove that he has not spoken against the Holy Ghost who in Paine strives with Christendom as in Christ he strove with the Jews" (p. 604). This "striving" against

the Law in order to redeem Life Blake saw represented by the
moment in the desert—the moment recorded and celebrated in
Milton's poem. The whole process of *Paradise Regained* is one
wherein Christ, turning within himself, consolidates in the figure
of Satan the errors of perverted Christianity and then annihilates
them. The act of turning inward and upward is portrayed insistently in the designs depicting Christ and his companions; it is
opposed to the contrasting gesture of Satan and his crew, who,
unlike the comparable array of figures in the title-page design for
the *Job* series, turn outward, look downward, to selfhood (see fig.
38).

Blake's interpretation of the wilderness story is not a common
one, but it is not a unique one either. Milton probably knew, and
Blake probably knew too, a painting previously alluded to in this
chapter, Botticelli's depiction of Christ's temptation in the Sistine
Chapel. The subject was rarely enough depicted so that this
rendition of it would have held the attention and interest of both
poets. In the lower portion of the painting is a boy carrying sticks
to a furnace; in the upper portion is a sequence of designs
depicting Christ's various temptations.[130] The picture has bewildered art historians, and perhaps the artist's intent is finally
elusive. But one can easily imagine what Milton and Blake might
have made of it. The overt reference to blood sacrifice in the lower
portion of the design is rendered unnecessary by what transpires in
its upper portion. Christ's journey into the desert draws an end to
the Old Testament ethic: it ensures that a philosophy of love will
reign over the law of sacrifice, which finds its fullest, most offen-
sive expression in the very story that Milton and Blake choose to
ignore—the story of Christ's crucifixion.

The main lines of such an interpretation are drawn in Blake's
depiction of Christ's baptism (see fig. 34). The center strip of the
design is highly conventionalized. Christ, standing in a stream, is
baptized by John, who takes a place to his right and who, with
thunder lines almost touching him, looks not toward Jesus but at
Satan. The moment depicted is the one described by Milton:

> . . . [the Baptist] on him baptiz'd
> Heaven open'd, and the likeness of a Dove
> The spirit descended, while the Fathers voice
> From Heav'n pronounc'd him his beloved Son.   (I. 29–32)

The zigzag lines of thunder, representing "the voice divine," establish Satan's perspective on the baptism, causing him to recall in council the time "When his fierce thunder drove us to the deep" (I. 35–36, 90). It is important that the Satanic perspective is introduced into this design; for we have, at this juncture in the poem, a clear instance of Milton's speaking through "the voice of the devil." When Satan says that John the Baptist "Pretends to wash off sin" and thus to prepare man for reception into heaven (I. 73–75), he reflects Milton's own view, shared by Blake, that John is an *Imposter* who represents the very ethic from which Christ is preparing to liberate mankind. For Milton, the event is not important, only what the event signifies, which, as MacKellar explains, is not the cleansing of sins but rather public avowal of one's commitment to live nobly *in this world.*[131]   Blake surely recognized that such a device was sometimes employed by Milton, and this recognition probably stands behind his observation in the 1793 *Prospectus* that Milton "could not publish [his] own works" (p. 670). There is the story, circulated by John Toland, that *Paradise Lost* was for a time suppressed; but what Blake's statement probably means is that Milton's manner of representing his ideas was greatly affected by their heretical cast. Thus in *Paradise Regained,* as MacKellar explains, what Milton had to say about the Baptism, because it was plainly "heretical," was assigned to the voice of the devil: Milton "could trust that competent readers would see in the present passage [*PR* I. 73–75] nothing more than a refutation of a very old story; and that only those most unfriendly readers would look for blasphemy, and for them there would be the fact that it was Satan who uttered the blasphemy."[132] Milton's vision was not mistaken, then, but oppression in his own time subjected his vision to distortion.

Along with John and Christ, Satan figures prominently in the depiction of the Baptism. Portrayed as a nude figure flying through air (this detail recalling the tenth design [see fig. 43] where Satan falls through air), Satan, identifiable by the serpent flying with him, rides over the cluster of figures (a man, woman, and child) who stand to Christ's left. The allusion is obviously to Milton's description of Satan, who "with envy fraught and rage/ Flies to his place" (I. 38–39). The figures themselves derive from the line informing us that Christ came to the Baptism amidst a throng of people (I. 75). In accordance with Milton's description, Blake pictorializes the throng through an encompassing age group, representing youth, adulthood, and old age; but he may also be elaborating upon Milton's text by pursuing the reference to Job (I. 147), for Blake introduces Job as the male figure in the throng, accompanied by a child and by a woman who bears striking resemblance to Mirth in the *L'Allegro* series. This resemblance is enhanced by the children in each corner of the design, whose hands are raised into the air; and it is perhaps confirmed by the woman, in the cluster of figures to Christ's right, who resembles Melancholy in the *Il Penseroso* series. Of the six figures witnessing the baptism, only Job and the children seem to comprehend its significance: Job because he has already undergone the experience that the Baptism presages; the children because only they, "the most Ignorant & Simple Minds," as Blake explains in his *Annotations to Thornton,* can comprehend "The Beauty of the Bible"— they "Understand it Best" (p. 657). Mirth and Melancholy look on, the one inattentively, the other reflectively.

Several observations are pertinent here. Blake presumably illustrated *L'Allegro* and *Il Penseroso* immediately before illustrating *Paradise Regained* and at the same time that he was preparing a final arrangement of *Songs of Innocence and of Experience.* Both Blake's songs and Milton's two lyrics are based on the themes of contraries and progression; both poets trace a journey from innocence to experience that culminates in the attainment of the prophetic strain. The progress charted in Milton's poems is precisely the progress Blake saw as he scrutinized Milton's poetry and the pattern of development it implied. In old age, Milton achieved unity of being, symbolized by the embracing figures in the last of the *Il Penseroso* designs; born out of the psychic wholeness was the vision of *Paradise Regained.* Mirth and melancholy, the struggling contraries, brought the poet to the threshold of the vision that informs his brief epic. In it, the divine vision is achieved as contraries are redeemed through the destruction of the negation, the spectral self. The very process that brought Milton to write the poem is what the poem and Blake's designs for it investigate. That process also finds its archetype in the Book of Job, which Milton alludes to in *The Reason of Church-Government* as the proper model for a brief epic poem. Blake, by portraying Job within the context of the Baptism, asserts the involvement of Milton's poem with its biblical prototype. The Book of Job provides not the outer structure but the inner form, the experience, that is the subject of *Paradise Regained.*

The Baptism, for Blake and for Milton, marks the emergence into experience, the start of a journey that completes itself in Jerusalem. Neither poet is orthodox in his understanding of the event, but the orthodox understanding of the event at least helps to bring into focus the experience to which the Baptism is a prologue. Traditionally, the Baptism is used to signify Christ's submission to the law, to represent an act of obedience to the Father, whose extension Blake recognized in the Satan of the Book of Job and the gospel accounts of Christ's temptation. This is why, in *Milton,* Urizen is represented as the Baptist who "stoop'd down/And took up water from the river Jordan: pouring on/To Miltons brain the icy fluid" (19:7–9)—an event that elicits from Milton not submission but a contrary act that destroys the very figure who would manacle him. Analogously, in *Paradise Regained,* Christ moves from the gospel of law, of punishment and affliction, to the gospel of love, of forgiveness and mercy. In the process, the Satan within is destroyed but so, too, is the God of wrath and vengeance of whom Satan is an emanation. The nude Satan of Blake's designs, who appears with his conventional attributes—the serpent in one instance (see fig. 34) and bat wings in another (see fig. 38)—is identical with the bearded Urizenic figure who sweeps over the banquet table (see fig. 39) and hovers over the sleeping Christ in the dream temptation (see fig. 41). The identity of the two figures is established by the portrayals of Satan in each of the three temptations—there is always the heavily muscled body, always the Urizenic beard (see figs. 35, 40, 43). Blake does here what he had already done in illustrating *The Book of Urizen:* through a "radical" contraction he allows us to see Milton's Satan and Milton's God "compacted into one."[133] That this Urizenic figure is an aspect of Christ himself, something within that must be overpowered and destroyed, is emphasized by the common attire of Christ in the baptism and Satan in the second temptation (see figs. 34 and 40).

The figure of the garment is as important a symbol in these designs as it was in those for *Milton;* and the ambiguity we earlier recognized in the image is evident in the first design, where the garments worn by John are old and tattered, contrasting with the white loin cloth worn by Christ. The progress of Christ's own enlightenment is marked by the increasingly scantier attire of Satan—first he is in robes, then in loin cloth, and finally, exposed for what he is, falls naked from the pinnacle (see figs. 35, 40, 43).[134] Not only do the garments signal Christ's heightened awareness of Satan, the enemy within; but the contrasting garments in the first design emphasize the poem's presiding theme, which involves casting off the garments of the law, those of religious orthodoxy, in order to don the garments of resurrection, those of the new religion founded upon love and forgiveness.

Blake uses his designs for *Paradise Regained* to make a statement not only about the meaning of Milton's poem but about his own idea of Milton and of where Milton stood in terms of the Christian tradition. Like Henry Fuseli, Blake believed that, because liberty, religion, and art are irrevocably involved with one another, until the recovery of true religion both liberty and the arts so dependent upon it are doomed; and with Fuseli, Blake would assent to the view that "Truth has been—and is—the destroyer of peace—and the parent of revolution." [135] So long as the ensuing revolution was mental, not corporeal, Blake could lend to it his support and allegiance. He could even be its instigator. For Blake, certainly, one of the great ironies of Milton criticism was that *Paradise Regained* had been invoked repeatedly to discredit Milton as a Christian, especially since, from Blake's point of view, it was Milton's brief epic, more than any other poem he wrote, that entitled his precursor to be called a Christian. In this poem, Milton finds the God whom he lost in childhood; and he redeems not only himself but the entire Christian religion as, eschewing corrupting orthodoxies, he returns to its origins.

Blake's idea of Milton, as it is projected by the *Paradise Regained* series, corresponds interestingly with William Ellery Channing's view of the poet. Like Blake, Channing sees Milton—as Milton saw himself when he wrote *De Doctrina Christiana*—as "an Apostle . . . to all the Churches of Christ." "Never was there a more unconfined mind," a poet with more of the "conscious dignity of a prophet," with so much "brightness" in his "prophetic visions." Milton participated in a Revolution that, instead

1. Blake's *Head of Milton.* *(The City of Manchester Art Galleries.)*

2. Faithorne's Crayon Portrait. (*Princeton University Library.*)

3. Milton Portrait Engraved by Marshall. (*Reproduced from "Poems of Mr. John Milton" [1645] by permission of the Folger Shakespeare Library, Washington, D.C.*)

4. Richardson's Frontispiece-Portrait.
(*Reproduced from "A Complete
Collection of the Historical,
Political, and Miscellaneous Works
of John Milton," ed. Thomas Birch
[1738]. A second edition, with
the same portrait, was published in
1753. By permission of the
Huntington Library, San Marino,
California.*)

5. DeLaunay's Frontispiece-Portrait.
(*Reproduced from the Foulis
edition of "Paradise Lost" [1776]
by permission of the Huntington
Library, San Marino, California.*)

6. Plate 1 of Blake's *Milton*,
   Copy B. (*By permission
   of the Huntington
   Library, San Marino,
   California.*)

7. Plate 1 of Blake's *Milton*,
   Copy C. (*Rare Book
   Division, The New York
   Public Library, Astor,
   Lenox and Tilden
   Foundations.*)

8. Plate 1 of Blake's *Milton*,
   Copy D. (*Library of
   Congress, Rosenwald
   Collection.*)

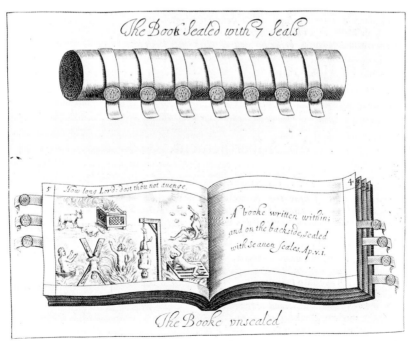

9. The Book of Revelation as a Picture-Prophecy. (*Reproduced from
   "The Works of Joseph Mede" [1664] by permission of the Huntington
   Library, San Marino, California.*)

10. Plate 13 of Blake's *Milton*, Copy B [Plate 16 in Copy D].
(*By permission of the Huntington Library, San Marino,
California.*)

11. Plate 16 of Blake's *Milton*, Copy D. (*Library of Congress, Rosenwald Collection.*)

12. Plate 15 of Blake's *Milton*, Copy A [Plate 18 in Copy D]. (*By permission of the Trustees of the British Museum.*)

13. Plate 18 of Blake's *Milton*, Copy D. (*Library of Congress, Rosenwald Collection.*)

14. Plate 29 of Blake's
    Milton, Copy B
    [Plate 32 in Copy
    D]. (*By permission
    of the Huntington
    Library, San
    Marino, California.*)

15. Plate 38 of Blake's
    Milton, Copy A
    [Plate 42 in Copy
    D]. (*By permission
    of the Trustees of
    the British
    Museum.*)

16. Plate 38 of Blake's *Milton,*
Copy B [Plate 42 in Copy
D]. (*By permission of the
Huntington Library, San
Marino, California.*)

17. Plate 42 of Blake's *Milton*, Copy D. (*Library of Congress,
Rosenwald Collection.*)

18. Plate 1 of *Jerusalem*, Copy E. (*From the Collection of Mr. and Mrs. Paul Mellon.*)

19. The Vision of the Candlesticks (Illustration for the Book of Revelation). (*Reproduced from the "Royal Universal Family Bible" [1780] by permission of the Harvard College Library.*)

20. A Balestra's
    Frontispiece, *Milton's
    Apotheosis.
    (Reproduced from "Il
    Paradiso Perduto"
    [1818]. This is the
    most recent
    reproduction of a
    design that
    accompanied editions
    in 1730, 1740, and
    1759. By permission
    of the Folger
    Shakespeare Library,
    Washington, D.C.)*

21. *Milton Triumphing
    Over Salmasius.
    (Reproduced from
    "Memoirs of Thomas
    Hollis" [1780] by
    permission of the
    Huntington Library,
    San Marino,
    California.)*

22. Illustration for Young's *Night Thoughts*, no. 537. (*By permission of the Trustees of the British Museum.*)

23. *Albion Rose* (line
    engraving). (*National
    Gallery of Art,
    Rosenwald
    Collection.*)

24. *Albion Rose* (color
    print). (*By permission
    of the Huntington
    Library, San Marino,
    California.*)

25. *Albion Rose* (color print). (*By permission of the Trustees of the British Museum.*)

26. Plate 76 of *Jerusalem*, Copy E. (*From the Collection of Mr. and Mrs. Paul Mellon.*)

27. Plate 2 of *Jerusalem*, Copy E. (*From the Collection of Mr. and Mrs. Paul Mellon.*)

28. Illustration for the
Book of Job, no. 3.
(*By permission of
the Huntington
Library, San
Marino, California.*)

29. Illustration for the
Book of Job, no. 6.
(*By permission of
the Huntington
Library, San
Marino, California.*

30. For *Comus* (water color, no. 7, early version) : [Sabrina Disenchants the Lady]. (*By permission of the Huntington Library, San Marino, California.*)

31. For *Comus* (water color, no. 7, late version) : [Sabrina Disenchants the Lady]. (*Gift of Mrs. John L. Gardner and George N. Black, Courtesy of Museum of Fine Arts, Boston.*)

32. For *Paradise Lost* (water color, no. 12, early version) : [The Expulsion]. (*By permission of the Huntington Library, San Marino, California.*)

33. For *Paradise Lost* (water color, no. 9, late version) : [The Expulsion]. (*Gift by Subscription, Museum of Fine Arts, Boston.*)

34. For *Paradise Regained* (water color, no. 1) : [The Baptism of Jesus].
(*Fitzwilliam Museum Collection.*)

35. For *Paradise
Regained* (water
color, no. 2) : [The
First Temptation].
(*Fitzwilliam
Museum
Collection.*)

36. For *Paradise
Regained* (water
color, no. 3) :
[Andrew and
Simon Peter].
(*Fitzwilliam
Museum
Collection.*)

37. For *Paradise
Regained* (water
color, no. 4) :
[Mary Meditating].
(*Fitzwilliam
Museum
Collection.*)

38. For *Paradise
Regained* (water
color, no. 5) :
[Satan in Council].
(*Fitzwilliam
Museum
Collection.*)

39. For *Paradise Regained* (water color, no. 6) : [The Banquet Temptation].
(*Fitzwilliam Museum Collection.*)

40. For *Paradise Regained* (water color, no. 7) : [The Second Temptation].
(*Fitzwilliam Museum Collection.*)

41. For *Paradise Regained* (water color, no. 8) : [Satan Inspiring Jesus' Ugly
Dreams]. (*Fitzwilliam Museum Collection.*)

42. For *Paradise Regained* (water color, no. 9) : [Morning Chasing Away the
Spectres of the Night]. (*Fitzwilliam Museum Collection.*)

43. For *Paradise Regained* (water color, no. 10) : [The Third Temptation].
(Fitzwilliam Museum Collection.)

44. For *Paradise Regained* (water color, no. 11) : [Jesus Ministered to by Angels].
(*Fitzwilliam Museum Collection.*)

45. For *Paradise Regained* (water color, no. 12) : [Jesus Returning to Mary].
(*Fitzwilliam Museum Collection.*)

of dampening his enthusiasm and fragmenting his vision, gave new vigor to both, says Channing; the Revolution subjected Milton to a trial from which he returned "exalted." Because he was a bold and inquiring spirit, Milton, had he been living during the early decades of the nineteenth century, would have been "among that class of Christians . . . who are too jealous of the rights of the mind, and too dissatisfied with the clashing systems of the age, to attach themselves closely to any party"; in matters of theology, Milton would have been committed to those who have "created a consciousness of defect" in religion and would require such "a manifestation of Christianity, as would throw all present systems into obscurity."[136] With these sentiments, Blake would have concurred. But Channing continues with statements from which Blake would have demurred, misreading Milton's Christology, or at least not pursuing it into *Paradise Regained,* and misconstruing the history of the Christian religion, seeing progress where Blake would see perversion:

> We now arrive at that part of Milton's work, in which his powerful mind might have been expected to look beyond the prevalent opinions of his day, but in which he has followed the beaten road almost without deviation, seldom noticing difficulties, and hardly seeming to know their existence. We refer to the great subjects of the moral condition of mankind, and of redemption by Jesus Christ.

> With respect to Christ's mediation, he supposes, that Christ saves us by bearing our punishment and in this way satisfying God's justice.

> . . . we are disappointed in finding the spirit of Milton satisfying itself with the degrading notions which prevailed around him. But we remember, that it is the order of Providence, that the greatest minds should sympathize much with their age, and that they contribute the more to the progress of mankind, by not advancing too fast and too far beyond their contemporaries.[137]

For all his perception about the character of Milton's genius and his art, Channing here provides an *apologia* which Blake would have dismissed. The great poet does not succumb to his age but outruns it: what Channing calls "providence" Blake would call "prostitution." But Blake would also have resisted the notion of progress that Channing finds in the history of religion and that leads him to attribute to Milton an even greater error:

> The great errour of Milton lies in supposing that the primitive church was meant to be a model for all ages.

The chief cause of Milton's failure was, that . . . he believed in the perfection of the primitive church and that Christianity, instead of being carried forward, was to be carried *back* to its original purity.[138]

What is for Channing "Milton's failure" is for Blake his great accomplishment. On the very grounds that Channing chooses to demean Milton, Blake wishes to celebrate him: the illustrations to *Paradise Regained* are part of a design to show how Milton broke with conventional forms of religion in order to expose the true form of which they are a perversion. In its particulars Milton's *De Doctrina Christiana* may not always be a reliable gloss to his final epic vision, but in purpose theological tract and epic poem agree: they both oppose "the false conclusions . . . wrung" from Scripture, attacking those who represent "the truth as error . . . while calling error . . . truth" (*Yale Milton*, VI, 120); they both correct those who would turn "the Christian religion completely upside down" (VI, 225).

In this regard, Blake's idea of Milton may be most illuminatingly glossed by turning to an anonymous essay published years after Blake's death but written in a spirit matching Blake's own conceptions. "In matters of religion," says its author, "many are proverbially afraid of new things. Had the fear existed before new things usurped the place of the old, it had been well. As it is, we have not only the state of things spoken of by the prophet, when men shall put darkness for light and light for darkness . . . , but we also have them . . . putting old things for new and new for old, clinging to the new things as if they were old, and crying out against the old things as if they were new."[139] This is emphatically the state of Milton criticism as Blake knew it, and it remains unsettlingly true of much Milton criticism today. Blake saw Milton laboring to remove such deceptions from the minds of the people; and he saw Milton's commentators, with equal diligence, laboring to preserve the same deceptions. Milton may have been partly at fault: he began his effort in *Paradise Lost,* and for a variety of reasons it was impeded there. However, Milton pursued his effort into *Paradise Regained,* and there it was triumphantly fulfilled. The first epic, if flawed, still places Milton at the head of his generation in literature and theology; the second poem, however—a poem of uninfected vision—places Milton at the head of all time in such matters. In his last epic, Milton takes the up-side-down world and turns it right side up. Here, in brief, we have the motive that led Blake to illuminate the poem—not in a spirit of contention but in one of collaboration and celebration. Like a later illustrator, Blake acknowledges that Milton is a guide to the real meaning of Holy Writ—a visionary who will himself make visionaries of the rest of us. [140] The designs for *Paradise Regained,* resting on these assumptions, imply insistently that Milton's poem must be read symbolically, its myth deciphered, before it can be understood.

Within Milton's poem, there are three major events—Christ's baptism, his temptations, and his return. Significantly, the first event to appear in each of the synoptic gospels, the first event referred to in Milton's poem, and the first event illustrated by Blake, is the baptism of Jesus. That event figures prominently in the two prologues to *Paradise Regained,* where it is presented as an announcement of a threshold experience, which characteristically involves the hero's withdrawal from civilization for the purpose of illumination. Jesus is baptized and leaves behind the wisdom of the law to embrace the wisdom of love. He makes his private departure into the wilderness where, by withstanding Satan's temptations, he achieves full self-knowledge and learns of his mediatorial offices. Christ's experience on the desert—the long temptation he undergoes—becomes for Blake, as it was later to become for Jung, a "sacred symbol": "the prototype of the only meaningful life, that is, of a life that strives for individual realisation." [141] That experience, entailing the birth of personality, has restorative effects upon both the individual and society: the individual acquires unity of being; society acquires an illuminated man to lead it.

The three major events in *Paradise Regained* balance with the three scenes of activity—the desert, the mountain-pinnacle, and the world of civilization. Related to these regions of tension and repose are the patterns of descent and ascent that dominate the poem. In retreating to the desert, Jesus separates himself from the world and symbolically journeys into the depths of his mind, where he experiences consciously the elemental struggles of existence. This descent is followed by an ascent, by the appearance of Christ on the pinnacle. Blake suggests that this descent into the self enables Christ to return to the plane of contemporary life, to re-entrench himself in civilization as one of its leaders and teachers. This return and the life this return implies are exactly proportionate to the depth of the hero's descent.

With gathering energy Milton's poem drives toward the climax on the pinnacle when Christ tells Satan, "Tempt not the Lord thy God," and Satan "smitten with amazement" falls (IV. 561–62). Blake focuses on that moment of triumph and complete self-realization, first by clustering five of his twelve illustrations within the fourth book of Milton's epic and then by making the illustration of Christ on the pinnacle (see fig. 43) the central design for that book. Christ's words on the pinnacle are, of course, the most ambiguous words in the entire poem. They have been taken to mean only that one must not make unnecessary demands upon God. But Blake, it seems, took them to mean much more. The poem began with an epiphany that Satan did not understand; it ends with an epiphany he does understand. Thus, stricken with the realization that he has been tempting divinity, Satan falls. At the same time, the pinnacle scene involves an epiphany for the reader; he now knows what has been suppressed throughout the poem. And most important, Christ's words indicate his own coming to awarness; he now comprehends that which he did not know before.

Blake is one of the very few illustrators, one of the very few interpreters, of *Paradise Regained* to recognize that Milton's poem does not end with the epiphanies signaled by the pinnacle scene, to comprehend that the final lines of the poem emphasize its meaning. Those lines are necessary; not, however, for the reason Walter MacKellar gives us, that in them "Milton achieves the quiet ending which both the patterns and parallel with *Paradise Lost* demand." [142] The parallel between the two epics is an inverted one; and the pattern of this poem, which has Christ returning to his mother's house, is not an echo of the ending to the first epic but an adumbration, albeit ironic, of the conclusion to *Samson Agonistes,* published with *Paradise Regained,* which has the fallen hero returning to his father's house. The epiphanies from the pinnacle are followed by the most heroic act of all. [143] Having learned of his divinity, Christ instead of passing away into ectasy returns to humanity. This is Christ's deed above heroic, what

Blake would call his "unexampled deed." By withstanding the temptation on the pinnacle Christ displays his enormous love for God; by returning home he displays his enormous love for man. Milton knew (and he makes this clear in *The Reason of Church-Government*) that Christ "came not to be minister'd to, but to minister" (*Yale Milton*, I, 824).

In his final illustration (see fig. 45), Blake quietly asserts the full meaning of Milton's poem. The design gathers details from previous ones: Mary has risen from the bench of contemplation where she meditates in the fourth design (see fig. 37); and though she occupies the same humble dwelling, her distaff is gone, as are the dying vines on either side of her shed. The palms, inconspicuous in the early design, are given more prominence here. Equally prominent are the figures of Andrew and Simon Peter, who recall the third design (see fig. 36), which, like the fourth, incorporates the image of the palms. There is no mention of Andrew and Simon Peter at this point in Milton's poem, and no allusion to palms that justifies Blake's depiction of them. Even so, these additions are faithful in spirit, if not in letter, to Milton's poem; and through them Blake makes his pictorial representation unfold poetic meaning.

Andrew and Simon Peter point toward Christ's ministry, which he is now ready to begin; they ensure his return to civilization, which he is to redeem through the gospel of love and forgiveness. The image of the palms is prominent, especially since it appears in this one set of illustrations as often as it does in the whole canon of Blake's poetry (see figs. 36, 37, and 45). [144] Interestingly, in the *Paradise Regained* series, only one other kind of tree is portrayed, the oaks of the second illustration (see fig. 35)—an important detail when we remember that in Blake's poetry the oak and the palm occur in conjunction, as the two trees standing on the edge of Beulah. The one is the tree of death that consigns man to the world of error; the other, the tree of life that enables him to enter eternity.

The palm image, associated in two of these designs with Mary, implies Blake's familiarity with the popular legend that tells of the palm trees bowing their branches to protect Christ's mother, and the related story that tells of how, with every bow, the palm tree destroys another idol standing in the way of the Christian vision.

This image of iconoclasm points to the iconoclastic enterprise that Christ is ready to undertake and that engages Milton himself as he writes his poem. As Blake explains in *The Everlasting Gospel,* Christ learns in the desert the value of "Spiritual Strife": he acquires "on the temples highest steeple" a knowledge of his divinity accompanied, paradoxically, by complete embracement of his humanity—something he learns "to adore" because it is the "Spirit of Life" (p. 511). And as Blake implies, by underlining the passage in Lavater's *Aphorisms on Man,* the knowledge Christ now achieves is the mark of his genius: "The discovery *of truth, by slow progressive meditation, is wisdom,*" says Lavater; "*Intuition of truth, not* preceded by *perceptible meditation, is genius*" (p. 576). With this knowledge, Christ returns to translate his vision, his fully developed understanding, into the gospel of love and forgiveness that he preaches. The palm, the symbol by which the multitudes recognize Christ as a prophet (Matthew 21:8), is also a symbol of the vision that, as prophet, Christ extends to them. Through his return, Christ enables vision to become act and ensures that other men, by comparable action, may come to dwell with him in eternity. The palms, then, through their historical association with Christ, symbolize the paradise he enables us to recover: they stand, in *Jerusalem,* on the edge of Beulah, at the gateway to eternity, signifying the perpetual giving of self that is prologue to "the Building up of Jerusalem" (plate 77). The palm continues to represent the pilgrim's progress toward Jerusalem—a progress that advances considerably with Christ's trampling down hypocrisy, with his drawing to an end the practice of martyrdom (a negative association of the palm), and with the triumph over sacrificial religion that the ending of this practice implies. Christ returns to his mother's house, from which he can lead us, in the perfect unity of his being, to his father's house—to Jerusalem.

The unity of being achieved by Christ in the wilderness is objectified in this final design by the return of Jesus to Mary, by the displacement of withered vegetation (see fig. 37) with the palms of life. There are, it is important to note, two palms, a detail which should cause us to remember that palm trees "grow in couples Male, & Female" and "the female is onely fruitfull" when her seeds are "mixt" with those of the male. In union, the palms "yield whatsoever is necessary to the Life of Man." At the same time that the tree represents the strife of life that "raise[s] . . . man upwards," thus symbolizing the resurrection in mortal life, it is "the emblem, or Hyeroglyphic of a Soldier Life," of a life that plays itself out in a theater of action.[145]

There is, however, a still more pointed meaning conveyed by the image of the palm. When it appears first in the *Paradise Regained* series (see fig. 36), it appears in the depiction of Andrew and Simon Peter, who stand before Jericho, "The City of Palms" (II. 21), an allusion in Milton's poem to the Book of Deuteronomy (34:3), to the chapter in which Moses' death and burial is reported. In his *Annotations to Watson,* Blake writes, "The laws of the Jews were . . . the basest & most oppressive of human codes. & being like all other codes given under pretence of divine command were what Christ pronounced them The Abomination that maketh desolate. i.e. State Religion . . . is the source of all Cruelty" (p. 607). In the moment on the desert, Christ, like Milton in plate 18 (see figs. 12 and 13) of the epic to which Blake gave his name, overthrows the primitive ethic of the Jews, represented by Moses as lawgiver and by Urizen and the Grecian architecture of the city seen in the distance behind Andrew and Simon Peter in the third design. This triumph, this revolution in religion, promised in the last chapter of Deuteronomy, is the subject of both Milton's poem and Blake's designs for it. One need not look for notes from the underground to explicate the biblical allusion in Milton's poem and Blake's design; the meaning of that allusion—its centrality to Milton's vision and Blake's pictorialization of it—is spelled out plainly by Martin Luther, who says that what the last chapter of Deuteronomy signifies is this:

. . . the power of the Law does not grow less through length of days or magnitude of deeds; but it always oppresses and rouses guilty consciences until it dies, that is, until it is done away with through Christ. . . .

When Christ came, says Luther, the old Law terminated "according to the passage in Hebrews (8:13): 'What is becoming obsolete and growing old is ready to vanish away' ";[146] it is *made* to vanish away, Milton and Blake would say, by Christ's triumph in the wilderness. To Christ, the old law, represented by Moses and Urizen, is made to yield: here in the desert it succumbs to the "greater Gospel" that Milton in his poetry, Blake in his, embraces.

Milton was not one of those whom he describes in *Of Reformation* as "preferring a foolish Sacrifice . . . to *Christs* example" (*Yale Milton,* I, 523). The priests of the church, as Milton explains in *The Reason of Church-Government,* have "made the crosse of Christ to be of none effect" by using it to nullify "the power and end of the Gospel" (I, 824); but Milton, as a true prophet of Christianity, quotes (and would have us quote) Christ in saying, "*I will have mercy and not sacrifice*" (*The Doctrine and Discipline of Divorce,* II, 355). Thus coming out of the wilderness of the self, Christ-Milton-Blake, armed with the gospel of love, can "Now enter, and begin to save mankind" (IV. 635).

Paradise Regained contains what was for Blake the highest, the fullest, the most intense, the most valuable mental experience imaginable. That internalized drama was, he thought, the center of the poem's interest and the basis of its unity. He presages those modern critics who locate "the really revolutionary moment in the history of the epic" [147] in Milton's poetry; but he would also have resisted the notion, all too common, that the "revolutionary moment" occurs with the publication of *Paradise Lost.* From Blake's point of view, Milton's brief epic was the first example of the truly modern *heroic* poem. If Milton's devastating treatment of the epic tradition in *Paradise Lost* had the effect of silencing the epic talent of future generations, the psychodrama of *Paradise Regained* had the opposite effect. Milton had taken the Book of Job as the model for his brief epic; his Romantic successors, the first of whom was Blake, took *Paradise Regained* for theirs, and for two reasons. The poem was free from the impedimenta of the classical epic tradition; and, as Blake read it, the poem retracted the terrifying theology of *Paradise Lost,* revealing Milton to be a broader and wiser man than was usually acknowledged, a more humane and moral man than ordinarily thought. In this poem, John Milton is shown falling from grace into humanity. [148]

From the few previous commentaries on Blake's Milton illustrations, some crucial questions have emerged: How closely related are Blake's illustrations and Milton's text? Do those illustrations move away from Milton's poetry in the direction of Blake's own private mythology, or are they instead literal renderings? Or are they rather symbolic statements containing more meaning than

has met the eye? To what extent is Blake working within traditions of illustration and criticism? What is the meaning of Milton's
poetry as Blake understood it? And closely related to that question: Do Blake's illustrations offer valid interpretations, or are
they an index to the reigning critical attitudes about Milton at the
end of the eighteenth century, the errors of which modern criticism has already exposed? With these questions this chapter has
been largely concerned.

Its conclusions, pointing toward a methodology for studying
Blake's designs, enable us to approach his Milton illustrations
anew. Besides dispelling the old notion that when multiple sets of
illustrations exist the early one relentlessly follows Milton's text
and the later one moves steadily away from it, this chapter has
shown that although the later sets become more symbolic they do
so as they push even closer to the text of Milton's poetry. It is,
therefore, the last set of illustrations to *Comus,* the *Nativity Ode,*
and *Paradise Lost* that provides the most complete statement on
the poem and offers the most reliable guide to interpretation.
Moreover, while Blake is obviously cognizant of various traditions
of illustration, and of traditions of interpretation as well, he works
with, not *within* them. Blake preserves the notion of interpretive
illustration that he inherited from the Renaissance biblical illustrators and saw practiced by eighteenth-century illustrators of Milton's poetry; but he also refuses to impose a typological interpretation upon a poem that resists it, or that may be confused by it.
Aware of the corrective function of much interpretive design,
Blake invoked that tradition, in most of his Milton illustrations, to
correct mistaken readings of Milton's poetry developed by eighteenth-century commentaries. He thereby returns to the visionary
experience of Milton's poetry that, though sometimes clouded by
the disfiguring mist of a cumbersome narrative, was most often
lost by the critic whose doors of perception remained closed. In
the process, Blake's illustrations remind us that "the critical history of a great literary work is incomplete unless it incorporates
inferences from the interpretation put upon the masterpiece by
artists";[149] his designs should also convince us that no responsible
history of Milton criticism can be written that does not take them
into account. Time after time, they assert an understanding of
Milton's poetry to which his critics still are strangers; behind them

lies an idea of Milton that modern critics are just beginning to recover. Blake's illustrations, together with his portrayals, unite in the perception that Milton was a revolutionary artist who laid to ruins the most oppressive forms of religion and politics. It is this "truth" about Milton—repressed in the eighteenth century and neglected in our own—that Blake sought to recover and that he invites us to explore.

CHAPTER THREE

"*Mental Prince*"

MILTON AS A REVOLUTIONARY

> I have come to change the old order.
>
> —Enkidu in *The Gilgamesh Epic*

> What the great Seers of Israel wore within;
> That was on them, and is on me . . .
>   . . . the veil of coming centuries
> Is rent,—a thousand years . . .
> Float from eternity into these eyes . . .
>   . . . I cannot all record
> That crowds on my prophetic eye . . .
>
> Dante in Byron's *The Prophecy of Dante*

WILLIAM BLAKE is the brightest star in the constellation of Romantic poets who dedicated themselves to the improvement of civilization through a "purifying and perfect revolution" that Milton, they thought, could help them accomplish. For all these poets, Milton, no slave of power, was "a power amongst powers" who, rather than obstructing genius, released it. That is why Shelley, along with Blake, called Milton an "awakener"—*the* awakener of entranced Europe, a philosopher of "the very loftiest powers," through whom both poets wished to legislate reform. With their contemporaries, they hoped to do for their own time what Milton had done for his: to "hit the new system of things a mighty mental blow."[1] None of these poets had, in his formative years, a knowledge of *De Doctrina Christiana,* except the assurance provided by Edward Phillips's *Life* that Milton wrote "A Perfect system of Divinity";[2] but they all possessed the understanding that the creation of "A Perfect system" was the ultimate

147

goal of all Milton's writing—a goal that Milton pursued in a spirit very much like Blake's. As Milton's "best knower" during the Romantic period, Blake was committed to devising his own system rather than to being enslaved by another man's and, beyond that, to using his system to effect the deliverance of mankind. This commitment led Blake, in *Public Address,* to designate himself "a Mental Prince"—an opponent of the princes of this world who by fostering "Tyranny" fettered "Human Life" (p. 569). Blake's phrase—"a Mental Prince"—tells us much about Blake himself; but it tells us something, too, about his idea of Milton, an idea epitomized in a phrase that identifies Blake's Milton with the Milton of the other poets of the Romantic era, a Milton whose lineaments were first drawn by Blake's onetime patron, William Hayley. Of the Romantic poets, Blake gave to new attitudes toward Milton their fullest embodiment, their most eloquent articulation. Blake's idea of Milton merits our attention, however, not just because an entire age's comprehension of the poet is summarized therein but because, in accordance with the dictum that genius outruns its age, Blake embodies, in pictures and in poems, truths about Milton repressed during the eighteenth century and still lost in the orthodoxies of modern criticism.

Though Milton has never been an unappreciated poet, he was in his own time a greatly misunderstood one; and he remains so today. In the seventeenth century and in the century that succeeded it, there was a single indisputable fact of literary criticism, sometimes noisily asserted, but more often, out of embarrassment, ignored: Milton was a revolutionary who, rather than observing orthodoxies, set out to subvert them and, in the process, subverted the very system of aesthetics that during the eighteenth century achieved the status of rule. In consequence, this immensely important dimension of Milton's art and thought was pushed into the distance as commentators directed their efforts toward surreptitiously snaring the poet in their own net of orthodoxy. This phenomenon of criticism, reappearing in the Victorian period, operated according to Wicksteed's law: "the works of inspiration are always being annexed by orthodoxy which hardens itself against every new incursion of the spirit."[3] The Romantics, especially Blake, resisted this direction in criticism; but their line of resistance was broken by those eminent Victorians who established the image of Milton as a conservative thinker, even while acknowledging the experimental character of his art.[4]

The Victorians' view of Milton persists in our own century, dominating much of its criticism; and though Robert West's essay, "Milton as Philosophical Poet," may cause us to say, "Victorianism is still too much with us," it must be credited with providing an admirable summary of a misunderstanding in which West himself participates:

> For Milton to be a philosophical poet does not mean, of course, that he was ahead of the philosophy of his time, as Proust may have been of his, or was even abreast of it. Milton seems to have had little sympathy with new ideas or ways of thought. . . . In fact, contemporary . . . experimentation [in ways of thinking] . . . seem[s] unimportant in Milton's scheme of thought. Milton was not interested in clearing away ancient preconceptions, except, perhaps, some of Aristotle's, which he looked on as crabbed. He was too authoritarian and too common-sense. . . . Milton was simply not detached enough or flexible enough of mind for a clear new philosophical vision. If, as Whitehead thought, philosophy is disclosure, fresh insight, the opening of windows, Milton can hardly be called philosophical. He was rather a superbly gifted confirmer of what his audience already believed and user of ways of thinking already established. . . . he was an advocate, not an instigator or discoverer.[5]

What West fails to acknowledge—and he is not alone— is that "the appearance of society's orthodoxies in a work of art does not subvert, or necessarily subvert, its revolutionary aims—what is important is not the artist's invocation of orthodoxies but the attitudes he assumes toward them."[6]

There is no quicker way to call West's view of Milton into doubt than to recall that Milton, on virtually every occasion when he speaks of tradition and custom, associates both with tyranny and error. "Error supports Custome," he says in *The Doctrine and Discipline of Divorce;* "Custome count'nances Error" (*Yale Milton,* II, 223). "Fraud of . . . traditions" (I, 520), "the broken reed of tradition" (I, 624), "idle traditions" (I, 641), "empty conformities" (I, 766), "unsavory traditions" (I, 895), "the old vomit of traditions" (I, 899)—rhetoric like this, bound to the belief expressed in *The Reason of Church-Government* that custom is "a tyrant" (I, 777), that tradition is a "perpetual cankerworme" (I, 779), betrays the conclusions that West invites us to accept.[7] Those conclusions present us with a dichotomy—with two Miltons, the one a conservative poet, the other a radical pamphleteer. It may be that we should contemplate such a Milton—one as full of postures as the John Donne who wrote the *Songs and Sonets,* one who with his left hand opposes the orthodoxies that with the right hand of his poetry he embraces. It may be that we should investigate a Milton whose poetry, like George Herbert's, is built upon a fundamental disjunction between the conventionality of a poem's content and the dazzling experimentations of its form. But it is not in directions such as these that William Blake points us. From him, we may glean a whole new set of premises, premises that lie behind the brilliantly elusive allegory of a Printing House in *The Marriage of Heaven and Hell.*

Milton figures so famously in *The Marriage of Heaven and Hell* that we may expect his art to have furnished the source for this allegory about creation, which encompasses the poet's relationship with tradition, the poem's involvement with the poet, especially with the faculty of genius, and finally the poem's relationship with its audience:

> In the first chamber was a Dragon-Man, clearing away the rubbish from a caves mouth; within, a number of Dragons were hollowing the cave,
>   In the second chamber was a Viper folding round the rock & the cave, and others adorning it with gold silver and precious stones.
>   In the third chamber was an Eagle with wings and feathers of air, he caused the inside of the cave to be infinite, around were numbers of Eagle like men, who built palaces in the immense cliffs.
>   In the fourth chamber were Lions of flaming fire raging around & melting the metals into living fluids.
>   In the fifth chamber were Unnam'd forms, which cast the metals into the expanse.
>   There they were reciev'd by Men who occupied the sixth chamber, and took the forms of books & were arranged in libraries.
>
> (plate 15)

The Dragon-Man, the "devilish" prophet, is joined in his labors by the other Dragons, by the sons of the prophets, whose task is to clear away the rubbish from the cave of tradition. This act enables the poet-prophet to discover the uncorrupted forms, represented by the viper folding round the rock and cave. When infused with inspiration from the eagle of genius and the eagle-like men (the prophets of tradition who are also a source of inspiration), these forms are transmuted by the new prophets, "Lions of flaming fire," into living fluids. The new, living form of prophecy is then cast by nameless publishers to the men of the sixth chamber, the prophets' audience, who rather than "eating," absorbing the prophecy, becoming imbued with its spirit, set themselves apart from it, making it into a book and then giving it a place in the stacks of a library. The prophets are the giants, the visionaries, who animate human existence, imparting meaning to it, though, paradoxically, they seem to live in chains, which are forged by "weak and tame minds" that resist their visions. Civilization manacles the prophet not only from without but from within: as one of the Prolific, then, the prophet, instead of accommodating himself to the Devourer he finds outside *and within,* must locate, isolate, and extirpate him, for the Devourer is intent upon destroying the very existence that the prophet would create. Such an allegory relates pointedly to Blake's idea of Milton.

For Blake, there are contradictions in Milton's vision that the poet eventually overcomes; they derive from a personality that is unintegrated, yet not so hopelessly unintegrated that we cannot discern a single posture shared by Milton's poetry and prose alike. For Blake, there is perfect unity in Milton's personality by the time he writes *Paradise Regained,* but the essential unity of his personality has already manifested itself in the harmony that exists between his radical vision and the form in which that vision is cast. For Blake, Milton devises new forms from old ones to encompass his radical politics and theology, and creates a new aesthetic system to support the new world order that he envisions. It is the unity of Milton's poetry and prose, the unity of his forms and their content, the unity of his ideology and aesthetics, that Blake notices. He, therefore, insists that we see Milton not as one who succumbed to the orthodoxies of his day but as one of those who attempted to "lay a new foundation of a more significant philosophy never to be overturned."[8]

REVOLUTIONARY ART

Too often it has been assumed that to be a revolutionary artist is to sever ties with tradition; and this assumption has generated a criticism that attends to a given artist, while eschewing the traditions, poetic and intellectual, that surround his work. To be a revolutionary, the argument goes, is to step beyond the confines of tradition and thus to require no attention within its context. Milton is a revolutionary artist, but we will not progress very far in our understanding of either his prose or his poetry unless we keep an eye steadily on the traditions that he assumes as contexts for his work. What, we must ask, was Milton's attitude toward them: did he accept, reject, or modify the traditions he invoked? Are there contexts we are surprised to find that Milton did not invoke; and if so, what is the meaning of conspicuous omissions? The need for asking these questions, for making these discriminations, is pointed to by both T. S. Eliot and W. B. Yeats, who, writing about poetry and tradition, use Milton and Blake as pivotal examples, each reaching strikingly different conclusions, even though both found their conclusions on a common premise. All poets are traditional in the sense that they employ conventions of poetry and traditions of thought to convey their visions; without tradition the poet is speechless, and without an intelligent understanding of tradition we are severely limited in our comprehension of poetry. It is tradition that enables the poet to think and to express himself, and it is his audience's awareness of tradition that enables it to read poetry comprehendingly. Yet from this ground of agreement, already explored in the Preface to this book, Eliot perceives Milton to be on the margins of tradition and Blake to have stepped well beyond them, whereas Yeats argues that Blake exists within the boundaries of a tradition that has Milton at its center. These different assessments of Milton and Blake derive from the different functions that Eliot and Yeats assign to tradition. Eliot's tradition is *changeless:* its function is to preserve values, to conserve orthodoxies; Yeats' tradition is *changing:* its function is to mark alterations in value and orthodoxy, to precipitate a radical transformation of them.[9]

Together, then, Eliot and Yeats provide a basis for distinguishing between conservative and revolutionary artists: the one encompasses tradition in a loving embrace, and the other uses tradition both creatively and subversively; the one confronts tradition with an attitude of acceptance, the other, with ambivalence. The revolutionary artist does not reject tradition but invokes it, salvaging what he can from it but subverting what is without value in order to wrest some meaning from life. For the conservative artist, what is important inheres in tradition; for the revolutionary artist, it must be newly created, the value of tradition being that it may be used as an agent in the artist's revolution: it may be made to yield up a new scheme of values, or it may be used against itself to destroy a system vacant of values.

When Coleridge acknowledged the power of Milton's epics, the tenderness of his pastorals, and the enchantment of *Comus,* he pointed to an aspect of Milton's art recognized in his own time but often ignored in ours:

[Milton] has left us models of excellence in every branch of his art. In the sublime epic, the noble drama, the picturesque mask, the graceful elegy, the vigorous sonnet,—in all he is equally great, equally beyond the reach of rivalry.[10]

Coleridge's perception, consonant with Milton's own intentions, is one of the major recoveries of recent Milton criticism. The self-consciousness with which Milton approaches his literary forms is as evident in his lyric poems as in his epics, creating the impression that he is openly engaged in "generic competition" that makes possible his "ultimate performance" in whatever form he employs.[11] This understanding is given eloquent articulation by Northrop Frye and is brilliantly expanded upon by Angus Fletcher.

It is no accident that Fletcher should see in Blake's *Comus* designs "a reading of *Comus* as a transcendental form"[12] —especially when one recalls Blake's assertion in his *Annotations to Reynolds:*

One Central Form Composed of all other Forms being Granted it does not therefore follow that all other Forms are Deformity.
All Forms are Perfect in the Poets Mind, but these are not Abstracted nor Compounded from Nature <but are from Imagination>[.]

(p. 637)

Nor is it an accident that Fletcher's study of Milton proceeds from the center of Frye's book on Milton's epics; for Frye, who identifies Spenser with conservative poetics, describes Milton as a revolutionary artist:

The radical or revolutionary artist impresses us, first of all, as a tremendous personal force. . . . His art has in consequence a kind of oratorical relation to him: his creative *persona* reveals his personality instead of concealing it. He does not enter into the forms of his art like an indwelling spirit, but approaches them analytically and externally, tearing them to pieces and putting them together again in a way which expresses his genius and not theirs. . . .

The revolutionary aspect of Milton also comes out in that curious mania for doing everything himself which led him to produce his own treatise on theology, his own national history, his own dictionary and grammar, his own art of logic. . . . Milton . . . is continually exploring the boundaries of his art, getting more experimental and radical as he goes on. . . . And just as the work of the radical artist is iconoclastic in its attitude to tradition, so it is destructive in its effect on tradition. . . .

The revolutionary artist does not have to be a social and political revolutionary as well, but he often is if he lives in a revolutionary time. . . . Every social revolution has the problem of establishing continuity with what it overturns, continuity of authority, of administration, of habit of life. For the revolutionary artist, it is precisely the continuity in tradition that he rejects in his art, and hence he tends to see his political situations also vertically, as a break with continuity.[13]

One cannot find a crisper, a more exacting formulation of Blake's idea of Milton; and one cannot imagine Frye's resisting the equation of his Milton with Blake's, especially after his modest acknowledgment that the school of modern criticism he is said to have fathered was really fathered by Blake.[14] Yet even here, one feels, there is an expansion of Frye's statement that Blake would require, a premise in it that Blake would reject, and an addition to it that Blake would want to make.

Milton was clearly not a spirit dwelling comfortably in the forms he employed. Whether writing a pastoral or a masque, an elegy or an epic, he broke with convention, creating his forms anew. Poetic forms were part of the tradition, an aspect of its tyranny, from which the poet tried to escape. Though Milton may never have written a philosophy of literary form, there is enough commentary in his prose and enough evidence in his practice as a poet to allow us to infer what his attitude toward literary form must have been.

"This very word of patterning or imitating," says Milton in *The Reason of Church-Government*, "betraies it to be a meere childe of ceremony" (*Yale Milton*, I, 765); liturgical forms, and by extension poetical forms, are, according to *Animadversions*, "a dull Opiat to the most wakefull attention" (I, 691), and are thus rejected in the language of *Areopagitica* as "rigid externall formality" and as "grosse conforming stupidity" (II, 564). Milton's whole discussion of liturgy may be used to gloss his conception of literary form: instead of slavishly imitating forms, the maker of poetry, like the practicer of religion, should each time modify them so that they become newly particularized forms. Moreover, in *An Apology for Smectymnuus,* Milton speaks disapprovingly of "the compelling of set formes" (I, 938), arguing that "shew of order, is the greatest disorder" (I, 937). And he explains in *Artis Logicae* that the orator-poet must be conscious of both the "archetype" and the "art"—of tradition (of its forms) and of the individual talent (of its manipulation of forms); the object of the artist is not to follow the norm but to deviate from it so as to "make something" (*Columbia Milton,* XI, 11, 15). All that Milton says, all that we can infer from his art, identifies him with those who believe that the poet must not "refuse to utilize the literary and artistic forms of the past"; for in his hands, we see that, in accordance with the doctrine of one revolutionary, "these old forms, remoulded and infused with new content, . . . become something revolutionary in the service of the people."[15] The shattering of forms is the shattering of revolution, as Herbert Marcuse explains; their rediscovery "is prerequisite for the liberation of man."[16]

The forms of poetry are devices for communication that may be used against the very systems that have disfigured them; but in the process they must be altered, restored to their pure condition, so that by contrast with what exists they may expose its perversity. The history of civilization, Milton implies, involves the disfiguration of God's universe and of all the forms that constitute it. God never intended to change his forms, never intended them "to be patch't afterwards, and varnish't over with the devices and imbellishings of mans imagination. Did God take such delight in measuring out the pillars, arches, and doores of a materiall Temple," Milton asks in *The Reason of Church-Government;* "was he so punctuall and circumspect in lavers . . . [and] altars" because he intended the perfect form to be changed (*Yale Milton,* I, 757)? The perversion of God's forms coincides with the perversion of society as a whole. The forms that have become an image of corrupted society, may, however, when transformed, become an instrument in its liberation: the revolutionary artist first engages in the transfiguration of forms and then uses those forms to transform his culture. His forms become, in the process, an image of the ideal to which the real world can then aspire.

Literary forms are a major part of the artistic tradition to which Milton was an heir; but they cannot be understood (and until they are understood, they cannot be effectively used) apart from their conventions, their ideologies, and their rhetorics. Every form has its own set of conventions that provides the poet with a principle of structure; but its structure is mechanical and ideally will be subdued by the living form, which is the poet's own invention. From tradition, then, the poet takes a rough scaffolding on which he mounts his vision. Every form has, besides, its own ideology, its own distinctive attitude toward human existence; and thus the poet cannot easily separate the form of his poem from the meaning he wishes to convey. Pastoral, for instance, is invested with a spirit of optimism that contrasts with the pessimism of the plaintive elegy; and tragedy supports a cyclical view of life that epic is bent upon breaking.[17] Finally, all literature is didactic, some of its forms more openly so than others, epic more than tragedy, satire more than either. Every form, then, has a rhetorical purpose and an accompanying rhetorical strategy peculiar to it. The purpose of epic is, from Milton's point of view, to inspire noble thoughts; the purpose of oratory, to fire men to action. The purpose of tragedy is to purge the mind of pity and fear; the purpose of pastoral, to leave man untroubled—calm of mind. To explore the boundaries of a form is thus to explore its structure, its ideology, and its rhetoric.

It is, therefore, not enough to say that the revolutionary artist alters the forms he inherits, unless it is made clear that in altering a form the poet elaborates its structure, modifies its ideology, while changing or intensifying its rhetoric. And even this is insufficient definition of the revolutionary artist's attitude toward form. A conservative artist is often content with bringing a single literary form to perfection; but a revolutionary artist like Milton ranges freely over all literary forms, taking special delight in consolidating them even as individually he alters them. These displays of virtuosity, and the flouting of tradition that often accompanies them, contribute to the revolutionary artist's effort to create a new tradition of poetry. The conservative artist takes a place comfortably within the traditions he receives; he is part of a continuum. The revolutionary artist, however, is concerned with "self-created 'poetic tradition' "[18] —with creating a tradition that his successors may use in the same way that his contemporaries used the orthodox traditions to which they were the heirs.

Every artist has his "original": Vergil his Homer, Milton his Spenser, Blake his Milton, Yeats his Blake. What distinguishes these relationships, one from the other, is the posture of subservience assumed by the conservative artist as opposed to the posture of contention assumed by the revolutionary artist. But subservience and contention are relative terms; and thus we find that Milton, for instance, was far more contentious in his relationship with Spenser than Blake was in his relationship with Milton, and for good reason: Spenser was locked into the orthodoxies from which Milton wished to liberate poetry; once it was liberated, a poet like Blake had a central tradition of revolutionary art in which he could work.

For the conservative artist, perfection of form does not involve transformation of form: it involves instead the recreation of the perfection already realized in the work of a precursor. For the revolutionary artist, perfection of form involves adjustment and alteration that are accompanied by new combinations and by fuller consolidations; the revolutionary artist, striving for new composite forms, is committed ultimately to "total form"—a conception that intervolves, that interrelates all forms.[19] The history of poetic form up to Milton reveals the process of exposure through which the potentialities of a form are unfolded; the inherent possibilities manifested by his precursors are then seized upon and actualized. In such moments, the forms of art undergo fundamental changes, develop new possibilities, that invite another great moment of transfiguration. Milton represents one such moment, Blake another.

The principle of consolidation is at the heart of what Angus Fletcher calls "the transcendental process." The poet is engaged in "generic competition"—he is intent upon outdoing his predecessors; and thus it becomes important to pursue his kinship with his predecessors—Milton's with Spenser and Shakespeare, Blake's with Milton; for in pursuing these relationships one discovers the pattern that is "archetypal for the poetry of transcendental forms"—a pattern that is part of "a single complex drive" which, encompassing multiple styles and forms "in a state of high, even ecstatic tension," pushes the poet beyond the forms of his precursors.[20] Transcendence of precursors, transcendence of their characteristic forms, is part of a larger purpose, however: the transcendence of the orthodoxies those poets purveyed and of the ideologies with which they invested the forms they used. Revolutionary art, Milton shows us, testifies to Marcuse's belief that as ideology it invalidates the dominant ideology.

There is a paradox to this transcendence, which is most easily delineated by the understanding, shared by Milton and Blake, that the history of poetry, like that of religion, is a history of corruption. Both Milton and Blake wished to return to original Christianity as it was laid down by Christ and his apostles, and both wished to return to forms of poetry as they were originally conceived. Herbert Marcuse speaks of Marx's embracing the idea of rediscovering "the true *Forms* of things, distorted and denied in the established reality."[21] Milton and Blake embraced the same idea, seeking to return to original Christianity and also to poetical forms uncorrupted by modern ideologies. For this reason, they rejected the classical for the Christian epic, whose traditions, both would have argued, are older than those traced to Homer and extended by him to Vergil. The classical epic perverted what was originally an open form into a closed form. It took the theme of return, traditional to epic poetry, and made it serve a cyclical conception of history. The Christian epic, in contrast, had used the same theme but developed it in terms of rebirth and resurrection, allowing it to be an agent in the breaking of the closed and cyclical structures of the classical epic. In the hands of Milton and Blake, then, what was understood by their respective ages as a classical form is transformed through a system of "storm and stress." A genre once used as a codifier of received values thus becomes the agent through which "the established universe" is shattered.[22]

This is not a common understanding: it does not, for instance, accord with the view of epic presented by Joan Webber (she makes no distinction between classical and Christian epic, emphasizing the subversive character of both); and most emphatically it does not agree with the conception of epic delineated by Walter Ong (unlike Webber, he sees Milton closing rather than opening the structure of heroic poetry).[23] From Ong's point of view, epic in its inception "projected an open cosmology," facing "outside itself, implying some other, some beyond."[24] During the Renaissance, however, especially under the aegis of Milton, epic joins with logic (with what Ong calls a system of closure), in the process losing a sense of the "beyond" and thus imposing closure on its once open cosmos. But this theory is controverted by the evidence of Milton's poems. They represent not so much a conjunction of epic with logic as a union of the heroic poem with prophecy; and prophecy opposes all systems of closure[25] —those represented by logical discourse and those with which the epics of Homer and Vergil were imbued. The *Iliad,* for example, does not show civilization evolving toward a new scheme of values; rather, it exhibits a hero recovering the ethic that, once having possessed, he is seen to surrender during the course of the poem. The two meetings with Lykaon are thus important—the first one attesting to Achilles' honor, the second, culminating in the brutal slaying of the suppliant, testifying to the loss of it. Yet Achilles' honor is recovered—in the moment when Hector's mutilated body is returned to his father. Simiarly, the point of Vergil's equating his Rome with its mythological past, the current leader with the nation's founder, is not to create a new system of values but to focus on the extent to which the modern age has departed from the ethic Vergil urges it to recover. In both epics the pattern is closed, but it is not in the Christian epic that Milton takes for his model, an epic whose concerns are not with conservation of a world order but with the creation of a new one, whose intent is not to extrapolate a value system from the present culture but to create one out of which a new culture may be born.

On the surface, the Miltonic epic may seem cyclical, especially in its return to old, uncorrupted forms and ideologies; but that return is motivated by the desire to find a new point of departure. The old forms and the value systems involved with them are subject to improvements effected by new revelations and inspired by on-going revolution. The Homeric and Vergilian epics postulate return to and acceptance of a prior condition. Milton, on the other hand, recreates the prior condition—Adam and Eve fallen, expelled into the wilderness—only to emphasize the superior position of modern man in a wilderness governed by the New Dispensation and to be governed, he hopes, by his New Revelation. In the classical epic, the accents fall on what is, which contrasts with what should be, which is what was. In the Christian epic, the accents are shifted to what may be, which is gauged in terms of past and present but which is, because of on-going revolution precipitated by new revelation, transcendingly better than both. Inevitably, in epic-prophecy, the poet's concern is not with endings, not with deaths, but with processes—the processes by which men and their civilizations continue to live. Without revelation there is no revolution—the one is the cause, the pattern, the effect, of the other. This message Blake took from Milton's epics and made the subject of his own. Neither Milton nor Blake could have known *The Gilgamesh Epic,* but one can imagine the sympathy both would muster for an epic alive with the revolutionary spirit that in the Homeric epic is written out of the genre.

From one position taken by Frye Blake would, we may suppose, demur: "The revolutionary artist does not have to be a social and political revolutionary."[26] Not all experimental artists have been proponents of revolution; this Blake realized, and this he would have seen as a sign of deterioration in culture, as an element of failure in the arts. He would not have disagreed with the position that "a common characteristic of the literature and art of all exploiting classes in their period of decline is the contradiction between their reactionary political [and theological] content and their artistic form." What revolutionary art demands "is the unity of politics and art, the unity of content and form, the unity of revolutionary political content and the highest possible perfection of artistic form."[27] To have a truly revolutionary art requires those various unities, and it is precisely those unities that Blake saw crystallizing as he traced Milton's vision from his early lyrics through his prose writings into his epics.

The conservative artist may be content with literary forms as he inherits them: his contentment is implicit in the fact that he can be an "indwelling spirit" in traditional forms, his goal being preservation not alteration of them, and in the fact that by assuming an order he asserts it. The first impulse of the defenders of order, as David Kubrin argues, is "to deny the possibility of other forms of existence, to claim that the *present* reality is *the only* reality, every manifestation or hint at the unchanging order of things [being] to them a most welcome ally in their defense of the *status quo.*"[28] This impulse is what the revolutionary artist tries to counter. In contrast to his conservative counterpart, he is restive; he shares in his culture's rage for order, but order for him is not something already achieved but something to be aspired to. He subscribes to Nietzsche's belief that only out of a chaos can a dancing star be born. Out of the chaos into which his culture has fallen, he must create a new order—an order that may be derived from the forms of the past but that is in no way represented by them. To alter traditional forms is to alter the very system of values by which a society has lived: to create a new form out of an old one is at once to acknowledge the continuity between generations and cultures and to insist that the continuity be broken in an act of vision that liberates society from its traditions while offering to it new ones—ones more nearly perfect and more enduring than those being replaced.

An addition to Frye's statement, then, seems to be called for. Revolutions imply wholesale change in a culture's values and institutions. For the poet, those values are enclosed within the forms that have been institutionalized by poets who have so often served as the upholders of orthodoxies, as the spokesmen for their culture's values. The shape of a poem indicates much about the shape of a poet's attitude toward tradition. The form is an order— a system of value and a structure in which the conservative artist acquiesces and against which the revolutionary artist struggles. There is, accordingly, a fundamental difference between the canons of conservative artists and those of revolutionary ones. The canon of the conservative poet is often a collection of disconnected poems—a series of unrelated imaginative moments; but the canon of the revolutionary artist is composed of an aggregate of poems inextricably involved with one another. Whereas the conservative poet presents a series of individual poems, the revolutionary artist creates a series of individual poems that comprise one grand, harmonious vision. The canon, not the poem, represents the radical unity of revolutionary art.

That Milton strove for this kind of unity, whose archetype is to be found in the Bible, is suggested first by his effort to subsume his prose writings within a grand design. In *Defensio Secunda,* Milton explains that the master-theme of all his prose efforts is "liberation of all human life from slavery":

> First, therefore, I addressed to a certain friend two books on the reforma-tion of the English church. Then . . . I replied to one of the bishops in two books [*Of Prelatical Episcopacy* and *The Reason of Church-Government*] . . . , while to the other bishop I made reply in certain *Animadversions* and later in an *Apology.* . . . [When the bishops] had at last fallen and troubled us no more, I directed my attention elsewhere, asking myself whether I could in any way advance the cause of true and substantial liberty, which must be sought, not without, but within, and which is best achieved, not by the sword, but by a life rightly undertaken and rightly conducted. Since, then, I observed that there are, in all, three varieties of liberty without which civilized life is scarcely possible, namely ecclesiastical liberty, domestic or personal liberty, and civil liberty, and since I had already written about the first, while I saw that the magistrates were vigorously attending to the third, I took as my province the remaining one, the second or domestic kind. This too seemed to be concerned with three problems: the nature of marriage itself, the education of the children, and finally the existence of freedom to express oneself.
>
> (*Yale Milton,* IV, i, 622–24)

To ask whether this "design" informed Milton's writings from the very beginning or whether it was, instead, an afterthought is beside the point. What is important is that it was conceived at all. A similar effort to interweave works was undertaken when Milton agreed to write *Lycidas,* presumably as a poem gathering together the themes of earlier poems in the Edward King memorial volume and then bringing them to resolution in his own consolation. [29] The same effort at entanglement is evident in the last poems, which take their design from the Bible. Once we recognize that the Bible is structured around three myths—one of creation and fall, another of wandering, a last of return and reintegration—then we can see the principle of unity that locks *Paradise Lost, Paradise Regained,* and *Samson Agonistes* in an enveloping pattern. The first poem, recounting the creation, explores the fall; the second, involving the theme of wandering, takes us to the threshold of vision from which apocalypse can be seen; the last, rather than envisioning apocalypse like the Book of Revelation, portrays in-stead a false apocalypse, unfolding the tragedy of precipitous action which, even if liberating to the individual, binds the rest of us down to the cycles of history. The centrality of *Paradise Regained* to Milton's vast design is suggested by the fact that into this poem Milton gathers the major themes of his early lyrics—the resurrection motif from *Lycidas,* the idea of temptation warded off from *Comus,* the concept of Christian heroics from *The Passion* and the *Nativity Ode,* and the theme of contemplation and action from *L'Allegro* and *Il Penseroso.* Like Blake's *Jerusalem,* then, Milton's brief epic may be seen as a consolidated work that synthesizes a whole complex of themes and that pursues the implications of those themes into a vision of paradise recovered.

Revolutionary art, whether Milton's or Blake's, did not fare well with the New Critics, perhaps for aesthetic reasons but more likely for ideological ones. In New Criticism are hidden ideological biases to which both Milton and Blake pose a challenge; and at the same time their works stand in defiance of the basic canons of New Criticism—that a work of art should be self-contained and self-enclosed, that it should possess an organic unity, which means finally, for both T. S. Eliot and F. R. Leavis, that the unity of a poem's form and content should be supported by the unity between its content and the values of the culture to which it is addressed.

It is too easily forgotten that what finally caused Eliot to withhold his admiration from Blake was not the poet's icono-clastic spirit *per se* but the fact that this spirit isolated Blake from "a framework of accepted and traditional values" that Eliot wished Blake's poetry to espouse. Blake, from Eliot's perspective, lacked the "gift of form which knows how to borrow,"[30] which is to say that he lacked the ability to alter forms while investing them with a received system of belief. In consequence, Blake's poetry, says Eliot, is "deprived of the advantages of culture" by the very fact that the poet indulged "in a philosophy of his own."[31]   F. R. Leavis extends the same objections to Milton. Leavis, it is often remembered, denied Milton a respected place in his great tradition of poetry, asserting that he suffered from a "defect of intelligence," a "defect of imagination."[32] Not until we peruse Leavis's essay on Pope, however, do we comprehend what defective intelligence in a poet means to this critic: it involves being out of touch with the past, "the complete rejec-tion" of it, in the case of Blake;[33] and in the case of Milton it involves deliberate avoidance of a tradition of poetry represented by Shakespeare and Spenser, by Donne and Jonson, whose content and forms derive their strength from the reigning values of "civilization." Milton's "defect of intelligence," like Blake's and Shelley's, lies, according to Leavis, in his defiance of the established "code of manners," in his avoidance of "the finest art and thought of the time."[34] Only when Milton is under Shakespeare's sway (Leavis thinks this happens in *Comus*), or when he is fully under Spenser's (Leavis says this happens in *Lycidas*), is his poetry to be countenanced.

Blake and Milton, one feels, would not have objected to Leavis's identifying poetry "with a crest of civilization" or his association of it with "the moral basis of society";[35] but both would have seen black where Leavis sees white, both would have seen in the line of wit an abrogation of the very values, aesthetic and ethical, that they sought to recover. Where Leavis discovered the civilized mind at its finest, Milton would have perceived—and Blake found— the mind distorted by the iron yoke of conformity into a grotesque travesty of what it once was and could once again become.

The principles of criticism formulated by Eliot and Leavis make it difficult to deal very seriously with poems that find their contexts in other poems and well nigh impossible to tolerate poems that instead of codifying the reigning system of belief wish to overturn it. That school of criticism, accordingly, produced major misunderstandings of Milton's poetry generated by those whose sympathies extended to Milton but whose principles of criticism did not reach beyond those of Eliot and Leavis. No one can deny that *Samson Agonistes,* taken in isolation (and it was probably written in analogous isolation, before *Paradise Lost* and *Paradise Regained*), is a drama of regeneration; but when it is set against *Paradise Regained* (and it was, after all, in this setting the the poem was published), ideological tensions develop that make it impossible to believe that *Samson* is anything other than what Milton tells us it is: *a tragedy* with a hero who locks men into the cycles of destruction rather than liberating men from such cycles. Set against *Paradise Regained* (its literary context) and the Book of Revelation (its biblical context), *Samson* is a play, grimly ironic, that adumbrates the tragedy of world history deriving from those who seek revolution through violence rather than through vision.

Ultimately, a radical aesthetic comes to dictate the forms a revolutionary artist will aspire to use, as well as the contexts he will aspire to create for them. In English art with revolutionary intentions, the Book of Revelation, usually regarded as a radical document, has been a primary context, a major source of inspiration; and invariably the revolutionary artist has turned to the form of poetry that lends itself best to the demand for a single comprehensive vision. Both Milton and Blake strove with lyric modes by way of developing a talent that would enable them to write within the visionary mode of the epic. I would not suggest that the epic poem was traditionally radical in ideology. If anything, the contrary is true: the epic poem became increasingly more reactionary in its content, increasingly bound up with elitist values. What began, presumably, as poetry for the people was converted, during the Renaissance, into poetry for the court. For precisely this reason, the revolutionary artist turns to epic, to what J. B. Broadbent calls an essentially "conservative" genre,[36] and proceeds to revise the form from the inside, altering its ideology while directing the poem to a new audience—still an elite, but a spiritual rather than a social elite.

By fastening our attention to Milton's preference for the daughters of inspiration over the daughters of memory, Blake leads us into yet another reason for the revolutionary artist's turning to epic. The classical epic, the line that extends from Homer to Vergil and from both into the Renaissance, derives from a theory of imitation; but another line of epic poetry that goes back, for the twentieth century, to *The Gilgamesh Epic* proceeds from the Bible and derives from a theory of inspiration. Milton's famous passage in *The Reason of Church-Government,* where he identifies the models for diffuse and brief epic poetry, along with tragedy, had it been written after *Paradise Lost* rather than before, would probably have identified the Pentateuch among the models for the long epic.

Not only does the new epic, as envisioned by Milton and later by Blake, proceed from inspiration; but it develops from the analogy between God and the poet as creators and the related one between

God's creation (the universe) and the poet's creation (his poem). As Tasso explains,

> . . . I consider unity in the heroic poem both necessary and possible to obtain, for, as in this wonderful masterpiece of God called the world the sky appears scattered over and divided by so great a variety of stars and, to descend then step by step, the air and the sea appear full of birds and fishes and the earth harbours so many beasts wild and tame, the earth where are found brooks and springs and lakes and meadows and plains and woods and mountains, here fruits and flowers there ice and snow, here dwellings and tillage there wilderness and terrors, yet for all this the world is one through folding into its bosom so many different things, its form and essence are one, and one the fashion in which its parts are joined and knit together with a kind of discordant harmony; and though nothing is lacking to it, nothing is there either superfluous or not necessary. So likewise I assert that the sublime poet . . . can indeed shape a poem in which as in a microcosm there are brought together [all things in the created universe, all aspects of human life]. . . . the poem . . . shall include all variety of substance [but] should nevertheless be one; the form and the fable one; and . . . all things should be put together so that one thing refers to another, one corresponds to another, one either by necessity or probability depend on another, so that the removal of a single part or its transference should ruin the whole.[37]

In *The Reason of Church-Government*, Milton employs language similar to Tasso's, talking of God as an architect and glancing at his "artfull symmetry" (*Yale Milton*, I, 758), an analogy he develops in *The Doctrine and Discipline of Divorce:* "there is indeed a twofold Seminary or stock in nature," says Milton, "flowing through the whole masse of created things, and . . . Gods doing ever is to bring the due likenesses and harmonies of his workes together"; "discords," "enmities," "agony and strife" are the terms Milton employs to describe that creation (II, 272). Moreover, in *Animadversions,* Milton attributes to inspired humans the capacity for "making a kind of creation like to Gods" (I, 721).

As Wordsworth was later to do, Milton employs an architectural metaphor to describe the interrelatedness of the poet's creation. Wordsworth writes,

> . . . the two Works [*The Prelude* and *The Excursion*] have the same kind of relation to each other . . . as the ante-chapel has to the Body of a gothic church. . . . [the] minor Pieces . . . will be found by the attentive Reader to have such connection with the main Work as may give them claim to be

likened to the little cells, oratories, and sepulchral recesses, ordinarily included in those edifices.[38]

Correspondingly, Milton says in *Areopagitica,*

And when every stone is laid artfully together, it cannot be united into a continuity, it can but be contiguous in this world; neither can every peece of the building be of one form; nay rather the perfection consists in this, that out of many moderat varieties and brotherly dissimilitudes that are not vastly disporportionall arises the goodly and the graceful symmetry that commends the whole pile and structure. Let us therefore be more considerat builders, more wise in spirituall architecture, when great reformation is expected.

(*Yale Milton,* II, 555)

For Tasso, as well as for Milton, Wordsworth, Shelley, and Blake, epic was the noblest kind of poetry because it gathered into itself and then reflected the enormous complexity, as well as the underlying unity, of God's creation, a creation in which multiple forms are subdued within an enveloping unity; and the epic poet was the noblest kind of poet because his creation, like God's, depended upon inspiration—it had a perfect idea behind it, an idea that existed not in the world outside the poet but one that was imprinted upon his mind from eternity.

The epic poem relied not on nature but on vision and thus symbolized man's intellectual and imaginative freedom from what was already in the world. It was therefore the mode of poetry that offered the best chance for reforming the world—for Milton it was doctrinal to the nation, and for Blake it justified his dictum that empire follows art. As an epitome of God's universe, the epic subsumes all forms and uses those forms to discharge the lightning that would roll the dark clouds of ignorance into the distance. This is the code of art that can be inferred from Blake's writings, that Blake found manifesting itself in Milton's poetry, and that is ultimately traceable to the Bible.

Not only *Paradise Lost,* but all of Milton's poems, and many of his orations, are gatherings of forms operating within a complex dialectic of styles and symbols. Milton's early lyrics all involve visionary modes, all search for the prophetic strain. *On the Morning of Christ's Nativity* cannot be fully, or even satisfyingly, understood if regarded only as an ode or a hymn: it belongs to the incidental genre of the nativity poem and is replete with the conventions of dream-vision poetry. Nor can *Lycidas,* with its "cosmological striving," be understood as just a pastoral elegy. It is that, but it is more, with its infusion of satire and its straining to burst the boundaries of the lyric mode to achieve the visionary dimensions of epic. This is all made clear in *Lycidas* through a cryptic shorthand—the address to Calliope (the muse of epic poetry) and the *ottava rima* stanza of the epilogue (the conventional verse form of the Renaissance epic). *Comus* may be a radical experiment, but then *Lycidas* is a more radical experiment still; for here Milton not only achieves the cosmic dimensions of epic, but he encompasses the structure of Revelation prophecy that he was later to use in his epics and in his tragedy. The culmination of these early experiments in form is *Paradise Lost;* yet Milton's epic achievement is to be located not in *Paradise Lost* alone but in the experiments of that poem which have their culmination in *Paradise Regained.* The first epic possesses a continuity with the epic of imitation, a continuity that in *Paradise Regained* is broken as Milton asserts a new continuity between this poem and the epic of inspiration.

It is not enough to say with John Shawcross that Milton's "break with tradition"[39] comes with the mixture of genres. The epic poem, from its very inception, was a mixture of genres. Homer joins epic and tragedy in the *Iliad,* and epic and romance in the *Odyssey.* Vergil's epic is also a "history," and Dante's epic also a "comedy." The Renaissance epic is distinguished by its fusion of genres—epic and romance in Boiardo, Ariosto, and Tasso; and epic, romance, *and pastoral* in Spenser and Sidney. Milton's epic is even larger in its compass, subsuming all the genres, small and large. Eve's love song in the fourth book is recognizable as an irregular sonnet, and the morning hymn of the fifth book as a well-formed ode. The speeches of the devils in the second book are grotesque perversions of oratorical form. Still further, within *Paradise Lost* there is a large infusion of masque, romance, and comedic elements; and there is, besides, the mock-epic of the first two books and the brief epic of the last two; there are the pastoral books and the tragic ones. When Milton acknowledged the pre-eminence of epic, then, he did not merely endorse a critical commonplace: he acknowledged that epic was at the apex of the genres because, in potentiality at least, it contained them all.

Such an argument does not discredit Shawcross's perception; it merely complicates a perception which we must extend. Milton clearly moves the epic poem into the realm of drama; this is true of *Paradise Lost* and doubly true of *Paradise Regained,* and this was doubtless understood by Blake and Shelley, and explains why Milton's brief epic is a model for Blake's "Visionary forms dramatic" and for Shelley's "lyrical drama." Yet it is not mimetic drama that Milton creates. He is finally an anti-mimetic poet, like the Romantic poets whom he served as a model; and thus he is less interested in the "action" of men than in the "drama" of the mind. One effect of assuming the conventions of multiple forms, and of then belittling them as Milton does in *Paradise Lost,* is to deny the poet (both himself and his successors) the structural support that generic conventions lend. *Paradise Lost* is a reassessment of all the genres it subsumes, and that reassessment involves an alteration, a perfection, of their ideologies, accompanied by a repudiation of their usual structures. Biblical prophecy—most notably Revelation prophecy—provides Milton with an alternative structure (or structures) and simultaneously enables him to intensify the dramatic element in his epics.

There are many points of correspondence between Revelation prophecy and Milton's conception of epic. Prophecy was understood to be a gathering of all the literary forms, and it possessed the same surface structures as epic. Just as epic was customarily regarded as a bipartite structure organized by elaborate patterns of parallelism or as a tripartite structure organized around principal characters or, in the seventeenth century, as a fivefold structure based on an analogy with drama, so Revelation prophecy had a similarly complex outer structure. It was a bipartite structure mounted upon two movements—one of tragic defeat, the other of spiritual triumph; it was a tripartite structure composed of a prologue, a prophecy, and an epilogue, or a quadripartite structure, both because it was organized around four universal time-distances and because the prophecy itself was composed of seven visions, each of them constituting a four-act drama. This may all suggest that what Stanley Fish represents as a fierce dialectic between outer and inner form in *Paradise Lost* is more exactly a dialectic between epic and prophecy or, more exactly still, a dialectic between the outer and inner forms of prophecy, the one controverting Milton's vision and the other organizing it.[40] More-over, in the understanding that epic and prophecy have the same identifiable and interpenetrating structures, the nagging questions posed by Michael Fixler disappear: "Why would Milton choose to leave his design obscure"? "What are we to make of the apparent epic structure"?[41] The answers to both questions are the same: Milton is following his source, not slavishly, but is extracting large principles from it and following them assiduously. The result is, as Blake explains it should be: "Mathematic Proportion ... [is] subdued by Living Proportion" (*Milton* 5:44).

Prophecy was dramatical not only in terms of structure, how-ever. In prophetical drama there was a cast of only two characters: the prophet and Christ, who transmitted the prophecy. The proph-et struggled first to apprehend the vision and then to hammer it into form, and thus he created a dramatical relationship with his audience, harassing it, exercising it, and thereby lifting it to his own level of perception. Moreover, though the cast of characters is reduced, there is an element of drama retained within the proph-ecy itself; for the usual characters of a play are replaced by perspectives that contend with one another as actors in a drama. This alliance between epic and prophecy transforms a mode of entertainment into a mode of enlightenment—a dome of pleasure becomes a palace of wisdom.

In terms of ideology, *Paradise Lost* expresses the poet's radi-calism not only in its rejection of epic structure but in its inversion of the hierarchy of styles: the plain style is assigned to God, the grand one to Satan. In the process Milton fractures the customary relationship between poet and audience. Though the epic poet often asserted artistic superiority over his audience, he seldom asserted moral authority over it; and this is because he took the values he celebrated from the audience he was addressing. Milton, however, claims both artistic and moral superiority, thereby mak-ing the poet the generator of the values by which a whole culture is asked to live. Milton may not have accomplished the revolution that his epic poems postulate; but in those poems, he "sowed a seed which has since taken root, and is ... growing up to a glorious harvest" in which Blake hoped soon to see "mankind exulting."[42] Milton, whatever his failings, must be credited with preparing "the minds of men for the recovery of their rights," with hastening "the overthrow of priestcraft and tyranny" that Blake saw on the horizon.[43]

A revolutionary artist, a radical thinker, Milton works *with*—rather than *within*—poetical traditions; and he establishes a perfect coincidence between his "virtuoso" forms and the revolutionary ideals with which he invests them. The image of Milton's idealized order is less the individual poem than the one grand poem to which all the individual poems contribute. *The one grand poem*—Milton's canon—is the poet's "ultimate . . . transcendental form."[44] Milton's radicalism may be profitably studied in the terms set down by Frye and Fletcher, but it may also be studied within a context established not by literary critics but by an avowed revolutionary:

... the literary and artistic works of the past are not a source but a stream; they were created by our predecessors and foreigners out of the literary and artistic raw materials they found in the life of the people of their time and place. We must take over all the fine things in our literary and artistic heritage, critically assimilate whatever is beneficial, and use them as examples when we create works out of the literary and artistic raw materials in the life of the people of our own time and place.[45]

That Blake possessed an understanding of Milton similar to the one I have outlined here is suggested not merely by his portrayals of Milton and his illustrations for Milton's poetry, but also by his epic manifesto. It aligns Blake's own epic theory with what may appear to be an underground aesthetic[46] of the eighteenth century, one that finds its fullest articulation in the writings of William Hayley. Furthermore, the understanding of Milton I have claimed to be Blake's own is expressed first in *The Marriage of Heaven and Hell* and then in *Milton*, where what Blake says has eluded understanding because the traditions informing these works have not been given adequate attention.

THE TRADITION OF REVOLUTION

Blake's deepest roots are in the epic tradition that was tied by Spenser and Milton to the tradition of prophecy—a tradition that, standing behind Blake's poetry from *Poetical Sketches* to *Jerusalem*, provides the best guide to understanding it. This is the tradition that Blake invokes, directly and contextually, when he describes his own poetry as "Sublime Allegory." In his celebrated letter to Thomas Butts, Blake speaks, probably of *Milton*, as "a Sublime Allegory, which is now perfectly completed into a Grand Poem. I may praise it," says Blake, "since I dare not pretend to be any other than the Secretary; the Authors are in Eternity. I consider it as the Grandest Poem that this World Contains. Allegory address'd to the Intellectual Powers, while it is altogether hidden from the Corporeal Understanding, is My Definition of the Most Sublime Poetry."[47]

The phrase "Sublime Allegory" identifies Blake with an aesthetic that is mounted upon Renaissance epic theory and practice, and upon the still unexplored tradition of prophecy. Epic and prophecy are not easy, and only the false prophet makes them seem to be:

... God sels nothing to Man without the price of lobour [*sic*], And howsoever the purblinde Ignorant, that only see with Corporal & not Intellectuall eies may surmise, yet Art is the fellow of sweat and labour and the Muses have no other Temples to dwell in but studious and laborious bosomes.[48]

The context in which Blake's phrase appears evokes, more particularly, the Milton tradition, which, "first of all ... a tradition of Revolution,"[49] brings Renaissance experimentation with epic to its fruition. When Blake says in the Butts letter that he wants "to be a Momento in time to come & to speak to future generations," he strikes the Miltonic pose of *Animadversions* and *Pro Populo Anglicano Defensio*, "tak[ing] up a Harp, and sing[ing] ... an elaborate Song" for "every nation and every age" (*Yale Milton*, I, 706; IV, i, 305). Nowhere is Milton's idea of the poet more grandly visible than in his Preface to the Second Book of *The Reason of Church-Government*, where, having described himself as "a Poet soaring in the high region of his fancies with his garland and singing robes about him," having laid down a plan for writing a diffuse and a brief epic, having promised, in the process, to spurn the epic rules, "which in them that know art, and use judgement is no transgression, but an inriching of art," having identified his muse with the Daughters of Inspiration (a passage that Blake himself quotes), and having spoken of beholding "the bright countenance of truth" (a passage that Blake echoes), Milton describes himself as God's "Secretary." Milton understood, as Blake did, that a "Secretary" was one "entrusted with the secrets or commands of God"; the "Secretary" was a prophet (*Yale Milton*, I, 808, 813, 820–22).

Milton's image, and Blake's, of the epic poet as "an amanuensis" is traditional; but the meaning those two poets assign to the image is not. Charles Rowan Beye has associated this image with Homer and with "the mechanical repetition of tradition" through a muse who, "as the daughter of Memory, is . . . the informal personification of the entire body of epic tradition, that reservoir of legend and technique" from which the epic poet created his poem.[50] The meaning that Milton and Blake attach to the image of the poet as amanuensis finds one analogue in Tasso, who, as Annabel Patterson suggests, allows "the artist to bypass Nature [and mechanical tradition], and to imitate directly the original Ideas of perfection by which the world was made."[51] Yet the image of the poet as amanuensis finds another, more immediately important, analogue in the tradition of prophecy. As Abraham J. Heschel explains,

> Lutheran dogmaticians of the seventeenth century developed the doctrine of verbal inspiration to the extreme: every word in Scripture was inspired and dictated by God; the prophets were merely the hands and pen-men of the Holy Spirit, *God's amanuenses*. Yet this monergistic doctrine of inspiration did not imply that God dehumanized His amanuenses and reduced them to mere mechanisms. They were not "unconscious," as the enthusiasts say of themselves and as the Gentiles imagine the ecstasy in their prophets. Neither is it to be taken as if the prophets did not understand their prophecies of the things which they were to write. . . . Inspiration embraces first of all a certain supernatural and extraordinary enlightenment of the mind.[52]

In isolation, Blake's definition of epic poetry as "Sublime Allegory" may seem less than curious; but, when set against Blake's other references to allegory, his use of the word "allegory" becomes puzzling. When Blake speaks of "Allegory around the Winding Worm" in *Jerusalem* (85:1), of "allegoric riches" in *The Song of Los* (6:18), or of "Allegoric Godship" in his *Annotations to Thornton* (p. 659), he is associating allegory with distortion, falsification, and perversion. More typically, however, Blake speaks of Generation—the world of experience, of twofold vision— as the "allegorical abode" (see *Europe* 6:7 and *Jerusalem* 50:2), associating allegory with fragmentation rather than with integration, with obfuscation rather than with revelation. When the word "allegory" is used by Blake with reference to art, these connotations are usually preserved and then amplified.

Blake's fullest discussion of allegory in relation to art occurs in his notebook-description of *A Vision of the Last Judgment,* where allegory is identified with fable and both are carefully differentiated from vision. The passage is worth quoting and remembering:

> The Last Judgment is not Fable or Allegory but Vision Fable or Allegory are a totally distinct & inferior kind of Poetry. Vision or Imagination is a Representation of what Eternally Exists. Really & Unchangeably. Fable or Allegory is Formd by the daughters of Memory. Imagination is Surrounded by the daughters of Inspiration who in the aggregate are calld Jerusalem < Fable is Allegory but what Critics call The Fable is Vision itself > The Hebrew Bible & the Gospel of Jesus are not Allegory but Eternal Vision or Imagination of All that Exists < Note here that Fable or Allgory [*sic*] is Seldom without some Vision Pilgrims Progress is full of it the Greek poets the same but . . . Allegory & Vision . . . ought to be known as Two Distinct Things & so calld for the Sake of Eternal Life Plato has made Socrates say that Poets & Prophets do not know or Understand what they write or Utter this is a most Pernicious Falshood . . .> [.]
>
> (p. 544)

Several pages later Blake jots down another note that provides a gloss on this comment. "Greek Fables," he says, "originated in Spiritual Mystery & Real Vision and Real Visions Which are lost & clouded in Fable & Allegory. . . . The Nature of my Work is Visionary or Imaginative it is an Endeavour to Restore <what the Ancients calld> the Golden Age" (p. 545). What Blake called "Sublime Allegory" in writing to Butts he here calls "Vision"; and as Hazard Adams suggests, if Blake, instead of saying "that allegory can contain 'some vision,' " had said "that vision can contain some allegory," his meaning would here be much less elusive.[53]

So perplexed was S. Foster Damon by Blake's use of the term "allegory" in the Butts letter that he concluded, "The one important exception when Blake used the word with approval seems to have been a slip of the pen."[54] The fact is that Blake, on another occasion, used the word approvingly. On an 1810 engraving of *Chaucer's Canterbury Pilgrims* he writes, "An Allegory of Idolatry or Politics." Blake clearly conceived of two kinds of allegory, two traditions of poetry, and in his letter to Butts invokes not only the tradition he wishes to embrace but the whole critical tradition behind it. The literary tradition surfaced in Chaucer but manifested itself most completely in Chaucer's successor, Spenser, and in the successor of both poets, Milton; the critical tradition took shape during the Renaissance and, though interrupted in the early years of the eighteenth century, was revived in the writings of John Hughes, Robert Lowth, Anselm Bayly, William Hayley, Thomas Taylor, and Henry Fuseli—all of whom provide illuminating glosses on Blake's definition of poetry in the Butts letter. These voices, when raised, were disregarded as they are generally disregarded still; yet they seem to be the voices that Blake in his theoretical statements echoes and in his poems follows. These voices all participate in the formation of a new aesthetic, based on Milton's achievement and Spenser's, that deserves more attention than it has received. Not to acknowledge this ignored tradition of commentary is to become a party to its repression, and to do that is to deny Blake the very contexts that illuminate his work.

Walter Jackson Bate has reminded us that "the split between 'popular' and 'sophisticated' art has always existed in cultivated societies, but it has become progressively greater since the seventeenth century."[55] What gives Milton uniqueness, in the eighteenth century, is that both "cultures," the sophisticated and the popular, paid considerable attention to his work. Ironically, the "culture" that was divesting Milton's poetry of its meaning, that was busy burying it under the weight of orthodoxy, is the one whose views persist into the twentieth century; the other "culture"—the one that strikes us today as a subculture—was intent upon wresting Milton's meaning from his poetry; and its Milton has not survived into our century, at least has not survived unimpaired. Yet such a Milton lived in the repressed tradition of commentary and, through that tradition, was extended to Blake—a Milton whose "example of defiance on behalf of the heroic continued to haunt the imagination." "It is because of this as much as anything," says Bate, "that, when the English poet got up courage to try the heroic, he adopted the Miltonic robes and stance with the Longinian belief, often justified, that confidence and spirit are contagious."[56]

What does it mean to be a Miltonic poet? This is the question that Hughes, Lowth, Bayly, Taylor, and Fuseli answered for Blake; and they answered it in much the same terms. Milton is an allegorist, a symbolist, who looks back for his aesthetic not to

Homer and Vergil but to the Bible. Milton's allegories are not simplistic but complex; they are of the sublimer kind that these critics identified variously with the Bible, with Dante, and with Spenser, all of whom wrote allegories in which the "whole literal Sense . . . is a kind of Vision."[57] By these critics, the words "epic" and "allegory" were used synonymously and the term "sublime" applied to both of them; moreover, all these concepts were defined by turning to the Book of Revelation and then identifying John's methods there with Milton's methods in his epics: in these two sources could be found the code of Christian art, the "medium" for conveying the spiritual sense of allegory. The Bible, especially the Book of Revelation, was one grand epic poem; and the Christian poet was urged, therefore, to follow Milton in imitating its prophecies. Milton was the poet who seemed to comprehend most fully the aesthetics of Christian art, and thus it was to him that poets were told to turn. From his epics, the poet could learn that epic and prophecy were indistinguishable, or should be, and that "a system of Art built on grandeur" required "a total revolution" in aesthetics.[58] Like so many revolutions, however, what was being called for was not a wholly new aesthetic but a return to an older one that, even if suppressed by neoclassicism, was very much alive during the Renaissance.

Don Cameron Allen has shown what "the discovery of Greek and Latin symbolical and allegorical interpretation taught the Renaissance";[59] and in the process he has provided a basis for understanding what this tradition, as used by Renaissance poets, taught artists like William Blake. Led away from contemporary theorists and back into the Renaissance epic tradition by William Hayley, Blake learned that "myth is allegory" and "allegory is myth," that when symbolic figures take form, when they are particularized, "allegory merges into myth" and "myth is created."[60] The ambiguity that surrounds the different senses in which Blake talks about allegory has its source in Renaissance attitudes toward allegory in the classical epic. For some commentators, allegory, as it was used by the ancients, "glided near the truth" but did not embody it. Such allegories were "proximate truth"; they transmitted truth inexactly, vestigially.[61] For others, the ancients wrote in metaphors not only to protect themselves but to preserve their theology from the corrupting distortions of vulgar minds. The same distinction is observed when the allegories of the ancients are distinguished from the allegories of the apostles. Renaissance commentators agreed that early epics and the scriptural books are "gatherings of allegories" and that Homer, Vergil, Ovid, Moses, David, the prophets, and Christ employed allegory to conceal their meanings.[62] But they also observed a fundamental difference between the classical habit of perverting truth through allegory and the Christian habit of concealing eternal truths in allegory so they could not be perverted by vulgar minds.

These distinctions lie behind Blake's conception of allegory and his identification of it with the epic poetry of Spenser and Milton. Homer and Vergil obscured truth; Spenser and Milton revealed it. To the extent that Homer and Vergil wrote allegories they managed to embody in them falsifications of eternal realities. Thus when Blake says in *On Homers Poetry* that those who seek unity in Homer "come out with a Moral like a sting in the tail" (p. 267) he is suggesting not only the desolating effects of the classical epic on human history but is questioning whether those who find continuous allegory unifying Homer's epics, and Vergil's, do not impose upon them something that is not actually there. Homer and Vergil were false prophets who may not have understood what they wrote or uttered, but Spenser and Milton, as true prophets, knew what they wrote; and to say otherwise involves, from Blake's point of view, a radical distortion of their achievement. Moreover, as true prophets, Spenser and Milton had both interpretive and creative functions to perform.

Blake's recollection that "Milton lov'd me in childhood & shew'd me his face" and his report to Henry Crabb Robinson that "I saw Milton in imagination and he told me to beware of being misled by his *Paradise Lost*"[63] set him within the tradition of commentators like Fulgentius, who tells "what Virgil, who visited him in a vision, said about the true meaning of his epic."[64] Like Renaissance commentators, Blake perceived the close connection between criticism and creation. What Fulgentius and later commentators did for Vergil, Blake is doing for Spenser, and even more for Milton, by imitating them and by illustrating their work.

For the Renaissance and for Blake, the creator and the interpreter are one, both participating in the creative act. God and the poet are analogous, and so are their creations. The poet's creation (the poem) repeats the original act of creation (the universe), which brought a difficult order out of chaos; but it also interprets the meaning of that creation. Moreover, the poet, especially the epic poet, imitates not only the original creation but also the poetical creations of his predecessors and in the process interprets their visions even as he moves beyond them. In this respect, the poet is like the prophet, who, proclaiming a new vision, serves simultaneously as an interpreter of it.[65] Blake is a poet-prophet of this order. Part of his commentary on his predecessors is corrective of their visions. This is especially true of what he says verbally and pictorially about Dante. But another part of his commentary, the principal part of it, is concerned with the visionary experience a poem affords—an experience that in Spenser and Milton is clouded over by an encumbering narrative. Blake is the first critic to offer a sustained symbolic interpretation of either poet, and he does this by ignoring the narrative and concentrating on the vision.

Blake, rather than shifting the direction in which Spenser and Milton moved the epic poem, follows to its logical conclusion the course set by them. Spenser and Milton, each in his own way, arrested narrative movement; but Blake virtually eliminates it. Northrop Frye remarks that the Spenserian stanza, "especially the final alexandrine, has a role rather similar to the engraved design in Blake: it deliberately arrests the narrative and forces the reader to concentrate on something else."[66] The point is valid, but it also ignores the more conspicuous device that serves the same ends. Spenser abandons a linear narrative, letting one plot-line intersect another; before one episode reaches its period, another interrupts it and is unfolded. Spenser uses this "device of interweaving,"[67] as Tasso did, to imitate the difficult order of God's universe, to create an image of immense diversity within an enveloping unity; but Spenser also uses the device to effect reflection and contemplation. Epic poetry had always required attention from its audience; with Spenser it begins to require effort.

What Spenser accomplishes through the alexandrine and through "interlacing," what Blake realizes through the pictorial design, is achieved by Milton through the various authorial intrusions that establish an antagonism between narration and commentary and that have the effect of goading the reader into an understanding of the visionary experience his poem records. Impeding the narrative flow is a distinctive contribution of Spenser and Milton to epic poetry, and it is one of the devices by which these poets together radically altered the epic mode. As Northrop Frye has observed, "Certain forms of art are ... designed to give us the strongest possible emphasis on the continuous process of creation," and "the most continuous form of poetry ever devised" was the "formulaic epic."[68] So continuous was the *Iliad* that the poet himself did not divide it into books. After the formulaic epic was superseded by the literary epic, the notion of continuing process was preserved by the introduction of romance structure. So continuous was Ariosto's *Orlando Furioso* that it could be extended endlessly and was interrupted only by the poet's death or by the obstructions to narrative movement added by the poet's commentators. In the oral epic and in the literary epic before Spenser and Milton, unity is achieved by adherence to the Aristotelian notion of imitative action. When this concept is disregarded, the usual epic continuity is disrupted and then replaced by the unity of design, a unity that does not preclude pauses or still-points. Following Spenser, Milton creates a tradition that demands contemplation of a work of art, and what Frye calls "Blake's plotless prophecies"[69] are a continuation of the same tradition.

Like all prophecies, *The Faerie Queene* is a unity, a "constitutive vision," that assimilates "poetic narrative to a steadily emerging vision"; and it is difficult, once one perceives the way in which individual books of Spenser's epic merge into one another, to reject "the impression that Spenser completed his epic," achieving in it a "continuous allegory" or vision.[70] The allegories of Spenser, Milton, and Blake (or, for that matter, the allegory of the Book of Revelation) are not continuous, if we mean by that designation that the reader moves uninterruptedly from the beginning to the end without being led into contemplation of separate panels of the poem; but the allegories of these works, once they are penetrated, establish the continuity of perspectives, and force upon us the perception that all coheres, all is integrated within a "Grand Poem" that *seems* a continuous vision.

What differentiates Spenserian allegory from that used by Milton and Blake is that Spenser's allegory predicates "agreement [between poet and audience] about the moral implications of a poetic theme"[71] and thereby eliminates the dramatic element that, in Milton and Blake, derives from the dialectical relationship between poet and audience. Spenser usually counts on a "stock response," whereas Milton, while continuing to use allegory, counts on a shared response between himself and a small coterie of readers who, with him, can penetrate the allegory and apprehend the vision that it articulates. Whereas Spenser, even in his cryptic allegories, presents attitudes that his whole audience shares, Milton summons his audience to a new understanding and finally to the acceptance of a new scheme of values.

In the Renaissance epic before Milton, the poet asserts a superiority over his audience, but he asserts an artistic rather than a moral superiority. For instance, as the narrative line in *Orlando Furioso* becomes increasingly more tenuous, as it becomes more fragmented, Ariosto becomes insistent that the poem is not without a systematic and deliberate plan; the effect is to assert the supremacy of his own will over that of his audience. Just as God regulates action in this world, so the poet regulates action in his poem; the poet contemplates the events in his poem from a position comparable to God's and, like God, metes out rewards and punishments. But Ariosto's poet has no moral superiority over his audience, which, as a certain social class of readers, generates the values, the moral norms, that his poem embodies. This theme of moral harmony between the poet and his audience is clearly articulated by Tasso; and such a theme persists in *The Faerie Queene,* but with a difference. As the poet's personal experience fades from the epic, so do references to his artistic superiority over his audience, still an audience composed of courtly, aristocratic readers. The effect is for Spenser to merge with his audience, which continues to provide the values the poem celebrates.[72] In the process, the dramatic potentiality of prophecy is dissipated because in Spenser, as in Dante, there is little antagonism between the poet and his audience and consequently little contention between the different perspectives that individual books furnish. In joining epic and prophecy, Spenser appropriates the structure but not the dramatic element of prophecy. But Milton, and Blake following him, makes of allegory "a form at once visionary and intensely dramatic."[73]

Believing with David Pareus that Revelation was a tragedy (i.e., a dramatic structure), Milton pursued the analogy between the play (God's vision) and the audience (the poet who receives God's vision).[74] Just as the poet, once receiving the vision, must struggle to penetrate it before he can presume to articulate and interpret it, so the audience, once it receives the poet's vision, must also struggle to apprehend it. The poet and his audience are, then, set in the same relationship as God and the poet; and the poem is, correspondingly, presented in dramatic form. When Blake speaks of "Visionary forms dramatic" on plate 98 of *Jerusalem* he is, indeed, providing "a climactic definition" of his composite art:[75] he is invoking the tradition of epic-prophecy, the Milton tradition, which sees the Book of Revelation and poems that adopt its structure, as *"Propheticall* Drama[s]" wherein the "diverse persons" of a play are replaced by "diverse *shews* and *apparitions,"* by visions, and wherein confrontations between characters are replaced by confrontations of perspectives.[76] Just as a play creates the *illusion* of continuous action, though it may be interrupted by interludes, so the epic-prophecy creates the *illusion* of continuous vision, though it too may be interrupted by authorial intrusions that interpret verbally (as in Milton) or pictorially (as in Blake). It is precisely this *illusion* of continuity that Blake tries to preserve in his designs, which, when viewed apart from the text, present both a "continuous allegory" and the poem's "darke conceit[s]"; it is the kind of continuity perceived when the text is read by itself, without the calculated interruptions that the full-page designs provide.

Blake's technique of using "darkness" as the way to "light," though more pronounced than Milton's, is still in keeping with Milton's own practice. The point of distinction between Milton and Blake as visionaries rests for some critics upon Milton's theory of accommodation, which, according to Geoffrey Hartman, involves "two different, even contradictory ideas." When Milton allows Raphael to liken spiritual to corporeal forms, "Raphael brings truth down to earth" but does so, says Hartman, as a way of lifting "an earthly mind to heaven." Because the first aspect of accommodation is "authoritarian and condescending," the Romantics, and especially Blake, are represented as opposing it; but since the second aspect of accommodation is "initiatory," the

Romantics, particularly Blake, are represented as embracing it: the idea of "initiating" into light through darkness, Hartman concludes, is the Romantic obverse to "the principle of accommodation" which depicts God darkening light that the human eyes are too weak to behold.[77] However shrewd, such a conclusion is misleading as it relates to both Milton's art and Blake's understanding of it.

The very issue that Hartman isolates and tries to tie to the Romantic understanding of Milton was in the early nineteenth century confronted and answered differently than Hartman proposes. William Ellery Channing is compelled to explain that to be "universally intelligible" is not the highest aim of art; for "a great mind cannot without injurious constraint, shrink itself to the grasp of common passive readers."[78] Milton did not even try for that sort of intelligibility, Channing says, but created instead "splendid confusion, dazzling to common readers, but kindling to congenial spirits"; and Channing concludes with an injunction that he credits Milton with having followed:

Let such writers as Addison (an honoured name) "bring down philosophy from heaven to earth." But let inspired genius fulfil its higher function of lifting the prepared mind from earth to heaven. Impose upon it no strict laws . . . Let it speak in its own language . . . Let it not lay aside its natural port, or dwarf itself that it may be comprehended by the surrounding multitude.[79]

The Romantics quote Milton's line from *Paradise Lost,* "fit audience find, though few" (VII. 31), with astonishing frequency; and Blake, of course, quotes the line in his 1809 Advertisement (p. 518), implying the kind of distinction that Hartman draws without implying that Milton's is a poetry of "condescension" in contrast to his own poetry of "initiation." That distinction is, in fact, analogous to the one Blake makes between the true and the false prophet: the one creates a symbolic language, and the other reduces the language of symbols to mere signs. Milton's whole purpose in frustrating narrative movement with authorial intrusions, in impeding narrative structure with "the traverse action"[80] of imagery, is to lift his reader to the level of vision rather than to accommodate his vision to the reader's lesser understanding. Blake's poetry is not totally without a narrative line; but, more pointedly than Milton's, it subordinates "narrative . . . to herme-

neutic structure."[81] Milton and Blake use this technique to transform their audience from a theater of readers into a house of
interpreters. This is my understanding of Milton, and I think
Blake's, but it is by no means a "modern" understanding of
Milton. Robert Lowth associates Milton with what he calls "that
sublimer kind of allegory, which . . . looks forward to a meaning
much more important than that which is obvious and literal," a
meaning "under a rind or shell" that is "interior" and "sacred."
This is the mode of allegory, says Lowth, that "prevails . . . in the
prophetic poetry" and that, opposed to "continued allegory," is
" 'like a light glimmering in a dark place, until the day dawn, and
the day-star arise.' "[82]

Milton and Blake, then, disrupt the traditional relationship between the epic poet and his audience. Both poets pursue the
analogy between God and the poet, but they understand the
analogy to imply more than the poet's artistic superiority over his
audience. God awakens the spirit of imagination in the poet who,
in turn, must awaken the same spirit in his audience. The authorial
intrusions, verbal and pictorial, have the same function in the epics
of Milton and Blake as the "songs" and "Hymnes" have in the
Book of Revelation; they exercise the minds of the readers, lifting
them from earthly to heavenly matters.[83] The poet's vision is
both something given and something received. The poet's role is to
fit his audience to receive his visions, which come not through
"dreamlike ease" but through "difficult, concentrated, sometimes
even painful attention. The vision has to be won," first by the
poet, then by his audience, through "devoted exercise," through
"an arduous process of contemplation."[84] What is true, in this
regard, of the poet Spenser is no less true of Milton and Blake. The
voice of each poet is controlled by a double purpose: it remains
faithful to the vision and, thus, tries to achieve the fullest possible
comprehension from the audience. Kathleen Williams rightly observes that "through the poet-narrator we are made aware of
poetry as . . . a divine rhetoric. The thing seen by the poet . . .
requires all his care and skill to convey it and ours as readers to
receive it. It is vision and rhetoric, the Orphic poet leading his
instructed and responsive listeners through the complex metaphor
in which he has captured his sight of harmonious order."[85] The
poet, then, presents a vision, one that he struggles to articulate and

that we must struggle to receive. The vision, once penetrated, extends to the audience a perfect scheme of values, which the audience is expected to adopt, and a plan for implementing reformation, which the audience is expected to execute. From Milton's point of view, and from Blake's, the poet possesses artistic superiority over his audience, but his real superiority resides in the fact that he is a generator of values rather than a confirmer of those that already exist.

Like Ariosto, Milton undertakes in *Paradise Lost* "Things unattempted yet in Prose or Rhime" (I. 16); yet unlike him, Milton pursues them not into an ironic vision but into what Blake calls "Divine Vision." Ariosto invokes the epic tradition and subjects it to ridicule, not because the form is irrelevant but because its traditional values are. *Orlando Furioso* proclaims the viability of the epic form and begs future poets to accommodate it to the values emerging in Renaissance culture. In *Orlando Furioso,* in Milton's epics, and in Blake's, there is "ironic disparagement operating,"[86] but in Ariosto it functions in one way and in Milton and Blake in quite another way. Ariosto's irony seeks to replace what was with what is; the irony of Milton and Blake seeks to replace what was *and what is* with a vision mounted on "original" Christianity, which has been, through history, scarred into an image of what both poets most deplore. Instead of adjusting their epic statements to the reigning values of their cultures, Milton and Blake urge their audiences to reorient the prevailing values of their cultures, a process which often requires discarding those values, so as to bring society in line with the poet's own moral vision. Ariosto's audience is composed of a social elite; Milton's, and also Blake's, of a whole culture, a small part of it capable of penetrating their visions, the largest part requiring education before it can comprehend.

Michael Murrin tells us that "the Renaissance allegorist could not ignore his audience, for it was part of his very conception of poetry. Not so the Romantics." A corollary of this historical phenomenon, says Murrin, is that whereas the Romantic poet "makes a new morality" the Renaissance poet "recalled old ones to his audience, values now almost forgotten."[87] These distinctions Murrin would use, presumably, to divide Blake from Milton; but for those two poets such distinctions are useful to note only because neither poet observes them.

Milton, the epic poet, has been celebrated as a "revolutionary" who, in *Paradise Lost,* "created new standards and conventions." "We cannot help thinking of the masterpiece as *being* the norm," says E. M. W. Tillyard, "when all the time it created the norm, doing thereby an original, maybe a daring thing."[88] Like so many literary historians who have acknowledged the revolutionary character of Milton's art, Tillyard fails to grasp the real nature of the revolution that Milton would precipitate. *Paradise Lost,* from Tillyard's point of view, continues to express "the undoubted voice" of Milton's age; it possesses what Tillyard regards as the essential feature of epic poetry, "choric quality," which, identifying Milton's philosophy with the main currents of thought in his own time, expresses "great and wide impulses that were at their height at periods just a little removed from the time of the man who expresses them."[89] Milton endorses, says Tillyard, "the generally held doctrines" of a slightly earlier age—a wide range of "group opinion." But *Paradise Regained* is another matter for that critic—it does none of these things and is therefore no epic either:

I turn finally to *Paradise Regained* only to give reasons for passing it over. How this poem should be labelled is doubtful. None of the traditional categories fit it. And the epic category fails to fit it most conspicuously. It is too short, confined, and simplified for the necessary epic variety and it quite lacks choric character. This is not to condemn the poem, which has its own perfection, but it is to assert that it has no place in the present context.[90]

Setting Tillyard's conclusions within the context of Murrin's observations, we are led to believe that *Paradise Lost* is a Renaissance epic and *Paradise Regained* a poem with peculiarly "Romantic" impulses; we are asked, especially by Tillyard, to see *Paradise Lost* as a poem which preserves close ties with its audience and *Paradise Regained* as a poem that severs the alliance between poet and audience.

In Milton and in Blake, a strong sense of elitism combines with a continuing interest in audience. This is the case with Milton, from the First Prolusion, where he chastises his audience for its ignorance, to *Paradise Regained,* where through Christ he says that his audience should bring to books "A spirit and judgment equal or superior" to those qualities possessed by their authors (IV. 324). What distinguishes Milton from his epic predecessors is the fact that his "fit" audience, in the words of *Pro Populo Anglicano Defensio,* is finally a "spiritual elite" (*Yale Milton,* IV, i, 330n) rather than a social class of readers. Though Milton knows that the full comprehension of his art is restricted to this "elite" he also uses his poetry to awaken the multitude. Through it Milton hopes to expand the consciousness of all readers and to bring them into an ever-widening group of "discerners"; he hopes to be "doctrinal and exemplary to a Nation" by opening the doors of perception, which will, in turn, transform the Lord's people into prophets.[91] When Milton saw that Empire would not follow him, he ceased trying to build Jerusalem in England's green and pleasant land and started instead to build mansions in Eternity.

Blake is Milton's first "fit" critic, the first commentator to attempt an unfolding of the Miltonic *vision;* and he does so not in the medium of the formal essay but through his epics, which in their imitation are criticism, and through his designs for Milton's epics, which are pictorial criticisms of the poems they accompany. Spenser, like his epic predecessors, allegorized a received tradition of beliefs, whereas Milton, and Blake following him, allegorize a radically new system that their audiences must be educated into accepting before the visionary experience can be unfolded.

However much the creator and the interpreter share, they employ strikingly different methods. The interpreter works with a knowledge of symbolism; the creator, to the extent that he is an interpreter, does too; but to the extent that he is a creator he also "eschews various symbols, which are without value, and employs those darker conceits, which circle and wind the meaning into obscurity"[92] —into an obscurity that hides the poet's vision from "Corporeal Understanding," protecting it from vulgarization, but that is still comprehensible to the initiated. The obscurity of Spenser and Milton, which Blake tried to imitate, is the same obscurity that clouds the allegories of the prophets and the apostles; it is the obscurity that Ariosto's commentator, as well as Tasso, as his own commentator, regards as an inextricable part of the epic poem, and the obscurity that Milton describes in *Defensio Secunda* as the "shadow" from which "the light of the divine countenance may shine forth all the more clearly" (*Yale Milton,* IV, i, 590).

John Harington's Preface to *Orlando Furioso* draws a distinction between the narration and the allegory, between what Blake calls the fable and the vision. Buried in the narration, says Harington, are the "deepe conceits" that transport the mind to the allegorical level of epic poetry. Moreover, Harington quickly distinguishes between two modes of allegory "natural" or historical allegory, which deals with terrestrial matters, and "heavenly" or what Blake calls "Sublime Allegory," which deals with what "Eternally Exists." Both modes of allegory he finds "hidden in . . . fiction."[93] Corporeal understanding digests the narrative and comprehends the historical allegory it contains, but only imagination penetrates the dark conceits that are windows opening into eternity. Tasso makes essentially the same distinction when he differentiates between "Actions" and "Allegorie." The former "regardeth the *Actions* of men subjected to outward senses" and does not consider the "discourses of the *Minde,* as they are inward." Allegory, on the other hand, represents mental actions that are "hidden and inward" and expresses them "obscurely . . . such as only the understanders of the nature of things can fully comprehend."[94]

The obscurity that critical theory and poetic practice identify with epic poetry is the obscurity that proceeds not from a muddled head but from the depths of understanding; it is not obscurity as opacity—that obscurity which Blake says in his *Annotations to Reynolds* "is Neither the Source of the Sublime nor of any Thing Else" (p. 647)—but obscurity that paradoxically breaks through opacity into the sublime clarity of true vision. This latter obscurity, which has its analogue in Milton's distinction, drawn in *Defensio Secunda,* between the blindness that "obscures the mind" and the blindness that fills it with "intellectual vision" (*Yale Milton,* IV, i, 589), is a point of contact between epic and prophecy, especially between epic poetry and the Book of Revelation, which, as one commentator puts it, contains "all the obscurities."[95] This obscurity is "a veil against the many" and a cloud for the sublime allegory concealed in "the tents of fiction."[96] Blake understood with Milton's nephew Edward Phillips (who may be echoing "the youthful Milton's remarks on the heroic epic"[97]) that "there is a kind of truth even in the midst of fiction. For whatever is pertinently said by way of allegory is morally [Blake would say "eternally"], though not historically true."[98] This is the perception Blake offers when he says in his description of *The Vision of the Last Judgment* that "what the critics call Fable or Allegory is seldom without some Vision"; it is the perception behind his method of illustrating and imitating Milton, which involves subduing the narrative, the fiction, in order to focus the poet's vision. However much Milton's recent critics have played down—or simply ignored—the fact, Milton's epics do not mark the end of the identification between allegory and epic. Blake comprehended, as did Milton's biographer John Toland, that in respect to allegory, Milton was not "behind any body."[99]

   Blake's poetry is, then, a poetry of obscurity; and its aesthetic basis derives from Blake's contemporaries and from those Renaissance poets and critics from whom Blake's contemporaries extracted their theories. For Blake, poetry was more—much more—than "allurement and delight"; more than interest, poetry demanded attention, and more than attention it required effort. John Hoole's contention that "allegory, which requires explanation, is certainly defective"[100] is contrary to Blake's own belief that unless poetry requires severe mental exertion it fails in its purpose, which is to cleanse the doors of perception. That belief Blake stated emphatically in a letter to Dr. Trusler, dated 23 August 1799:

> You say that I want somebody to Elucidate my Ideas. But you ought to know that What is Grand is necessarily obscure to Weak men. That which can be made Explicit to the Idiot is not worth my care. The wisest of the Ancients considerd what is not too Explicit as the fittest for Instruction because it rouzes the faculties to act. I name Moses Solomon Esop Homer Plato [.]
>
> (p. 676)

This is the ideal that Spenser and Milton achieved through allegory, the ideal that Blake, ensconcing himself in their tradition, aspired to. This is also the principle of art that enables us to penetrate the intellectual density of both *The Marriage of Heaven and Hell* and *Milton*.

BLAKE'S MILTON

   "The prophetic poet," Angus Fletcher has written, "is uniquely sure of himself, and this he shows by allowing his utterance to be enigmatic and obscure on its surface, knowing that the immediate surface of the riddle is supported by an underlying clarity."[101]

Since the time of Alexander Gilchrist, *The Marriage of Heaven and Hell* has received special acclaim among Blake's works; but it has also been denied, even by Gilchrist, the "underlying clarity" that Fletcher promises from prophecy. Gilchrist acknowledges that *The Marriage of Heaven and Hell* is "the most daring in conception and gorgeous in illustration of all Blake's works" but argues that these wild utterances "defy description and interpretation."[102] Moreover, even if it was once said that *The Marriage of Heaven and Hell* is the central work in Blake's canon, "the most complete and concise expression of his philosophy that can be found,"[103] it has since been urged that the work represents a set of attitudes that Blake "had repudiated" by the time he came to write the major prophecies,[104] that in it there is "too much damning, too much praising, too little art."[105] Against this tradition of criticism, the following observations should be offered.

Blake's first great prophecy, *The Marriage of Heaven and Hell*, contains a major statement on Milton, anticipating the one in *Milton* and possessing a clarity that has eluded most readers, because they have mistaken the work's genre and, ignoring its contexts, have not penetrated its meaning. Previous misinterpretation requires that our attention be turned, first, to Blake's strategies in *The Marriage of Heaven and Hell* and the contexts he develops for it. Neither has been scrutinized; yet only after each has been can we begin to assess the place of Milton in this work. And as we begin to explore strategies and contexts, we should acknowledge immediately that *The Marriage of Heaven and Hell* is not a prose satire but a prophecy;[106] it is not about the inversion of moral categories but about the formation of the prophetic character. The work's subject dictates its form, and its form reveals its subject, which, in an unexpected setting, is identified by John E. Grant:

> There have been many accounts of what *The Marriage of Heaven and Hell* is about. I say it is about the education of the Prophetic Character. Blake is committed to showing how much pain and dislocation such an education demands. Though he was honest about the magnitude of the task, he was glad to join with Moses and Milton in praying that all the Lord's people become prophets.[107]

The Marriage of Heaven and Hell takes as its objective the transformation of an entire civilization into a nation of visionaries; and therefore it requires of its prospective readers a knowledge of prophecy, an understanding of its inner workings.

The chief obstacle in the way of our understanding prophecy, says Abraham Heschel, is our concentration on the theology of the Bible, which has caused us to ignore the prophet's role in the prophetic act, to ignore both his "response" and "the human situation" that produces it:

The prophet's task is to convey a divine view, yet as a person he *is* a point of view. He speaks from the perspective of God as perceived from the perspective of his own situation. We must seek to understand not only the views he expounded but also the attitudes he embodied. . . .[108]

We must also recognize with Heschel that the prophet is a generator of insight and that "insight is breakthrough, requiring much intellectual dismantling and dislocation":

It begins with a mental interim, with the cultivation for the unfamiliar, unparalleled, incredible. . . . Insight is accompanied by a sense of surprise. What has been closed is suddenly disclosed. It entails genuine perception, seeing anew.[109]

Though the human situation may alter, the pattern of the prophet's response does not. The problem for him is not that he lives in a world vacant of meaning but that he inhabits a world deaf to meaning. This situation provokes his consternation; and thus, while the prophet "always begins with a message of doom [see plate 2 of *The Marriage of Heaven and Hell*]," he invariably "concludes with a message of hope and redemption [see plate 25]."[110] The prophet says "No to his society, condemning its habits and assumptions, its complacency, waywardness, and syncretism"; but nay-saying is not the prophet's real function. "The ultimate purpose of the prophet," says Heschel, "is not to be inspired, but to inspire the people; not to be filled with passion, but to impassion the people."[111] Just as poets have their forms which provide them with structures, ideologies, and rhetorics, the prophet has his—the form of prophecy brought to its perfection by Saint John when he wrote the Book of Revelation.

Blake was, as Hazard Adams said a decade ago, a "master" of this "prophetic line";[112] and though he displays a knowledge of prophetic structure, based upon the Book of Revelation, as early as *The French Revolution* (1791), a work whose publication intersects with the composition of *The Marriage of Heaven and Hell* (1790–1793), his mastery of the form does not display itself until the latter work.[113] *The Marriage of Heaven and Hell* is a magnificent, yet troubled, manifestation of Blake's understanding of the elements that coalesce in the structure of the Book of Revelation—a recognition that helps us distinguish between this work and the *Songs of Innocence and of Experience,* which were prepared concurrently with *The Marriage of Heaven and Hell.* What differentiates these works "is not tone alone but total difference of genre": the prophecies, of which *The Marriage of Heaven and Hell* is Blake's first exquisite example, "can no more be judged as lyrics with elephantiasis," says Adams, "than can Revelation be considered as a puffed up twenty-third psalm."[114]

The Book of Revelation draws upon previous prophecy, inverting its patterns, correcting and amplifying its visions. A medley of forms and styles, Saint John's prophecy is composed of seven separate panels, each containing a vision with a commentary, the seventh vision distinguishing itself from the rest by virtue of its special clarity. The seven visions, in turn, are framed by a prologue and an epilogue. Though a new prophecy, Revelation serves as a commentary on older ones; it invokes contexts that it interprets and projects a vision requiring interpretation similar to that which it provides for previous prophecy. Within the prophecy itself there is repetition, accompanied by a movement from obscurity to clarity, from shadowy types to truth. Its structure is dramatic in the sense that the prophecy replaces confrontations of character with confrontations of perspective and creates an antagonism between the prophet and his audience, who relate to one another in the same way that the prophet relates to the source of his vision. Just as the prophet was made to struggle to receive a vision and then to translate it, so his audience, being extended a vision, is made to struggle to comprehend it.

The Marriage of Heaven and Hell follows these principles assiduously. It assumes the status of commentary on Swedenborg's *Heaven and Hell,* Milton's *Paradise Lost,* and, most important (for it etches this context into plate 3), the prophecy of Isaiah. It is written in both poetry and prose, like earlier prophecy, and is, as has recently been suggested, a medley of forms:

The Marriage of Heaven and Hell contains seven successive statements or illustrations of the concept of contraries, each relatively short, bearing a distinctive shape or form, and showing a discrete manifestation of the eternal contraries in conflict in human life and culture. These versions of the contraries in a medley of genres—a poem, a proclamation, an argument, a critique, history, allegory, and philosophical statement—have in common a limitation of meaning imposed by their form. Blake was able to transcend these limitations, however, in the myth of *A Song of Liberty* . . . Thus, the nonmyth shapings of the concept of contraries in *The Marriage,* which have limited reference, culminates in the fuller, more inclusive mythic formulation achieved in *A Song.*[115]

The critic is right to isolate these forms and to conclude that Blake was "motivated to create new forms." The "new" form of *The Marriage of Heaven and Hell,* however, is more than a medley of forms; it is a prophecy, many of whose themes are derived from Isaiah's prophecy and whose structure is modeled upon that of the Book of Revelation.

The context of Isaiah is firmly established in plate 3. By pointing specifically to Chapters 34 and 35, Blake isolates a small prophecy within a larger one whose patterns, both generically and thematically, give shape to *The Marriage of Heaven and Hell.* Bishop Lowth comments perceptively when he explains that this prophecy within a prophecy is apocalyptic, dealing literally and historically with the fall of Babylon but figuratively and anagogically with last things: a vision of destruction is succeeded by a vision of the new heaven and new earth; the Last Judgment is prologue to the moment when the eyes are unclosed, the ears opened, and the heavenly Jerusalem obtained. But Lowth can speak for himself:

The two chapters make one distinct prophecy: an intire, regular, and beautiful poem, consisting of two parts: the first containing a denunciation of Divine vengeance against the enemies of the people, a Church of God; the second describing the flourishing State of the Church of God, consequent upon the execution of those judgements. The event foretold is represented as of the highest importance, and of unusual concern: all nations are called upon to attend to the declaration of it; and the wrath of God is denounced against all the nations; that is, all those that had provoked to anger the defender of the cause of Sion. Among those Edom is particularly specified. . . . Accordingly the Edomites were, together with the rest of the neighbouring nations, ravaged and laid waste by Nebuchadnezzar. . . . By a figure, very common in the prophetical writings, any city, or people, remarkably distinguished as enemies of the people and kingdom of God, is put for those enemies in general. . . . It seems therefore reasonable to suppose . . . that this prophecy has a further view to events still future; to some great revolutions to be effected in later times, antecedent to that more perfect state of the kingdom of God upon earth, and serving to introduce it . . .[116]

Blake's prophecy, in terms of its patterns and emphases, reverses the prophecy of Isaiah. The first vision of *The Marriage of Heaven and Hell* refers to "a new heaven" falsely prophesied by Swedenborg, and its penultimate vision concludes with a portrayal of the triumph of Nebuchadnezzar; but this inversion of pattern finds its precedent in the Book of Revelation, which itself reverses the patterns of previous prophecy. Blake derives much of his thematic content from Isaiah, along with many of his formal patterns; but these themes and patterns are folded into the seven-part structure of Revelation prophecy. Here the distinction between prophecy and apocalyptics is useful: the one converts downward into history, the other outward into eternity; the one takes as its objective the reformation of man, the other, upon man's reformation, the creation of Jerusalem.[117] Therefore, in *The Marriage of Heaven and Hell,* Blake will do what Swedenborg could not do: Blake will make good the promises of his predecessor.

This observation brings us to the central concern of Blake's prophecy. An acknowledged context for *The Marriage of Heaven and Hell,* the Book of Isaiah provides one passage that corrects the usual misreadings of Blake's prophecy, a passage over which Blake would certainly have lingered: "Wo unto them that call evil good, and good evil; that put darkness for light, and light for darkness; that put bitter for sweet, and sweet for bitter" (5:20). Blake's concern is not with making a simple inversion of usual moral categories but with reassessing them. *The Marriage of Heaven and Hell* is not, like the later prophecies, an exploration of evil but rather a redefinition of good through a system of contraries that, interacting, bring man to the threshold of vision. However, as Blake explains in *Milton,* the struggle of contraries must be redeemed by destroying the negations, which impede the progress implied by contraries.

Those who have read *The Marriage of Heaven and Hell* as an inversion of moral categories are, in relation to Blake, like the Jews accusing Saint Paul of having "turned the world upside down" (Acts 17:6). The tradition of revolution to which both Milton and Blake belong assumes, as Blake does in his inscription for Design 101 in the Dante series, that "In Equivocal Worlds Up & Down are Equivocal" (p. 668); it postulates that when man falls he falls into an upside-down world, whether it be the wilderness into which Adam and Eve are exiled, alluded to by Rintrah, or the Night of Albion. This tradition involves "overturning, questioning, revaluing"[118] —activities which are part of a revolutionary effort to turn what has become an upside-down world right side up. The revolutionary is thus not opposed to order but is so deeply committed to it that he envisions a new order, which he locates in the past before corruption set in and which, by elimination of corruption, he hopes to re-establish in the present. As a revolutionary, Milton engaged in the process of "questioning," living "in a state of permanent dialogue with radical views";[119] and Blake, a kindred spirit, was involved in a continuous dialogue with his favorite poet, sometimes pointing to failings of Milton's radicalism but more often deriving inspiration from his mentor. Both kinds of dialogue are evidenced in *The Marriage of Heaven and Hell.*

Blake's prophecy begins with a cry of indignation and culminates in a vision of apocalypse; paradise is lost only to be regained. The song of Rintrah, entitled "The Argument," introduces a sevenfold prophecy, which has as its epilogue, "A Song of Liberty"; and, as in the Book of Revelation, the early portions of the prophecy are more doctrinal than prophetic, the first two visions—the one biblical and Swedenborgian, the other Miltonic—establishing the context for and the concerns of the succeeding visions. The prophecy itself, which has been described as an "unorthodox structure,"[120] is organized according to a traditional pattern:

Prologue: Plates 1–2.

I Vision   Plate 3, paragraph 1.
  Commentary   Plate 3, paragraphs 2–4.

II Vision   Plate 4.
   Commentary   Plates 5–6, through "Note."

III Vision   Plates 6–10.
    Commentary   Plate 11.

IV Vision   Plates 12–13.
   Commentary   Plate 14.

V	Vision	Plate 15.
	Commentary	Plates 16–17, through ". . . are our Energies."
VI	Vision	Plates 17–20.
	Commentary	Plates 21–22, through ". . . candle in sunshine."
VII	Vision	Plates 22–24, through ". . . as Elijah."
	Commentary	Plate 24, "Note."

Epilogue: Plate 25.

The Marriage of Heaven and Hell has all the external features that Bishop Lowth points to as hallmarks of prophecy. In accordance with the Hebrew alphabet, it is built on units of 22: the opening prophecy, like the one in Isaiah, disconnected from the major prophecy, contains 22 lines; the central prophecy is composed of 22 different systems of lines (plates 3–24); the epilogue, which is yet another isolated prophecy, is also composed of 22 units—20 verses, plus the colophon and the choral speech. There are the additional features of bold elliptical expressions, abrupt change of person, wild vacillation of verb tenses—all identified by Lowth as characteristic of prophecy. There is, finally, the intermingling of prose with poetry, the poetry strained to achieve the character of prose and the prose bursting through its boundaries into lyrical flights.[121]

Like the Book of Revelation, *The Marriage of Heaven and Hell* has a dramatic structure, organized around a double perspective that is defined by the work's title and its title-page design and is represented within the prophecy itself by the Devil and the Angel. They symbolize the relationship that we as audience share with Blake the prophet. The real dialectic of *The Marriage of Heaven and Hell* occurs not in the prophecy itself but in the antagonism Blake establishes between it and its prospective audience. But, again like the Book of Revelation, this primary dialectic is internalized and then mirrored in a cast of five characters: Rintrah, the objective voice of plate 3, the Devil, the *I* persona, and the Angel. Within the prophecy, the dialectic represented by the Devil and the Angel finds its fullest expression in the voice of plate 3, which embraces all contraries and announces not only the "philosophy" that informs this prophecy but the apocalypse it hopes to accomplish.

The dialectic of *The Marriage of Heaven and Hell* is also figured by Rintrah and the *I* persona, who identifies so closely with the voice of the Devil. Rintrah roars the song with which *The Marriage of Heaven and Hell* commences—a song that in four stanzas, recreating the four great time distances in the Book of Revelation, summarizes the history of western civilization from the fall to the French Revolution, whose intimations of apocalypse the prophecy itself explores. Rintrah has been understood variously—as "the spirit presiding over the late eighteenth century,"[122] as a "convinced and uncompromising mystic," [123] as "revolutionary wrath," [124] as "the lion spirit of egoism"; [125] he has also been described mistakenly as "a son of Urizen" [126] and very pointedly as Blake's representative of prophetic tradition, an Elijah figure, the wrathful spirit of prophecy driven into the wilderness. [127] Rintrah later appears as one of the sons of Los, as a representative of the class of men identified by Blake as the reprobate, a class comprising the prophets who have been consigned to the wilds by the elect, that class of men now in control of society and represented in *The Marriage of Heaven and Hell* by Swedenborg and his like. In the topsy-turvy world after the fall, "the sneaking serpent" appears as the just man; and the just man appears as the villain. The confusions of *The Marriage of Heaven and Hell* find an analogue later in the Bard's song of *Milton,* where the true prophet Milton is mistaken for the false prophet Satan.

David Erdman asks us to pass quickly by Rintrah, who "plays no further part after his roaring in the prologue" and thus "must remain unidentified."[128] Yet one should not bypass Rintrah without at least acknowledging that his song recalls a passage from Joel, which might well serve as an epigraph to it: "The Lord roars from Zion,/And utters His voice from Jerusalem/And the heaven and earth shake" (4:16). Rintrah's roaring, coupled with this biblical passage, reminds us that "prophecy is more than knowledge acquired by inspiration. It is not a quiet insight, a simple act of apperception. It is a startling event: a thunder in the world and a lightning in the soul."[129] It may or may not be helpful to look into Blake's later prophecies to ascertain what Rintrah signifies here; but it is certainly useful to recall the Hebraic associations of his name and to pursue his associations with Rimmon, his probable prototype, whose name, meaning "roarer," identifies the storm god of Babylonian mythology and, in Christian mythology, "a fallen archangel," who in his fallenness became associated with "conform[ing] to . . . reprehensible custom."[130] The "roarer" of Blake's poem is the *unfallen* prophet, the revolutionary, an association preserved by the figure of the pomegranate which is Rimmon's insignia—the ripe fruit splitting open and showing on the inside the red seeds of revolution and of the apocalypse attendant upon it, even while recalling the Paradise from which the prophet has been exiled. Moreover, Rimmon is allegedly the one devil who rather than hardening into evil is returned to heaven. He alone achieves the "marriage" of heaven and hell that is the subject of Blake's prophecy, and this last association gives Blake the added advantage of establishing immediately the infernal perspective that persists in the voice of the Devil and in the *I* persona, whose sympathies are clearly with this perspective.

If Rintrah is of that class known as the reprobate, the *I* persona belongs to the class known as the redeemed. The two voices together represent the two voices of prophecy, which Milton, in *The Doctrine and Discipline of Divorce,* describes in language appropriate to Blake's purposes here. Having established Christ as perfect prophet, as the figure who comprehends all prophets and all prophetic attitudes, Milton explains that Christ speaks "sometimes by a milde and familiar converse . . . ; otherwhiles with bitter and irefull rebukes." But Milton is moved to explain further that "this coole unpassionate mildness of primitive wisdome" is not enough "in times of opposition when . . . new heresies," along with "old corruptions," are arising; in times like these "Zeale" is needed "whose substance is ethereal, arming in compleat diamonds . . . [to ascend] his fiery Chariot drawn with two blazing Meteors figur'd like beasts . . . , resembling two of those four which *Ezeciel* and S. *John* saw, the one visag'd like a Lion to expresse power, high autority, and indignation, the other of count'nance like a man to cast derision and scorne upon perverse and fraudulent seducers . . ." Milton then concludes: "Thus did the true Prophets of old combat with the false; thus Christ himselfe the fountaine of meeknesse found acrimony anough to be still galling and vexing" (*Yale Milton,* I, 899–900).

This passage is important as a gloss on *The Marriage of Heaven and Hell* not only because it helps to locate and explain the prophetic postures assumed in the work, but because it identifies the central concerns, as well as the strategies, of the work. The voice of indignation (Rintrah's voice) is a complement, a prologue, to the voice of the Devil, critical of Milton, and to the *I* persona, derisive of Swedenborg. In times that try men's souls, when societies have sunk into corruption, when the doors of perception have been closed, the calm voice of the true discerner is not enough. His consciousness is present in *The Marriage of Heaven and Hell,* but his voice is not the one through which its prophecy is given fullest expression.

The Marriage of Heaven and Hell is a brilliantly experimental work; but it may not be, artistically, a wholly successful one for precisely this reason: Blake sympathizes, but does not fully identify, with the principal voices in the prophecy; they represent two of the many prophetic postures, all of which Blake the prophet comprehends, but the full array of these postures is not integrated within the prophecy itself; nor are the distinct perspectives associated with these postures. The perspective of the Devil is fully developed through his own voice, through his proverbs, and through the *I* persona, who has been converted to his party. Yet Blake's title promises a "marriage," and the marriage theme is reinforced by the doctrine of contraries introduced on plate 3; but even so the Angel is an incidental figure in the prophecy—one not acting but being acted upon, one whose perspective, rather than being developed as a contrary to the Devil's, is annihilated in the "marriage" that occurs at the end of the prophecy when Devil and Angel meet in an embrace.

It is useful, therefore, to distinguish this prophecy from later ones in terms of their different strategies. In *Milton,* as we have already seen, different perspectives are fully developed within the poem itself; they are reinforced by its accompanying illustrations. In *The Marriage of Heaven and Hell,* one perspective—the Devil's— is elaborated by the prophecy, and the other—the Angel's—is merely assumed of Blake's audience of prospective readers. The consciousness of the true prophet, who subsumes all prophetic postures and their related perspectives, can be attributed to Blake as Blake would attribute that consciousness to Milton; but that consciousness does not exercise the kind of control over this prophecy that it was later to achieve in *Milton* and *Jerusalem*. We can, to be sure, infer a rhetorical strategy from *The Marriage of Heaven and Hell,* but its success is another question. *The Marriage of Heaven and Hell* involves a double strategy: to expose the false prophets, eliminating the negation they represent; and to accomplish through prophecy the struggle of contraries by which the organs of perception are cleansed and the apocalypse finally achieved. Sometimes called a work about apocalypse, *The Marriage of Heaven and Hell* is more exactly about the way in which apocalypse is realized—by annihilating erroneous doctrines as a prelude to the assimilation of new perspectives.

Within this context, we can begin to explore the role of Milton in *The Marriage of Heaven and Hell;* and this we can do best by first recognizing that, like all prophecy, *The Marriage of Heaven and Hell* submits to multiple levels of interpretation. The dialectic of the work—the struggle of contraries that pervades it—is represented literally by the Devil and the Angel. All other levels of meaning derive from and relate back to this system of meaning, in accordance with Bishop Lowth's contention that "whatever senses are supposed to be included in the Prophet's words, Spiritual, Mystical, Allegorical, Anagogical, or the like, they must all intirely depend on the Literal Sense. This is the only foundation upon which such interpretations can be securely raised; and if this is not firmly and well established, all that is built upon it will fall to the ground."[131] Mythologically, the terms of Blake's distinction in *The Marriage of Heaven and Hell* point inward and outward. Psychologically, the contraries are represented by energy and reason or, when translated into Freudian terms, by the id and super-ego. Historically, the contraries are represented by Milton and Swedenborg, the true and false prophet respectively. Milton represents the Devil's, Swedenborg the Angel's, party. This dialectical tension in Blake's prophecy is indigenous to its subject and form. A remark by Abraham Heschel is pertinent:

A dialectic tension in the prophet's consciousness has its source in the dualism of his experience. He is both active and passive, free and forced. He is free to respond to the content of the moment; he is forced to experience the moment, to accept the burden of his mission. Thus the effect of the impact of imagination is to evoke in him both a sense of freedom and a feeling of coercion, an act of spontaneity and an awareness of forced receptivity. This note of dialectic tension is of essential significance in the structure of the prophetic personality.[132]

The note of dialectical tension, we might add, characteristically reflected in the structure of prophecy itself, is mirrored in *The Marriage of Heaven and Hell* by the opposition established between Milton and Swedenborg.

It is finally not very helpful to say that *The Marriage of Heaven and Hell* is a criticism of Milton and Swedenborg, unless we are prepared to discriminate between the criticisms leveled against each figure. Swedenborg is the object of ridicule; Milton, the subject of the Devil's mild ironies. The criticism of Swedenborg is registered by the voice of the *I* persona, whereas the criticism of Milton is assigned to the voice of the Devil, a voice that is distanced from Blake's own, incapable of articulating the subtleties that Blake himself comprehends. The basis of this opposition of Swedenborg and Milton, though not spelled out, is clear enough on reflection. Swedenborg promised a new heaven in 1757, the year of Blake's birth; and in 1790, thirty-three years after Swedenborg's announcement, Blake pronounces Swedenborg's heaven to be his own hell. The man who began his life as a visionary was shorn by the churches; by the end of his career he had become bound down to an orthodoxy, institutionalizing his teachings, codifying his errors. The pattern of Swedenborg's life, Blake saw, was an image in reverse of Milton's. Having identified himself in early life with orthodoxy, Milton moved steadily away from it. This history was accepted by all parties; indeed it was widely enough accepted so that Dr. Johnson could expound it as a commonplace.[133] Yet the intellectual history of the two "prophets" pointed to still other patterns distinguishing them from one another.

Yeats is quite correct in observing that *The Marriage of Heaven and Hell* "is certainly a reply to ... [Swedenborg's] 'Heaven and Hell'."[134] Swedenborg introduced *A Treatise Concerning Heaven and Hell* with an epigraph—"Where there is no Vision, the people perish .../He that hath ears to hear, let him hear"; but ironically his work promoted the very dichotomy between heaven and hell, good and evil, that Blake saw as an obstacle to vision. In contrast,

Milton developed as a leitmotif in his prose works the notion that all the Lord's people could become prophets and in *Paradise Regained* laid down the vision through which such an objective could be accomplished. Swedenborg, though he represented himself as a visionary, espoused the orthodoxies from which Milton's hatred of custom and tradition had freed him; Swedenborg was therefore, from Blake's point of view, "the eternal type of prophet who becomes a new kind of priest, and by becoming a church loses his imaginative strength,"[135] in contrast to Milton, who, by divorcing himself from organized religion, acquired his strength of vision. As a member of the Angel's party, Swedenborg wrote to uphold the orthodoxies that Milton, as a member of the Devil's party, wished to subvert.

In *The Apocalypse Revealed,* Swedenborg distinguishes between the hell called "the Devil," by which he means the hell created by those "who are in the love of self," and the hell called "Satan," by which he means the hell created by those who live by "falsities" and "who are in the pride of their own intelligence."[136] Thus, in plate 21 of *The Marriage of Heaven and Hell,* Swedenborg stands self-condemned: he is among the angels who "have the vanity to speak of themselves as the only wise"; he "boasts that what he writes is new," says Blake, "tho' it is only the Contents and Index of already publish'd books." Swedenborg moved from a revolutionary posture into orthodoxy, from the valley of vision into the prison of selfhood, finally embracing the Calvinistic doctrine of predestination that in *Paradise Lost* Milton disavows.[137] Milton, in contrast, moved the other way—beyond orthodoxy, outside selfhood, into the divine vision of *Paradise Regained.* All this would be commonplace to the literati of the eighteenth century, offering a mitigating perspective on the criticism directed against Milton, criticism which has seemed both outrageous and mistaken to so many modern readers.

We should be aware, at the outset, that the purpose of *The Marriage of Heaven and Hell,* unlike that of *Milton,* is criticism rather than celebration—the exposure of error by way of leading men into the divine vision. But we should also recognize that the attitudes adopted toward Swedenborg and Milton are qualitatively different, an awareness, which, coupled with the understanding that much else in *The Marriage of Heaven and Hell* softens the criticism of Milton, suggests that Blake's fit audience will not require the bold histrionics of plates 5 and 6.

There are various analogues for the doctrine of contraries that pervades *The Marriage of Heaven and Hell*—too many to rehearse here. One of them is of special importance, however. In *The Reason of Church-Government*, Milton comments, "if we look but on the nature of elementall and mixt things, we know they cannot suffer any change of one kind, or quality into another without the struggl of contrarieties" (*Yale Milton*, I, 795). By itself, the passage seems little more than another analogue. It has the rhetorical advantage, however, of distinguishing Milton from Swedenborg, who, as Martin Nurmi reminds us, did not perceive "the necessity of the contraries to Human Existence"[138] —a necessity that Milton and Blake acknowledge. When we recall the context in which Milton's statement appears, in a work that instructs England to "rub her eyes" and man to "open his eyes to a higher consideration of good and evil" (I, 834, 836), in one that divides into two parts, the first celebrating the theme of liberation through contraries, the second the theme of vision through contraries, the entire work culminating in an image of mental warfare producing apocalypse—when we recall all this, *The Reason of Church-Government* emerges as yet another source for the thematic materials and their arrangement in Blake's prophecy.

Milton acknowledges time and again in *The Reason of Church-Government* that though sects and parties are limiting to vision they are necessary to perception. Those who will not allow dissent, those who are opposed to contraries, are, as Milton explains in *Areopagitica,* "the troublers, . . . the dividers of unity" who effect "the forc't and outward union of cold and neutrall, and inwardly divided minds" (*Yale Milton*, II, 550–51). The agents of repression are those responsible for truth's perversion: Truth was once "a perfect shape most glorious"; but then her "lovely form," says Milton, was hewn "into a thousand peeces, and scatter'd . . . to the four winds. From that time ever since" men have had to gather truth "limb by limb still as they could find them. We have not yet found them all . . . , nor ever shall we," Milton concludes, "till her Masters second coming; he shall bring together every joynt and member, and shall mould them into an immortall feature of lovelines and perfection" (II, 549). Milton devoted his entire career as a polemicist to the recovery of lost truths. Armed with the weapon of truth, Milton says in *Animadversions,* he can "throw down your *Nebuchadnezzars* Image and crumble it like the chaffe of the Summer threshing floores" (I, 700). Annihilating falsehood, mastering lost truths, marrying them into a unity—these are the objectives of Blake in *The Marriage of Heaven and Hell;* and they are figured through *"Nebuchadnezzars* Image" on its penultimate plate, an image that must be broken before the marriage state can be achieved. If Milton thought that the marriage of truth would not occur until the Apocalypse, Blake thought the Apocalypse would not occur until such a marriage had been accomplished; and that state could not be achieved until what Milton calls the "third existence," and Blake the "negation," had been destroyed. There are subtle distinctions to be made between Blake and Milton, but on the matter of contraries both poets are in complete accord.

There is no place in the Gospel, according to *The Reason of Church-Government,* which insists upon annihilating sects and parties, not even "in those places where dissention was most rife" (*Yale Milton,* I, 780). To destroy factions, to annihilate contraries, Milton concludes, is to bring "all the diameters of schisme" together and to "knit [them] up in the center of one grand falshood" (I, 783); their abolition by Prelaty, or by what Blake would call the party of the angels, "is the very disease we groan under; and never can be to us a remedy but by removing it selfe" (I, 791). Prelaty, in short, is the negation that must be destroyed to redeem the contraries; and though Blake does not articulate the concept of a negation in *The Marriage of Heaven and Hell,* he clearly understood it, and only through it can we comprehend the triumph over the angel that occurs at the end of his prophecy—a triumph that instead of refuting the doctrine of contraries insures its survival.

That the idea of "party" should figure as prominently as it does in *The Marriage of Heaven and Hell* is not surprising when we remember that Milton's own doctrine of contraries is prefaced, in *The Reason of Church-Government,* with the observation that sects and schisms are "the throws and pangs that go before the birth of reformation" (*Yale Milton,* I, 795) and followed by the reminder that "Tis not rebellion that ought to be the hindrance of reformation, but it is the want of this which is the cause of that" (I, 798). It is "rebellion," the attendant strife of contraries, that in Milton's pamphlet and Blake's prophecy push "reformation . . . forward with all possible diligence and speed" (I, 800).

It is not just Blake's general conception of contraries that we find elucidated in Milton, but its particulars as well. Milton defines Blake's contraries of love and hate, formulated on plate 3 of *The Marriage of Heaven and Hell*, in *The Doctrine and Discipline of Divorce*, explaining that he means "not that Hate that sins, but that which onely is naturall dissatisfaction and the turning aside from a mistaken object" (*Yale Milton*, II, 253). Hate, elsewhere in the same work, is "the mightiest divider" (II, 345) but, in this context, is a natural aversion, not a negation, though Milton comprehends that "two contraries" can meet "their own destruction" through "a third existence . . . or some evil Angel which wreaks havoc in *marriages* and in the world." The "third existence," he concludes, is the cause of "jarre and discord that end in rancor and strife"; it is not a contrary, but an "opposite both to marriage and to Christianitie" (II, 280).

That Blake observed a similar distinction between contraries and what opposes them is shown on the design to plate 30 of *Milton*, which carries the inscription, "Contraries are Positives/A Negation is not a contrary." This distinction Blake confronted, even before writing *The Marriage of Heaven and Hell*, among Lavater's aphorisms, in the contention that "there are but three classes of men—the retrograde, the stationary, the progressive";[139] and Blake himself implies a comparable distinction in his *Annotations to Lavater*, explaining that "Vice . . . is a Negative" not always corresponding with "what the laws of Kings & Priests have calld Vice," that "the hindering of act in another . . . is Vice but all Act [< *from Individual propensity* >] is Virtue," and concluding that "whatever is Negative is Vice" (p. 590). What the Angel at the end of *The Marriage of Heaven and Hell* relinquishes, then, is not the positive but the negative in the Christian vision; he relinquishes not action but all that impedes action and thus enables the struggle of contraries to resume. The strategy of this work is clarified by the epigraph to *The Four Zoas*, where, quoting Ephesians, Blake says that our contention is with the spirit of evil in things heavenly (I, p. 3). As Jackie DiSalvo argues, Blake translates this biblical text into "his own dialectical vision in his prophecies, where he asserts that it is false consciousness, religious 'Mystery' and the 'spirit of evil in things heavenly' " that beg for elimination.[140] These are the impediments to progress and vision that are cast off by the Angel when on plate 24 he joins with Blake's Devil.

The strategy of *The Marriage of Heaven and Hell* is also elucidated by Harold Bloom's discussion of Blake's three classes of men—the reprobate, the redeemed, and the elect. The first are "avatars of prophetic tradition," like Rintrah and the objective voice of plate 3 or like the Milton of the early prose tracts and *Paradise Regained;* the second are struggling, like the Milton of *Paradise Lost,* for redemption. The redeemed—"a cultural battleground on which the prophets and the upholders of a repressive society meet in combat"—are, in terms of *The Marriage of Heaven and Hell,* the *I* who has cast aside the negative aspects of Christianity and the Angel who makes the same gesture by the end of the poem, as well as the audience, which is expected to undergo the same conversion in the course of reading the prophecy, casting off the trappings of orthodoxy just as the *I* persona casts off Swedenborg and the "election" he symbolizes. The redeemed, however, are not only those who have sided with the elect but those of the Devil's party, who also stand in need of redemption. When, as Bloom explains, "the Redeemed embrace the Reprobate, then contraries meet, and progression takes place."[141] This struggle is central to the prophet's experience: like Blake and Milton, all potential prophets must divest themselves of their electness, symbolized in *The Marriage of Heaven and Hell* by Swedenborg: but those of the Devil's party must similarly come to share in the perspective of the redeemed. Because *The Marriage of Heaven and Hell* is addressed primarily to one "party," it emphasizes the perspective of that party over all others. That this prophecy is designed to convert those of one party should not obscure the fact that those of the other party, like the Devil, also require redemption; they too must be involved in the mental expansion produced by struggling contraries. Blake's Devil may be more enlightened than his Angel; but he never exhibits the enlightenment characteristic of the true visionary.

Despite such observations as "Active Evil is better than Passive

Good" in *Annotations to Lavater* (p. 581) and "Good & Evil are here both Good & the two contraries Married" among the *Annotations to Swedenborg* (p. 594), we can conclude that it is not Blake's reading of Lavater and Swedenborg but his reading of Milton that inspired and influenced his prophecy. Milton contends in *The Doctrine and Discipline of Divorce* that "Excesse [is] cur'd by contrary excesse" (*Yale Milton,* II, 281), thus providing Blake with the master-theme of the proverbs of hell: excess, not prudence, leads to the palace of wisdom. And from Milton's insistence in *Areopagitica* that "truth separated from truth . . . is the fiercest rent and disunion of all" (II, 564), Blake derives the basic supposition of his entire prophecy: the necessary marriage of the fragmented truths represented by Devil and Angel alike. Moreover, *The Reason of Church-Government,* supplying Blake with a complex of themes, also provides a strategy for developing them.

The reader is "a central figure" in the plot of both Milton's pamphlet and Blake's prophecy, whose common purpose is to inspire an audience to "exchange one way of knowing for another,"[142] forcing it to take a place in "one of two categories, [with] those who have recourse to reason" or with "those who do not"[143] or, in terms of Blake's *The Marriage of Heaven and Hell,* with those who apprehend truth discursively, *reasonably,* like the Angel, or with those who apprehend it intuitively, *energetically,* like the Devil. Both Milton's pamphlet and Blake's prophecy employ the same strategy—"the devaluing of . . . reason"—pushing the reader to "the very center of the 'action,'" poising him "somewhat uneasily between the contending parties, [and] their modes of apprehension."[144] The hierarchy of values that emerges from both works develops in terms of a dichotomy between reason and the energy to produce vision, a vision that should place the reader on the side of those who see with "illumined eyes" and against those who see with "the worldly machinery" of reason.[145] Both works, then, move toward discrediting reason and celebrating vision. This strategy, in turn, conditions the structure or structures of both works.

What Stanley Fish says about *The Reason of Church-Government* pertains equally to *The Marriage of Heaven and Hell:*

In effect, *The Reason of Church Government* has two structures . . . : an outer structure that promises rational argument, progressive clarification, and encapsulated knowledge; and an inner structure whose points are made at the expense of the other's promises. . . . The structure or structures of the tract reflect exactly . . . the minds of the two classes of readers to whom Milton continually refers, one in bondage to the fleshly world and therefore to reason and prelacy, the other illumined . . . [as is] the poet-speaker himself. It is to the latter reader that the radical unity of the piece . . . is at once apparent.[146]

Blake's prophecy, like Milton's pamphlet, has all the hallmarks of reason and order, concepts reinforced by the theme of satire that pervades the work and by the strict organization evident on its surface. Its initial argument is developed by the voice of the Devil, by the proverbs of hell, and by the amplifications of each of the memorable fancies.

But this outer, mechanical structure is opposed to and finally subdued by the inner, living form of prophecy which forges the work's "radical unity." *The Marriage of Heaven and Hell* reveals the same progress evident in *The Reason of Church-Government*— a progress given precise definition by Fish in his further comments on Milton's pamphlet:

Its true medium . . . is the reader's consciousness. I return . . . to the idea of a progress . . . : not, of course, to the "ratiocinative progress" . . . but to a progressive enlargement of understanding. . . . the reader who negotiates these . . . pages is not following an argument. . . . The reader proceeds in space and time and from point to point, but always to find the same unchanging essences . . . shining through their local manifestations. . . . The reader may be getting nowhere, but from the vantage point provided by his enlarged understanding, nowhere is equivalent to everywhere.[147]

Blake's reader, like Milton's, is fixed in the same place; but in the very act of being immobilized, of being made several times to confront the same materials, his ability to evaluate, to comprehend, them changes, until what was obscure bursts into the clarity of Blake's final vision, which is succeeded by "A Song of Liberty," prognosticating a universal liberty achieved by the liberated consciousness, a consciousness produced by the experience of prophecy itself.

Finally, Blake has derived the focus for his own prophecy from Milton's prose works collectively. Repeatedly, Milton's pamphlets develop around the opposition between the true and false prophet; the latter must be mocked, says Milton in *An Apology for Smectymnuus,* in order "to teach and instruct the . . . misledde people"

(*Yale Milton,* I, 903); the true prophets must employ the devices of satire and irony in order "*to rip up the wounds* of Idolatry and Superstition" (I, 903). At a loss until it is able to discover the true prophets and to be wary of the false prophets (I, 931), civilization depends on its visionaries to make this discrimination, which explains why, in *The Marriage of Heaven and Hell,* the ability to detect the false prophet is rendered as a primary theme.

Blake's criticism of Milton—of the Milton who wrote *Paradise Lost*—is in *The Marriage of Heaven and Hell* set within a framework of allusion to Milton's prose works. The resonances of these allusions qualify the criticism leveled against the poet by Blake's Devil. His criticism, we should remember, has qualifications imposed on it by the larger context of this prophecy, which in turn imposes qualifications on the conventional belief that Blake "writes the *Marriage,* as he was later to write *Milton,* to rectify the errors of a thinker he loves, whose influence upon him is immense." [148] The influence of Milton on Blake is indisputable, and so is Blake's admiration for Milton. In *The Marriage of Heaven and Hell,* Blake focuses on the Milton who in *Paradise Lost* sometimes stands in the posture of error; but Milton did not always write from a posture of error, as both his early prose tracts and *Paradise Regained* testify—works invoked by the context of allusion built up around plates 5 and 6 of Blake's prophecy. [149]

As we turn to plates 5 and 6 of *The Marriage of Heaven and Hell,* we should also remember that the words spoken here are assigned to the Devil and that they constitute a commentary upon the philosophical abstractions of the preceding plate. The commentary, specifying the errors of "All Bibles and sacred codes" as they emerge in *Paradise Lost,* holds those errors responsible for the failings of Milton's vision:

> Those who restrain desire, do so because theirs is weak enough to be restrained; and the restrainer or reason usurps its place & governs the unwilling.
> And being restrained it by degrees becomes passive till it is only the shadow of desire.
> The history of this is written in Paradise Lost. & the Governor or Reason is call'd Messiah.
> And the original Archangel or possessor of the command of the heavenly host, is calld the Devil or Satan and his children are call'd Sin & Death.

But in the Book of Job Miltons Messiah is call'd Satan.

For this history has been adopted by both parties.

It indeed appear'd to Reason as if Desire was cast out, but the Devils account is, that the Messiah fell. & formed a heaven of what he stole from the Abyss.

This is shewn in the Gospel, where he prays to the Father to send the comforter or Desire that Reason may have Ideas to build on, the Jehovah of the Bible being no other than he, who dwells in flaming fire. Know that after Christs death, he became Jehovah.

But in Milton; the Father is Destiny, the Son, a Ratio of the five senses. & the Holy-ghost, Vacuum!

Note. The reason Milton wrote in fetters when he wrote of Angels & God, and at liberty when of Devils & Hell, is because he was a true Poet and of the Devils party without knowing it [.]

The first point to make about this critique is that Blake does not misunderstand Milton, even if his predecessors and his Devil do.

There is some distortion both in the Devil's argument and in his commentary on it. The context for the argument is sharply delineated:

All Bibles or sacred codes. have been the causes of the following Errors.

1. That Man has two real existing principles Viz: a Body & a Soul.

2. That Energy. calld Evil. is alone from the Body. & that Reason. calld Good. is alone from the Soul.

3. That God will torment Man in Eternity for following his Energies.

(plate 4)

Yet this context is distorted, and its distortions are nicely focused by Abraham Heschel, who writes:

The Bible knows neither the dichotomy of body and soul nor the trichotomy of body, soul, and spirit . . . It sets up no hierarchy in the inner life, nor does it tend to compartmentalize the soul. . . . To put it in different terms: the mind is not a member apart, but is itself transformed into passion. For the two "do not dwell separate and distinct, but passion and reason are only the transfiguration of the mind toward the better or the worse." Nor does the Bible share the view that passions are disturbances or weaknesses of the soul, and much less the premise that passion itself is evil, that passion itself is incompatible with right thinking or right living.[150]

Milton and Blake knew this, but Blake's Devil does not.

The Devil's argument is solid:

But the following Contraries to these are True

1 Man has no Body distinct from his Soul for that calld Body is a portion of Soul discernd by the five Senses, the chief inlets of Soul in this age

2 Energy is the only life and is from the Body and Reason is the bound or outward circumfernce of Energy.
3 Energy is Eternal Delight [.]

(plate 4)

Not the argument, but the context within which it is offered, distorts the Angel's (orthodoxy's) point of view. Christianity, traditionally, asserted the neutrality, not the evilness, of the body, though some sects, notably the Puritans, moved in the direction the Devil suggests, giving to his perspective a measure of validity but not redeeming it from partiality. Moreover, there is the insinuation here that Milton conforms to orthodox lines as the Devil draws them, when, in fact, Milton in *Tetrachordon* assaults the Gnostics for their "little reading, and lesse meditating" (II, 579), arguing here as elsewhere against their position that the body is evil, and that hence desire and energy are evil.[151] Milton acknowledges the delights of the body as openly as Blake does and, in *Paradise Lost,* revolutionizes the story of the fall by introducing sexuality, approvingly, to the garden before the fall occurs.[152] In this sense, then, the Devil's critique is misleading, and it has also proved misleading by inviting the inference that Satan is Milton's hero. Whatever else these plates may say, they do not say that Satan is the hero of *Paradise Lost.* This is a misreading of Milton for which some eighteenth-century commentators and some modern ones must be held accountable; it is a misreading of Blake for which some in the Milton establishment are responsible.[153]

Blake's criticism of Milton is double-edged. On the one hand, it is straightforward and involves the aesthetics of Milton's poem. Reason and its bedfellow theology, in *Paradise Lost,* repress energy and depress vision, with the result that the early books are a triumph of imagination, while the last ones represent a failure of it. Such criticism is commonplace in the eighteenth century, different not in kind but only in degree from Thomas Newton's famous observation:

The reader may have observed that these last two books fall short of the sublimity and majesty of the rest; and so likewise do the two last books of the Iliad, and for the same reason, because the subject is of a different kind from that of the foregoing ones. The subject of these two last books of the Paradise Lost is history rather than poetry. However we may still discover the same great genius, and there are intermix'd as many ornaments and graces of poetry, as the nature of the subject, and the author's fidelity and strict attachment to the truth of Scripture history, and the reduction of so many and such various events into so narrow a compass, would admit. It is the same ocean, but not at its highest tide; it is now ebbing and retreating. It is the same sun, but not in the full blaze of meridian glory; it now shines with a gentler ray as it is setting.[154]

On the other hand, Blake's criticism is ironic and attacks the theology of Milton's poem.

The first interpretive problem arises in the line, "But in the Book of Job Miltons Messiah is call'd Satan." That is, Christ in *Paradise Lost* is present only in his divine aspect and serves as an instrument of God for inflicting pain and suffering; he participates in the horror of Christianity from which, in his human aspect, he will liberate himself and mankind. The Christ of *Paradise Lost* and the Satan of the Book of Job perform identical roles, are manifestations of the same deity, are in each instance administers of punishment. For this reason, the Devil identifies Christ and Satan, confident that his history is acceptable to "both parties." In the sense that Satan in the Book of Job is not yet an "evil" being (but a messenger of the Lord for testing the obedience of man), that Christ performs similar roles in *Paradise Lost* and is said, too, to have worked through Old Testament heroes—in this sense, "both parties" can agree on the identification.[155] The next statement is even more enigmatic, "It indeed appear'd . . . " The reference is to the routing of the rebel angels in the sixth book of Milton's epic—an event that involves separation of the Father and the Son, reason from energy; and this separation precipitates division in the deity, the fall of both its members. Thus when Satan, the reservoir of divine energy, is expelled, Godhead falls, and Christ loses his energy, becoming a "ratio of the five senses," a reasoning circumference rather than a center of energy. Reason divorced from energy is impotent, and energy by itself is formless. The fallen perspectives related to these interpretations and represented in *The Marriage of Heaven and Hell* by the Devil and the Angel are limiting, for each of them now exists apart from the other and each has become identified with a "party."

The Devil's next observation is more enigmatic still: "Know that after Christs death, he became Jehovah." Here the Devil simply inverts the history to which Blake elsewhere subscribes. Christ undergoes Incarnation, journeys into the desert, to redeem the energy of which he has been emptied. He emerges a perfectly integrated personality, having cast aside the law of obedience for the gospel of love. After his death, he does indeed return to the Father; and the Father becomes like the Son rather than the Son's becoming like him: the God of Wrath, Jehovah, becomes a God of Mercy, Jesus. This is the history of God from an eternal perspective, but from another perspective this history has been inverted: God continues to be conceptualized as an angry, vengeful deity and Christ, identified with him, has anger and vengeance imposed on his own character. This is the distorted view of history and the one the Devil expresses. The Devil, in other words, advances his critique from the perspective of history rather than eternity; and consequently what he says is historically, but not eternally, true. This distinction, drawn by Blake himself, is also recognized by Hazard Adams when he says that to crucify Christ upside down "means that Blake believes the historical development of Christianity has been toward the reassumption of an all-surrounding . . . abstract moral law. Thus the historical Christ of the modern church is the upside-down man, while the upright Christ is the perpetually immediate visionary act."[156]

The Devil's short critique terminates with a Note, the conclusion of which is "true" only in an ironic sense. Milton, in poems like *Comus* and *Paradise Lost,* exhibits a distorted vision that aligns him with the Devil's perspective from which the inference of the Note is drawn. The voice of the Devil is not "the voice of the whole man";[157] to say that it is, is to confuse the voice of the Devil with Blake's own, forgetting that Blake's Devil is "a partisan spokesman telling partisan truth . . . [that] is incomplete."[158] The Note focuses the partiality of the Devil's vision, which on the one hand is brilliantly penetrating and on the other intriguingly mistaken. At this point it is useful to recall a remark by Shelley from which Blake, one feels, would have demurred.

Shelley writes that "the poetry of Dante may be considered as the bridge thrown over the stream of time, which unites the modern and antient World. The distorted notions of invisible things which Dante and his rival Milton idealised," says Shelley, "are merely the mask and the mantle in which these great poets walk through eternity enveloped and disguised. It is a difficult question to determine how far they were conscious of the distinction which must have subsisted in their minds between their own creeds and that of the people."[159] Both Dante and Milton, as Blake understood them, were conscious of what they wrote; the difference between them is that Dante codifies the reigning system of belief, is consciously conservative in his ideology, whereas Milton, attempting to replace specious orthodoxies with a new system of values, is openly revolutionary in his posture. Blake, like Shelley, perceived that *Paradise Lost* "contains within itself a philosophical refutation of that system, of which, by a strange and natural antithesis, it has been a chief popular support."[160] But unlike Shelley, Blake would not have countenanced Socrates' claim that "Poets & Prophets do not know what they write or Utter"; this belief, says Blake, in *A Vision of the Last Judgment,* "is a most Pernicious Falshood" (p. 544). Milton, in short, was consciously of the Devil's party, openly and unashamedly a revolutionary, though he was not always conscious of the failings in vision that his own unintegrated personality introduced into his epic. When Milton became conscious of his failings, however, he eliminated them, creating the purely visionary work of *Paradise Regained.*

Blake's Devil always speaks forthrightly; but sometimes, as here, he speaks from a partisan point of view and thus as mistakenly as the angels whom he is assailing. Milton repeatedly warned against confusing the voice of a persona with the voice of a poet. In *An Apology for Smectymnuus,* he wrote, "the author is ever distinguisht from the person he introduces" (*Yale Milton,* I, 880). Blake clearly shared this sentiment; for in an annotation to Swedenborg's *A Treatise Concerning Heaven and Hell,* he wrote, "Thus fools quote Shakespeare: The Above is Theseus's opinion Not Shakespeares. You might as well quote Satans blasphemies from Milton & give them as Miltons Opinions" (p. 590).

In *The Marriage of Heaven and Hell,* Blake's Devil distinguishes between Milton's conscious and unconscious meanings at the same time that he calls Milton "a true Poet." Therein lies one of his errors; for, from Blake's point of view, a true poet, who is also a prophet, knows and understands what he says. There is, nevertheless, an element of truth in what the Devil says; and even if the Devil himself does not perceive that truth, Blake does. When the

Devil identifies Milton with "the Devil's party" he employs a commonplace of political rhetoric—a favorite device of the Puritan revolutionaries and their adversaries. As Christopher Hill explains, the phrase is part of "the old vocabulary of abuse,"[161] its history being a story of transference. During the Civil War, the royalists represented "the devil's party"—a phrase that after 1660 was appropriated by the royalists themselves and deployed against the revolutionaries.[162]   Moreover, the appellation has a history of association with Milton. Salmasius identified Milton with the diabolical party, and Milton employed the same tactic in attacking Alexander More. After the Restoration, it became increasingly dangerous to associate either the powers of state or religious institutions with the devil; but it was common enough for conservative forces, both during the Restoration and throughout the eighteenth century, to employ that rhetorical weapon in dealing with political radicals and religious dissenters. Indeed, Blake's Devil is not the first eighteenth-century "critic" to apply the label to Milton; nor is Blake the first writer of the age to make polemical use of the voice of the Devil.

   In defending Milton as the hero of political radicalism, as the creator of "the *mode* of the Revolution, as well as the *principles* of it" that then pertained, Thomas Hollis printed two answers to criticism of *Paradise Lost* from the *London Chronicle,* both of which establish that by 1764 it was a cliché to refer to the Whigs, or the republicans, as belonging to "the party" of the devils or the "diabolical party."[163]   When Blake's Devil adopts this vocabulary and introduces it into his critique of Milton, he is, in effect, transforming a rhetoric of abuse into a rhetoric of praise. A term of disapprobation becomes here a term of praise, and it imparts a dimension to the Note on plate 6 that is seldom observed: to say that Milton is of "the devil's party" is to say that he is both a political radical and a religious dissenter. In both capacities, Milton held Blake's unflagging admiration. In this connection, one should also notice that during the 1780's Charles Dibdin published a weekly periodical called *The Devil,* the first number posing the question, "Can the Devil speak truth?"—a question informing the revolutionary perspective of *The Marriage of Heaven and Hell.* And so, too, does the answer provided for this question: the Devil's way, we are advised, is to turn the world upside down; here the same dichotomy is drawn between Devil and Angel, and because Devil and Angel alike subscribe to party principles both are said to represent partial perspectives.[164] Dibdin's objective, like Blake's, is to find truth that transcends the partiality of party affiliation.

Blake is a supreme ironist, engaged in *The Marriage of Heaven and Hell* in the same kind of ironic play that Milton engaged in with Satan. When Satan says in *Paradise Lost* that "The mind is its own place, and in it self/Can make a Heav'n of Hell, a Hell of Heav'n" (I. 254–55), he articulates sentiments with which Milton himself can agree. The irony lies in the fact that what is true from the human perspective is not true from a demonic one, just as what the Devil says in *The Marriage of Heaven and Hell* may be true from the perspective of history, but it is not true from the perspective of eternity that the prophet enjoys. The irony in the remark made by Blake's Devil lies in the fact that Blake, in possession of a larger consciousness and thus aware of subtleties that his devil does not perceive, has him use a term of abuse and apply that term approvingly to Milton. In this sense, the Devil is to Blake what Milton's Beelzebub is to Satan and what Satan sometimes is to Milton—a spokesman who never exhibits the same largeness of mind as the figure with whom he is identified. When, echoing the vocabulary of Milton's Beelzebub in *Paradise Lost* (II. 368), the Devil says that Milton was of "the Devil's party," he points to precisely those qualities (sublimity, majesty, and energy) which both Milton and Blake could admire if they were invested in a "moral" character. In *Paradise Regained* they are; in *Paradise Lost,* they are not; and thus Satan, whom Blake will later represent as Milton's spectre, his selfhood, must be repudiated. At the same time, Blake's Devil, without knowing it, makes a statement with which Blake can agree, so long as we read "knowing" where the Devil says "without knowing it."[165] To associate Milton with "the Devil's party" is to acknowledge, from Blake's point of view, precisely what the Devil seems to deny: that Milton was consciously radical in his politics and in his theology, a view that makes a great deal of sense when we return the Devil's quip to the larger context of *The Marriage of Heaven and Hell* and read it in terms of the rhetorical strategy that Blake here employs.

The Marriage of Heaven and Hell is cast in the form of prophecy.

It is about the formation of the prophetic character, and it is structured around the opposition between the true prophet and the false prophet—an opposition exploited by Milton himself in his most abusive political pamphlets. It also takes its argument of contraries, its themes of spiritual perception and apocalypse, and its purpose of transforming an entire civilization into a nation of visionaries from Milton's early prose works. To perceive the Miltonic context Blake gives to *The Marriage of Heaven and Hell* is the first step toward understanding his rhetorical strategy. Milton's vision may have failed him in *Paradise Lost,* but not so completely as the Devil suggests and not in quite the sense he means. The pattern of Milton's life, as we have already observed, provided Blake with a neat contrast to the pattern of Swedenborg's: whereas Swedenborg established a sect, subverting the revolutionary character of his early thought and embracing the Calvinistic notion of predestination that Blake so deplored, Milton moved steadily away from institutionalized religion, in *Paradise Lost* casting off Calvin's odious doctrine and in *Paradise Regained* formulating a radically new version of Christinaity. When this pattern of opposition is discerned, we see Blake's Milton emerging from *The Marriage of Heaven and Hell* not as a target of ridicule but as a type of the true prophet—the true prophets belonging to no "party."

Herein lies the final irony of the Devil's commentary, which is there, in *The Marriage of Heaven and Hell,* as a statement on the philosophy of union that the Devil expounds, a philosophy that *Paradise Lost* is said to disregard. It turns out, however, that the political divisions and consequent partisan perspective represented by the Devil are just another manifestation of the philosophical opposition between body and soul that institutionalized Christianity is said to espouse and that *Paradise Lost* is accused of supporting. Finally, what we can perceive from the eternal perspective that Blake's Devil does not share with the poet is that Swedenborg, whatever his ideological leanings, was always a "party" man—a "turncoat," to be sure, who moved from the radical left to the conservative right. Milton, on the other hand, reversed the pattern. *Paradise Lost,* Blake knew, was a flawed poem, but not a regressive one: the poem is fundamentally a radical, not a reactionary, document, though it contains some failings of vision that may be regarded as vestigial traces of earlier orthodox leanings. *Paradise Lost,* like *Comus,* is a poem divided by contradictions,[166] obfuscated by orthodoxies, that Milton transcends in *Paradise Regained.* There the personality has become integrated, divisions are bridged: the poet achieves the unity of being that enables him to step into the divine vision and to translate it exactly.

Blake's understanding of Milton's intellectual development distinguishes him from those who believe that Milton "does not belong with those broadly human . . . artists, who reflect . . . every phase of life . . . but with the intense, austere and lofty souls whose narrowness is likewise their strength," from those who believe that Milton's place "is beside Dante, the Catholic Puritan."[167] Blake sees in Milton's poetry multiple reflections of Renaissance life—its hopes, ideals, values, and beliefs—and invites us to consider what Milton's attitude is toward those aspects of Renaissance culture. As a critic of Milton, Blake represents the Shelleyan ideal of the commentator who is "impanelled by Time from the selectest of the wise of many generations."[168] Committed not to representing the already formed opinion of mankind as it relates to Milton but to asserting an understanding of his own that will shape a new understanding of the poet, Blake exposes the visionary dimensions of Milton's art, thus taking his place in the company of those enlightened commentators who by the time of Blake's death were proclaiming:

His [Milton's] mind was too independent and universal to narrow itself to human creeds and parties. He is supposed to have separated himself in his last years from all the denominations around him. . . . He would probably stand first [today] among that class of Christians . . . who are too jealous of the rights of the mind, and too dissatisfied with the clashing systems of the age, to attach themselves closely to any party; in whom the present improved state of theology has created a consciousness of defect, rather than the triumph of acquisition. . . . we should rejoice in such a manifestation of Christianity, as would throw all present systems into obscurity.[169]

Blake would have agreed with Wordsworth's claim that Milton "was like a Star, who dwelt apart"[170] so long as it was understood that Milton was not out of touch with his age, with its artistic traditions and philosophical predispositions, but, acknowledging them, working through them, managed at the same time to transcend them. Milton, Blake understood, borrowed from other poets; but his poems were formed not from borrowings but from "the sublime patterns of his own mind";[171] engaging constantly in dialogue with the "parties" of his own time, he became "more and more of a radical idealist—a revolutionist without a party."[172] Milton was, like Blake, a prophet; and with Blake and other students of prophecy he believed that the spirit of prophecy, "addicted to no one Sect, or Party, among men," reveals itself to be "a common Father to all."[173]

If on occasion, as in *Comus* and *Paradise Lost,* Milton's mind was confined by orthodoxy, it was finally, when he wrote *Paradise Regained,* freed from it. In *Paradise Lost,* Milton may have assumed the form of a slave, he may have suffered under, even while reflecting, the tyrannical orthodoxies of his own time; but Blake would ultimately say of Milton what Milton in *Pro Populo Anglicano Defensio* said of Christ: "he never failed to preserve the heart of a liberator" (*Yale Milton,* IV, i, 375). Indeed, by his slavery and suffering, Milton, like his Christ, tried to win all proper freedoms; like his Christ, Milton was the champion of political freedom, the great political prophet of the modern world. Finally, there is no better guide to Blake's idea of Milton than Milton's idea of himself—the self-portrait of *Defensio Secunda,* which presents the poet as "the focal point of the world's struggle for freedom,"[174] as the hero of political radicalism and religious dissent, the deliverer who projects the morning beam of reformation that will bring the nation into freedom. Milton possessed the spiritual eye of the true discerner and tried, as Blake tried in *The Marriage of Heaven and Hell,* to make his eye the eye through which the rest of the world might see. When that eye is opened in the populace— and it was to open that eye that Milton wrote *The Reason of Church-Government* and Blake wrote *The Marriage of Heaven and Hell*—the kingdom will be at hand and the people will be "standing at the dore": then, as Milton says in *Animadversions,* the voice of the Bride may call them, then will "all creatures sigh to bee renew'd" (I, 707). That is the Milton whom Blake celebrates as the Awakener in his brief epic and the Milton who created the tradition of poetry which Blake embraces and of which he was the first, and is still the most brilliant, exponent.

Milton, it has been suggested by Harold Bloom, was "a colossal Covering Cherub, who prevented the Romantics from certain achievements."[175]   The contrary is true. From Milton, Blake learned not to be contained by tradition but to achieve freedom through it. Thus Milton, who initially seemed a burden to the poet, became his liberator—the liberator not of Blake only but of all the poets who are generally subsumed under the rubric of "the Romantics." But Bloom's thesis, recently elaborated into an expansive statement on the Blake and Milton relationship, requires our final attention and then our disavowal.

"Forward Thro' Eternity"

Clear the eyes of the mind from all dusts of earth; leave the tumults of crowds and the clamour of words; follow the angel in spirit into the desert; ascend with the same angel into the great and high mountain; there you will behold high truths hidden from the beginning of time and from all generations. . . . For we, called in these latest times to follow the spirit rather than the letter, ought to obey, going from illumination to illumination, from the first heaven to the second, and from the second to the third, from the place of darkness into the light of the moon, that at last we may come out of the moonlight into the glory of the full Sun.

—Joachim of Fiore

EVEN BEFORE Blake's *Milton* was printed, the importance of Milton to Blake was asserted by Benjamin Malkin, who wrote that not only the Book of Revelation but Milton "may well be supposed to engross much of Mr. Blake's study."[1] The literary relationship was not attended to until this century, when those who recognized the knit of identity between Milton and Blake were quickly countered by those who preferred to stress their differences. Denis Saurat has explored the biographical parallels that associate the two poets; and Northrop Frye, the literary patterns uniting them.[2] More recently, Jackie DiSalvo has taken us to a different vantage point, identifying the ideological divisions that distinguish Blake from Milton.[3] DiSalvo's dissociation by politics has become, under the aegis of Harold Bloom, dissociation by psychology: a cocksure Milton is set against an anxiety-ridden William Blake.[4]

The burdens of the past, the anxieties of influence, according to

Bloom, were not felt by Shakespeare or Milton but represent a phenomenon belonging to "the cosmos of the greatest post-Miltonic poets."[5] These later "Satanic" poets responded to their precursors—*as Blake responded to Milton*, we are told—by deliberately "misreading" so as "to clear imaginative space" for themselves. This line of argument winds into Bloom's thesis:

> *Poetic Influence—when it involves two strong, authentic poets,—always proceeds by a misreading of the prior poet, an act of creative correction that is actually and necessarily a misinterpretation. The history of fruitful poetic influence, which is to say the main tradition of Western poetry since the Renaissance, is a history of anxiety and self-saving caricature, of distortion, of perverse, wilful revisionism without which modern poetry as such could not exist.*[6]

By way of introducing this assertion, Bloom bows to Blake, from whom he claims to derive his theory and to whom he turns for its clarification and verification: "Blake . . . remains the most profound and original theorist of revisionism . . . and an inevitable aid in the development of a new theory of Poetic Influence."[7] Haunted by the spectre of Milton, father of the "ruminative line" of English poetry and "the central problem in any theory and history of poetic influence in English," Blake repudiated his mentor in order to join "the visionary and prophetic line" of poetry, which runs "from the relative mildness of Spenser's temperament down through the various fiercenesses of Blake, Shelley, Browning, Whitman, and Yeats."[8] In releasing himself from Milton, Bloom continues, Blake ceased to be a "victim" and became a "poet"; in the process, he engaged in fierce, brazen, but "creative," misinterpretation of his mentor, the purpose of which was to let Blake assert his own integrity, his own uniqueness.

Bloom, I think, is wrong,[9] though we should concede immediately that Blake provides ample evidence to make it *appear* that Bloom is right. There is the spirit of contention with which Blake approaches most of the poets he illustrates, as well as his open avowal, cited by Bloom, that he must create his own system rather than be enslaved by another man's, coupled with his practice of invoking traditions only to use them against themselves. But over and against this evidence, there is the relationship Blake assumes with Milton, together with the obvious fact, lost to Bloom but not to Blake, that the tactics of subversion Blake employs are not his invention but Milton's.

A THEORY OF INFLUENCE

Comprehension of the Blake-Milton relationship, as we have seen, depends upon the critic's ability to distinguish that relationship from Blake's relationships with other poets. The posture that Blake strikes in relation to Homer, Vergil, Dante, Young, Blair, and Gray is different from the one he assumes toward Milton. The commentary required by a true prophet involves, for the most part, elucidation; that required by false prophets entails more: their "visions," demonic parodies of true revelation, must be turned on end, must be radically revised, so much so that the new prophet will, most of the time, be reversing the "visions" of the false prophet. Yet in this activity, the new prophet is not an abuser of another's vision but a disabuser of the distortions it contains. An analogy employed by Bloom provides the quickest refutation of his own argument. The opposing aspects of poetic influence, says Bloom, may be symbolized by the negative image of "the flowing in of an occult power exercised by humans . . . upon humans" or by the positive image of "stars [operating] upon humans."[10] Given these terms, it is noteworthy that when Blake chooses in *Milton* to verbalize, even to pictorialize, his relationship with his hero he chooses the image of a star (see, e.g., fig. 14; also 15:47–50)—chooses it fully conscious of one commonplace of prophetic literature: "Stars are ministers not masters";[11] rather than darkening the prophet's vision they cast light upon it. The proof text is found in the Book of Revelation, where Christ appears as the morning star because "he illuminates mens wils and understandings," he gives to men "perfect illumination and lightning."[12] Blake's point is that Christ revived revelation rather than caused its cessation, and the last poet to possess it was Milton; hence Blake's willingness to subject himself to Milton's influence in full sympathy with the prophetic dictum that the precursor, even if mistaken, is not an oppressor but a liberator, that, as John Smith puts it, "under the beams of the greater," the prophet submits to his "irradiations and influence."[13] Deeply rooted in

prophetic tradition, then, there may be found a theory—a psychology—of influence that is contrary to the one formulated by
Bloom; in terms of this tradition, Bloom's theory, insofar as it is
founded on Blake's encounters with Milton, may be put to rest.

Some poets have doubtless responded to tradition as scoffingly
as did Wallace Stevens: " . . . I am not conscious of having been
influenced by anybody and have purposely held off from reading
highly mannered people like Eliot and Pound so that I should not
absorb anything, even unconsciously."[14] But there are other
poets, Blake among them, who responded to tradition as Ralph
Waldo Emerson did: "Every book is a quotation; and every house
is a quotation out of all forests and mines and stone quarries; and
every man is a quotation from all his ancestors."[15] Versed in
prophetic tradition as he was, Emerson might have added that
every new prophecy is a quotation out of all previous prophecy.
Such an observation, in any event, takes us to the very heart of a
tradition founded on the belief that prophecy is "Inter-Connected
and Progressive" in character.[16] The principles governing prophetic tradition are much like those governing epic tradition,
especially as they are defined by W. F. Jackson Knight when he
explains that "Homeric poets" subscribe to the belief that the
artist should take over as much as possible from his predecessors.
There is, however, a paradox attendant upon such a belief: the
artist who embraces it "appears to retain and compress the power
of the old," but also produces something new, "which can be very
new, and quite unrecognizable, because there have been so many
alterations to the old material which is still richly retained."[17]
Even if Blake might be reluctant to identify himself with a
tradition of "Homeric poets," he would be willing, one feels, to
preserve Knight's concept under the rubric of "Miltonic poets." In
all Blake's art, verbal and pictorial, a principle of integration is
operative, Blake seeing himself as a great consolidator (see *Jerusalem,* plate 3) and setting himself, most emphatically, within the
tradition of Milton. Blake's works contain frequent quotations
from Milton's own, those quotations coagulating within a work to
provide its context.

However similar epic and prophetic poetry may be with respect
to design, they differ decidedly in terms of what motivates the
design: for the epic poet, poetic integration is a device for mem-

ory; for the prophetic poet, it is a device of inspiration. A chain with many links, prophecy looks backward and forward, each new prophecy casting greater illumination on the past even as it receives illumination from it. Each new prophecy proceeds by taking stock of earlier prophecy (of the fulfillment it has received) by way of ascertaining what is yet to be made, such retrospectives causing prophecy to adhere to "the old channels," to maintain "the original impress," thus "develop[ing] under relations already settled and known, not by the introduction of others essentially different and new." This process ensures interconnectedness even as it promises renovation: it "tells of the way to a sonship condition" at the same time that it "lays open . . . the prospect of a sonship inheritance."[18]

Insofar as Bloom's notion of misinterpretation is relevant to this tradition, it is relevant because it describes a condition imposed on prophecy by those who consider individual "visions" as distinct from, rather than as an embodiment and extension of, tradition. The prophet makes two assumptions about his art: one is that he must offer a sharper articulation of his precursor's visions; the other, that he is the recipient of a new revelation which he is charged with purveying. In the first instance, he functions as a commentator; in the second, as a creator. As a commentator, his relationship to his precursors is complicated by their shared "humanity." Neither new prophet nor old is perfect, and both work within a form that is, by design, highly enigmatic. Therefore, one obligation of the new prophet is to offer full elucidation of his predecessor. Presumably a part of the older prophet's vision has already been penetrated; thus the new prophet concentrates on what is still hidden or on what has been misunderstood. In the process, he refocuses, recreates, an old vision, intent not upon burying it in his own reinterpretation, but upon releasing it from the misinterpretations of others, some of which may be traceable to the mental failings of the prophet himself but most of which result from the "unfitness" of his audience. Prophecy, then, is both "progressively embodied" and "progressively unfolded."[19] In consequence, the new embodiment, the full elucidation, is prelude to the new revelation that will find its own parodists and distorters and that will thus require yet another prophet to do for the new prophet what he has done for the old one.

The prophet is a commentator, but he is also a creator and, as creator, finds his prototype in Christ, not Satan. When it comes to talking about Milton, I do not think it will take us very far to assign much credence to Bloom's "experiment" with *Paradise Lost,* which involves reading the epic "as an allegory of the dilemma of the modern poet, at his strongest"—an allegory where-in "Satan is that modern poet, while God is his dead but still embarrassingly potent . . . ancestral poet":

Adam is the potentially strong modern poet, but at his weakest moment . . . Of the living poets in the poem, Satan has Sin, Adam has Eve, and Milton has only his Interior Paramour . . . invoked magnificently four times in the poem. Milton has no name for her . . . Satan, a stronger poet even than Milton, has progressed beyond invoking his Muse.[20]

At least such an effort will not take us very far—will seem not "apparently frivolous" but "frivolous indeed"—if we devise an allegory that so completely violates Milton's text. Allegory, after all, is founded upon a text whose details shape and support it. *Paradise Lost* is, from one perspective, an allegory about creation—about God's creation of the universe and Milton's creation of a poem. Neither creates out of nothing, and neither's creation is independent of tradition or of inspiration. The strong poet—Milton and his prototype Christ—receives an idea that he executes. Both are, in a Blakean sense, "copyists" not "imitators," the imitators being what Satan is in Milton's poem, "God's ape,"[21] a false prophet who produces bad facsimiles of God's Heaven in his Hell and of God's thunderbolt in his cannon. The Satanic poet, in this sense, is not the Romantic poet but Milton's neo-classical "imitator." *Paradise Lost* offers mythic models for poetic influ-ence—one for Satanic poets and another for prophetic ones; and it is with the latter model that Milton and Blake associate them-selves. This model reinforces the idea that it is in the "son" that the "father" shines "Most glorious . . . /Substantially expressed," "without cloud/Made visible" (III. 139–40, 385–86). The poetic son manifests the qualities, clarifies the vision, of his poetic father; like the "son" in *Paradise Regained,* he provides "glimpses of his Father's glory" (I. 93).

Blake's commitment to such a view of poetic influence is openly stated in *Milton,* where the Seven Angels of the Presence weep over Milton's shadow and then, as the Seven Eyes of God, enter his sleeping body, causing Milton to arise and walk with them through Eden "as an Eighth Image Divine" (14:42–15:1–7). Milton, by the end of the poem, is designated one of "The Eight Immortal Starry-Ones" (34:4) and with them becomes "One Man Jesus the Saviour" (42:10–11). Through this imagery, derived from the Book of Revelation, Blake identifies Milton as the last in a line of prophets, symbolizing through him the highest peak of imaginative development. Through Milton, man passes from the Seventh Eye of Jesus to the Eighth Eye of his Second Coming, Milton epitomizing the "inward-turning" process that culminates in apocalypse, in the achievement of the highest state of mental freedom, which is finally no state but human existence itself. The Seven Eyes, the Seven Spirits, the Seven Angels of John's Apocalypse were traditionally associated with the building of Jerusalem; by adding Milton, who is the Starry Eighth, to this assemblage, Blake makes clear whom he sees as the city's master-builder.

In *Milton,* Rintrah and Palamabron are mythic types of two historical types (Whitefield and Wesley) of Saint John's "two Witnesses" (22:55–56); but the archetypal witness is the Bard ("Let the Bard himself *witness*" [13:50; my italics]). From Blake's point of view, he and Milton are the principal historical types for the last age, Blake concluding that it is not the priests of the church but the poet-prophets who are the fullest approximations of John's two witnesses. To know who the witnesses are and to know what they represent is to understand more completely Blake's idea of Milton and of himself in relation to Milton. The witnesses are the openers and purveyors of Christ's Gospel who, warring with Antichrist as Milton does on plate 18 (see figs. 12 and 13), elevate spiritual over mental warfare. Their story, as told by Saint John, epitomizes the meaning of Blake's poem.

What John portrays as a natural death was understood as a political, spiritual death; and, correspondingly, what he depicts as a natural resurrection was comprehended as a political, spiritual resurrection involving a complete overthrow of the reigning hierarchy. The point is made succinctly by Henry More: as soon as the two figures begin witnessing to the truth, they are assaulted or suppressed, *"politically* killed, as their Resurrection also is *Political."*[22] The two witnesses, then, testify to the spirit of prophecy and, like Milton and Blake, embody it; rather than predicting the future, they witness to the truth of a new birth, opening and expounding the Bible, especially the New Testament, and thus precipitate a revolution that reforms the world. The witnesses are alive, reborn, only when their visions are turned into life and practice in us, only when the reigning orthodoxies, the false doctrines, cease to slay man and are instead slain by him.

The witnesses of the Book of Revelation recall all the famous pairs of prophets in the Old Testament—Moses and Aaron, Elijah and Elisha, Zerubbabel and Joshua—who envision the new Jerusalem; they also anticipate later pairs of prophets who will construct it. Charged with "measuring, building, and finishing the temple," these new prophets are authenticated by their apparel— by the doffing of filthy garments and the donning of white ones stained with blood (see figs. 10 and 11).[23] In his crucifixion, Christ literally died; but his witnesses in theirs only die metaphorically—Milton by succumbing to the politics of violence through his participation in regicide and Blake by acquiescing in the politics of withdrawal through his retreat to Felpham. Yet, like the witnesses, both poets rise again, in their own lives and in their followers who profess the same cause ("so John Baptist rose up in the spirit of Elias; and when Christ preached, they thought John was risen from the dead"); and their rising signals a "great turn of things"—a "hastening to the New Jerusalem."[24] As men's deliverers from tyranny and servitude, the two witnesses, the most recent of them, historically, being Milton and Blake, "pull downe errours and wicked vices"[25] —they are revolutionaries. This perception takes us to the heart of Bloom's misconception: he translates social and political radicalism into mental perversity; he suppresses the motive force behind Milton's poetry and Blake's—their respective commitments to witnessing to the truth. Within this context we can best comprehend Blake's encounters with Milton, both in pictures and in poems; and within it we can best judge the theory of poetic influence that Bloom claims to extrapolate from those encounters.

Critical theory, like poetry, is not created *ex nihilo;* it is inextricably bound to literary texts and must finally be tested against them. If the Blake-Milton relationship generates a theory of poetic influence, an understanding of relationships between poets (and I think it does), then that theory, presumably, finds articulation somewhere in the Blake canon and can be verified—or at least can be accounted for—by taking into consideration all we know about this particular relationship. This Bloom does not do, but his omissions point to the task this book has undertaken.

The whole thrust of *The Anxiety of Influence* is toward hardening Eliot's famous pronouncement into an orthodoxy. For Eliot, Milton was a bad influence, could only be a bad influence, on poets who would follow in his footsteps. For Bloom, Milton is the Great Inhibitor, the Covering Cherub, who oppressed the very poets who came under his sway. One wonders, in contemplating the thesis of Bloom's book, whether it does not have its roots in Thomas DeQuincey's famous essay, where, having described Milton as "a power amongst powers," he proceeds to speak of those "original minds" who "quelled and repressed" by their own excellence "other minds of the same cast. *Mere despair of excelling him* . . . drove back others who pressed into the arena."[26] The *him* to whom DeQuincey refers is not Milton, but Butler, from whom Milton, as a strong poet, is distinguished. Whereas Butler "quelled and repressed," Milton, "in that mode of power which he wielded," was able to act upon other poets; rather than stifling their talents, he animated them.[27] My own study of Milton and Blake has proceeded from DeQuincey's perception. But even so, Bloom's book raises a question about which there is still more to say. If Bloom's Milton is not Blake's Milton, then what was Blake's Milton like? This question we have come a long way toward answering by scrutinizing a portrait and various portrayals of Milton, by examining the illustrations Blake prepared for Milton's poetry and the statement Blake makes about Milton in *The Marriage of Heaven and Hell.* All that we have said so far, though at odds with Bloom's conclusions, is in perfect accord with William Hayley's Milton and with the idea of Milton that informs the epic to which Milton lends his name.

HAYLEY'S MILTON

Alexander Gilchrist's remark that Hayley is not mentioned "but to be injuriously spoken of, and the worst construction put upon his motives," is less true now than it was in our antecedent

century.[28] In the past, it was fashionable to cast derision Hayley's
way whenever his name was introduced in conjunction with
Blake's; but this prejudice, codified in the nineteenth century, is
beginning to disappear in our own. Northrop Frye, who once
argued that there is little we can learn from Hayley and who
portrayed this "conceited dilettante" as "a representative of Au-
gustan culture" with a "solid body of organized taste" standing
behind him,[29] has now recanted, allowing that there is something
we can learn about Blake from a study of Hayley. "The immediate
effect of Hayley on Blake," says Frye, "was to sharpen his sense
and increase his knowledge of the epic tradition,"[30] a position
that was doubtless shaped by an understanding resembling H. T.
Swedenborg's when he tells us that Hayley is "almost unique
among the critics of . . . [the eighteenth] century" because he
dissociated himself from "those who were concerned with systems
and theories and established methods" and leveled a "frontal"
attack upon "the established approach to the epic."[31] Clearly,
Hayley sympathized with Henry Fuseli, who believed that "the
epoch of rules, of theories, poetics, criticisms in a nation, will add
to their stock of authors in the same proportion as it diminishes
their stock of genius: their productions will bear the stamp of
study, not of nature; they will adopt, not generate."[32] And like
Fuseli, Hayley returned to Milton because he represented "the
genuine principles of Art" that since his time had disappeared
from the national character of England and that had been lacking
on the Continent as well.[33] Frye's altered opinion, coupled with
advances in literary history, has provoked James Rieger's enjoinder
that we desist from idle "chatter about the dead"[34] and has
inspired two critical studies—one showing the depth of Hayley's
influence on Blake's epics and the other demonstrating that
Blake's Hyle is not Hayley.[35]

Through these various discussions, we have been brought to the
understanding that Hayley, in *An Essay on Epic Poetry,*[36] resur-
rects the epic tradition, which Blake himself explores, then uses,
with a facility not displayed by any of the so-called Miltonic poets
of the eighteenth century. What distinguishes Blake from them is
his adherence to a dictum like Petrarch's: "We should make use of
another man's inner quality and tone, but avoid his words. For the
one kind of similarity is hidden and the other protrudes; the one

creates poets, the other apes."[37] But more important still, at least for our present purposes, Hayley, in *The Life of Milton,*[38] forges an attitude toward the poet compatible with Blake's own, an attitude that in *Milton* Blake elaborates and extends. Hayley is indisputably the best knower of the Milton tradition, of its inner workings, before Blake; and thus it is not surprising to find a striking continuity between Hayley's Milton and Blake's and between the Milton of *The Marriage of Heaven and Hell* and the poet celebrated in *Milton.* These last pages are devoted not to a full-scale commentary on *Milton,* which requires another book, but to these continuities, which emerge from the understanding that Milton is a poet, revolutionary in his attitudes toward all traditions, artistic and intellectual alike, who, instead of being the Great Inhibitor, is the agent who freed Blake from the tyrannies of art and of history.

Frederick Pierce has proposed that Hayley's *Life of Milton* provided the immediate inspiration for Blake's *Milton.* Yet Pierce has defined Blake's debt to Hayley inexactly and has interpreted Blake's poem mistakenly. According to him, "the central theme of Blake's epic was suggested by two passages in Hayley's *Life*"[39] : one which reads, "I am persuaded his [Milton's] attachment to truth was as sincere and fervent as that of the honest Montaigne, who says: 'I would come again with all my heart from the other world to give any one the lie, who should report me other than I was, though he did it to honour me' "; another which says, "Milton, adorned with every graceful endowment, highly and hollily accomplished as he was, appears, in the dark colouring of Johnson, a most unamiable being; but could he revisit earth in his mortal character, with a wish to retaliate, what a picture might be drawn, by that sublime and offended genius, of the great moralist, who has treated him with such excess of asperity."[40] Moreover, Hayley also suggests that "a work of literary retaliation" is imminent.[41] Pierce's conclusion is that Blake, profoundly affected by Hayley's *Life,* took imaginative hints from it. In *Milton,* says Pierce, Blake is concerned with rescuing his poet-hero not from his own erroneous teachings, but from "the degraded misinterpretation of his thoughts by readers and critics who could not rise to his level."[42] But one cannot maintain that only Milton's commentators *and not Milton* are the objects of Blake's criticism. The poem suggests otherwise. During the eighteenth century, Milton was discussed as a man, an intellect, and an artist. In *Milton,* Blake criticizes his hero on all three counts, suggesting that the whole destiny of man is threatened by one erring poet, but also that all men may participate in his redemption.[43] Through Milton's six-fold emanation Ololon, Blake underscores Milton's domestic shortcomings. By having Los behold "the Cloud of Milton [his intellectual fault] stretching over Europe" (21:36) and by having Rintrah and Palamabron tell Los about Milton's "Religion," Blake acknowledges Milton's errors as a thinker:

> The Shadowy Female shudders thro' heaven in torment inexpressible!
> And all the Daughters of Los prophetic wail: yet in deceit,
> They weave a new Religion from new Jealousy of Theotormon!
> Milton's Religion is the cause: there is no end to destruction!
>
> (22:36–39)

Finally, by including a Preface that rebukes Milton for having been "curb'd by the general malady & infection from the silly Greek & Latin slaves of the Sword,"[44] Blake extends his criticism to Milton the artist. But even so, Pierce calls our attention to two significant aspects of Blake's poem: its ultimate concern with Milton's redeeming strengths and its retaliatory character. One need not argue that the idea of Milton's returning to this world was so uniquely Hayleyan as to constitute a debt (with important analogues in the eighteenth century, this idea was, during the Romantic period, a commonplace of Milton criticism); nor need one insist that Blake, like Hayley, is writing an answer to Dr. Johnson's *Milton.* The connection is more general. Hayley formulated in his *Life of Milton* a view of the poet that was impressed upon Blake's mind (as it was upon the minds of many Romantics); and further, whereas Hayley wrote specifically in response to Dr. Johnson, Blake is answering all those eighteenth-century biographers, critics, and editors who falsified both Milton and his poetry, blocking from view the spiritual form of the poet.

For Blake and for Hayley, Milton was "a poet of the most powerful, and, perhaps, the most independent mind that was ever given to a mere mortal,"[45] Milton's audacious independence of mind and his republican sympathies manifesting themselves most conspicuously in his prose, but emerging in his epic endeavors as well. In the final estimate of both, however, Milton's distinguishing characteristic was his religious enthusiasm. It was "the prime director of his genius" as exhibited in *Paradise Lost* and *Paradise Regained,* the latter poem representing "the truest heroism, and the triumph of Christianity."[46] Blake's interest, like Hayley's, though it extended to Milton's early lyrics and prose tracts, finally turned on *Paradise Lost* and *Paradise Regained;* for it was in these poems that Milton enabled England to rival "antiquity in the highest province of literature," the epic, which he "extended and ennobled."[47]

If Blake read Hayley's *Life of Milton* during the Felpham years (and he probably did), he read the 1796 edition, to which "Conjectures on the Origin of the Paradise Lost" was appended.[48] And if he derived a general point of view toward Milton—or found presented there one that coincided with his own—he also gleaned from this newly added essay a deeper understanding of Milton's epic achievements and a more precise comprehension of Milton's place in epic tradition. Hayley defended the sixth book of *Paradise Lost* as an imaginative "transport" and used it, along with Milton's claim in Book IX that his epic was not less but more heroic than the poems of Homer and Vergil, to support the contention that as much as Milton "delighted in the poetry of Homer, he appears to have thought ... that the Grecian bard ... has too great a tendency to nourish that sanguinary madness in mankind, which has continually made the earth a theatre of carnage." Homer, says Hayley interpreting Milton, was "accessary to the innumerable massacres with which men ... have desolated the world."[49] Thus *Paradise Lost* and *Paradise Regained* are to be viewed as poems that exhibit "an abhorrence for the atrocious absurdity of ordinary war" and thereby embody "a purer religion" accompanied by "greater force of imagination."[50] The idea of Milton elaborated here had already been sketched out in *An Essay on Epic Poetry.*

The principal perception to emerge from Hayley's *Life of Milton* is the insistence that Milton is a revolutionary artist—one who embodies in the epic form a radical version of Christianity. Earlier, Hayley had suggested that Milton's revolutionary character influenced the very forms he was using—forms that Milton radically altered without destroying their essential identity. This realization is central to *An Essay on Epic Poetry,* intended by Hayley to revolutionize the epic tradition and to encourage young poets to utilize the form. The concept of epic poetry articulated in this work profoundly affected Blake, whose epic compositions give form and body to Hayley's abstractions.

In *An Essay,* Hayley sets out to "examine and refute the prejudices" that contributed to "the neglect of the Heroic Muse" and "to kindle" in England's poets "a warmer sense of national honour, with ambition to excel in the noblest province of poesy."[51] Hayley's five verse epistles envision a new kind of epic poetry, which will unshackle the poet from "imitation" and "the rules," and offer a plan on which the young poet "Might build his glory" (IV. 156). While the epic poet often assumes the conventions of his predecessors (usually to his own peril), the "true" epic poet, Hayley argues, is concerned ultimately with perfecting earlier techniques at the same time that he experiments with new ones. He uses the conventions of form only to trample them; he supersedes in his poetry the visions of his predecessors. Consequently, it is not the "epic paradox"[52] that fascinates Blake or Hayley but instead the revolutionary aspect of epic poetry. Previous epic poets, with the exception of Milton, were enslaved by systems— intellectual and poetical. However, the "true" epic poet, an iconoclast and a visionary, is born "to disown" every law and system and to be ruled "by Fancy's boundless power alone" (III. 155– 56).[53] A supreme example of the poet who bursts the fetters of epic rule, who extends beyond "its mimic reign," Milton, by refusing "to rehearse/The sacred, old, traditionary verse" (I. 3, 167–68) greatly expanded the possibilities of epic poetry while displaying freedom of thought and energy of mind.

Blake believed with Hayley that insofar as the poet needs models he should emulate the most perfect examples of the literary forms he is using. Homer and Vergil were parasitic; so was Dante.[54] Milton, on the other hand, was a perpetual source of creative energy. Even when working with borrowed materials, he managed to leave the imprint of his genius upon them. This Blake thought especially true of the literary forms with which Milton worked. Ode, masque, pastoral, tragedy, brief epic, or diffuse epic—all were stunningly transformed by Milton who, spurning imitation as a form of enslavement, elevated originality as a symbol of freedom. For Blake the lyric poet, this realization meant returning to the

Nativity Ode, L'Allegro and *Il Penseroso,* and *Comus* (all of which he illustrated) and to *Lycidas* (which he often echoes). For Blake the epic poet, it meant turning to *Paradise Lost* and *Paradise Regained,* the subjects of his finest, most provocative Milton illuminations. Blake's intention, however, is never to present a carbon copy of Milton's poems but instead to extract from them techniques that he can perfect and a vision that he can extend.

It has recently been suggested that "the whole modern conception of evolution and change of genres themselves—[is] so easy to talk about theoretically, so difficult to insinuate into the habitual response of those whose task is to create or perform rather than to reflect or devise. Our modern sense that genres are not stratified as God-given has ... done something to free the artist." But, concludes Walter Jackson Bate, "I do not believe that the liberating influence of the critical theory of the evolution of genres *per se* had much direct effect on the poet himself ... till later in the nineteenth century, and then largely because of romantic models."[55] The models that effect the change that Bate describes are not Romantic but Miltonic; and the "liberating influence" of critical theory, derived from such models, is precisely the debt that Blake owes to Hayley. Hayley's theory of the epic as a revolutionary form—and the precepts related to his theory—are reflected with striking clarity in Blake's epic achievements.

An Essay on Epic Poetry, besides describing a new kind of epic poetry, presents definite recommendations, traceable to Milton, concerning the direction epic poetry ought to take:

1. Improved characterization will necessitate the poet's exploring man himself, particularly the complexities of the human mind; it will also hold out the opportunity for making women, who have been relegated to the position of incidental characters, major participants in the epic.
2. Psychological probing will involve the introduction of more meaningful action into the poem, which, in turn, will require the shearing away of celestial machinery and the tightening up of narrative structure by spurning "faint Allegory's feeble aid" (V. 182).
3. Each new poem ought to embody "New Forms of Beauty and Disorder" and encompass the "Extremes of Harmony and Dis-

cord" (III. 114—15). Each new poem ought to replace mechanical with organic form.

4. Since "Heaven and Hell" can yield nothing more, the epic poet
should search for a "new mythology" which will become at
once the "copious spring of visionary force" and the "new
machinery" of the epic poem (V. 268—70); replacing the epic
conventions that previously provided a rough scaffolding on
which to erect the poem, the "new mythology" will yield an
organic form.

5. The new epic should take on a story of national import, should
celebrate England and her people. Its master-theme ought to be
freedom, and that theme ought to have various points of reference—political, social, religious, and artistic. The new epic
should embody republican ideals and protest against repression.

That these recommendations shaped Blake's epic-prophecies, especially *Milton* and *Jerusalem,* should be self-evident. One of these
suggestions, concerning the structure of epic poetry, is of special
concern, however; for through the form of *Milton* Blake indicates
the subject of his poem, providing an emblem of what Milton's
achievement involves, of what his attitude toward the poet is. The
initial impression of planned disorder created by *Milton* is quickly
checked by the discovery of careful symmetry and balance both
within and between books, by the discovery of a "dark conceit"
that holds the poem together. It has been said that the "bloated
structure" of *Milton* "depresses" and "distorts" Blake's theme.[56]
In fact, the poem's structure reinforces its theme.

THE MILTON OF *MILTON*

If *Milton* does not achieve the same splendid mythic and philosophical condensation as *Jerusalem,* it is, nevertheless, a perfect
realization of Hayley's theory of structural unity within the epic
mode. The poem's two books are parallel in design. Book I is
concerned with the making of the poet, Book II with the making
of the poem—subjects that Blake regards as indistinguishable.
Imagination and inspiration converge within the poet to make the
poem; the poet is thus himself a true poem.[57] As the second book
of *Milton* commences, the poet and the poem are symbolically

represented by the lark and the nightingale; but by the end of the book the nightingale, or the idea of the poet, has disappeared within the lark, or the idea of the poem. Out of the nightingale's (the poet's) suffering and woe comes the poem which is a perpetual song of joy. And the parallelisms do not end here.

The Songs of Beulah in Book II find their structural analogue in the Song of the Bard in Book I. In each instance, the songs provide the immediate philosophical context for the book they preface: the Song of the Bard evolves a theory of psychological types, and the Songs of Beulah enunciate Blake's philosophy of contraries and his conception of states and individuals. In each book, the songs are followed by a descent—the descent of Milton in Book I, the descent of Ololon, his female emanation, in Book II; and each book rises to a moment of vision—Book I ends with a vision of the time-world, Book II with a vision of eternity of which the time-world is an image. Moreover, *Milton* is composed of three carefully articulated thematic units, each of them practically equal in length and precisely parallel in pattern and each carefully marked off by Blake with full-page illuminations. The poem's first thematic division is composed of the initial sixteen plates, the second of the next sixteen plates, and the last of the eighteen plates that compose Book II. Each thematic division begins with a descent and ends with a union. Part I begins with the poet's petitioning the Daughters of Beulah to descend "down the nerves" of his arm and enter the portals of his brain; it ends with the union of the Bard and Milton. Part II begins with the descent of Milton into himself and culminates in the union of Milton with Blake and Los with Blake. Part III describes the descent of Ololon and draws to its period as Milton and his emanation join.[58]

This symmetry of design is accompanied by elaborate patterns of repetition,[59] which, calculated to imitate the order of the universe, suggest the image of the perfect circle that, turning endlessly upon itself, is a symbol of the poem's unity and of the poet who like a god is both its center and circumference (this is exactly so in *Milton*) and that, perpetually expanding, symbolizes the mind which is forever enlarging so as to comprehend all mystery. As the poem's "dark conceit," the circle serves as a hieroglyph for the poem's "action"—the expansion of consciousness that enables Milton to stand transfigured in the poem's conclusion and that enables Blake to experience so movingly intimations of that time when "All Animals upon the Earth" will "go forth to the Great Harvest & Vintage of the Nations" (42:39; 43:1).[60] With his usual incisiveness, Coleridge reminds us that literary forms, replete with conventions, possess their own unity; but that unity is "addressed pre-eminently to the outward senses" rather than to imagination. The poet who shears away conventions and thereby deviates from conventional forms so as to recreate them appeals to imagination at the same time that he presses toward the contemplation of man's "inward nature, and the workings of the passions in their most retired recesses."[61] Blake, working with the same premises, makes poetical structure serve thematic ends by creating, in accordance with Hayley's suggestion, a perfect coincidence between them. Blake, while dichotomizing mechanical and living forms, does not forsake the one in order to achieve the other. His goal, as he explains it in *Milton,* is to subordinate mechanical to living form (5:44); and this goal is realized by developing "two orders," which, as E. H. Gombrich explains, "interact": "the formal symmetries impart a sense of ease to the intricate group which, in turn, reinforces our feeling of balance."[62]

The circle is Blake's "dark conceit": it is both "design" in Blake's poem and emblem of what the poem means; but one cannot take the image with only its traditional associations and expect to ascertain from them the meaning of Blake's poem or the way this image relates it. The circle was, as George Poulet has pointed out, a conventional image of both God and his creation. In the nineteenth century, according to Poulet, it became an image not of processes external to man but of the mental processes that evolve within him.[63] The meaning that Poulet here assigns to the circle is a meaning that Blake himself exploits—not as an innovator of symbolic meaning but as a borrower of the meaning from Milton. It is clear, both from Blake's design for the sixth book of *Paradise Lost,* which is present in both sets of illustrations for the poem, and from his separate design of God creating the universe, which was later appropriated as a frontispiece for *Europe,* that Blake perceives the prominence of the circle image in *Paradise Lost,* a prominence that the image does not achieve until the central books of Milton's epic. These books, we should remember, involve the education of Adam; and their major symbol is thus an image of what the books themselves record—the expansion of man's consciousness by way of forearming him against the temptations that follow.

In *Milton,* the circle image also advances the poem's meaning, serving as an emblem for a psychic drama, the expanding awareness, that Milton experiences. But the image relates even more subtly to the thematic content of the poem. It is, after all, an adjunct of the poem's mechanical structure: it is inscribed, as it were, by the poem's symmetries, which are finally opposed by and subdued within the living form of its mythology. This is precisely Blake's point: the true revolutionary releases man from the cycles of history rather than confining him to them. The poem acknowledges expanded consciousness as an agent in Milton's redemption, but Milton's redemption involves his assuming the role of the Awakener—a role that commits the poet to bursting through cyclical patterns in order to achieve apocalypse. This role can be performed, finally, only by those who commit themselves to the mental warfare that redeems contraries and that, redeeming them, allows the hero and those who follow him to experience transcendence. This theme, monumentally important, is announced in the Preface to *Milton,* which was included in only Copies A and B of the poem.

The Preface delineates Blake's objective in writing *Milton,* which is to further the cause of freedom in every department of life and art, while celebrating the glory of the English nation in whose green and pleasant land Jerusalem will be built. Milton, of course, provides Blake with a precedent for celebrating the English as the second chosen people and the poet as their deliverer. He began *Paradise Lost* by equating England with Israel and himself with Moses. Blake, therefore, introduces *Milton* with a lyric that makes similar claims. England, he promises, will be the great agent in the apocalypse and the poet—a new and more successful Moses—will be the nation's awakener and guide. Like Hayley, Blake was convinced that the prophecy of England's regeneration described in the white heat of Milton's early prose tracts would be accomplished. This end his own "prophecies" serve; but their success depends first upon avoiding the failings of Milton, which Blake explores in *The Marriage of Heaven and Hell* and takes notice of in

Milton; it depends upon engaging a whole nation in the experience of conversion that enabled Milton to articulate the vision of *Paradise Regained*—a conversion that Blake insinuates in *The Marriage of Heaven and Hell* and documents in the poem to which Milton's name is given. Appropriately, the opening lyric is a song of *the* bard: the conception is Milton's, though the formulation and execution are Blake's own.

Plate 2 of *Milton* contains not only a lyric but a prose statement that develops a context in which the lyric may be read. Ostensibly the statement identifies two traditions of poetry, one traceable to Homer, the other to the Bible; it places Milton in the latter tradition while acknowledging that his poetry, like Shakespeare's, was afflicted by the artistic tyrannies generated by the classics. This criticism is then thrown into relief by the address to the "Young Men of the New Age," wherein Blake assumes the Miltonic pose of addressing himself not just to his own age but to future ones. Furthermore, the attack on the inhibitions artistic tradition places on poetry is in keeping with the revolutionary manifesto that Milton appends to *Paradise Lost* and that, through Christ, he delivers in *Paradise Regained.* This prose preface comes to its period with the formulation of the theme that is threaded through the accompanying lyric: the instigation of the mental warfare that will culminate in the nation's renewal. What we should observe, then, is that Blake does create a series of dichotomies here: classical versus Christian art, the poetry of imitation versus the poetry of inspiration, the present generation versus future ones, physical versus mental warfare. Insofar as these dichotomies involve Milton and Blake, it has seemed that they, too, are set in opposition—the first poet laboring under the tyrannies of art, the second liberated from them. Yet the spirit of contention evident here is not between Milton and Blake but between Milton the poet and Milton the pamphleteer. This dichotomy, the same one that appeared in *The Marriage of Heaven and Hell,* is reinforced by the lyric poem, which directs attention away from Milton the oppressed artist to Milton the liberator and awakener. Through this dichotomy, Blake represents the fundamental contradictions in Milton's vision. Blake is not saying, as Jackie DiSalvo argues, that "the conflicts we feel" in a poem like *Paradise Lost* "are related to contradictions in Milton's politics"[64] but that such contradictions emerge from the conflicts between the radicalism of Milton's politics and his sometimes reactionary theology.

It has recently been argued that "in the epic tradition of the West, in the *Iliad* and the *Aeneid*, the 'true' God sends down real weapons in the service of his favored warrior. By contrast to Blake, who interiorized the struggle, Milton is a non-visionary . . . poet. There is in Milton no sentiment such as the Blakean 'mental fight,' which seems in fact to have derived as an imagined response to the failure of the historical Commonwealth."[65] Such a statement ignores the symbolic reading of the sixth book of *Paradise Lost,* which Hayley, we know, engaged in and which Blake, judging from the iconography of his illustration for this book, probably observed. But more distressing still, such an observation betrays an ignorance of Milton's prose that Blake did not share. The concept of "mental fight," a master-theme in Milton's prose, derives not from a recognition of the Commonweath's failure but from Milton's efforts to build it.

Such a theme, Blake surely knew, was a hallmark of prophetic literature, even at times a basis for distinguishing between the true and false prophets. The latter, like Samson, hurl a nation into ruins; the former, like Milton, "having neither *Sword* nor *Spear,* but *the Spirit of the Living God,*" having broken "*their Spears into Pruning-hooks, and their Swords into Sithes,* . . . *have* learned to *War no more.*"[66] Or, in this regard, William Lilly's pictorial prophecy is also pertinent, beginning like Blake's *Milton* with an image of the sword, moving toward a vision of thrashing and harvesting (see plate 50 of *Milton*), and concluding with the portrayal of three men engaged not in physical combat but in sparring discourse. So often in prophetic literature, this theme is reinforced by contrasting Samson and Christ; and in this prophetic literature the promise is always the same: "those people shall be delivered from the Sword" who rather than fighting with a "Carnall Sword . . . are redeemed out of it."[67]

In *The Reason of Church-Government,* celebrating mental warfare as "the approved way which the Gospell prescribes," Milton urges the use of "spiritual weapons" for "warfare, not carnall, but mighty through God to the pulling downe of strong holds, casting down imaginations, and every high thing that exalteth it selfe against the knowledge of God" (*Yale Milton,* I, 848). This passage flows into Milton's peroration, which commences with an allusion to Christ who in the Book of Revelation goes forth "on the white Horse with his bow . . . conquering, and to conquer" (I, 850). The image of the bow is here, by design, an image for the spiritual warfare Milton has been urging. Again in *Areopagitica,* Milton speaks of the "wars of Truth," of grappling with truth in "a free and open encounter" (II, 561–62), having spoken in *The Doctrine and Discipline of Divorce* of "our Christian warfare" (II, 228), a concept that is central to Milton's later Defenses.

In *Defensio Secunda,* Milton exalts himself as mental warrior above the common soldier, explaining that defending truth by intellect is more noble than defending it by arms. Mental fight, he says, is "the only defence truly appropriate to man" (*Yale Milton,* IV, i, 553). The man who would advance the cause of other men's freedom, "which must be sought, not without, but within," will employ "not . . . the sword, but . . . a life rightly undertaken and rightly conducted" (IV, i, 624). No one, says Milton, should believe "it more glorious to smite the foe than to instruct himself and others in the knowledge of heavenly things, or think it more noble to practice warlike rather than the evangelical combat" (IV, i, 648). The only purpose of warfare is "to dispel all errors from the mind and impart the heavenly light of truth to whomever He will"; the proper goal of man is not "to sow and reap [corporeal] warfare" but to instigate the spiritual warfare that will culminate in the building of Jerusalem (IV, i, 649). Finally, in *Pro Se Defensio,* Milton returns to the idea of how he may best serve the state, concluding that, armed with eloquence, he will "venture into the sun, and dust, and field of battle, now to exert real brawn, brandish real arms, seek a real enemy" (IV, ii, 795). This is the Milton whom Blake celebrates as the Awakener—the one whom Blake portrays on plate 18 of *Milton,* in deliberate contrast to the biblical Samson, tearing down the tablets of Urizenic law, a Milton who at least in one version of the plate, the very first version, shows the marks of having ventured into the sun and dust (see figs. 12 and 13). E. H. Gombrich has observed that what is particularly puzzling in the history of painting is the "obtrusion of the artist's own likeness into the portrait."[68] Historically, what is remarkable about Blake's portrayals of Milton is the degree to which Milton's own self-portraits determine Blake's representations of him. It is appropriate that the prefatory lyric for *Milton* should be a song of *the* bard who is the poem's hero. The concept behind the poem and the images that comprise it are Milton's own, and they derive not from the prose works alone but from *Paradise Lost* as well. Moreover, the concluding prayer, "Would to God that all the Lords people were Prophets," is one that Milton himself employs as a leitmotif in his prose, nowhere more eloquently than in *Areopagitica,* where he anticipates the time when "the great prophet may sit in heav'n rejoycing to see that memorable and glorious wish of his fulfill'd, when not only our sev'nty Elders, but all the Lords people are become Prophets" (II, 555–56).

Blake's *Milton* derives from the understanding that the prophet's inner life is not wholly his own but reflects the inner life of a whole people, as well as the relationship of those people to the objective world. The poem, furthermore, observes Milton's dictum, enunciated in *Defensio Secunda,* that the epic poet should undertake "to extol, not the whole life of the hero . . . but usually one event of his life," as well as Milton's corresponding suggestion that if the purpose is to celebrate a nation, then the orator or poet should settle upon "one heroic achievement of . . . [his] countrymen" (*Yale Milton,* IV, i, 685). Blake's *Milton* pursues a double purpose: one is to locate the decisive turning point in Milton's life, which, as we have already said, comes with the writing of *Paradise Regained* and then to mythologize it; the other is to relate that moment of redemption to the renewal of the entire human race which comes with "the Great Harvest & Vintage of the Nations" promised in the poem's final plate. At the time Blake wrote *Milton,* he may have felt that Milton's inner life was too singularly his own; but the purpose of his poem is to translate a too singular pattern into a universal one. That is why Milton wrote *Paradise Regained* and why Blake, assuming a place in his tradition, wrote *Milton.*

Blake's epic not only anatomizes and mythologizes a moment in Milton's life, but it defines the significance of that moment. Therefore, Blake must necessarily explore the obstacles to vision that Milton in this moment overcomes. There are the poet's personal failings both in friendship and in marriage, both as father and as husband; there are the political, actually theological, mistakes that led Milton to defend the regicides and the obviously theological ones that disturbed the focus of *Comus* and *Paradise Lost.* All these failings and errors are dispelled in Milton's moment of triumph—a moment in which Blake sees not only an individual regeneration but the potential, at least, for a general resurrection. *Milton is the cause.* Without him, without the pattern of experience he represents, the building of Jerusalem is a vain hope. This is why we must finally see *Milton* and *Jerusalem* contiguously, the first poem being a gateway into the other, its hero being no other than the city's architect.

The metaphor of the gate or door is an important one—so important that it is pictorialized on plate 1 of *Jerusalem* (see fig. 18). The biblical allusion, though not always observed, is obvious:

> Verily, verily, I say unto you, He that entereth not by the door into the sheepfold, but climbeth up some other way, the same is a thief and a robber.
> But he that entereth in by the door is the shepherd of the sheep. . . .
> Then said Jesus unto them again, Verily, verily, I say unto you, I am the door of the sheep. . . .
> I am the door: by me if any man enter in, he shall be saved, and shall go in and out, and find pasture.
>
> (John 10:1, 2, 7, 9)

The significance of the door is no less obvious: it represents both an initiation and a consummation; it involves relinquishing the past in order to find a new life. The door is the temple gate of Jerusalem, thus the plate introducing Blake's poem; it is approached by all pilgrims in solemn procession on the Feast of the Tabernacles. Yet the door is, finally, only a metaphor: the real door, traditionally, is Jesus, signifying salvation, redemption, and resurrection through him; it is an emblem of the Crucifixion, for when Christ extended his arms on the cross he became the door through which all Christians entered into marriage with the Lamb. In this historic moment, portrayed in *Jerusalem* as a perpetually recurring event, Christ opens himself to us and, repeating his gesture, opening ourselves to him, we enter Jerusalem—both the poem and the "state" the poem enshrines. Here, in Blake's poem, these traditional associations acquire new meanings. The figure entering the door is Los;[69] the door or state he is entering—and we with him are entering—is "the Door of Death" or the state called Milton, the state of self-annihilation and eternal death (*Milton*

32:26–27). Milton entered into that state when he embraced the vision of *Paradise Regained,* Blake entered it when he united with Milton in the preceding epic, and we enter it through the poem *Milton* which is our doorway into *Jerusalem.*

Milton is, to be sure, "a symbolic epic unified by the theme of regeneration through the Imagination";[70] whether there is a "flaw" in its unity remains to be seen. Morton D. Paley regards "the inclusion of a prophecy concerning Orc which is neither fulfilled nor otherwise accounted for" as a major structural fault in the poem. The reason for the inclusion of this prophecy, says Paley, "must be that when Blake began *Milton* he had not yet made his final disposition of the Orc symbol in *The Four Zoas.* He still hoped somehow to reconcile Orc's revolutionary energy with the regenerative Imagination symbolized by Jesus, Milton, and the inspired Los." The "old Prophecy" concerning Orc, as Paley observes, is mentioned twice in the poem, both times in the first book:

> At last when desperation almost tore his heart in twain
> He recollected an old Prophecy in Eden recorded,
> And often sung to the loud harp at the immortal feasts
> That Milton of the Land of Albion should up ascend
> Forwards from Ulro from the Vale of Felpham; and set free
> Orc from his Chain of Jealousy . . .
>
> (20:56–61)

> I recollect an old Prophecy in Eden recorded in gold; and oft
> Sung to the harp: That Milton of the land of Albion
> Should up ascend forward from Felphams Vale & break the Chain
> Of Jealousy from all its roots . . .
>
> (23:35–38)

Paley concludes that "the prophecy is never fulfilled in *Milton,* for its fulfillment would have no relation to reality."[71]

Such a reading disregards the nature of prophecy, as Blake understood it. Prophecy is a sublime allegory, not predictive of the future but relating to the here and now; its reference points, finally, are not history but the inner life of man. We do not dismiss the quick references to Orpheus in *L'Allegro, Il Penseroso,* or *Lycidas* as irrelevant; and neither should be disregard these two references to Orc. Milton's poetry draws upon a received mythology, which provides a context for the allusions Milton makes to it.

Blake's poetry proceeds from a private mythology that offers a context for any allusions Blake makes to it. Milton knew that "an author borrows from himself"—this he makes clear in *An Apology for Smectymnuus* (*Yale Milton,* I, 906); and Blake's poetry makes such borrowings necessary.

One need not read all Blake's early prophecies to interpret this one. It is the meaning, not the name, that Blake asks us to recall. Orc is from the very beginning the spirit of revolution that Blake identifies with the cyclical process of history. As the Awakener, Milton not only exposes those recurring patterns but points the way out of them. His triumph is analogous to Zeus's triumph in Hesiod's *Theogony,* a work Blake admired and one that provides the best introduction to the large design of Blake's own mythology.[72] Milton's triumph is achieved, the old prophecy fulfilled, in the moment that the powers of Urizen and Orc are restored to their unfallen state. "Milton's struggle," Paley reminds us, "is not to destroy Urizen but to make him a part of the whole human identity";[73] and this perception has its corollary. The poet must redeem not only Urizen—he must redeem Orc as well; and he does this not by repressing or forgetting him and thus perpetuating the cycles of destruction, but by liberating him, by integrating him, thereby redeeming the spirit of revolution that Orc as Luvah is made to serve. In this moment of integration, Milton experiences his transfiguration.

If there is any doubt about the fulfillment of this prophecy in *Milton,* we need only turn to plate 18 (see figs. 12 and 13), which equates Milton's triumph over Urizen with the moment when the prophecy relating to Orc is fulfilled. *We* may see in this moment only Milton's triumph over Urizen, but Ololon sees in it much more: "I see thee strive upon the Brooks of Arnon . . . /I behold Los & Urizen. I behold Orc & Tharmas;/The Four Zoa's at Albion & thy Spirit with them striving/In Self annihilation giving thy life to thy enemies" (40:4, 6–8). That a prophecy is being fulfilled is underscored by the figures in the upper portion of the design (five of them in Copies A, B, and C; six in Copy D; see figs. 12 and 13), who with horns, timbrels, and harp dance upon a hill. In the upper portion of this design, then, is the company of prophets, traditionally represented in groups of six or twelve (see 1 Samuel 5–6), which Blake had invoked iconographically in his *Head of*

Milton (see fig. 1). The instruments held by the dancers are those associated in the Bible with praise and with prophecy (see, e.g., 1 Chronicles 13:8 and 25:1). Yet 2 Chronicles provides an even more pointed gloss on these figures: the Levites are said to play their instruments at the moment of sacrifice (5:12–13)—in Chronicles during a moment of blood-sacrifice, in Blake's poem in a moment of self-sacrifice, the very word, "Self-hood," being broken by the placement of Milton's foot in the midst of it. Since the dancing musicians appear as female rather than male, Blake may also wish us to recall the women in Exodus, playing and dancing, in the moment of glorious triumph. Moreover, the association of these figures with Milton's sixfold emanation (his three wives and three daughters) is inevitable when we remember, through iconographic association, the story of Jephthah rending his clothes as he is met by his daughter, who is playing timbrels and dancing: Jephthah is committed to putting to death his daughter, who first goes off for two months, lamenting her virginity. Milton's doctrine of chastity, which had oppressed him, his wives, and his daughters, is, in his moment of triumph, overcome, Milton annihilating the tyranny of the law (Urizen), one of whose tyrannies is "the Chain of Jealousy" that binds Orc. In this moment of personal apocalypse, Urizen *and Orc* are restored to their proper places in the human psyche, enabling Milton to begin the work of man's redemption. With him, England may now move toward apocalypse—and we, Blake's readers, may now enter the gates of Jerusalem. In *Milton*, one prophet salutes another, Blake's intention being not, presumptuously, to alter or improve Milton, but to celebrate him as the architect of the city that Blake is ready to execute as a poem.

The version of Blake's idea of Milton that Harold Bloom asks us to accept is different from the one presented here. Originally under Milton's sway, Blake wrote *The Four Zoas* "in the formal shadow of *Paradise Lost*, and *Milton* less darkly in the shadow of Job and *Paradise Regained*"; but in *Jerusalem*, Blake bursts beyond the tyrannies with which Milton afflicted him, going "at last for prophetic structure to a prophet, to the priestly orator, Ezekiel, whose situation and sorrow most closely resembled his own." Blake "followed Milton, to the line of prophecy," Bloom allows; but he finally casts off the counterfeit Milton for the authentic Ezekiel, crossing over, in the process, "from the theatre of mind to the orator's theatre of action."[74] It is not possible to find a formulation that more boldly defies the delineation of Blake's Milton advanced in this book; but Bloom's formulation also defies the fundamental attitudes toward Milton that can be gleaned from Blake's portrayals of Milton and illustrations for his poetry, not to mention Blake's own writings.

Literary relationships are fragile affairs, and it is difficult to find one of consequence in which mutual admiration is not accompanied by contention and competition. Indeed, the spirit of contention is indigenous to the epic tradition in which both Milton and Blake situated themselves. Within this context we can perhaps better assess the prominence of these elements in the relationship that Blake establishes with Milton. Earlier we pointed to the fact that Dante, as he approached the divine vision, dismissed Vergil as his guide. Following the Dantean precedent, Milton, at first very quietly, assumes an antagonistic relationship with Homer. Blake, in contrast, walks with Milton through eternity.

Within the classical epic tradition, there was always a powerful sense of continuity, created by letting one epic poem join with another. The *Odyssey* picks up with a figure whose story is not completed in the *Iliad;* the *Aeneid* does too. The tradition of epic continuity persisted into the Renaissance; and thus we find Boiardo beginning a poem that Ariosto continues but leaves unfinished, inviting a successor to do for him what he did for Boiardo. In keeping with this tradition of continuity, Milton threads the first book of *Paradise Lost* into the last book of the *Odyssey.* Homer's poem ends with the descent of the dead suitors into the underworld and with an assertion of cosmic order and justice, which are acknowledged by the suitors as they submit to their punishment. Milton's poem begins where Homer's concludes—with the claim of divine providence by the poet, a claim that is denied by the fallen angels who have just arrived in the hell of their own making; rather than submitting to their fate as the suitors did, the devils resist it. What strikes us about these corresponding books of epic poetry is not similitude but dissimilitude. Milton's purpose is to invoke the principle of continuity only to destroy it; and lest we mistake his purpose, in the prologue to Book IX he boldly asserts the rupture his epic creates within the epic tradition.

The great writers of Christian epic have been adamant in their desire to transcend their precursors; they have not tried to hide their antagonisms but have openly acknowledged them—Dante expressed his toward Vergil, Milton revealed his toward both Homer and Vergil. Blake did not conceal his disagreements with Milton; but those disagreements are, by any standard, less fierce than those felt by Dante or Milton toward their predecessors. Indeed, Blake's disagreements with Milton became less and less an obsession as his comprehension of Milton's vision enlarged and intensified. Blake's admiration of Milton's poetry centered in *Paradise Lost* and *Paradise Regained,* where the traditions of oratory and prophecy converge upon the epic mode. In *Jerusalem,* Blake sits comfortably within the Milton tradition. The poem begins where *Paradise Regained* ends, with the story of an individual redemption and with an assertion of the values of love and forgiveness that Milton's brief epic recovers. The third plate concludes with a discussion of versification that takes up, literally, where the one appended to *Paradise Lost* terminates; and this plate concludes by distinguishing the three styles of oratory that Milton himself identifies in his prose and weaves into the fabric of his epic vision. *Jerusalem* is not a correction of Milton's vision but an extension and amplification of it, an envisioning of the universal redemption that *Paradise Regained* and *Milton* presage. Blake, rather than divorcing himself from Milton, is in this poem deriving inspiration and strategy from him; and thus if we are going to proceed toward an intelligent reading of it, or of any other poem Blake wrote, we will have to consider not the "anxieties" of an influence but its "dynamics."

Further study of the literary relationship of Blake and Milton, or of the larger question of Blake's association with tradition, should proceed from Northrop Frye's incisive observation:

... the quality of art never improves. But it may increase in conscious awareness of the implications of vision as the work of a growing body of predecessors accumulates and is, however haphazardly preserved. Milton is not a better poet than Sophocles because he follows him in time, but his ability to use Sophocles may have given him a more explicit understanding of what his imagination saw. To pursue this point ... would be to anticipate the theme of Blake's poem on Milton ... [75]

Blake's adherence to this principle is affirmed by his response to one of Lavater's aphorisms. When Lavater writes, "*Who seeks those that* are greater *than himself, their greatness* enjoys, *and forgets his greatest* qualities *in their greater ones, is* already *truly great,*" Blake responds, "I hope I do not flatter myself that this is pleasant to me" (p. 577). The notion that Blake suffered under the anxiety of influence, that he was obsessed by a drive to transcend Milton, even at the cost of misrepresenting and misinterpreting him, is antithetical not only to the spirit of Blake's rejoinder to Lavater but to the principle of art that Blake enunciates in *A Descriptive Catalogue:* "To suppose that Art can go beyond the finest specimens of Art that are now in the world," says Blake, "is not knowing what Art is; it is being blind to the gifts of the spirit" (p. 535). Indeed, Bloom's notion of poetic influence negates the message that Blake allows to climax first *The Marriage of Heaven and Hell* ("The worship of God is. Honouring his gifts in other men each according to his genius. and loving the greatest men best" [plates 22–23]) and then *Jerusalem,* where in almost identical words he appeals, "Go, tell them that the Worship of God, is honouring his gifts/In other men: & loving the greatest men best, each according/To his Genius" (91:7–9).

Blake, his own words testify, was not psychologically crippled by Milton; rather, he had both the joy of seeing divine countenance in Milton more distinctly than in any prince or hero and the capacity to forget his greatest qualities in Milton's greater ones. The donning of the bright sandal in *Milton* occurs in a crucial moment—the moment of union between Blake and Milton; and it should be understood in terms of the convention of prophecy which, recognizing that "to walk without sandals is a sign of great poverty or deep mourning," asserts that, conversely, to strap on the sandal is a sign that the prophet, no longer impoverished, has achieved an integrated personality, is about to throw " 'his whole self into his prophecy,' " making " 'not his lips alone, but his whole personality,' " the vehicle for the divine word.[76] Milton, "in full possession of all his prophetic faculties,"[77] is the ideal that Blake aspires to become, that he does become in this moment of union. In this moment Blake does what Dante would not do—with his precursor he "walk[s] forward thro' Eternity" (21:14).

Notes/Index

Notes

Chapter 1: "HIS LINEAMENTS DIVINE": BLAKE'S PORTRAIT AND PORTRAYALS OF MILTON

1 Malcolm C. Salamon, *British Book Illustration Yesterday and Today* (London: Studio, 1923), p. 10.

2 Morse Peckham, "Blake, Milton, and Edward Burney," *Princeton University Chronicle,* 11 (1950), 114.

3 These designs are reproduced by Irene Tayler in *Blake's Illustrations to the Poems of Gray* (Princeton: Princeton Univ. Press, 1971), pls. 4 and 5 of *Ode for Music.*

4 The phrase is William Michael Rossetti's; see Alexander Gilchrist, *Life of William Blake,* 2nd ed., 2 vols. (London: Macmillan, 1880), II, 212.

5 Irene Tayler makes essentially the same observation about Blake's *Head of Spenser:* " . . . the center portrait shows what Hayley wanted shown, a likeness of the 'natural' man, as nearly as possible correct in historical detail. But imposed on this is the suggestion that Spenser was in real life too much of the queen's man"—a suggestion conveyed by the accompanying iconography (*Blake's Illustrations to the Poems of Gray,* p. 104).

6 See *William Blake's Heads of the Poets,* ed. William Wells (Manchester: City of Manchester Art Galleries, 1971), p. 23. The leaves of the garland are identified by Rossetti in Gilchrist, *Life of William Blake,* II, 212.

7 The portraits derived from this model are reproduced by John Rupert Martin, *The Portrait of John Milton at Princeton and Its Place in Milton Iconography* (Princeton: Princeton Univ. Library, 1961). My point is not that Blake had in hand the crayon portrait from which he made his own. Faithorne provides two prototypes, a line engraving and a crayon portrait, that stand behind many eighteenth-century portraits. Blake's portrait belongs to the lineage deriving from the crayon portrait; and the most recent portrait in this lineage, before Blake's own, was Cipriani's, which was drawn directly from the Faithorne crayon portrait (see *William Blake's Heads of the Poets,* p. 23, and the accompanying booklet, *"For Friendship's Sake": William Blake and William Hayley,* p. 9). For the most part, Wells is accurate, though he traces Blake's portrait only to the line engraving and not to the crayon portrait that probably precedes it. The history of Milton portraiture is very complicated; and it may be, as Robert R. Wark suggests, that there is a "lost study by Faithorne" that should also be taken into account (see *Early British*

Drawings in the Huntington Collection 1600–1750 [San Marino: Huntington Library, 1969], pp. 9, 55–56). Wark's point has particular
reference to the Vertue portrait but has little pertinence to Blake's
unless one assumes, first, that Wark's conjecture is a fact and, second,
that Blake's portrait is drawn directly from Vertue's. Neither assumption
seems warranted.

8 Martin, *The Portrait of John Milton,* p. 8.

9 Ibid., p. 11. Two comments by Blake are pertinent. In a letter to William
Hayley, dated 26 November 1800, he claims to be "Absorbed by the
poets Milton, Homer, Camoens, Ercilla, Ariosto, and Spenser, whose
physiognomies have been my delightful study"; and in another letter to
Hayley, dated 28 May 1804, he acknowledges that he had "the happi-
ness of seeing the Divine countenance in . . . Milton more distinctly than
in any prince or hero." See *The Romantics on Milton: Formal Essays
and Critical Asides,* ed. Joseph Anthony Wittreich, Jr. (Cleveland: Press
of Case Western Reserve Univ., 1970), pp. 37–38.

10 J. B. Trapp's essay, "The Iconography of the Fall of Man," in *Ap-
proaches to "Paradise Lost,"* ed. C. A. Patrides (Toronto: Univ. of
Toronto Press, 1968), pp. 223–65, outlines the biblical tradition. For
Pigne's design, see *Paradise Regained,* 5th ed. (London: J. Tonson,
1713); and for the Cheron title-page design, see the first volume of *The
Poetical Works of Mr. John Milton,* 2 vols. (London: Jacob Tonson,
1720). For the first of the two Richardson portraits, see the volume by
Richardson and his son, *Explanatory Notes and Remarks on Milton's
"Paradise Lost"* (London: James, John, and Paul Knapton, 1734); the
frontispiece portrait, unsigned, appears in James Paterson's *A Complete
Commentary on . . . Milton's "Paradise Lost"* (London: R. Walker,
1744).

11 See Clara Erskine Clement, *A Handbook of Christian Symbols and
Studies of the Saints,* ed. Katherine E. Conway (1886; rpt. Detroit: Gale
Research Co., 1971), p. 199.

12 Rossetti, in Gilchrist, *Life of William Blake,* II, 211.

13 See the first chapter of Behrendt's unpublished dissertation, "Liberating
the Awakener: William Blake's Illustrations to John Milton's Poetry"
(Univ. of Wisconsin, 1974), pp. 19–20. The art of Blake's portrait
involves a set of deliberately ambiguous images. The bay and the oak
leaves, traditionally the emblems of the poet and the prophet respectively (see Rupert Taylor, *The Political Prophecy in England* [New
York: Columbia Univ. Press, 1911], p. 47), imply within the context of
Blake's own symbolism a criticism of Milton. For an analogous pairing
of images, for much the same purpose, see Thomas Taylor, *Christs
Victorie over the Dragon* (London: Printed for R. Dawlman, 1633),
where it is suggested that ivy in conjunction with oak signifies purity
mixed with corruption (p. 309).

14 "Say First! What Mov'd Blake? Blake's *Comus* Designs and *Milton,*" in
Blake's Sublime Allegory: Essays on "The Four Zoas," "Milton," and

"Jerusalem," ed. Stuart Curran and Joseph Anthony Wittreich, Jr. (Madison: Univ. of Wisconsin Press, 1973), p. 249.

15 "The Mask and the Face: The Perception of Physiognomic Likeness in Life and in Art," in *Art, Perception, and Reality,* ed. Maurice Mandelbaum (Baltimore: Johns Hopkins Univ. Press, 1972), pp. 12–13, 17.

16 These associations are developed by George Herbert in his famous poem from *The Temple.*

17 *Mystagogus Poeticus, or the Muses Interpreter,* 5th ed. (London: J. Martyn, 1672), p. 338.

18 *Oratio in Laudem Artis Poeticae* (ca. 1572), tr. Walter Allen, Jr., and William Ringler (Princeton: Princeton Univ. Press, 1940), p. 45.

19 For a discussion of this point, see my note, "Milton's *Idea* of the Orator," *Milton Quarterly,* 6 (1972), 38–40; and for a discussion of the harp image, which corroborates what I have said here and which shows this whole tradition extending into Blake's own time, see Emanuel Swedenborg, *The Apocalypse Explained According to the Spiritual Sense,* 5 vols. (New York: John Allen, 1846–47), n. 323. Finally, the palm and bay leaves may be said to reinforce the identification of Milton as a prophet inasmuch as they are, according to Ross, the symbols of Apollo in his capacity as prophet (*Mystagogus Poeticus,* p. 28); and the pipes, of course, in their association with Pan, define the shepherd as a prophet.

20 See Maurice Bowra's presidential address, *The Prophetic Element* (London: English Association, 1959), pp. 4, 6.

21 "Of Prophecy," in *A Collection of Theological Tracts,* ed. Richard Watson, 6 vols. (London: J. Nichols, 1785), IV, 347–48.

22 See *Wonderful Prophecies, Being a Dissertation on the Existence, Nature, and Extent of the Prophetic Powers in the Human Mind,* 6th ed. (London: n.p., 1795), p. 4.

23 I have deliberately quoted Hayley as he is quoted by John Evans, "Sketch of the Life and Writings of John Milton," in *Milton's "Paradise Lost"* (London: C. Whittingham, 1799). This edition, illustrated by Edward Burney, was a popular one, and Evans's sketch was often reprinted. What is remarkable is the rapidity with which Hayley's observation became a commonplace of a new understanding of Milton. Evans acknowledges, for instance, that his own perspective on Milton is "chiefly indebted" to Hayley's (pp. ix, xiv).

24 *Symbols, Signs, and Their Meaning* (London: Leonard Hill, 1960), p. 233. See also George Ferguson, *Signs and Symbols in Christian Art* (New York: Oxford Univ. Press, 1954), p. 45.

25 *The Apocalypse Explained,* n. 458.

26 Max J. Friedländer, *Landscape, Portrait, Still Life, Their Origin and Development,* tr. R. F. C. Hull (Oxford: Bruno Cassirer, 1949), p. 232. Friedländer's perspective on portraiture, acknowledged by Mario Praz in *Mnemosyne: The Parallel Between Literature and the Visual Arts,* Bollingen Series 35: 16 (Princeton: Princeton Univ. Press, 1970), p. 171, is

brilliantly elucidated by E. H. Gombrich, "The Mask and the Face," in *Art, Perception, and Reality,* pp. 1—46. All Blake's efforts in portraiture are directed toward breaking what William M. Ivins, Jr., calls "the tyranny of rule." By the end of the eighteenth century, Ivins explains, "someone invented the physionotrace—a contraption with which it was possible . . . to make quick and easy tracings of profiles and transfer them to the copper in small size" (*Prints and Visual Communication* [Cambridge, Mass.: Harvard Univ. Press, 1953], p. 84). This is the system of rationality that, in his portraiture, Blake rejects.

27 *Landscape, Portrait, Still Life,* p. 155.

28 Within this context, it should be noted that even as Blake presses beyond the conventions of Milton portraiture he often observes the tradition of parting Milton's hair in the middle and letting his locks fall gently over his shoulders. With regard to plate 42, S. Foster Damon has observed that "the sexual nature of the moment is clearly indicated" in Copy A but "suppressed" in subsequent copies (*William Blake: His Philosophy and Symbols* [Boston and New York: Houghton and Mifflin, 1924], p. 432).

29 See Kenneth Clark, *The Nude: A Study in Ideal Form,* Bollingen Series 35: 2 (Princeton: Princeton Univ. Press, 1956), esp. pp. 49, 51, but also pp. 173—224. The images of Milton in the various versions of plates 1 and 16 are complementary, the poet's nudity being glossed here by lines like those in the prophecy of Merlin, where it is explained that "putting off . . . [the] garment" signifies that "naked shall he vanquish him against whom when clad he might not prevail" (quoted by Taylor, *The Political Prophecy in England,* p. 12). Nonetheless, once one has entered Blake's *Milton,* it becomes increasingly evident that Milton's nudity also epitomizes Blake's criticism of the poet; for Revelation commentary yields another tradition of meaning for nudity, using it to signify man in a state of error. Within this tradition, "Nakedness" implies a process whereby man is stripped of his garments and "his shame . . . layd in open view" (see Thomas Brightman, *The Revelation of S. John* [Leyden: Printed by John Class, 1616], p. 191). Blake himself draws out some of the implications of nudity in his commentary on *The Vision of the Last Judgment* where he writes, "Naked we come here . . . & naked we shall return. but while clothed with the Divine Mercy" (p. 689).

30 W. J. T. Mitchell makes an important comment: "The title-page presents Milton's descent from the point of view of the 'Heavens of Albion' . . . The second plate presents the same event from the perspective of time and space: at approximately the same point in the page where Milton's hand thrusts inward on the title-page, his blazing star bursts out on plate 2" ("Style and Iconography in the Illustrations of Blake's *Milton,*" *Blake Studies,* 6, i [1973], 53).

31 In the text of this section, references to the designs for *Milton,* unless otherwise indicated, correspond to the plate sequence in the Trianon

edition, which reproduces Copy D of the poem in color-facsimile (London, 1967). References to the text of the poem, as previously indicated, are to the Erdman edition, which, because it does not number full-page designs, does not correspond with Copy D. In quoting passages from *Milton,* in order to achieve precision in indicating where the text occurs in relation to a design, I have inserted in brackets the corresponding plate number of Copy D. Thus 15 [17]:47–48 means plate 15, lines 47–48, in the Erdman edition, corresponding to plate 17 in Copy D.

32 "The Iconoclastic Enterprise: Blake's Critique of 'Milton's Religion'," *Blake Studies,* 5, i (1972), 16.

33 See, e.g., Kenneth A. Strand, *Reformation Bible Pictures: Woodcuts from Early Lutheran and Emserian New Testaments* (Ann Arbor, Mich.: Ann Arbor Publications, 1963), p. 31.

34 These quotations from Homer and Shakespeare, identified by Elizabeth Luther Carey, are written on a single page of the British Museum copy of *Europe; see The Art of William Blake* (New York: Moffat and Yard, 1907), p. 46 (my italics); and see also *Prophecies of the Reverend Christopher Love* (Boston: Samuel Hall, 1793), p. 6.

35 See David Pareus, *A Commentary upon the Divine Revelation of the Apostle and Evangelical John,* tr. Elias Arnold (Amsterdam: C. P., 1644), pp. 161–64.

36 *The Apocalypse Explained,* nn. 517–19.

37 Thomson's Preface, accompanying his edition of 1738, is reprinted in *Areopagitica,* ed. T. Holt White (London: Printed for R. Hunter, 1819), p. lxxvii.

38 *The Apocalypse Explained,* n. 538.

39 Ibid., n. 533.

40 Ibid., n. 536. The identifications of Milton with the angels of the Apocalypse, made here and in the two preceding paragraphs, find their precedent in prophetic tradition as it is described by Marjorie Reeves (see *The Influence of Prophecy in the Later Middle Ages: A Study of Joachimism* [Oxford: Clarendon Press, 1969], esp. pp. 193, 209, 232–33, 354, 443). As Reeves points out, in reference to Joachim's three ages of the world, each age is symbolized by a prophet who is represented as an angel sent to mankind from heaven—the first age by Moses, the second age by Elijah, the third by yet another historical figure, whom Blake would name as Milton, elevating him into the eschatological position of an apocalyptic angel (cf. ibid., pp. 143, 154). There is, besides, a tendency among Revelation commentators to associate the third and fifth angels of the Apocalypse, some identifying and others contrasting them with the Mighty Angel (see, esp., William Fulke, *Praelections upon the Sacred and Holy Revelation of S. John,* tr. George Gyffard [London: Thomas Purfoote, 1573], p. 55; George Giffard, *Sermons upon the Whole Booke of the Revelation* [London: Printed by Richard Field and Felix Kingston, 1599], p. 165; Junius, *The Apocalyps, or Revelation of S. John* [Cambridge: John Legat, 1596], pp. 98,

100; and Richard Bernard, *A Key of Knowledge for the Opening of the Secret Mysteries of St. Johns Mysticall Revelation* [London: Felix Kyngston, 1617], p. 34). Plates 1 and 16 of *Milton* invoke this tradition, Blake contrasting the darkened angel of plate 1 with the resurrected angel of plate 16. Both these plates find an important analogue in Blake's depiction of the Mighty Angel of the Apocalypse, reproduced most recently by Harvey Stahl and Bruce Daryl Barone in *William Blake: The Apocalyptic Vision* (Purchase, N.Y.: Manhattanville College, 1974), pl. 21. Stall, in his note to this design, is needlessly bewildered by the seven horsemen, and he is certainly mistaken in his description of the Mighty Angel as "an immense Urizenic figure." The background figures recapitulate the seal prophecy, the horses deriving from the text relating to the first four seals and the figures themselves owing to the seven angels, all of them having fallen into error; *they* are the "Urizenic" figures in Blake's watercolor and in John's prophecy, contrasting with the Mighty Angel, the eternal man. A similar contrast, developed in *Milton,* is evident when plates 1 and 16 are juxtaposed.

41 James Bicheno, *The Signs of the Times; or the Dark Prophecies of Scripture Illustrated by the Application of Present Important Events* (West Springfield, Mass.: Printed for Richard Dawson, 1796), p. 65. (Bicheno's treatise, though published in America, was written in England between 1793 and 1795.) This symbolism, also accepted by Swedenborg, was used by Bicheno to emphasize the universality of prophetic language, the image, he allows, being used more generally to signify war and often the multitudes (p. 75). These associations are in keeping with Blake's statement, for Milton's "erroneous doctrine" involved a retreat, however unwitting, into the pagan ideology of Homer and Vergil, an ideology that desolated Europe with wars; and in the very act of casting off his "erroneous doctrine" Milton frees the multitudes who have been afflicted by it. Milton, in alliance with Blake, is thus demonstrating what Bicheno describes as the ultimate responsibility of a great nation, a responsibility into which it is educated by prophecy: the overturning of "oppressive systems, and form[ing] of new ones" (p. 90).

42 Jean H. Hagstrum, "Christ's Body," in *William Blake: Essays in Honour of Sir Geoffrey Keynes,* ed. Morton D. Paley and Michael Phillips (Oxford: Clarendon Press, 1973), p. 150.

43 See the anonymous tract, *Catastrophe Mundi: or, Merlin Reviv'd* (London: n.p., 1683), pp. 61–65.

44 In a special issue of *Blake Studies,* edited by Karl Kroeber, two essays, among a group of fine ones, deal with Blake's *Milton* illustrations. See Mitchell's essay, cited in note 30 above, and David V. Erdman's "The Steps (of Dance and Stone) That Order Blake's *Milton,*" *Blake Studies,* 6 i (1973), 73–87. Both essays move indiscriminately from copy to copy, neither observing the kinds of iconographic distinctions drawn in the subsequent pages of this chapter. Such discriminations, however, are observed by Erdman in the careful annotations he provides for the

Milton designs in *The Illuminated Blake* (Garden City, N.Y.: Doubleday, 1974)—a volume that appeared after my own book had gone to the printer. Thus, here I can only give notice to a volume that, for its scholarly thoroughness and for the brilliance of its individual perceptions, merits the attention of every serious student of Blake's designs. There is, generally, agreement between my descriptions of designs and Erdman's; yet our interpretations, while they are complementary, do not overlap, and in one crucial detail, relating to plate 16, Erdman's description is incomplete: it is true that in Copy D "the white clothes and belt stand out sharply" (p. 232), but it should also be observed that those garments, bloodstained in Copy D, are colored black in Copies A, B, and C, though there is a sense of lightening as one moves from A to C.

45 John E. Grant has a point when he says that since "some of Blake's 'ideas' were probably never fully articulated in his own writings," we shall not get very far in our understanding of his pictures "if we aim to find some verse adequate to serve as a caption for each of them" ("You Can't Write About Blake's Pictures Like That," *Blake Studies*, 1, ii [1969], 194). Yet this statement, upon scrutiny, requires refinement. Blake's pictures, it is true, are not mere redactions; those accompanying a text (those for *Milton*, let us say) or those implying a text (for example, those for Milton's poetry), nonetheless, relate to their text even as they amplify it. The process here is like the one involving emblems: "no part of the emblem—figure, epigram, caption, or adage— was supposed to translate any other: rather all the elements were by their special means to point inward to a single idea, supported in part by all of them" (see Rosalie L. Colie, *The Resources of Kind: Genre-Theory in the Renaissance,* ed. Barbara K. Lewalski [Berkeley and Los Angeles: Univ. of California Press, 1973], p. 37). Similarly, in Blake's illuminated books, text and design, constituting a plate, collaborate to express a common idea. In the designs for *Milton,* there is, without exception, a point of intersection between design and text, though that point of intersection often lies somewhere between plates rather than always within a single plate, a line here relating to a design there. Indeed, on occasion, the point of intersection may even lie between poems. For instance, plate 42 of *Milton* looks backward to *The Four Zoas* and forward to *Jerusalem,* the design here relating to the text there. Students of Blake have been aware of the process of interweaving, involving the text, that relates one poem to another; occasionally, as is the case with plate 42, the designs themselves participate in the interlacing that links poem with poem.

46 Plate 19 is an interestingly allusive one. The severed head of Urizen, as Leslie Tannenbaum has suggested to me, recalls the earlier line, "Charles calls on Milton for Atonement" (5:39), as well as Milton's triumph portrayed on the preceding plate—a triumph mythologized by the detail of the severed head, which "is an attribute of David, who, after striking down Goliath the Philistine with a stone . . . , struck off . . . [his head]

with a sword" (Ferguson, *Signs and Symbols in Christian Art,* p. 66). By drawing an analogy between Milton's triumph and David's, Blake is able to distinguish Milton's early triumph over the king, over the Urizenic principle without, from his triumph here over the Urizenic principle within. Blake would not have hesitated to use Byron's words, if he had known them: "Milton's politics kept him down" (*The Romantics on Milton,* p. 517). But, of course, Blake would not mean the same thing that Byron meant in this comment on Milton. It is not Milton's political "radicalism" that Blake objects to; it is rather the way in which Milton's political positions were infected by the Urizenic principle within that caused Blake alarm. From Blake's point of view, Milton's triumph over Charles was a Pyrrhic victory; this one over Urizen complete and consequential.

47 Four copies of *Milton* survive: Copy A in the British Museum; Copy B in the Henry E. Huntington Library; Copy C in the Rare Book Divison of the New York Public Library; and Copy D in the Lessing J. Rosenwald Collection in the Library of Congress. Erdman, in *Poetry and Prose,* suggests that Copies C and D were "both completed near the time of printing of D (on 1815 paper)" (p. 728). Erdman's dating raises but does not resolve a question posed by my own discussion. Copies A and B are similar, making essentially the same kind of "critical" statement. Copy C, though often more complicated in its iconography, belongs, in terms of its "critical" perspective, with those earlier copies. Copy D, however, is radically altered; it makes a decidedly different statement, celebrative rather than critical in character. One may argue that Blake's attitude toward Milton was so complicated that it took Copies C and D to represent it adequately. But I think that it may be argued, much more cogently, that Copy D represents a final attitude toward Milton, that it is the product of new opinions, not altered principles. There is no doubt in my mind that Copy C succeeds Copies A and B; but it is very possible that it belongs in time closer to them than to Copy D. Besides the Trianon edition of Copy D, there is a color facsimile of Copy A, prepared by William Muir and published in Edmonton in 1886. Copies B and C, except for individual plates, have never been reproduced, though I am currently preparing a color-facsimile of Copy B, with variant plates, to be published by the Blake Foundation of America. Erdman's *The Illuminated Blake* provides a virtual facsimile, in black and white, of Copy A, drawing later plates from Copy D and on one occasion (for plate 37) substituting the plate from Copy C for the one in Copy A.

48 See Ferguson, *Signs and Symbols in Christian Art,* pp. 64–66.

49 Robert N. Essick comments provocatively in "Blake and the Traditions of Reproductive Engraving," *Blake Studies,* 5, i (1972), 68; and so does Northrop Frye as he asks about the relationship between physical appearance and mental form—a relationship he explains by turning to Exodus, "which tells how Moses went up to Mount Sinai and was permitted to see the 'back parts' of God. These back parts are tradi-

tionally interpreted as the material world" (*Fearful Symmetry: A Study of William Blake* [Princeton: Princeton Univ. Press, 1947], p. 349). Related to plate 1, the passage from Exodus may suggest that Blake portrays here that part of Milton, that part of his vision, which will be burned away, leaving the spiritual form of plate 16. Also pertinent is Revelation 1:12—John's "I turned back" (John's turning his back), which signifies, says William Perkins, "his preparation or entrance into the vision" (*Lectures upon the Three First Chapters of the Revelation* [London: Printed for Cuthbert Burbie, 1604], p. 84), an act that enables the prophet to become like Christ, as Milton does in the final version of plate 16, just as Christ, in turning to man, becomes "like the Son of Man." This initial plate, then, summarizes Blake's "criticism" of Milton, but it would be a mistake to assume that the statement it makes is wholly negative, for anyone familiar with the language of Revelation prophecy will probably remember that to be without garments and with a cloud is to be a manifestation of God's glory: "there is no such glory in the robes of any prince as there is in Christ cloathed with a bright cloude," says William Fulke (see *Praelections upon the Sacred and Holy Revelation of S. John,* p. 62). Moreover, to come in clouds was understood to constitute (1) a sign of conversion and (2) a sign of the Last Judgment (see, e.g., Henry More, *An Exposition of the Grand Mystery of Godliness* [London: Printed for W. Morden, 1660], p. 212). More, though he argues against it, summarizes the very reading of the Book of Revelation that Blake in his prophecies develops: the Passion, Resurrection, and Ascension are a "Representation of something to be performed within us, namely his *Crucifixion,* or our mortifying of the old man, his *Resurrection,* or our *rising* to newness of life, his *Ascension into Heaven* . . . , or our entrance into a rule and reign in the Heavenly Being with Christ in the Spirit . . . " (p. 252).

50 *Catastrophe Mundi,* pp. 60–61. For another picture-prophecy, see *Le Prognostic de Paracelse: Prophétie en 32 Figures et Textes,* tr. J. Weber-Marshall (Paris: J. Oliven, 1948). This whole tradition is traceable to the Book of Revelation, which was often regarded as a picture-prophecy (see, e.g., Joseph Mede, *The Key of the Revelation,* tr. Richard More, 2nd ed. [London: Printed for Phil. Stephens, 1650], the illustration between pp. 26 and 27; see also fig. 9). This tradition was popularized by Joachim of Fiore (see Reeves, *The Influence of Prophecy in the Later Middle Ages,* esp. pp. 27, 73, 79, 84).

51 For Frosch's thesis, see *The Awakening of Albion: The Renovation of the Body in the Poetry of William Blake* (Ithaca: Cornell Univ. Press, 1974); and for the opposite tendency, far more popular among modern Blakeans, see John E. Grant, "Visions in *Vala*: A Consideration of Some Pictures in the Manuscript," in *Blake's Sublime Allegory,* pp. 141–202.

52 *Mythologies,* tr. Annette Lavers (1970; rpt. New York: Hill and Wang, 1972), p. 110.

53 Hagstrum, "Christ's Body," in *William Blake: Essays,* p. 129.

54 *Catastrophe Mundi,* p. 99, quoting from Paul Grebnar's 1582 prophecy.
55 *The Signs of the Times,* p. 10.
56 Swedenborg, *The Apocalypse Explained,* n. 533. Swedenborg substantiates his own interpretation of the smoke in Revelation with references to Genesis 15:17, 19:28; Exodus 19:17–18, 20:18–19; Psalm 18:7–8; and 2 Samuel 22:8–10.
57 It should be noted immediately that the errors Milton rolls back in the form of smoky clouds are not the poet's errors alone, but the mistakes of those commentators who perverted his vision in much the same way that Milton may be said to have perverted God's vision. In this regard, we should remember that Blake was not unique in portraying Milton enveloped by a mist. William Hayley, in *The Life of Milton* (1796), emphasizes, not the insufficiencies of Milton's vision, but the inadequacies of those who would interpret Milton's vision; he says that political animosity, especially Dr. Johnson's, threw "a mist over the bright intellect of Milton" ([Gainesville, Fla.: Scholars' Facsimiles and Reprints, 1970], p. 104). Similarly, in his own Preface to *Areopagitica,* T. Holt White speaks of the "dark . . . cloud of prejudice which eclipsed the luster of MILTON'S name" (p. lviii). Blake would not, like White and Hayley, have wholly exonerated Milton: the reactionary politics of Milton's interpreters have perverted his vision, but so too has the Urizenic principle within the poet himself.
58 Philip Hofer, *Baroque Book Illustration: A Short Survey* (Cambridge, Mass.: Harvard Univ. Press, 1951), p. 9; see also Otto Benesch, *Artistic and Intellectual Patterns from Rubens to Daumier as Shown in Book Illustration* (Cambridge, Mass.: Harvard College Library, 1943), p. 11.
59 The garments, somewhat lightened in color in Copy C, are still predominantly black and gray. In this regard, it is noteworthy that the last five illustrations Blake did for *Il Penseroso* depict Milton wearing darkly colored garments; contrast these portrayals of Milton with the two in *L'Allegro,* nos. 3 and 6. Both sets of illustrations are reproduced by Adrian Van Sinderen in *Blake: The Mystic Genius* (Syracuse: Syracuse Univ. Press, 1949); and they are interpreted perceptively by John E. Grant in his two-part essay, "Blake's Designs for *L'Allegro* and *Il Penseroso,*" *Blake Newsletter,* 4 (1971), 117–34, and 5 (1972), 190–202.
   Also pertinent to the argument here is the alteration of Milton's hair as we move from Copy C to Copy D. In the first instance, in plate 13 (16 in Copy D) Milton's hair is straight; in the second it is curled into long locks. Correspondingly, in plate 1 of Copy C, Milton's hair is heavily curled, but it is very straight in Copy D. Here, as in the different versions of *Albion Rose,* the straight hair is a mark of the fallen state, the curled hair, a mark of the state of redemption.
60 See Keynes's note to this plate in the Trianon *Milton,* unpaginated notes following the poem; and see also Pareus, *A Commentary upon the Divine Revelation,* p. 24. There appears to be evidence of gold tinting in

this facsimile that is not really evident in Copy D, from which it was made. However, in Copy D, the garment in Milton's right hand has a streak of gold extending in a vertical line beside it. Possibly this device is meant to suggest the golden girdle of the Apocalypse; whether or not this is so, the white garments constitute a sufficiently explicit allusion to the Book of Revelation. Interestingly, Blake illustrated this moment in 1780 (see fig. 19); and, interestingly, too, when Albion arises from his couch at the end of *Milton,* his bosom is said to be "girt with gold" (39 [44]:42).

61 I quote from Behrendt's dissertation, "Liberating the Awakener: William Blake's Illustrations to John Milton's Poetry," p. 28. A detail supplied by Ferguson, in *Signs and Symbols in Christian Art,* corroborates this identification: the mandorla around Milton's head is a symbol "given to Christ in pictures of the Last Judgment, and, on certain occasions, to the Virgin Mary, as in representations of the Assumption" (p. 148). Blake's point is that, a last judgment having passed over Milton, he now stands resurrected. Mitchell, though he does not distinguish between different versions of plate 16, notes that it represents "perhaps Milton's best moment in the poem and in the designs as well," Blake alluding, "in the text, to Jesus's offering of himself as a sacrifice in *Paradise Lost* and, in the design, to treatments of Jesus shedding the grave-clothes of his Resurrection" ("Style and Iconography in the Illustrations to Blake's *Milton,*" p. 54). Perhaps the best gloss on this design is provided by Blake himself. In plate 16 Milton is depicted just as Jesus is depicted in Blake's *Vision of the Last Judgment*—"surrounded by Beams of Glory" (compare the representation of Milton here with the portrayal of him in plate 45); and in his commentary on that painting Blake suggests why: in the Divine Humanity, "the Nature of Eternal Things [is] Displayed," all things "beam[ing] from him," because "*as he himself has said All dwells in him*" (pp. 551–52). The same commentary, in its discussion of cloud imagery, relates the iconography of plate 1 to the event recorded on plate 18: Blake explains that "those who are in Eternity" appear in clouds "when any thing of Creation Redemption or Judgment are the Subjects of Contemplation." Moreover, says Blake, the reason they so appear is that they are in the act of "Humiliating . . . Selfhood & . . . Giving up all to Inspiration" (p. 553).

Milton might well bear an inscription like the one appended to H. Niclas's *The Prophecy of the Spirit of Love* (1574): "Beholde/I will send mine Angell or Messenger/which shall prepare the way or make-plaine the Path." Christ, in his coming, brings the "Propheacie of his Spirit of Love," a prophecy that his messengers, like Milton, also bring to light, their discovering in their moment of descent that the "Cleernes of God" wholly shone about them and that their "understanding [became] brighter then the Sunne" (sigs. A2, A3–[A3ᵛ]). The following scriptural texts are relevant—Malachi 3–4, together with the first chapters of Matthew, Mark, and Luke—all of them pointing to what Blake's design pictorializes: "a Spiritual Man . . . clothed with the Spirit of God and the Trueth" (sig. D4ᵛ). Implicit in Blake's depiction is the prophetic theme that God's mercy infuses the "Poet's Breast with a Prophetic Muse," the poet thereupon becoming charged with the duty of leading a people wandering in darkness and error back into the light (see the first two prophecies, dated 1623 and 1628, in *An Exact Collection of Many Wonderful Prophesies* [London: Printed for J. Baker, 1714]).

62 See *Poetry and Prose,* p. 730. One should recall, in this context, the *I* of *The Marriage of Heaven and Hell* who flings himself into the body of the sun and there clothes himself "in white" (plate 19). Plates 1 and 16, as we have already observed, are contrasting images; yet plate 1, with Milton's right hand extended into heaven, anticipates the moment of redemption recorded on plate 16. The Angel of the Bottomless Pit and the Mighty Angel, both associated with clouds, were generally understood as being deliberately contrasting images etched by John's visionary hand (see, e.g., John Bale, *The Image of Both Churches* [1548; rpt. London: Thomas East, 1570], pp. 139–[139ᵛ]) recalling not only the Mighty Angel of the Apocalypse but the Angel in Daniel, where it is promised that men who are darkened will, through travail, become tried, purified, and white. (Blake's inscription, "I return from flames of fire tried & pure & white," is a close paraphrase of the following verse from Daniel: "Many shall be purified, and white, and tried" [12:10]). Those who are shall, like Blake's Milton, shine "like the stars" (12:3).

63 See "The Figure of the Garment in *The Four Zoas, Milton,* and *Jerusalem,*" in *Blake's Sublime Allegory,* pp. 119–39. Harold Bloom anticipates Paley when, in *Blake's Apocalypse: A Study in Poetic Argument,* he speaks of "the contrasting garments, Memory and Inspiration" and then observes that "if there is a single central image in *Milton,* it is the garment" ([New York: Doubleday, 1963], p. 358). The garment image is also central to the Book of Revelation, and it is certainly made central to the prophecy in Swedenborg's commentary on it. In a beautiful irony, then, Blake takes a Swedenborgian theme and uses it against its popularizer in *The Marriage of Heaven and Hell,* plate 3. Like Blake, Milton also uses "linen" to figure orthodoxy and priestcraft; see, e.g., *Areopagitica,* in *Yale Milton,* II, 564.

64 Paley makes an important comment: " . . . we frequently find the same images viewed from different perspectives in both *Milton* and *Jerusalem,*" especially in "moments of extraordinary importance"; for Paley's remarks quoted above in the text and here in the note, see "The Figure of the Garment in *The Four Zoas, Milton,* and *Jerusalem,*" in *Blake's Sublime Allegory,* pp. 130, 132.

Paley's argument gathers considerable strength not from the literary analogues he cites (Shakespeare and Carlyle) but from the tradition of prophecy where the filthy garments are habitually contrasted with the white garments dipped in blood. This contrast of garments is no less prominent in secular than in biblical prophecy. See, for example, the prophecy by T. Dutton (*A Collection of Prophetical Warnings of the Eternal Spirit* [London: Printed for B. Bragg, 1708]), which anticipates the time when, having purged their own errors and those of their civilization, "the Sons of God shall shine out . . . as the Sun" (p. 47). The redeemer of mankind, says Dutton, "will come, cloth'd with glorious Majesty, shining, . . . shining in . . . white Robes" (p. 45). Thus Dutton's admonition: "Oh, throw away then your filthy Robes. Come ye to him with White Garments on" (p. 51). In the same volume, see the prophecy by M. Keemer (esp. pp. 101—2) and the one by J. Potter, which suggest that, like Christ, men are known by the color of their garments, those "travelling in . . . Greatness . . . [and] Majesty" identifiable by garments "stained with . . . Blood" (p. 147).

In biblical prophecy and commentary, the garment theme is equally prominent. In *The Arte of Prophecying,* for instance, William Perkins introduces the theme by way of demonstrating that comparable images are used in prophecy to emphasize distinctions, his examples being new sandals and old ones, filthy garments and white ones (*The Works of . . . Mr. W. Perkins,* 3 vols. [Cambridge: Printed by Cantrell Legge, 1613], II, 659). Revelation commentators like Bullinger, Marlorate, Traheron, Giffard, Mayer, Burton, and More develop the same point. On the significance of white garments, which, according to Bernard, cannot be assumed until Christ's, or man's, triumph over his enemies (*A Key of Knowledge,* p. 264) and which are regularly associated with regenerated bodies and with the commencement of glory, see Fulke, who says that such garments belong to the "conquerers" and are assumed when they return from battle, in their moment of "rising out of . . . sleep" (*Praelections,* p. 20, and also pp. [47^v]—48). According to yet another commentator (anonymous), when the white garments are stained with blood they indicate that the hero, having undergone Christ's sacrifice by annihilating his own selfhood, stands redeemed; the white garments are an emblem for those who are released from the powers of darkness by intellectual warfare (see *A Briefe Exposition of the XI. XII. and XIII. Chapters of the Revelation* [London: Printed by M. Simmons, 1651], pp. 60, 67).

65 *The Apocalypse Explained,* nn. 457, 537.
66 Ibid., n. 196.
67 Ibid., n. 395.
68 Ibid., n. 64.
69 See Perkins, *Three First Chapters of the Revelation,* sig. A and p. 323.
70 Ibid., p. 265.
71 Swedenborg, *The Apocalypse Explained,* n. 65.
72 Ibid.
73 Perkins, *Three First Chapters of Revelation,* pp. 105—6.

74 See *Iconography of Christian Art,* tr. Janet Seligman (Greenwich, Conn.: New York Graphic Society, 1971), p. 146.

75 Many, like John of Damascus, were enraged by this comparison (see ibid., pp. 146–47).

76 "Christ's Body," in *William Blake: Essays,* p. 154.

77 Bloom, *Blake's Apocalypse,* p. 310. See also Thomas Frosch's discussion of "anti-perspectivism" as "a technique of multi-perspectivism" in Blake's epics—a discussion that, making the eye subordinate to the ear, fails to grasp the relevance of this technique to Blake's pictorial art (*The Awakening of Albion,* esp. pp. 115–18).

78 *Time and Free Will: An Essay on the Immediate Data of Consciousness,* tr. F. L. Pogson (London: G. Allen and Unwin, and New York: Humanities Press, 1971), pp. 196–97.

79 "*America:* New Expanses," in *Blake's Visionary Forms Dramatic,* ed. David V. Erdman and John E. Grant (Princeton: Princeton Univ. Press, 1970), p. 109. In a subsequent discussion of this plate, however, Erdman eradicates its ambiguity (see "The Steps [of Dance and Stone] That Order Blake's *Milton,*" pp. 82–84), which is happily preserved by Mitchell (see "Style and Iconography in the Illustrations of Blake's *Milton,*" pp. 62–63), who follows the suggestion of Michael J. Tolley (see "Some Blake Puzzles—Old and New," *Blake Studies,* 3, ii [1971], 124).

80 "Blake's Use of Gesture," in *Blake's Visionary Forms Dramatic,* p. 184. On the same page, Warner makes an additional observation, which qualifies simplistic interpretations that have been imposed on this design: "Blake often draws the figure on a bierlike stone just above the water," which "at best" connotes "Generation—or perhaps in the case of *Milton* 42, Beulah—and at worst the fall, a spiritual death." Harold Bloom also comments pertinently when he explains that "the ambiguities of Beulah" are "totally explored" in *Milton (Blake's Apocalypse,* p. 341). If the male figure is Milton (or Albion), he is the Milton (or Albion) who has not yet purged himself of selfhood; if the female figure is Ololon (or Jerusalem), she is the Ololon (or Jerusalem) who still shows traces of the female will. It is simply wrong to say, as Kathryn Kremen does, that plate 42 is "*entitled* 'The Moment of Inspiration' "; and it is downright misleading to say that it portrays the figures in the "*fury* of Poetic Inspiration" (*The Imagination of the Resurrection: The Poetic Continuity of a Religious Motif in Donne, Blake, and Yeats* [Lewisburg: Bucknell Univ. Press, 1972], p. 192 [my italics]). In plate 42, Milton/Albion is portrayed out of the same impulse that led Blake to depict Moses and Abraham in *The Vision of the Last Judgment.* As Blake explains in his lengthy commentary on that painting, these biblical figures are to be understood as "the States signified by . . . [their] Names, the Individuals being representatives or Visions of those States" (p. 546).

In *The Illuminated Blake,* David Erdman calls our attention to Blake's "matching" of pictures in *Milton* (see pp. 232, 267). A related device is that of taking an inter-linear or marginal design and later translating it into a full-page illustration. One example occurs on plates 17 and 32, and another is evident when plate 30 of Copy A is seen in the context of plate 42. The border that frames this plate (and it appears only in Copy A) has for its bottom panel three figures, each apparently in a different state of consciousness, lying on sepulchers. The theme of awakening into a new life is intensified by the rising figures in the side panels and by the angels sounding the trumpets of apocalypse in the top panel of the border. What is here portrayed marginally is gathered into focus in the full-page design of plate 42.

In terms of the sequentiality of plates in *Milton,* the ambiguity of the male figure here, depending on whether we identify him as Milton or Albion, points to the first or last moments of the poem—to the moment when Milton is inspired by the Bard's Song or to the moment when Milton transfigured inspires Albion. I am aware of the dangers of talking about sequentiality in this poem, especially as they are pointed out by Morton D. Paley, when he writes, "The secret of understanding the poem is to realize that it all takes place in a moment of time and that there is therefore no real sequence of events" (*Energy and Imagination: A Study of the Development of Blake's Thought* [Oxford: Clarendon Press, 1970], p. 238). At the same time, I think it is important to recognize what Blake says: "Events of Time start forth & are concievd . . . /Within a Moment" (*Milton* 29:2–3). The poet who anatomizes such a moment, as Blake does in *Milton,* must, like Eno, take the moment and draw it out in time (see *The Four Zoas* I, p. 9, ll. 9–11). As Erdman observes, Blake's "visualizable" dramas stress his "departure from narrative but not from progression" ("*America:* New Expanses," in *Blake's Visionary Forms Dramatic,* p. 95).

E. H. Gombrich's discussion of the artist's "refusal" to "freeze" his subject into a "mask and settle into one rigid reading" is pertinent to all Blake's portrayals of Milton in the various copies of *Milton.* Plate 42 (38 in earlier copies) is a superb example of the metamorphoses that an individual design and its subjects may undergo. Each copy of the design is different, each has its own ambiguities, and each contributes, when the designs are lined up chronologically, by order of composition, to the overall effect of dawning light. Though Michael Tolley properly notes "the parallelism between Milton on his death couch and Albion on his," he also confuses the different versions of plate 42, observing that they depict the "hopelessness of the moment *before* dawn" ("Some Blake Puzzles—Old and New," p. 124 [my italics]). Such a statement is true for Copy A but not for Copy D. Different versions of this plate may have their own deep structure, inviting us to attend to "what is constant behind the changing appearance" (E. H. Gombrich, *Norm and Form:*

Studies in the Art of the Renaissance, 2nd ed. [London and New York: Phaidon, 1971], pp. 42, 44–45); yet the different versions of this plate relate to one another as the successive frames of a motion picture do.

81 I quote from a gloss Grant provides on Erdman's essay, "*America:* New Expanses," in *Blake's Visionary Forms Dramatic,* p. 109n. It is true that the eagle is not menacing in Copy A, but it becomes menacing in subsequent copies. One cannot ignore its associations with the tyrannical Sky-God Zeus, nor its role as tormentor of Prometheus. Yet in Copy D, with the sunlight streaking its wings, these negative associations are mitigated (they do not, however, disappear); and only here, through biblical associations, textual and iconographic, are the positive associations of the eagle developed and confirmed. The iconographic associations of the eagle with prophecy and with angels in the Apocalypse make it possible, indeed desirable, to identify the eagle of Copy D with Milton, inspirer and awakener (Milton has already been associated in plates 1 and 16 with angels of the Apocalypse, specifically with those portrayed iconographically as eagles); and these associations, finally, reconcile this image with that of the Lark-angel which figures so prominently in *Milton.* This identification of the eagle with Milton is quite in keeping with prophetic tradition where the eagle invariably symbolizes some historical figure (see Taylor, *The Political Prophecy in England,* pp. 112–13), and may have been encouraged by the fact that, as Pierre Bayle reports, Milton's home was located at the sign of the eagle in London (*A General Dictionary, Historical and Critical,* rev. ed. [London: Printed by James Bettenham, 1738], VII, 576). Moreover, if I am right that the iconography for this plate, and others, is drawn from the Book of Revelation, then it is important to remember that the angel-eagle flying in the midst of heaven flies there because, as various commentators explain, he is "waighed down with . . . errours" (Brightman, *The Revelation of S. John,* p. 364)—but not hopelessly so, for he signifies "truth . . . reviving" and in the process casting off "the burden" of error that has depressed it (ibid., p. 614). Just as some commentators identify the third and fifth angels of the Apocalypse with the Mighty Angel, so others identify this eagle with him (see, e.g., John Mayer, *Ecclestica Interpretatio* [London: John Haveland, 1627], p. 444). Compare the eagle here with the one that appears on plate 15 of *The Marriage of Heaven and Hell,* noting that the ambiguity of the picture there is captured within the figure of the eagle in *Milton.* The sun-streaked wings of the eagle in Copy D identify it with this earlier eagle of genius (for an opposing view, erring in some of its particulars, see Michael J. Tolley, "Some Blake Puzzles—Old and New," pp. 123–24). See also John Adlard, *The Sports of Cruelty* (London: Cecil and Amelia Woolf, 1972), pls. 6a and 6b for depictions of eagle-headed men and pp. 120–21 for discussion of them. Besides the exegetical tradition that identifies eagles with historical personages, there is the literary tradition

noted by Donald R. Howard (Chaucer portrays Vergil an as eagle); see "Flying through Space: Chaucer and Milton," in *Milton and the Line of Vision,* ed. Joseph Anthony Wittreich, Jr. (Madison: Univ. of Wisconsin Press), forthcoming. For the eagle in Milton iconography, see Martin, *The Portrait of John Milton,* pls. 15 and 23.

82 Francis Klingender, *Animals in Art and Thought at the End of the Middle Ages* (London: Routledge and Kegan Paul, 1971), p. 214.

83 See Swedenborg, *The Apocalypse Explained,* n. 281.

84 Ibid.

85 Bishop Haymo quoted by John E. Hankins, "Spenser and the Revelation of St. John," in *Essential Articles for the Study of Edmund Spenser,* ed. A. C. Hamilton (Hamden, Conn.: Archon Books, 1972), p. 55. See also *The Faerie Queene,* I. xi. 34.

86 See H. Flanders Dunbar, *Symbolism in Medieval Thought and Its Consummation in "The Divine Comedy"* (New Haven: Yale Univ. Press, 1929), esp. pp. 215–16, 299. In plate 42, there may also be, as Leslie Tannenbaum has proposed to me, a suggestion of Ololon's descent to awaken Los and Enitharmon (34 [29]:46). Los is Blake's archetypal poet, and Ololon is earlier depicted with "brooding wings" ready to renew the world to "Eternal Life" (21 [23]:55–56). The moment of descent is the moment of dawn indicated by the sunlight on the wings of the eagle.

87 *The Bestiary: A Book of Beasts,* tr. and ed. T. H. White (1954; rpt. New York: G. P. Putnam's Sons, 1960), pp. 105, 197.

88 Friedländer, *Landscape, Portrait, Still Life,* pp. 247, 262.

89 *Milton and English Art* (Manchester: Manchester Univ. Press, 1970), p. 251.

90 Romney's drawing appears as an engraved frontispiece for volume 1 of *The Poetical Works of John Milton, with a Life of the Author,* ed. William Hayley (London: J. and J. Boydell and G. Nicol, 1794–97); Westall's design appears in the same edition as an illustration for Sonnet XXIII (see III, 189). By 1800, Fuseli had also depicted *Milton's Wife Pleading and Imploring for His Pardon,* though he did not include the painting in his Milton Gallery (see Pointon, *Milton and English Art,* p. 252). There is, then, a tradition taking shape when Blake begins *Milton;* what should be acknowledged is that Blake stands near its inception. Indeed, he may stand in its forefront. So prominent was the subject in Milton biography that Blake may, like Romney, have been inspired by it in plate 10 of *The Marriage of Heaven and Hell,* where the Devil (Milton?) is dictating to scribes (Milton's daughters?). This identification is encouraged by the fact that this prophecy, both verbally and visually, is profoundly influenced by Milton. For the former, see Chapter III of this book; and in relation to the latter, note that in one copy of *The Marriage of Heaven and Hell* the figure on the pyramid in plate 20 is identified with Satan on Mount Niphates and that one of the figures on

plate 24 is "walking on waves, wind filling his scarf," thus recalling *Lycidas,* perhaps deriving this motif from it (see David V. Erdman, with Tom Dargan and Marlene Deverell-Van Meter, "Reading the Illuminations of Blake's *Marriage of Heaven and Hell*," in *William Blake: Essays,* pp. 197n. and 200). The parodic intent of plate 10 of *The Marriage of Heaven and Hell* is clear enough, though rather than following Erdman et al. in describing it as "vaguely" parodic of God on Judgment Day, I prefer to think of it as directly parodic of a famous episode in Milton's life (see ibid., p. 182). Indeed, it seems to me that the Erdman reading of this plate is problematical in the extreme: it is not enough to say that "the active Devil is on his knees, with his wings open" (they are bat wings!). This plate makes greater sense if it is understood as a pictorialization of Blake's entire criticism of Milton, which is presented verbally on plates 5 and 6: Milton is of the Devil's party and is thus depicted in hell; the bat wings signal the poet's errors, especially his theological ones, which resulted in his surrendering, at times, his inspiration to the daughters of memory, with Milton shown here turned toward a daughter of memory as he ignores the daughter of inspiration on his left.

It may be, too, that plate 33 of *Milton* belongs to the same tradition of portraiture; however, the figures (all of them) are so lightly sketched that I do not feel comfortable following Erdman in making a formal identification of the central two figures with Milton and Ololon (see "The Steps [of Stone and Dance] That Order Blake's *Milton*," p. 80). Moreover, I have followed Geoffrey Keynes in identifying the figures on plate 45 with Milton and Ololon (see Trianon facsimile, endnotes), rather than Erdman (ibid., p. 84) and Mitchell ("Style and Iconography in the Illustrations of Blake's *Milton*," p. 56), who identify the figures as Milton and Urizen. Blake is generally precise in his depictions, observing, not violating, textual detail. Milton and Urizen strive *upon, among,* the Brooks of Arnon, Milton labors *in* the ocean; then appears the full-page design, showing Milton coming to the banks of the Arnon, then the lines, "Before Ololon Milton stood & percievd the Eternal Form/Of that mild Vision" (40 [46]:1–2). Urizen is in the waters, Ololon on the banks, kneeling in Copy C against a green hill, which in Copy D is transformed into a plateau. From this vantage point, from her perspective, we behold the event already portrayed on plate 18 (see figs. 12 and 13). In "Some Blake Puzzles—Old and New," Michael J. Tolley notes the feminine quality of the standing figure who is Milton (p. 123). Tolley's perception corroborates my own interpretation, this plate, through the feminine quality attributed to the poet, implying that he has achieved union with his emanation rather than suggesting that he is still struggling with Urizen. This plate, like all the others portraying Milton, probably owes something to the Book of Revelation, especially the last verse of the twelfth chapter, where it is said that *he* stands on the sand, the *he,* as commentators point out, referring not to the beast who is warring but to the prophet John. The beast, of course, is in the sea warring with a woman, the Church, of which Milton is a manifestation; but in Blake's design Milton is shown on the sand, having completed his warfare, uniting again with Ololon.

91 It should be noted, in regard to the portrayal of Milton composing with Newton looking on (see note 3 above), that these two mental giants had previously been joined together, not in a single drawing but in companion pictures, by George Romney (see Pointon, *Milton and English Art,* p. 253).

For earlier depictions of Milton's apotheosis, see, e.g., the Cheron title-page design (cited above in note 10), and the title-page design by A. Balestra in *Il Paradiso Perduto* (Verona: Alberto Tumerani, 1730). Balestra's design accompanied editions published in 1740, 1759, and 1818 (see fig. 20). Of special interest is an anonymous design illustrating Milton's apotheosis as it is described in the prologue to the accompanying stage version of *Comus* and as it is announced in the famous epigraph by Dryden. Homer and Vergil present the garland of victory to Milton, over whose head a winged muse plays a lyre (see *Comus, a Mask,* 2nd ed. [London: Printed for W. Feales, 1785]). The frontispiece design by John Flaxman, depicting Milton on a throne, also belongs to this category of Milton drawings; see *Latin and Italian Poems of Milton,* tr. William Cowper and ed. William Hayley (Chichester: J. Johnson, 1808). The involvement of illustrations depicting Milton inspired with the prologues, especially the prologue to Book I, of *Paradise Lost* is confirmed by William Harvey's frontispiece design, which gathers this subject, along with Satan calling up his legions, into a single illustration; see *The Poetical Works of John Milton* (London: George Routledge, 1853). Finally, the obvious fact should not be ignored: Milton is portrayed four times as a star, which is, as John Rainolds notes, the symbol of man's apotheosis, a meaning established by the Book of Daniel, where it is said, "those who are wise shall shine like the brightness of the firmament . . . , like the stars for ever and ever" (12:3). The star, if we accept the associations developed by Rainolds, is the emblem for those who open the windows onto Eternity (*The Prophecy of Obadiah Opened and Applied* [1613; rpt. Edinburgh: James Nichol, 1864], p. 16). The fullest discussion of star imagery in the Book of Revelation is provided by Taylor, *Christs Victorie over the Dragon,* pp. 81–85, also pp. 226–27.

92 "The Apotheosis of Milton, A Vision," *Gentleman's Magazine,* 8 (1738), 223–35, 469, 521–22; 9 (1739), 20–21, 73–75. (This last installment is mistakenly marked, "To be continued.") For the attribution, see *Monthly Review,* 77 (1787), 69; but note, too, that John Hawkins included this piece in volume 11 of *The Works of Samuel Johnson* (London: Printed for J. Buckland, 1787–88). It is noteworthy that the Milton entry in the first edition of Bayle's *A General Dictionary* (1697) takes no notice of the fact that Milton is the author of *Paradise Lost*

(such notice, however, is given to Milton in a supplementary note to the revised edition from which I am quoting); instead, the first sentence of the entry alludes to the poet as "the famous Apologist of the beheading of Charles I" (VII, 567).

93 *Disembodied Laughter: Troilus and the Apotheosis Tradition* (Berkeley and Los Angeles: Univ. of California Press, 1972), pp. 37–38.

94 Ibid., p. 47.

95 Ibid., pp. 66–67.

96 Ibid., p. 76.

97 See Lady Eleanor Audeley, *Strange and Wonderfull Prophesies* (1649), in *The Old Collector's Miscellany,* ed. Charles Hindley (London: Reeves and Turner, 1873), p. 7.

98 "Blake and the Traditions of Reproductive Engraving," p. 68.

99 Ibid., n. 15.

100 The Preface originally appeared as plate 2, and it appeared only in Copies A and B.

101 See *Memoirs of Thomas Hollis,* comp. Francis Blackburne (London: Privately printed, 1780), and Hayley's *Life,* in the first volume of *The Poetical Works of John Milton.* This expurgated version of Hayley's *Life* was followed in 1796 by a second edition with all deleted passages restored; see *The Life of Milton* (with Introduction by Joseph Anthony Wittreich, Jr.). See also Philip Neve's *Cursory Remarks on Some of the Ancient English Poets, Particularly Milton* (London: Private printing, 1789).

102 William Riley Parker, *Milton: A Biography,* 2 vols. (Oxford: Clarendon Press, 1968), II, 1065. Edward J. Rose also perceives pattern in Milton's life, but a pattern different from the one I am here describing; see both "Blake's *Milton*: The Poet as Poem," *Blake Studies,* 1, i (1968), 16–38, and "Blake's Illustrations for *Paradise Lost, L'Allegro* and *Il Penseroso*: A Thematic Reading," *Hartford Studies in Literature,* 2 (1970), 40–67.

103 *The Romantics on Milton,* p. 96. Though S. Foster Damon believes that "Blake never troubled about being accurate about such dates," it appears that Blake was more accurate than Damon thinks (*William Blake: His Philosophy and Symbols,* p. 404). There is, for instance, a precision to the "bright pilgrimage of sixty years" that Damon misses when he tries to tell us that Milton lived in the body for sixty-six, not sixty, years (p. 413); and there is a comparable precision to Blake's saying that Milton "walkd about in Eternity/One hundred years" (*Milton* 2 [3]:16–17)—a precision noted by Harold Bloom, when he tells us that "Milton had died in 1674. One hundred years later the young Blake began to write poems in Milton's tradition worthy of the master" (*Blake's Apocalypse,* p. 308). In the first instance, Blake points to the moment when Milton began to correct his own vision; in the second instance, he points to the moment when he himself began to correct that part of Milton's vision still obstructed by the poet's eighteenth-century commentators.

104 *The Romantics on Milton,* p. 96. It should be noted in this regard that the revised structure of *Paradise Lost* turns the epic, quite literally, into a Christocentric poem. This structural revision, affecting the second edition of the poem, published in 1674, may not have been conceived of before the completion of *Paradise Regained;* in fact, the theology of the second poem may have contributed to the new Christocentric character of the first epic.

105 *A True Coppie of a Prophesie Which was Founded in Old Ancient House of One Master Truswell ... Whereunto is Added Mother Shipton's Prophesies* (London: Printed for Henry Marth, 1642), p. 4.

106 *A Collection of Ancient and Moderne Prophesies* (London: Printed for John Partridge and Humphrey Blunden, 1645), p. 26. Lilly's prophecy was first published in 1644.

107 Ibid., pp. 31–32.

108 Ibid., pp. 33–35.

109 I have here adopted language from Rose, who, asserting "the consistency of Blake's view of Milton," argues that the same motives lie behind both the Dante and Milton illustrations; see "Blake's Illustrations for *Paradise Lost, L'Allegro,* and *Il Penseroso:* A Thematic Reading," pp. 60–61.

110 I quote from *Comus: A Masque* (London: A. Millar, 1750), p. 5, but John T. Shawcross informs me that this prologue accompanies the second, third, and fourth editions of John Dalton's adaptation (all dated 1738) and may accompany the first edition (same date), which neither of us has been able to check. The prologue is not in the Dublin, 1738, edition but is included in the fifth edition (1740) and the sixth edition (1741), as well as in another edition of 1741 and one of 1744(?). Most editions after 1750 carry the prologue, which in spirit differs so greatly from the adaptation itself that one suspects Dalton was not its author. It is also noteworthy that this prologue emphasizes Milton's unwillingness to accommodate his poetry to "the judgment of a trifling age" but "To choicer spirits he bequeath'd his page" (p. 4).

111 See "Say First! What Mov'd Blake? Blake's *Comus* Designs and *Milton,*" in *Blake's Sublime Allegory,* pp. 233–58.

112 Pointon, *Milton and English Art,* p. xxvii.

113 *Transformations in Late Eighteenth Century Art* (Princeton: Princeton Univ. Press, 1967), p. 154.

114 See *Pro Populo Anglicano Defensio,* in *Yale Milton,* IV, i, 574–75, esp. n. 115.

115 Taylor, *Christs Victorie over the Dragon,* p. 622. Taylor observes some pages later that "selfe-love" is the greatest enemy of the Christian (p. 637).

116 Anon., *A Short Survey of the Kingdom of Christ Here on Earth with His Saints* (London: Printed by M. Fabian, 1699), p. 56.

117 *Blake's Apocalypse,* p. 329. It should be noted that Michael Phillips misinterprets Marvell's poem when he says that Marvell was "the first to *associate* the poet [Milton] with the figure from Judges" ("Blake's Early

Poetry," in *William Blake: Essays,* p. 21 [my italics]). Marvell *disso-ciates* Milton from Samson.

118   See Jackie DiSalvo's important essay, " 'The Lord's Battells': *Samson Agonistes* and the Puritan Revolution," *Milton Studies,* 4 (1972), 39–62.

119   Northrop Frye explores the connection between Samson and Milton as revolutionary figures in "Agon and Logos: Revolution and Revelation," in *The Prison and the Pinnacle: Papers to Commemorate the Tercentenary of "Paradise Regained" and "Samson Agonistes" 1671–1971,* ed. Balachandra Rajan (London: Routledge and Kegan Paul, 1973), pp. 135–63. However, Frye attributes to Milton a simplicity of statement in *Samson Agonistes* that the play itself, and the next section of this chapter, call into question: "some of us," says Frye, may "catch a glimpse of a boundless energy [in *Samson*] which, however destructive to social establishments, is always there, always confronting us, and always the same, and yet has always the power to create all things anew" (p. 163). The driving force in Milton is *creative,* but whether the same force rules Samson is disputable.

120   See the Book of Job (1:20), and see also Swedenborg's remarks on hair as a symbol in the Book of Revelation (1:14). Hair, he says, defines "the Divine Being in ultimates"; thus those who are bald, says Swedenborg, are "abusers of the Word" who have committed themselves to "wicked purposes" (see *The Apocalypse Explained,* n. 66). Blake, in plate 18 (see figs. 12 and 13), invokes this tradition of meaning that gathered around the Samson story; but, wanting to contrast Samson and Milton in a way favorable to the latter, he does not assiduously observe the tradition. Only on plate 18, where he is equated with Samson, does Milton appear with short hair. To the extent that Milton was an "abuser" of the Word, the plate draws upon the tradition summarized by Swedenborg and derives meaning from it; but Blake's real point is that the battle Milton now wages, the triumph he is about to experience, is qualitatively different from and superior to the supposed triumph of Samson. During the early nineteenth century, it was not unusual to associate Milton with Samson. In an anonymous essay entitled "A Critique of Paradise Regain'd," in *Poetical Works of John Milton* (London: Suttaby, Evance, and Fox, 1821), Milton is labelled as the "Samson among Poets" (p. xiv). Yet this common association was not one that Blake wished to encourage or to preserve. For a contrary (and I think mistaken) opinion, see Rose, "Blake's Illustrations for *Paradise Lost, L'Allegro,* and *Il Penseroso:* A Thematic Reading," p. 61.

121   Erdman, *"America:* New Expanses," in *Blake's Visionary Forms Dramatic,* p. 92.

122   "Blake's 'Glad Day,' " *Journal of the Warburg and Courtauld Institute,* 2 (1938), 65.

123   Ibid., p. 68.

124 *Symbol and Image in William Blake* (Oxford: Clarendon Press, 1957), p. 10.

125 In *William Blake* (New York and Washington, D.C.: Praeger, 1970), Raine mistakenly assumes that the line engraving was "made" in 1780 and then proceeds to describe it as "the first work to show those inestimable Blakean qualities of joyous energy and elegance of form" (p. 91). Mitchell displays a comparable confusion as he identifies the picture he is talking about by inscription and then proceeds to base his commentary on the color print that carries no inscription ("Blake's Composite Art," in *Blake's Visionary Forms Dramatic*, p. 77).

126 See Keynes, *Engravings by William Blake: The Separate Plates* (Dublin: Emery Walker, 1956), p. 7, and Gilchrist, *Life of William Blake*, I, 32.

127 *Engravings by William Blake*, p. 7.

128 *Blake: Prophet Against Empire*, rev. ed. (Princeton: Princeton Univ. Press, 1969), pp. 7, 206, also pp. 10, 25.

129 See *Memoirs of Thomas Hollis*, p. 624, and Hayley, *The Life of Milton*, p. 162. By the end of the eighteenth century, largely because of the influence of Hollis and Hayley, it was customary to date *Samson Agonistes* in the early 1660's and to read the poem autobiographically and historically; see, e.g., John Evans, "Sketch of the Life and Writings of John Milton," in *Milton's "Paradise Lost"* (London: C. Whittingham, 1799), p. xiv.

130 The most eloquent plea for a revisionist interpretation of the play is provided by Irene Samuel, "*Samson Agonistes* as Tragedy," in *Calm of Mind*, pp. 235—37.

131 John Sutherland, "Blake and Urizen," in *Blake's Visionary Forms Dramatic*, p. 246.

132 Aileen Ward, "The Forging of Orc: Blake and the Idea of Revolution," in *Literature in Revolution*, ed. George Abbott White and Charles Newman (New York: Holt, Rinehart, and Winston, 1972), p. 217.

133 "*Samson Agonistes* as Tragedy," in *Calm of Mind*, p. 253. Milton's influence on Blake's conception of Samson is evident in the early sketch called "Samson"; see *Poetry and Prose*, pp. 434—36, and Harold Bloom's observations in *Blake's Apocalypse*, p. 22.

134 *Fearful Symmetry*, pp. 215, 224—25.

135 One version of Samson pulling down the pillars is included in this volume (see fig. 22); the other is lost. Blake's first depiction of Samson was engraved after a design by Stothard and shows Samson discovered by three Philistines while he sleeps on Delilah's knees; see *The Poets of Great Britain*, British Library, XIII (London: John Bell, 1783), frontispiece. For Blake's other Samson illustrations, see the companion pieces, *Samson Breaking His Bonds* and *Samson Subdued* (1805); the first design is reproduced by G. E. Bentley, Jr., *The Blake Collection of Mrs. Landon K. Thorne* (New York: Pierpont Morgan Library, 1971), pl. 29; and the second is reproduced by Darrell Figgis, *The Paintings of William*

Blake (New York: Charles Scribner's Sons, 1925), pl. 82. This latter design owes a considerable debt to the Stothard design mentioned above.

136 "Good-Bye to Orc and All That," *Blake Studies*, 4, ii (1972), 135.

137 Ibid., p. 137.

138 Ibid., p. 149.

139 See Erdman's "A Note on the 'Orc Cycle'," in *Blake's Visionary Forms Dramatic*, pp. 112—14. Michael J. Tolley, I think mistakenly, extends Erdman's argument about the Orc cycle to *Europe*. Orc is not Christ, says Tolley, but neither is he in *Europe* a villain; Blake "had not yet projected Orc's perversion: his Prophecy was written in the hope that Orc would continue to expand" ("*Europe:* 'to those ychain'd in sleep'," in *Blake's Visionary Forms Dramatic*, p. 145n.).

140 "Blake's Composite Art," in *Blake's Visionary Forms Dramatic*, p. 79. Like Mitchell, Janet Warner notes that Urizen and Orc, in plates 8 and 10 of *America*, are in poses that, mocking one another, also link the two figures together ("Blake's Use of Gesture," in *Blake's Visionary Forms Dramatic*, pp. 181—82).

141 "Urizen: The Symmetry of Fear," in *Blake's Visionary Forms Dramatic*, p. 161n.

142 "*America:* New Expanses," in *Blake's Visionary Forms Dramatic*, p. 97.

143 Warner, "Blake's Use of Gesture," in *Blake's Visionary Forms Dramatic*, p. 188.

144 Besides the second state of the line engraving and the two color prints, reproduced here as figs. 23, 24, and 25, there are two pencil sketches—a front view of Albion, reproduced in *Pencil Drawings by William Blake*, ed. Geoffrey Keynes (London: Nonesuch Press, 1927), pl. 1; and a back view of Albion, reproduced in the same volume, pl. 2. There is also the first state of the line engraving reproduced by Laurence Binyon in *The Engraved Designs of William Blake* (London: Ernest Benn, 1926), pl. 4. Geoffrey Keynes submits that the two states of the line engraving are not to be distinguished. Dismissing the usual argument that one state carries the inscription while the other does not, he observes that the inscription, once accompanying the first state, "has been cut away," but even so "the tops of the first two letters, *Al,* can still be seen" (*Engravings by William Blake*, p. 6). The two states of the color print may be differentiated by Albion's hair: in the Huntington version, Albion's hair is sparse, and is shown in patches; in the British Museum version, the hair, very full, is softened into short golden locks.

145 Blunt, "Blake's 'Glad Day'," p. 66. Students of Blake's art, and especially of this problematical design, should take counsel from a letter by Leonardo quoted by E. H. Gombrich, in *Norm and Form*, p. 59: "Now have you never thought about how poets compose their verse? They do not trouble to trace beautiful letters nor do they mind crossing out several lines so as to make them better. So, painter, rough out the arrangement of the limbs of your figures and first attend to the move-

ments appropriate to the mental state of the creatures that make up your picture rather than to the beauty and perfection of their parts." As Gombrich explains, "The sketch is no longer the preparation for a particular work, but is part of a process which is constantly going on in the artist's mind; instead of fixing the flow of imagination it keeps it in flux" (p. 61). Interpreters of Blake's art should remember that "certain motifs which have a clear symbolic significance in the finished version grow out of entirely different forms" and that the artist, therefore, may be projecting "new meaning into the forms he saw in his old discarded sketches" (p. 61). As with Leonardo, so with Blake: "it is the act of creation that matters to him"; "the more the sketch can stimulate the imagination the better can it fulfil its purpose" (p. 62). The sketches of *Albion Rose* relate in one way to the color print and in quite another way to the line engraving.

146 *Engravings by William Blake*, p. 7.
147 Ibid., p. 8.
148 David V. Erdman, "The Dating of William Blake's Engravings," *Philological Quarterly*, 31 (1952), 339–40, and see also *Prophet Against Empire*, p. 11.
149 Erdman concedes that in his various publications he has been "guilty of moving about impulsively" as he has tried to date *Albion Rose* (see David V. Erdman, "Dating Blake's Script: the 'g' hypothesis," *Blake Newsletter*, 3 [1969], 11); but it is clear from this essay and from the revised version of *Prophet Against Empire*, p. 10n., that Erdman favors a late date for the line engraving.
150 Erdman, *Prophet Against Empire*, p. 7.
151 *Engraved Designs*, p. 38. See also Digby, *Symbol and Image*, pp. 9–13.
152 "Blake and the Traditions of Reproductive Engraving," pp. 63–64. Behind Essick's reading is Mona Wilson's interpretation of *Albion Rose* as in "some sort a portrait of the young Blake" (*The Life of William Blake*, ed. Geoffrey Keynes [London and New York: Oxford Univ. Press, 1971], p. 14). It is noteworthy that in *America* it is Urizen who pours down the rain or sleet represented on the poem's title page (see Erdman, "*America*: New Expanses," in *Blake's Visionary Forms Dramatic*, p. 103); and it should be observed, too, that in *Europe* "two fine young nudes . . . blast pestilential hail over the page" (Tolley, "*Europe*: 'to those ychain'd in sleep'," in *Blake's Visionary Forms Dramatic*, pp. 115, 130). The allusion in *Europe* is to the "hail" of Exodus 9:18, recalling "the Egyptian pattern of a despotic Pharaoh imposing slavery on his people and then himself suffering all the effects of the plague before the people could be liberated" (ibid., p. 132). The analogy between the Pharaoh and Samson is obvious and should be extended to encompass the fallen Albion of Blake's line engraving. Blake seems consistent in his employment of rain and dark clouds as images of destruction, this significance associated by Isaac Newton and others with the universal language of prophecy. See, e.g., Bicheno, *The Signs of the*

Times, p. 75, who quotes Newton's equations of clouds with war, hail and heavy rain with " 'a tempest of war descending from the heavens and clouds politic' "; and see, too, John Napier, who equates hail with "selfe-love," the state of Satan (*A Plaine Discovery of the Whole Revelation of Saint John* [Edinburgh: Printed by Robert Walde-grave, 1593], p. 142).

153 *Engravings by William Blake,* p. 9.

154 See, e.g., C. H. Collins Baker, *Catalogue of William Blake's Drawings and Paintings in the Huntington Library,* rev. by Robert R. Wark (San Marino: Huntington Library, 1969), pl. XII.

155 Aileen Ward, "The Forging of Orc," in *Literature in Revolution,* p. 209.

156 See Robert R. Wark, *Rowlandson's Drawings for the English Dance of Death* (San Marino: Huntington Library, 1966), p. 13.

157 Ward, "The Forging of Orc," in *Literature in Revolution,* p. 211n.

158 Warner, "Blake's Use of Gesture," in *Blake's Visionary Forms Dramatic,* p. 177.

159 Ibid., pp. 185, 189. Also relevant is "Blake's Figures of Despair: Man in His Spectre's Power," in *William Blake: Essays,* where once again Warner offers an important theoretical statement whose consequences for *Albion Rose* she does not explore: "In Blake's art, it is always necessary to distinguish between representations of man in the power of the Spectre, and thus in the state of Despair, and representations of the Spectre itself . . . The visual images for the Spectre include recognizable Satanic figures . . . [and] bat-winged hovering forms . . . " (p. 215). The resemblances between the figure in Blake's line engraving and the Satan in both *Satan in His Original Glory* and the two versions of *Satan Calling up His Legions* should be noted; and the bat-winged moth should be regarded as a decisive detail, indicating, not that Albion is the Spectre, but that he, like Milton's Samson, is in its power. Finally, for an important statement on hand symbolism in Blake's poetry and prose, see Edward J. Rose, "Blake's Hand: Symbol and Design in *Jerusalem,*" *Texas Studies in Literature and Language,* 6 (1964), 47–58; he notes that the figure of Hand appears first in *Milton,* and there only twice (p. 50), but the symbol of the hand is of longer duration, used by Blake to symbolize a "man's . . . mental life" (p. 58).

160 Anthony Blunt, *The Art of William Blake* (Morningside Heights, N.Y.: Columbia Univ. Press, 1959), p. 82.

161 It is through the details of hair and hair style that Blake makes an association between Samson and Albion of his line engraving, Milton of plate 16 in *Milton,* and Albion of the color print. Hair standing out from the head is associated with the rays emanating from the head of the sun god. Milton clearly knew that the Old Testament Samson was often identified with the ancient sun god who lost his power when his "rays" were shorn. See Barbara Harrell Carson, "Milton's Samson as *Parvus Sol,*" *English Language Notes,* 5 (1968), 171–76.

162 *The Art of William Blake,* p. 46. In the quotations, I have added italics for emphasis.

163 Edward J. Rose, "Blake's Human Insect: Symbol, Theory, and Design," *Texas Studies in Literature and Language,* 10 (1968), 215.

164 Ibid., p. 216.

165 Ibid., p. 224.

166 See Erdman, "*America:* New Expanses," and Warner, "Blake's Use of Gesture," in *Blake's Visionary Forms Dramatic,* pp. 92, 184, 187. John Grant observes that "bat-wingedness is never a favorable sign in Blake's pictorial symbolism, partly because of the overwhelmingly sinister image of the bat-winged spectre in *Jerusalem* 6" ("Visions in *Vala:* A Consideration of Some Pictures in the Manuscript," in *Blake's Sublime Allegory,* p. 194).

167 *Milton and English Art,* p. lx.

168 References to the illustrations by Hayman and Metz may be found in Pointon, *Milton and English Art,* pp. 54, 74. Though Pointon mentions Westall, she does not allude to his illustrations for *Samson Agonistes (Samson Meditating* and *The Messenger Reporting Samson's Catastrophe),* which are reproduced in *The Poetical Works of John Milton,* ed. Hayley; nor does she mention these other volumes containing illustrations for *Samson:* Burney's depiction of Samson and Dalila in *Milton's "Paradise Regained"* (London: T. Longman, 1796), and Stothard's depiction of Samson and Dalila and Graham's of Samson meditating in *Samson Agonistes,* British Library (London: George Cawthorn, 1796).

169 Pointon does not mention this anomalous illustration, which was reproduced in the fourth volume of *The Poetical Works of John Milton,* British Poets (Edinburgh: Apollo Press, 1779).

170 *Memoirs of Thomas Hollis,* p. 624. Erdman makes an important comment: "Blake must have seen some of these materials and heard a good deal about Hollis; he is said to have engraved some of the plates in the *Memoirs*"; and Erdman continues, "we may be sure that the Milton he encountered in the vortex of Thomas Hollis was Milton the republican, anticipator of Wilkes and Liberty" (see *Prophet Against Empire,* pp. 34–35). In the radical literature of the late eighteenth and early nineteenth centuries there are many other precedents for portraying Milton as a revolutionary; see, e.g., Richard Price, "A Discourse on the Love of Our Country" (1790), in *British Radicals and Reformers 1789–1832,* Keutsch English Texts (Tübingen: Max Niemeyer, 1971), p. 11. And in the same volume there are examples of Samson being portrayed as a revolutionary; see, e.g., Thomas Babington Macaulay, "The Present Administration" (1827), p. 109. Milton and Blake stand together in their understanding of the ambivalent character of Samson's action and in their acute delineation of it.

171 Frye, *Fearful Symmetry,* p. 326.

172 *The Resolved Mans Resolution* (London, n.p., 1647), p. 1.

173 Frosch, *The Awakening of Albion*, p. 84.

174 *Three First Chapters of the Revelation*, p. 272.

175 Frye, "Agon and Logos: Revolution and Revelation," in *The Prison and the Pinnacle*, p. 140.

176 Balachandra Rajan makes the same point in " 'To Which is Added *Samson Agonistes*—'," in *The Prison and the Pinnacle*, p. 97.

177 I adapt a point made by Leslie Brisman, *Milton's Poetry of Choice and Its Romantic Heirs* (Ithaca: Cornell Univ. Press, 1973), p. 196.

178 William Perkins, *A Declaration of the True Manner of Knowing Christ Crucified* (London: Printed by John Legate, 1611), p. 2; but see also pp. 6–7, 53–54.

179 "Blake's Early Poetry," in *William Blake: Essays*, p. 13.

180 Ibid., p. 17.

181 Ibid., p. 23. Following Blake's other commentators, David Bindman says that it is "likely" that "the date of 1780 on the *Glad Day* engraving refers to a lost first state, or at least the date of Blake's original idea" ("Blake's 'Gothicised Imagination' and the History of England," in *William Blake: Essays*, p. 44). We know from Blake that most if not all of the pieces in *Poetical Sketches* were completed by 1777, though publication did not occur until 1783. Is it possible that "Samson" is a late piece (1780?); is it perhaps the referent of the 1780 date on the line engraving, Blake alluding through the later picture-prophecy to this early prophecy, of which the line engraving is a pictorialization?

182 *A Key of Knowledge*, pp. 34–36; see also p. 76, where Samson is invoked as a type of the Great Dragon and Delilah as a type of the Great Whore.

183 West's poem, originally published in *Poems and Plays* (1799), is reprinted in *The Works of the English Poets from Chaucer to Cowper*, 21 vols. (London: J. Johnson, 1810), VII, 347.

184 Andrew Wright, *Blake's "Job": A Commentary* (Oxford: Clarendon Press, 1972), p. 21. Interestingly, particularly in view of Janet Warner's observations on "gesture," one of Satan's hands is turned upward, the other downward. See also note 159 above.

185 Compare plates 1 and 16 of *Milton* (see figs. 7 and 10) with plates 18 and 21 of Blake's *Job* series, reproduced by Wright, *Blake's "Job"*, pp. 44, 50; and notice, too, that this motif of turning inward and upward dominates Blake's title page for the *Job* series, also reproduced by Wright, ibid., p. 2.

186 C. H. Collins Baker, "William Blake, Painter," *Huntington Library Bulletin*, 10 (1936), 137.

187 For views that oppose my own, see Paley, *Energy and Imagination*, pp. 195–99, and see also John Grant's review of Paley's book in *English Language Notes*, 9 (1972), 214–16. Blake's paintings—*Pitt Guiding Behemoth* and *Nelson Guiding Leviathan*—are reproduced by Anthony Blunt in *The Art of William Blake*, pls. 46c and 46d.

188 *Memoirs of Thomas Hollis*, p. 532. For Robinson's report of the conver-

sation, see *The Romantics on Milton*, pp. 96–97. It should be noted, however, that Robinson is much more explicit in his query than most published versions of this account suggest: "I ventured to ask, half ashamed at the time, which of the three or four portraits in *Hollis's Memoirs* (Vols in 4to) is the most like—He answ^d ['] They are all like, At different Ages—I have seen him as a youth And as an old man with a long flowing beard[.] He came lately as an old man . . .[']" (*Blake Records*, ed. G. E. Bentley, Jr. [Oxford: Clarendon Press, 1969], p. 317). This remark probably caused S. Foster Damon to see in plate 1 of *Milton* "a nude youth with a Christ-like beard" (*William Blake: His Philosophy and Symbols*, p. 429). The only copy of *Milton* to show any evidence of a beard on this plate is B, and then this evidence is not at all conclusive.

189 *The Romantics on Milton*, p. 96.

190 Blake would certainly have learned from Hayley about the bondage in which an author is held by his publisher. Hayley's *Life of Milton* was published first in the expurgated edition of 1794. For a discussion of Hayley's difficulties with his publisher and for an account of the differences between the 1794 and 1796 editions of this *Life*, see my Introduction to Hayley's *Life of Milton*, esp. pp. vii–x.

191 See *The Life and Posthumous Writings of William Cowper*, 3 vols. (Chichester: J. Johnson, 1803–4), and *Cowper's Milton*, 4 vols. (Chichester: J. Johnson, 1810).

192 See *A Complete Collection of the Historical, Political, and Miscellaneous Works of John Milton*, 2 vols. (London: A. Millar, 1738). A second edition was issued in 1753.

193 See *The Romantics on Milton*, p. 95.

194 See Tayler, "Say First! What Mov'd Blake? Blake's *Comus* Designs and *Milton*," in *Blake's Sublime Allegory*, pp. 233–58.

195 Tayler, *Blake's Illustrations to the Poems of Gray*, p. 80, and see also pp. 9–10. I am in full sympathy with what Tayler says about Gray, but I do not think that what she says about him can be extended to Milton without a shift in accent as one observes the shifting attitude of Blake toward his mentor.

196 A striking example of an engraver altering the designs of an artist occurred when Pierre Fourdrinier engraved the Aldrich-Medina-Lens illustrations for *Paradise Lost* (London: Jacob Tonson, 1725). See my note, "Milton's 'First' Illustrator," *Seventeenth-Century News*, 35 (1975). Fourdrinier's new conception of Satan may be less compatible with Milton's poem; but it is quite compatible with a view of Milton and his devils articulated a year later by Daniel Defoe—a view that had already begun to prevail. "I admire Mr. *Milton* as a Poet," says Defoe; "yet . . . he was greatly out in matters of History, and especially the History of the *Devil*." Indeed, from Defoe's point of view, Milton has taken so much liberty with the Devil that Defoe feels compelled to "pursue the duty of an Historian" and to correct Milton's "mischief" (*The Political*

History of the Devil [London: T. Warner, 1726], pp. 27, 36). Like Defoe, Fourdrinier seems intent upon *correcting* Milton's vision rather than upon representing it with the accuracy achieved by Medina; and it is in this contention between illustrator and engraver that the Satanist controversy begins—at least in the visual arts. The problems of illustration attendant upon such a situation are discussed by William Ivins, *Prints and Visual Communication,* where he explains that "with very few exceptions" the eighteenth-century publisher presented "pictures which were at one and two removes from the visual statements made by their titular makers"; and their makers, we should add, were often one or two removes from the texts they were illustrating. All one could hope for was that a text, and then an illustration for it, would be represented "in a generally adequate way, and that the iconographic detail was more or less truthful" (pp. 88–89). These tyrannies, so carefully described by Ivins, are the ones that were broken in the nineteenth century through the agency of Blake.

197 *"Clinamen* or Poetic Misprision," *New Literary History,* 3 (1972), 382–83. Bloom's views are more fully developed in *The Anxiety of Influence: A Theory of Poetry* (New York: Oxford Univ. Press, 1973), esp. pp. 5–45.
198 "Blake and Milton," in *The Divine Vision: Studies in the Poetry and Art of William Blake,* ed. Vivian de Sola Pinto (London: Victor Gollancz, 1957), pp. 91–96.
199 See *Shelley: A Critical Reading* (Baltimore: Johns Hopkins Press, 1971), esp. pp. vii–ix.
200 *Cowper's Milton,* IV, 394.

Chapter 2: "THE HOUSE OF THE INTERPRETER": BLAKE'S MILTON
         ILLUSTRATIONS

  1 Within this chapter, I range freely over Blake's designs, many of which I have been unable to reproduce in this book. Rather than pausing after every reference to indicate where a specific design can be found, I point the reader *now* to the headnote for Appendix B in *Calm of Mind: Tercentenary Essays on "Paradise Regained" and "Samson Agonistes,"* ed. Joseph Anthony Wittreich, Jr. (Cleveland: Press of Case Western Reserve Univ., 1971), pp. 331–34, which provides a comprehensive list of sources where reproductions of Blake's Milton designs appear. I have also alluded in this chapter to the tradition of illustration for *Paradise Regained* that I have recreated in Appendix A of *Calm of Mind,* pp. 309–29.
  2 I adopt language from Clyde Taylor's review of John Beer's *Blake's Humanism,* in *Criticism,* 11 (1969), 101.
  3 Ralph Cohen, *The Art of Discrimination: Thomson's "The Seasons" and*

the Language of Criticism (Berkeley and Los Angeles: Univ. of California Press, 1964), p. 253; see also pp. 2–5, 441–48.

4 *Landscape, Portrait, Still Life, Their Origin and Development,* tr. R. F. C. Hull (Oxford: Bruno Cassirer, 1949), p. 168.

5 *Biographia* (London: J. Johnson, 1799), p. 505.

6 Philippe Soupault, *William Blake,* tr. J. Lewis May (New York: Dodd and Mead, 1928), p. 48. Nor should one forget Blake's remark in *A Descriptive Catalogue* that many of his visions were translated into "pictures . . . all containing mythological and recondite meaning, where more is meant than meets the eye" (p. 522).

7 If there is not total agreement on the date for the illustrations to *Paradise Regained,* there is at least a consensus. In *The Art of William Blake* (Morningside Heights, N.Y.: Columbia Univ. Press, 1959), Anthony Blunt postulates a later date, ca. 1820–1821 (p. 83); in *The Paintings of William Blake* (London: Ernest Benn, 1925), Darrell Figgis suggests a much earlier date, ca. 1808 (p. 69); so does George Wingfield Digby in *Symbol and Image in William Blake* (Oxford: Clarendon Press, 1957), p. 65. But Geoffrey Keynes in *John Milton: Poems in English with Illustrations by William Blake, Miscellaneous Poems* (London: Nonesuch Press, 1926), p. 278, Thomas Wright in *The Life of William Blake,* 2 vols. (Olney: Wright, 1929), II, 26, and Mona Wilson in *The Life of William Blake* (New York: Ballou, 1933), p. 220, agree that the illustrations were made about 1816.

John E. Grant makes the same argument for the *L'Allegro* and *Il Penseroso* series that I make for the *Paradise Regained* illustrations: those for Milton's companion poems, he says, come last and are an epitome of Milton's vision (see "Blake's Designs for *L'Allegro* and *Il Penseroso,*" *Blake Newsletter,* 4 [1971], 118). No supporting evidence is offered there for his assertion; nor is any forthcoming in the second half of the essay, also published in *Blake Newsletter,* 5 (1972), 190–202. There is no effort to explain the circumstance that Mirth and Melancholy may, indeed, be the female figures portrayed in the first design for the *Paradise Regained* series (see fig. 34) and no acknowledgment of any relationship between the designs for Milton's twin lyrics and those for his brief epic. Finally, it is less important to dispute the chronology of the designs than to perceive the sequential relationship between them. The illustrations for *L'Allegro* and *Il Penseroso* record the poet's struggle to achieve the prophetic strain, the divine vision; those for *Paradise Regained* are an articulation of the vision itself. These two sets of designs, then, relate to one another just as *Milton* and *Jerusalem* do. Blake is not alone in perceiving this progression in the companion poems or in discerning a relationship between them and *Paradise Regained:* some published versions of Handel's musical setting carry an apocalyptic fourth part, which celebrates "the conqu'ring Hero" as prophet, king, and priest (see, e.g., *"L'Allegro" ed "Il Pen-*

seroso" as Performed at Ranelagh-House [London: J. and R. Tonson, 1759]).

8 The phrase is Northrop Frye's; see *A Study of English Romanticism* (New York: Random House, 1968), pp. 3–49.

9 "The Altering Eye: Blake's Vision in the *Tiriel* Designs," in *William Blake: Essays in Honour of Sir Geoffrey Keynes,* ed. Morton D. Paley and Michael Phillips (Oxford: Clarendon Press, 1973), p. 65.

10 *Poems in English,* p. 272.

11 "Say First! What Mov'd Blake? Blake's *Comus* Designs and *Milton,*" in *Blake's Sublime Allegory: Essays on "The Four Zoas," "Milton," and "Jerusalem,"* ed. Stuart Curran and Joseph Anthony Wittreich, Jr. (Madison: Univ. of Wisconsin Press, 1973), p. 235.

12 Ibid., p. 239.

13 Ibid., p. 240.

14 See the important essay by Barbara Breasted, "*Comus* and the Castle-haven Scandal," *Milton Studies,* 3 (1971), 201–24.

15 John T. Shawcross's probing essay is complementary to Tayler's; see "Milton and Diodati: An Essay in Psychodynamic Meaning," in a special issue of *Milton Studies,* ed. Albert C. Labriola and Michael Lieb (Pittsburgh: Univ. of Pittsburgh Press, 1975). Also pertinent is Jackie Di Salvo's statement, "William Blake on the Unholy Alliance: Satanic Freedom and Godly Repression in Liberal Society," *The Wordsworth Circle,* 4 (1972), 212–22.

16 *Illustrations in Roll and Codex: A Study of the Origin and Method of Text Illustration* (Princeton: Princeton Univ. Press, 1947), p. 171. Ronald Paulson, in an important methodological statement, echoes my point, observing that an illustration has access not only to a text but to an iconographic tradition paralleling it (see "The Tradition of Comic Illustration from Hogarth to Cruikshank," *Princeton University Library Chronicle,* 35 [1974], 56).

17 Weitzmann, *Illustrations in Roll and Codex,* p. 171. Herbert Marcuse sees "marked silence," omission, as an important ingredient of revolutionary art; from the calculated omission, revolutionary art derives much of its power, and through it delivers a considerable part of its message (*Counter-Revolution and Revolt* [Boston: Beacon Press, 1972], p. 96).

18 *Illustrations in Roll and Codex,* p. 183.

19 "Say First! What Mov'd Blake? Blake's *Comus* Designs and *Milton,*" in *Blake's Sublime Allegory,* p. 237.

20 *The Romantics on Milton: Formal Essays and Critical Asides,* ed. Joseph Anthony Wittreich, Jr. (Cleveland: Press of Case Western Reserve Univ., 1970), p. 299.

21 *The Poetical Works of John Milton,* ed. Henry John Todd, 2nd ed., 7 vols. (London: Printed for J. Johnson, 1809), VI, 413. Tayler's conjecture that "the chief allusion is probably to Medea"—that "Blake merely literalizes and makes explicit the connection" (see "Say First! What Mov'd Blake? Blake's *Comus* Designs and *Milton,*" in *Blake's Sublime*

Allegory, p. 237) takes credibility from the fact that the Medea-Comus association was a commonplace in the eighteenth century; see, e.g., Charles Dibdin, *The Devil* (London: Denew and Grant [1786]), p. 116: "Neptune's chariot may be that of Medea, the spirit of Comus, Hecate, or almost any other, altered and drawn by sea horses."

22 *Poetical Works*, ed. Todd (1809), VI, 415, 418.

23 Tayler, "Say First! What Mov'd Blake? Blake's *Comus* Designs and *Milton*," in *Blake's Sublime Allegory*, p. 239.

24 Ibid., p. 238.

25 See Pointon's index, *Milton and English Art* (Toronto: Univ. of Toronto Press, 1970). For the new designs listed above, see *Comus, A Masque* (London: Printed for W. Lowndes and S. Badon, 1790)—Dighton's design is dated 1777; *Comus*, in *Bell's British Theatre* (London: Printed for John Bell, 1777); *Comus, A Masque* (London: Printed for J. Wenman, 1777); *The Cabinet of Genius* (London: Printed for C. Taylor, 1787); *Comus, A Masque* (London: Printed for the Proprietors, 1791)—this volume contains both the Burney and the DeWilde designs; *The Poetical Works of John Milton*, 4 vols. (London: Printed for J. Johnson, 1801)—Rigaud's design is in the third volume. The history of *Comus* illustration is much like the history of illustration for *L'Allegro* and *Il Penseroso*: illustrators of both poems seem to have been less concerned with interpreting poetry than with using it as an occasion for complimentary portraits. Pointon's incomplete catalogue of Milton's illustrators lists designs by Francis Hayman (1752), George Romney (1770), Alexander Runciman (1773), Robert Smirke (ca. 1780), and Richard Westall (1797, 1816)—most of them complimentary portraits. However, there are other designs for *L'Allegro* and *Il Penseroso*, unnoticed by Pointon, that are of real interest. There is, first of all, the background to the frontispiece portrait of Milton, engraved by William Marshall and included in *Poems of Mr. John Milton* (see fig. 3). The background depicts children dancing in the shade of a tree to the music of a piper. Second, there are two illustrations—one shows the poet embracing the world; the other, the poet rejecting it—included in *Paradise Regained*, 5th ed. (London: Printed for J. Tonson, 1713). The first of these designs is signed by Nicholas Pigne. Third, in *The Cabinet of Genius*, there are designs by C. Taylor for both *L'Allegro* and *Il Penseroso*, one entitled *Morning* (it portrays the wandering poet beneath the elms), the other called *Evening* (it depicts children dancing in the shade to the music of a piper who sits in a tree, with a cluster of old people looking on). Finally, there are two other illustrations, both by Stephen Rigaud, in *The Poetical Works of John Milton*, 4 vols. (London: Printed for J. Johnson, 1801). The fourth volume contains depictions of both Mirth and Melancholy.

26 See pp. iv–v of the 1791 edition, cited in note 25.

27 For Hayman's design, see *Paradise Regain'd*, ed. Thomas Newton (London: Printed for J. and R. Tonson, 1752).

28 *Comus, A Masque* (London: Printed for A. Millar, 1750), pp. 5–6, 11.
29 Ibid., p. 5.
30 See J. B. Broadbent's essay, "The Nativity Ode," in *The Living Milton,* ed. Frank Kermode (London: Routledge and Kegan Paul, 1960), pp. 12–31.
31 Gertrud Schiller, *Iconography of Christian Art,* tr. Janet Seligman (Greenwich, Conn.: New York Graphic Society, 1971), p. 59.
32 *"Europe:* 'to those ychain'd in sleep'," in *Blake's Visionary Forms Dramatic,* ed. David V. Erdman and John E. Grant (Princeton: Princeton Univ. Press, 1970), p. 145.
33 Westall's design appears in the third volume of *The Poetical Works of John Milton,* ed. William Hayley, 3 vols. (London: Printed for J. and J. Boydell and G. Nicol, 1794–97).
34 *Poems upon Several Occasions* (London: J. Dodsley, 1785), p. 282.
35 Ibid., pp. 282–83.
36 The subjects Blake illustrates are highly conventional. Two of them, according to C. H. Collins Baker, are new: Satan and Raphael entering Eden, and the Crucifixion. It should be remembered, however, that Satan and Raphael had previously been depicted in Eden; and thus Blake merely revises the moment being pictorialized. Moreover, though Blake is the first to present the Crucifixion among his *Paradise Lost* designs, he is not the first to depict the subject in illustrating Milton's poetry (see note 88). See Baker's two-part essay, "Some Illustrators of Milton's *Paradise Lost* (1688–1850)," *The Library,* 5th ser., 3 (1948), 1–21, 101–19, and also the index to Pointon's *Milton and English Art,* which provides supplementary materials. Despite their diligence, both Baker and Pointon have missed numerous published illustrations that antedate those by Blake. The list is too long to be reported here, but it can easily be assembled by looking at the following items in my own list of Milton illustrations in the forthcoming *Milton Encyclopedia,* ed. William B. Hunter, Jr., et al.: "Anonymous designs, 1736," "Balestra et al., 1740," "Piazetta et al., 1742," "Gillray, 1782," "Gillray, 1787," "Gillray, 1790–92," "Burney, 1795," "Gillray, 1795–98," "Burney, 1802," "Gillray, 1803–5," "Chapman–Craig, 1804," "Monsiau, 1805," "Uwins, 1811," "Massard, 1812," and "Flaxman, 1819." But even this catalogue requires an addendum: eight anonymous designs appear in *Le Paradis Terrestre,* an imitation of Milton by Madame D. B. (London: n.p., 1760); the subjects illustrated are Adam and Eve in their bower, the expulsion of the rebel angels, Satan calling up his legions, Adam and Eve in Eden, Raphael calling to Adam and Eve, Adam conversing with Raphael, the temptation of Eve, and Adam and Michael on the hill.
37 See both "Blake's Illustrations to *Paradise Lost,*" *Blake Newsletter,* 3 (1969), 57, and, in the same publication, "A 'Minute Particular' Particularized: Blake's Second Set of Illustrations to *Paradise Lost,*" 6 (1972), 44–46.
38 "A 'Minute Particular' Particularized," p. 46.
39 *Seven Lectures on Shakespeare and Milton by the Late S. T. Coleridge,*

ed. John Payne Collier (London: Chapman and Hall, 1856), pp. 65–66. The comment was frequently repeated by Coleridge; see *The Romantics on Milton,* pp. 201, 215, 242, 247.

40 Blake mentions this edition in a letter to Thomas Butts, dated July 6, 1803; see *The Romantics on Milton,* p. 38. In *The Life of William Blake,* Mona Wilson suggests that this illustration to *Paradise Lost* "follows closely Hogarth's treatment on the same subject" (p. 210); however, Geoffrey Keynes was the first critic to postulate that debt (see "The Nonesuch Milton," *The Nation and Athenaeum,* 39 [1926], 697). But in *Blake: Prophet Against Empire,* rev. ed. (Garden City, N.Y.: Double-day, 1969), David V. Erdman argues that Blake's largest debt is to James Gillray (pp. 221–23). Hogarth's design is reproduced by Samuel Ireland in *Graphic Illustrations of Hogarth from Pictures, and Drawings, in the Possession of Samuel Ireland,* 2 vols. (London: R. Faulder, 1794–99), I, facing 179; Gillray's is reproduced as plate 50 in *The Works of James Gillray: 582 Plates and a Supplement Containing the 45 So-called "Suppressed Plates"* (1851; rpt. New York: Benjamin Blom, 1968).

41 *Milton's Life and Poetical Works with Notes by William Cowper,* ed. William Hayley, 4 vols. (Chichester: Printed for J. Johnson, 1810), II, 453–54.

42 John E. Grant reminds us that before painting his sets of illustrations to *Paradise Lost* Blake did a separate design of "The Lazar House" in which he attempted "to analyze the human consequences of the Fall" ("You Can't Write About Blake's Pictures Like That," *Blake Studies,* 1, ii [1969], 196).

43 In *William Blake, Poet and Painter: An Introduction to the Illuminated Verse* (Chicago: Univ. of Chicago Press, 1964), Jean Hagstrum writes (I think mistakenly), "Even the four Zoas, who appear broodingly in the sky at the time of the expulsion, are not the four horsemen of the Apocalypse, but fallen gods yearning for the day that will restore their primal unity" (p. 126). At least, in the tradition of biblical illustration, the four horsemen have been involved previously in an expulsion scene (see, e.g., Kenneth A. Strand, *Reformation Bible Pictures: Woodcuts from Early Lutheran and Emserian New Testaments* [Ann Arbor, Mich.: Ann Arbor Publishers, 1963], p. 31). Blake accomplishes the contrast of beginning and end, of defeat and triumph, by appropriating the iconography of expulsion from the Book of Revelation, which does involve the four horsemen, to the expulsion scene in Genesis, which does not usually involve them.

44 "John Martin and the Expulsion Scene of *Paradise Lost,*" *Studies in English Literature 1500–1900,* 1 (1961), 70.

45 "Some Illustrators of Milton: The Expulsion from Paradise," in *Milton Studies in Honor of Harris Francis Fletcher,* ed. G. Blakemore Evans et al. (Urbana: Univ. of Illinois Press, 1961), pp. 65–66.

46 Leslie Brisman, *Milton's Poetry of Choice and Its Romantic Heirs* (Ithaca: Cornell Univ. Press, 1973), pp. 245, 246.

47 Friedländer, *Landscape, Portrait, Still Life,* p. 169.

48 See the reproductions provided by Leonard D. Ettlinger, *The Sistine Chapel Before Michelangelo: Religious Imagery and Papal Primacy* (Oxford: Clarendon Press, 1965), esp. pl. 9.

49 Kurt Weitzmann, *Ancient Book Illumination,* Martin Classical Lectures, No. XVI (Cambridge, Mass.: Harvard Univ. Press, 1959), p. 31. Blake's interest, of course, is less in the narrative than in the vision accompanying it; Karl Kroeber's essay is pertinent (see "Graphic-Poetic Structuring in Blake's *Book of Urizen," Blake Studies,* 3 [1970], 7—18).

50 Weitzmann, *Ancient Book Illumination,* p. 31.

51 See Tayler, "Say First! What Mov'd Blake? Blake's *Comus* Designs and *Milton,"* in *Blake's Sublime Allegory,* p. 233, and Mitchell, "Blake's Composite Art," in *Blake's Visionary Forms Dramatic,* p. 58.

52 *"America:* New Expanses," in *Blake's Visionary Forms Dramatic,* pp. 92—93.

53 Weitzmann, *Ancient Book Illumination,* p. 1.

54 *"America:* New Expanses," in *Blake's Visionary Forms Dramatic,* p. 111.

55 Strand, *Reformation Bible Pictures,* pp. 14, 92.

56 Tayler, "Say First! What Mov'd Blake? Blake's *Comus* Designs and *Milton,"* in *Blake's Sublime Allegory,* p. 235.

57 Ben F. Nelms, "Text and Design in *Illustrations of the Book of Job,"* in *Blake's Visionary Forms Dramatic,* pp. 341—42.

58 *English Illustration: The Nineties* (London: Faber and Faber, 1935), p. 247.

59 Especially interesting for the subtle interplay of illustration and "decoration" are the designs by Louis Cheron in *The Poetical Works of Mr. John Milton,* 2 vols. (London: Printed for Jacob Tonson, 1720); those by Balestra et al. in *Il Paradiso Perduto,* 2 vols. (Paris: Giovanni Alberto Tumerani, 1740); and those by Craig in *Paradise Lost,* 2 vols. (London: Albion Press, 1804). For interpretive "decorations" after Blake, see Jane E. Giraud, *The Flowers of Milton* (London: Day and Haghe, 1846); the designs for *Paradise Lost* present the poem as an exploration of evil, and those for *Paradise Regained* repeatedly identify the brief epic with the drama of the Crucifixion.

60 *A History of Book Illustration: The Illuminated Manuscript and the Printed Book* (Berkeley and Los Angeles: Univ. of California Press, 1969), p. 15; see also Philip Hofer, *Baroque Book Illustration: A Short Survey* (Cambridge, Mass.: Harvard Univ. Press, 1951), p. 5.

61 "Blake's Illustrations for *Paradise Lost, L'Allegro,* and *Il Penseroso:* A Thematic Reading," *Hartford Studies in Literature,* 2 (1970), 40.

62 R. Margaret Slythe, *The Art of Illustration 1750—1900* (London: Library Association, 1970), p. 9.

63 On the Opie design, see G. E. Bentley, Jr., and Martin K. Nurmi, *A Blake Bibliography* (Minneapolis: Univ. of Minnesota Press, 1964), p. 154. Robert N. Essick has pointed out to me the extent of Blake's alterations of Fuseli's *The Fertilization of Egypt.*

64 *Ancient Book Illustration,* p. 1 (my italics).

65 Robert Weaver, "The Future of Illustration," in *The Illustrator in America*, ed. Walter Reed (New York: Reinhold, n.d.), p. 268.

66 Ibid.

67 Philip Hofer, *The Artist and the Book 1860–1960 in Western Europe and the United States* (Boston: Museum of Fine Arts, and Cambridge, Mass.: Harvard College Library, 1961), p. 7.

68 *William Blake, Poet and Painter,* p. 10. The same assumption lies behind Michael Phillips's essay, "Blake's Early Poetry," where it is argued that, since the eighteenth century read *Samson Agonistes* in such a way so, too, did Blake (see *William Blake: Essays,* esp. pp. 20–25).

69 Weitzmann reminds us that book illustration, in ancient times and now, "begins only after [the text] has become sufficiently popular and widespread" (p. 2). "The first condition for a text to be illustrated," he reiterates, "is its popularity" (p. 31).

   See the Latin translation by William Hog, *Paraphrasis Poetica in Tria Johannis Miltoni, Viri Clarissmi, Poemata, viz. Paradisum Amissum, Paradisum Recuperatum, et Samsonem Agonisten* (London: J. Darby, 1690); also the anonymous *On the Resurrection in Imitation of Milton,* in Francis Peck's *New Memoirs of the Life and Poetical Works of Mr. John Milton* (London, 1740), separate pagination, and the anonymous *Jesus: A Poem in the Blank Verse* (London, 1745). There are, in addition, numerous eighteenth-century translations of Milton's brief epic into both French and German.

70 See [Bernard Routh], *Lettres critiques a Mr Le Comte sur le Paradis Perdu et Reconquis de Milton* (Paris, 1731); Richard Meadowcourt, *A Critique on Milton's "Paradise Regain'd"* (London: Printed for Henry Lintot, 1732); the anonymous *An Essay upon Milton's Imitations of the Ancients in His "Paradise Lost," with Some Observations on the "Paradise Regain'd"* ([London], 1741). A second edition of Meadowcourt's critique, printed for A. Millar, was published in 1748 under the title *Critical Dissertation with Notes on Milton's "Paradise Regain'd."* An anonymous prose translation of *Paradise Regained, The Recovery of Man,* was published in 1771 (London?); but the first separate English edition of the poem, published in London by Toplis and Bunney, did not appear until eight years later. The first American edition of *Paradise Regained,* published along with *Paradise Lost,* was issued in Philadelphia in 1777.

71 London: J. and R. Tonson, 1752, pp. 3, 49. Newton is quoting from John Jortin's *Remarks on Spenser's Poems* (London: J. Whiston, 1734), p. 172; but see also Newton's Preface, p. [i], and his note, pp. 186–87.

72 The comments by Thyer and Warburton are quoted from Newton's edition, pp. 3–4. Warburton raises an objection to *Paradise Regained* implied earlier (1705) by John Dennis, who thought that Milton in his brief epic "err'd wildly" in his religion (*Milton: The Critical Heritage,* ed. John T. Shawcross [London: Routledge and Kegan Paul, 1970], p. 134).

73 Wordsworth is reported to have thought *Paradise Regained* "the most

perfect in *execution* of anything written by Milton" (*The Prose Works of William Wordsworth,* ed. Alexander B. Grosart, 3 vols. (London: Edward Moxon, 1876], III, 430); and Shelley's enthusiasm for the poem is communicated in a letter to John Gisborne: Byron's *Cain,* he says, "contains finer poetry than has appeared in England since the publication of Paradise Regained" (*The Letters of Percy Bysshe Shelley,* ed. Frederick L. Jones, 2 vols. [Oxford: Clarendon Press, 1964], II, 388). Thomas Medwin, recollecting this comment, observes that *Paradise Regained* is a work that Shelley "frequently read and compared to the calm and tranquil beauty of an autumnal sunset, after the meridian glory and splendour of a summer's day" (*The Life of Percy Bysshe Shelley,* ed. H. Buxton Forman [London: Oxford Univ. Press, 1913], p. 263). For other appraisals of *Paradise Regained* by the major Romantics, both poets and critics, see the index to my edition, *The Romantics on Milton;* and see also Stuart Curran, "The Mental Pinnacle: *Paradise Regained* and the Romantic Four-Book Epic," in *Calm of Mind,* pp. 133–62. For a typically eighteenth-century response to the poem, see the imaginary dialogue between Tasso and Milton, wherein Tasso, conceding he erred in revising *Gerusalemme Liberata* into *Gerusalemme Conquistata,* attributes to Milton the still greater error of "preferring that *mean* performance of yours the Paradise Regained to your Paradise Lost" (see *Il Tasso* [London: R. Baldwin, 1762], pp. 10–11).

74 *The Life of Milton,* in *The Poetical Works of John Milton* (1794–97), I, cxxv–cxxvi. Hayley's distinction between Milton's two epics probably caught the eye of Blake, as it caught the eye of Coleridge, who marks the passage with three check marks in his 1796 copy of Hayley's *Life* (see my facsimile edition, and Introduction [Gainesville, Fla.: Scholars' Facsimiles and Reprints, 1970]). Coleridge's copy is now in the Henry E. Huntington Library (Catalogue No. 144952). For his views on this matter, Hayley may owe something to William Cowper, who by 1826 was being cited by Todd to represent the notion that *Paradise Regained* is complete. Cowper had used the *Iliad* and the *Aeneid* to explain that, in *Paradise Regained* as well as these epics, the "action has proceeded so far as to pass the cardinal event upon which all that was to follow must happen." In this sense, *Paradise Regained* is as complete as these earlier epics, for after "the Tempter was defeated, Man was put into a state of *regaining Paradise,* as Christ thereby stood enabled to perform all the parts of his mission and purposes" (*The Poetical Works of John Milton,* 3rd ed., 6 vols. [London: C. and J. Rivington, 1826], IV, 307).

75 London: T. Cadell and W. Davies, 1795, pp. i, iv (a second edition of Dunster's volume was issued in 1800). But Dunster also refers to *Paradise Regained* as a "companion" poem to *Samson Agonistes* (p. v). For fuller discussion of the critical tradition accumulated by *Paradise Regained* during the eighteenth century and the Romantic period, see the introduction to my facsimile edition of Meadowcourt's *Critique* and Dunster's edition of the poem (Gainesville, Fla.: Scholars' Facsimiles and Reprints, 1971).

76 *Poetical Works,* ed. Todd (1801), IV, 355; (1809), V, 310.
77 *The Prose Works of John Milton, with a Life of the Author,* 7 vols. (London: J. Johnson, 1806), VII, 487, 489.
78 *The Poetical Works of John Milton* (1801), I, 33–34.
79 *Poetical Works of John Milton* (London: Suttaby, Evance, and Fox, 1821), pp. iii, xii.
80 Ibid., p. xiii. Jean Hagstrum fully grasps the significance of Blake's portrayals of Christ in the *Paradise Regained* series: Milton's poem, says Hagstrum, provides the "nearest" literary prototype for Blake's Christ, Blake, though, going "beyond even the Milton of *Paradise Regained* in humanizing the Son of God" ("Christ's Body," in *William Blake: Essays,* p. 133).
81 *Paradise Regained and Other Poems* (New York: Solomon King, 1831).
82 Walter MacKellar, *The Poems of John Milton* (London: Routledge and Kegan Paul, forthcoming).
83 Ibid.
84 From 1800 to 1803, Blake lived on Hayley's estate at Felpham. During that time, Hayley taught Blake some Latin and Greek, and the two probably discussed Milton from time to time. For a list of the holdings in Hayley's library, which contained a sizable Milton collection, see *A Catalogue of the Very Valuable and Extensive Library of the Late William Hayley, Esq.* (Sold at auction by Mr. Evans), February, 1821. Hayley's copy of the Dunster edition is in the William Andrews Clark Memorial Library, Los Angeles. And for discussion of Blake's reading of Milton, see John Beer, *Blake's Visionary Universe* (Manchester: Manchester Univ. Press, and New York: Barnes and Noble, 1969), pp. 23–25.
85 "Blake, Milton, and Edward Burney," *Princeton University Library Chronicle,* 11 (1950), 114, 126. In *The Art of William Blake,* Anthony Blunt postulates that Blake "borrowed more extensively and more systematically from the work of other artists than did any of his contemporaries" (p. 32); see also *Blake's Pencil Drawings,* ed. Geoffrey Keynes, 2nd ser. (London: Nonesuch Press, 1956), p. ix. The "minute particulars" of the tradition of illustration involving *Paradise Regained* are provided in Appendix A of *Calm of Mind,* pp. 309–29.
86 "The Iconography of the Fall of Man," in *Approaches to "Paradise Lost": The York Tercentenary Lectures,* ed. C. A. Patrides (Toronto: Univ. of Toronto Press, 1968), pp. 253, 224–25. Trapp's conclusions are easily borne out by looking through the sixty volume, extra-illustrated Kitto Bible in the Henry E. Huntington Library (Catalogue No. 49000). The temptations of Christ, as represented by Matthew, Mark, and Luke, are copiously illustrated—especially the first one—by biblical designers. The illustrators of *Paradise Regained* relied so heavily upon this tradition that in many instances their designs are scarcely more than copies of earlier biblical illustrations. But Blake, even when he used a traditional subject, transformed, in an important way, the concepts that he inherited from tradition; his greatest debt to the traditions of biblical

illustration and eighteenth-century Milton illustration lies not in his borrowing of detail but in his adaptation of a technique. Acutely sensitive to traditional typology, which relates the temptations of Adam to those of Christ and which sees in any one of the latter temptations the whole sequence, the biblical illustrator customarily brought only the first temptation of Christ into focus but at the same time might represent the others marginally (see, e.g., Kitto Bible, XXXIV, 6362; XXXIX, facing 7184, 7183 verso, 7207; XLVIII, 8636, 8750). Blake also uses the device of typology—not as his precursors did, to confirm a tradition of theology, but to indicate Milton's departures from it. Thus, where the technique appears in Blake's illustrations, as in the sixth and seventh designs, it serves to suggest the continuity of the banquet and kingdoms temptation (in the first instance) and to call attention to Milton's gathering of the three temptations into the extended second temptation (the second instance). See also notes 99 and 100.

87 *Norm and Form: Studies in the Art of the Renaissance,* 2nd ed. (London and New York: Phaidon, 1971), p. 20.

88 As C. H. Collins Baker observes, Blake is the first illustrator to present the Crucifixion, with Christ bruising the head of the serpent, as a subject for *Paradise Lost* (see "Some Illustrators of Milton's *Paradise Lost,*" p. 119); however, Blake is not the first to use the subject in his Milton illustrations. Blake's predecessors often chose the subject as the first illustration (generally a frontispiece) to *Paradise Regained,* thereby stressing the continuity between the two epics. Blake, on the other hand, uses the subject only where Milton's text fully justifies its use, that is, in Book XII of *Paradise Lost.* That illustration is obviously affected by those done previously for *Paradise Regained,* but in conception and execution it surpasses those earlier renderings. Previous illustrators show the serpent twined around the foot of the cross and a skull lying to the side of it (Christ is ordinarily carrying the cross rather than suspended from it); Blake shows the nail piercing Christ's foot also piercing the head of the serpent. The only comparable conception that I have seen is in the Kitto Bible, XLI, 7673, where the base of a crude cross is shown going through the head of the serpent. The illustration, designed by P. J. de Loutherbourg, may have been known to Blake, since de Loutherbourg, a contemporary of James Barry, exhibited a design for *Paradise Lost* at the Royal Academy in 1782. Baker's contention ignores the fact that, while no illustrator depicts the Crucifixion in the context of Book XII of *Paradise Lost,* many illustrators represent the subject, usually in relation to Books III and VI. For examples, see Medina's illustration for the third book in *Paradise Lost,* 4th ed. (London: Printed for Jacob Tonson, 1688); Cheron's tailpiece for the sixth book in the first volume of *The Poetical Works of Mr. John Milton,* 2 vols. (London: Printed for Jacob Tonson, 1720); Crozati's design for the third book in the first volume of *Il Paradiso Perduto;* and Craig's tailpiece for the tenth book in the second volume of *Paradise Lost,* 2 vols. (London: Albion Press, 1804).

89 Gombrich, *Norm and Form*, p. 22.

90 Ibid., p. 25. One must not dismiss too quickly this tradition of cosmic painting. It clearly does not represent the mode of the Milton illustrations, but it is the mode of the one design for Chaucer's *Canterbury Tales* and of the one design for Spenser's *The Faerie Queene*. These designs are an active complication of this artistic tradition. Rather than preparing one design for each of Chaucer's tales, or one design for each book of Spenser's epic, Blake provides but one illustration for each poem—an illustration that compresses, through both allusion and iconography, the major thematic content of what is, in each instance, an exceedingly long poem. In these designs, Blake outdoes the typical "synoptic" illustrator, creating designs that should be studied as a great culmination in the history of cosmic painting.

91 Rose, "Blake's Illustrations for *Paradise Lost, L'Allegro,* and *Il Penseroso*: A Thematic Reading," p. 56.

92 Ibid., p. 66.

93 For a standard portrayal of Christ receiving food from the angels, see Charles Le Brun's *Christ in the Wilderness* reproduced by Joan Evans, *Monastic Iconography in France from the Renaissance to the Revolution* (Cambridge: Univ. Press, 1970), pl. 89. For two examples of the angels gathering Christ's blood, see the Crucifixion paintings by Paolo Veneziano and Bernado Daddi. Both paintings are in the National Gallery of Art, Washington, D.C.

94 According to Gilchrist, Linnell tried unsuccessfully to sell the illustrations to Sir Francis Chantrey (see *The Life of William Blake,* 2nd ed., 2 vols. [London: Macmillan, 1880], I, 378, 400). See also G. E. Bentley, Jr., *Blake Records* (Oxford: Clarendon Press, 1969), pp. 338–39, 604, 607.

95 *Letters of William Michael Rossetti Concerning Whitman, Blake, and Shelley, to Anne Gilchrist and Her Son Herbert Gilchrist,* ed. Clarence Gohdes and Paull Franklin Baum (Durham, N.C.: Duke Univ. Press, 1934), p. 11.

96 *Life of William Blake, "Pictor Ignotus,"* 2 vols. (London and Cambridge: Macmillan, 1863), I, 335. The passage quoted is underscored by Rossetti in his copy of Gilchrist's *Life,* which is now in the Houghton Library, Harvard University (see Catalogue No. *EC75/B5815/W863$_g$ [B]).

97 *Life of William Blake* (1863), II, 215.

98 The Keynes quotation is from "Notes on the Illustrations," *On the Morning of Christ's Nativity: Milton's Hymn with Illustrations by William Blake* (Cambridge: Univ. Press, 1923), p. 32.

99 *Poems in English,* pp. 278–79. Jean Hagstrum notes and explains another apparent deviation: in his sixth design, wishing to emphasize the "sensual" nature of Christ's temptation, Blake deviates from Milton's rendering of the banquet temptation by including the female figures; they can, however, be accounted for in terms of Milton's text, Blake drawing them from Milton's description of the temptation as it is proposed by Belial but then rejected by Satan (see "Christ's Body," in

William Blake: Essays, p. 133). Yet such an observation should be accompanied by another: as Christ beholds Satan's banquet he sees "distant ... /Under the Trees ... /Nymphs of *Diana's* train, and *Naiades*/With fruits and flowers from *Amalthea*'s horn,/And Ladies of th' *Hesperides*" (II. 353–57). Such is the splendor in Milton's poem that Christ in Blake's design beholds.

100 The image of the "crown" looks forward to the kingdoms sequence that follows and makes clear that Blake saw Milton compressing the entire temptation sequence within the second temptation. For a thoughtful discussion of the temptation motif—its tradition and Milton's deviations from that tradition—see Elizabeth Marie Pope, *Paradise Regained: The Tradition and the Poem* (Baltimore: Johns Hopkins Press, 1947), pp. 51–69.

101 "Blake, Milton, and Edward Burney," p. 126.

102 Many previous illustrators depicted different phases of the long second temptation, but Blake is the only illustrator of the poem, so far as I know, to conflate the entire kingdoms sequence within a single design. For this reason, I have thought it appropriate to treat the design as a new subject.

103 Pointon, *Milton and English Art,* p. xxxix.

104 *The Harmonious Vision: Studies in Milton's Poetry* (Baltimore: Johns Hopkins Press, 1954), p. 110. This is not to say that Blake and Hayley could not join with Charles Dunster in perceiving points of contact between *Paradise Lost* and *Paradise Regained* when the two poems are seen together: the emblematic serpent which moves through the designs to *Paradise Lost* as a kind of "visual melody" reappears, less magnificently to be sure, in the designs to *Paradise Regained* (figs. 41 and 42); the winged Lucifer of the *Paradise Lost* series turns up in the fifth of the *Paradise Regained* designs (see fig. 38) but without his earlier grandeur. Blake, then, is emphasizing dissimilitude rather than similitude between the two poems; and his primary concern seems to be with showing the unity, connection, and perfection that exist in *Paradise Regained* and which the view of the poem as simply a sequel to *Paradise Lost* ordinarily denies it. Blake, of course, apprehends the entanglement of the poems in Milton's canon which together comprise his "vision." His point is simply that *Paradise Regained,* and every other poem, retains its own integrity at the same time that each contributes to a larger vision that the poems together constitute.

105 Philip James, *English Book Illustration 1800–1900* (London and New York: King Penguin Books, 1947), p. 8.

106 This was not the case when, on another occasion, Blake illustrated the same subject, but a different aspect of it. Regrettably, the Frick Museum did not allow reproduction of this item in its collection, but this alternate design has previously been reproduced, between pp. xxviii and xxix in John Bunyan, *The Pilgrim's Progress,* ed. G. B. Harrison (New York: Spiral Press, 1941). This design is discussed in a forthcoming essay

by James T. Wills, " 'For I discern thee other then thou seem'st': An Extra Illustration for Blake's *Paradise Regained* Series," *Blake Studies*. I agree with Geoffrey Keynes's observation in *The Pilgrim's Progress* that this is "a rejected design for *Paradise Regained*—rejected because another quite different version, which agreed more closely with the text, was eventually included in that series" (p. xxviii). This conjecture fits the pattern of revision we have traced through Blake's other Milton designs (for an opposing view, see Wills's forthcoming essay). It is as if Blake, having completed this design, used it as a basis for others—its conceptions and its iconography. The cloud appears, with a different set of faces, in the depiction of Jesus' ugly dream; the nude Satan (the accompanying idea of evil undisguised) and the star-like nimbus (with its visionary associations) are incorporated into the depiction of Christ on the pinnacle. The suggestion of this initial design, that Christ's prophetic powers are here fully developed, is inappropriate to this moment in Milton's poem but is, of course, appropriate to the pinnacle scene. A poem about the formation of the prophetic character, *Paradise Regained* (as well as Blake's tenth illustration for it) locates visionary maturity in the culminating moment of the third temptation. Now, having become a prophet, having perfected his visionary capacity, Christ may take up his ministry—he may begin to prophesy.

107 *Milton's Brief Epic: The Genre, Meaning and Art of "Paradise Regained"* (Providence: Brown Univ. Press, 1966), esp. pp. 3–129; see also Curran, "The Mental Pinnacle: *Paradise Regained* and the Romantic Four-Book Epic," in *Calm of Mind*, pp. 133–62.

108 Northrop Frye perceives the dramatic aspect of brief-epic poetry in *Fearful Symmetry: A Study of William Blake* (Princeton: Princeton Univ. Press, 1947), p. 405.

109 MacKellar, *The Poems of John Milton* (forthcoming).

110 "A Dissertation on the Sixth Book of Virgil's Aenis," in *The Works of Virgil*, ed. Joseph Warton, 4 vols. (London: Printed for R. Dodsley, 1753), III, 53, 59.

111 *Paradise Regained: The Tradition and the Poem*, p. 51. What Pope neglects to point out is that many biblical illustrators before Milton paired Adam's temptations and Christ's (see, e.g., Kitto Bible, XLVIII, 8634). Orthodox theology, however, is undisturbed, since the temptation in the wilderness is seen merely as a "type" of the Crucifixion at which time Paradise is recovered. In other words, the suggestion implicit in this pairing—that Paradise was regained in the desert—never was absorbed into orthodoxy. Milton does not exploit this typological association between the temptation and the Crucifixion, though of course he exploits others, as the proem to the brief epic indicates and as Lewalski (see note 107) so competently demonstrates. It should be remembered that "Nonconformism in religion was at a low ebb after 1660. . . . an era of theology had left people weary of such squabbling; and, more important still, dissent was equated with rebellion and civil strife"—thus

the subtlety of Milton's strategy (see David Kubrin's study, *How Sir Isaac Newton Helped Restore Law 'n Order to the West* [Madison: Privately printed, 1972], and, for the quotation cited above, Roland N. Stromberg, *Religious Liberalism in Eighteenth-Century England* [London: Oxford Univ. Press, 1954], p. 14).

112 See Kitto Bible, XXXIV, 6357, 6362; XXXIX, 7207.

113 See Ettlinger, *The Sistine Chapel,* pl. 9.

114 *The Poems of John Milton* (forthcoming). Christopher Hill notes that in Milton paradise is regained in the desert, not on the cross, and observes, quite properly, that this is a "radical treatment" of the Christ myth (see *The World Turned Upside Down: Radical Ideas During the English Revolution* [New York: Viking Press, 1972], p. 322).

115 *Milton's Poetry of Choice,* p. 193.

116 Ibid., p. 195. Milton's own posture is sharply drawn in *De Doctrina Christiana:* in the very moment that he allows the inviolability of Scripture he acknowledges the validity of on-going revelation against which only "an impious wretch" would dare "to raise so much as a murmur . . . , let alone a sustained protest" (*Yale Milton,* VI, 204).

117 *The Matter of Britain: Essays in a Living Culture* (London: Lawrence and Wishart, 1966), p. 101. See also Hill, *The World Turned Upside Down,* p. 299. Since completing this chapter, I have read Ira Clark's essay, which argues that John's gospel is "the primary inspiration for *Paradise Regained*" (p. 1): Milton, in his brief epic, repairs the "hiatus" in John's gospel, "almost as if he were supplying a manuscript loss," at the same time that he takes from John both the dogma and the literary matrix for his poem (pp. 4, 6). Resisting the radicalism of Milton's undertaking, Clark's essay falls into apologetics ("Milton supplemented the Bible" but "was not presumptuous or sacrilegious" [p. 5]), concluding that in the moment of identity on the pinnacle Milton's poem comes to its period: "Milton's poem is complete, for his account of the Son of Man's crucial recognition of who he is precisely supplies the hiatus in the fourth Gospel" (p. 15). See "*Paradise Regained* and the Gospel according to John," *Modern Philology,* 71 (1973), 1–15, for Clark's full argument. And for an interpretation alive to dimensions of Milton's poem excluded by Clark's conclusion, see Irene Samuel, "The Regaining of Paradise," in *The Prison and the Pinnacle: Papers to Commemorate the Tercentenary of "Paradise Regained" and "Samson Agonistes" 1671–1971,* ed. Balachandra Rajan (London: Routledge and Kegan Paul, 1973), pp. 111–34. Samuel contends that to read *Paradise Regained* "as a 'Who am I?' poem is to limit it . . . ; to read it as a 'How am I to live?' poem is to see it . . . as the mimesis of a universal action, a program for every man" (p. 126).

118 *Milton and the Christian Tradition* (Oxford: Clarendon Press, 1966), p. 132. In this passage Patrides is quoting from J. S. Whale's *Christian Doctrine* (Cambridge: Univ. Press, 1941), p. 75.

119 Ibid., pp. 141–42.

120 "Comment on Art and Reformation," in *Symbols in Transformation: Iconographic Themes at the Time of the Reformation,* comp. Craig Harbison (Princeton: Princeton Univ. Art Museum, 1969), p. 11. See also note 17 above.

E. L. Marilla, as we have already observed, is quite mistaken when he says that Denis Saurat was "the first to recognize the problem" in Milton's omitting the subject of the Crucifixion from *Paradise Regained,* but quite right in saying that "there is a need for a clear definition of Milton's conception of the Crucifixion" ("Milton and the Crucifixion," *Études Anglaises,* 22 [1969], 7). It is questionable, however, whether a "clear definition" emerges from Marilla's essay, which takes into account *De Doctrina Christiana,* along with Books III and XII of *Paradise Lost,* while ignoring Book VI of the epic and dismissing as irrelevant the "negative evidence" supplied by *Paradise Regained.* The Crucifixion, says Marilla, "does not appear" in the brief epic "for the simple reason that the context provides no place for it" (p. 10). Lurking behind this conclusion, and indeed behind the entire essay, is the assumption that Milton, once he formulated an attitude, never changed it. A statement from plate 19 of *The Marriage of Heaven and Hell* provides a corrective: "The man who never alters his opinions is like standing water, & breeds reptiles of the mind."

In a recent essay, "Milton on the Exaltation of the Son: The War in Heaven in *Paradise Lost,*" *ELH,* 36 (1969), 215–31, William B. Hunter, Jr., draws our attention to the typological dimensions of the sixth book of *Paradise Lost:* in a single moment Milton collapses all time—past, present, and future. The Battle in Heaven, depicted in the first moments of time, points forward to the War in Heaven of the Apocalypse; moreover, the three-day battle recalls the period from Christ's death to his resurrection. Hunter's perception, though it may strike us as novel, lies behind much eighteenth-century illustration and commentary, where repeatedly the cross is introduced as part of the iconographic detail in illustrations for this book (see note 88 above). What is important, however, is not that the Crucifixion is alluded to but that, in alluding to it, Milton felt compelled to hide the concept in the basement of his poem. It was understood by Thomas Hollis and by William Hayley, for instance, that this central book of Milton's epic was the best guide to the poem's revolutionary spirit and doctrine. Hollis read the book as historical allegory, but Hayley read it somewhat differently (for Hollis's allegorization of Book VI, see *Memoirs of Thomas Hollis,* comp. Francis Blackburne [London: Privately printed, 1780], p. 623, and for Hayley's interpretation, see "Conjectures on the Origin of the *Paradise Lost,*" in *The Life of Milton* [1796], pp. 270–76. This essay was not included with the 1794 *Life*). In his allegory, through the parody of corporeal warfare, Milton hurls into ruins the classical epic tradition. In it, we might add, he also subdues the doctrine of the Crucifixion, which gathers round itself a primitive ethical scheme that is disruptive to the "great argument" his poem advances. That Blake saw in a book that described physical warfare an assertion of his own concept of mental fight is suggested by the iconography in his illustration for the sixth book of Milton's epic (see also the imagery in the lyric that introduces *Milton,* plate 2, and the similar imagery in the poem included with the letter to Thomas Butts, dated 22 November 1802 [p. 693, esp. ll. 78–80]). In this sense, the sixth book of Milton's epic involves a critique of the ideology that customarily asserts itself in epic poetry and of the one that lay at the very heart of Christian orthodoxy. The attitude insinuated here is openly expressed in the brief epic. One cannot overestimate the significance of the Crucifixion's being omitted from a poem whose title announces it as its subject.

121 *Symbols in Transformation,* p. 24.

122 Schiller, *Iconography of Christian Art,* pp. 143–44.

123 I adopt language from Hayley's *Life of Milton* (1796), p. 277.

124 *The Romantics on Milton,* p. 532.

125 I quote from Calton's note reprinted by Dunster in his edition of *Paradise Regained,* p. 262.

126 For Frye's comments, see *Anatomy of Criticism: Four Essays* (Princeton: Princeton Univ. Press, 1957), p. 96, and *The Return of Eden: Five Essays on Milton's Epics* (Toronto: Univ. of Toronto Press, 1965), pp. 118–43; and for Schultz's, see "A Fairer Paradise? Some Recent Studies of *Paradise Regained,*" *ELH,* 32 (1965), 275–302.

127 For an excellent discussion of this point, see Patrides, *Milton and the Christian Tradition,* pp. 149–52.

128 *The Hero with a Thousand Faces,* Bollingen Series, 17 (New York: Pantheon Books, 1949), p. 349; but see also pp. 315–64.

129 The phrase is Harold Boom's; see *Blake's Apocalypse: A Study in Poetic Argument* (Garden City, N.Y.: Doubleday, 1963), p. 362.

130 I am grateful to Philipp Fehl, Department of Art History, University of Illinois, for calling this particular depiction to my attention.

131 *The Poems of John Milton* (forthcoming).

132 Ibid. On the matter of suppression, see William Riley Parker, *Milton: A Biography,* 2 vols. (Oxford: Clarendon Press, 1968), I, 600–601, and II, 1107, n. 26.

133 See Brisman, *Milton's Poetry of Choice,* p. 206.

134 Blake here observes a distinction between nudity and nakedness; the tradition is explored by Kenneth Clark, *The Nude: A Study in Ideal Form,* Bollingen Series, 35: 2 (1956; rpt. Princeton: Princeton Univ. Press, 1972), pp. 3–29.

135 *Remarks on the Writings and Conduct of J. J. Rousseau* (London: T. Cadell, 1767), sig. b^v.

136 Channing's essay first appeared in *Christian Examiner and Theological Review,* 3 (1826), 29–77. I quote from the second edition, issued as a separate pamphlet, *Remarks on the Character and Writings of John Milton*

(London: Printed for Edward Rainford, 1828), pp. 5, 7, 9, 25, 35.

137 Ibid., pp. 39–40.

138 Ibid., pp. 43, 46.

139 *The State of the Dead* (Battle Creek, Mich.: Steam Press, 1866), p. iii.

140 See the unpaginated introductory notes by Frederick Thrupp, *Paradise Lost* (London: Hardwicke and Bogue, 1879).

141 Carl G. Jung, *The Development of Personality*, tr. R. F. C. Hull, Bollingen Series, 20 (New York: Pantheon Books, 1954), p. 181.

142 *The Poems of John Milton* (forthcoming).

143 For Blake, it seems that Christ's deed above heroic is his decision to return to civilization as its leader and redeemer; contemplation, then, is merely a prologue to action. Interestingly, Blake's *Milton* takes *Paradise Regained* as its model in a more exact, but also in a much different, sense than is usually acknowledged. Both poems involve the interior journey, the descent into the self, which ends with the hero's return to civilization. The focus of the poets is different, however; Milton concentrates upon the journey, whereas Blake stresses the idea of return. In a very real sense, *Milton* begins where *Paradise Regained* leaves off. I would argue, then, that it is the illustrations to *Paradise Regained* that provide the best guide for reading *Milton,* although Susan C. Fox has suggested that if *Milton* is "derived from any Miltonic pattern, it is from the two brief poems which reflect and reinforce each other, 'L'Allegro' and 'Il Penseroso' " ("The Structure of a Moment and Parallelism in the Two Books of Blake's *Milton,*" *Blake Studies,* 2, i [1970], 21).

144 For Blake's references to palm in his poetry, see *The Four Zoas,* I, p. 18, ll. 11–13, and *Jerusalem* 18:19–20; 23:24–25; 59:5–9.

145 These details are assembled by Henry Oxenden; see Folger MS V b. 110, quoted by kind permission of the Folger Shakespeare Library. See also Charles M. Skinner, who summarizes most of these associations of the palm and who emphasizes that, in association with Christ, the palm signifies "the dark mind" being enlightened; it is a symbol of man's release from the grave, of his resurrection and salvation (*Myth and Legends of Flowers, Trees, Fruits, and Plants in All Ages and in All Climes* [Philadelphia and London: J. B. Lippincott, 1911], pp. 207–8). Palms, according to Henry More, signify victory over Satan—"victory over the *Beast, his Image and his Mark*" *(Apocalypsis Apocalypseos; or the Revelation of St. John the Divine Unveiled* [London: Printed for J. Martyn and W. Kettilby, 1680], p. 66).

146 *Lectures on Deuteronomy,* tr. Richard R. Caemmerer, in *Luther's Works,* ed. Jaroslav Pelikan and Daniel Poellot, 54 vols. (St. Louis: Concordia, 1960), IX, 310.

147 Peter Felix Hägin, *The Epic Hero and the Decline of Heroic Poetry: A Study of the Neoclassical English Epic with Special Reference to Milton's "Paradise Lost,"* ed. H. Lüdeke (Basel: Cooper Monographs, 1964), p. 44.

148 The BBC tercentenary film, "Paradise Restored: The Argument Being the Fall of John Milton from Grace into Humanity" propounds, without acknowledging it, a Blakean thesis. The film was shown in Great Britain on 8 November 1974.

149 Svendsen, "John Martin and the Expulsion Scene of *Paradise Lost*," p. 64.

Chapter 3: "MENTAL PRINCE": MILTON AS A REVOLUTIONARY

1 The first phrase is Walter Savage Landor's, quoted from "Galileo, Milton, and a Dominican," *Imaginary Conversations,* ed. Charles G. Crump, 6 vols. (London: J. M. Dent, 1891), IV, 386; the second is Thomas De Quincey's, the next two are Shelley's, and the last is from Keats—all of them quoted from *The Romantics on Milton: Formal Essays and Critical Asides,* ed. Joseph Anthony Wittreich, Jr. (Cleveland: Press of Case Western Reserve Univ., 1970), pp. 478, 539, 537, 556. These phrases figure in an important way in my essay, "Milton, Man and Thinker: Apotheosis in Romantic Criticism," *Bucknell Review,* 16 (1968), 64–84.

2 *The Early Lives of Milton,* ed. Helen Darbishire (London: Constable, 1932), p. 61.

3 Joseph Wicksteed, *Blake's Innocence and Experience: A Study of the Songs and Manuscripts* (London and Toronto: J. M. Dent, and New York: E. P. Dutton, 1928), p. 163. The revolutionary character of Milton's art and thought has not been sufficiently attended to in our century, but neither has it been ignored. Three earlier studies provide a context for my own: Edgell Rickword's "Milton: The Revolutionary Intellect," in *The English Revolution 1640: Three Essays,* ed. Christopher Hill (London: Lawrence and Wishart, 1940), pp. 100–132; G. Wilson Knight's *Chariot of Wrath: The Message of John Milton to Democracy at War* (London: Faber and Faber, 1942); and, most important, Merritt Y. Hughes's "Milton as a Revolutionary," in *Ten Perspectives on Milton* (New Haven: Yale Univ. Press, 1965), pp. 240–75. Knight properly chides Rickword for making no effort to relate the principles expressed in Milton's prose to his poetry; and Hughes, responding to Knight, corrects his excesses and repairs his omissions. My own contribution to this discussion proceeds from Hughes's belief that the "prophetic message" of the prose works culminates in Milton's epics (p. 243). Hughes argues properly that until we examine "the sterner, historical, revolutionary implications" of Milton's prose we will not be able to throw the poet's "true, revolutionary character into high relief" (p. 242). Such an effort requires, as Hughes acknowledges, that we take into account "Milton's mixed role as both religious prophet and political philosopher in the Puritan Revolution" (p. 247) and that we do this, first, by studying the antiprelatical tracts, which are so often ignored by those who would study Milton as a revolutionary. This effort was begun

by William Blake: he first asked the question—Where shall we place Milton in the revolutionary process that has been under way in England?—and thus I shall tie my own discussion to Blake's penetrating inquiries and answers.

4 For a useful general survey of Milton criticism, see James Thorpe, *Milton Criticism: Selections from Four Centuries* (London: Routledge and Kegan Paul, 1951), pp. 3–19; and for more particularized discussions, see the following: John T. Shawcross, *Milton: The Critical Heritage*, 2 vols. (London: Routledge and Kegan Paul, 1970, 1972), I, 1–34, II, 1–39; Wittreich, ed., *The Romantics on Milton*, pp. 3–32; and James G. Nelson, *The Sublime Puritan: Milton and the Victorians* (Madison: Univ. of Wisconsin Press, 1963), esp. pp. 126–51.

5 West's essay appears in *Th' Upright Heart and Pure: Essays on John Milton Commemorating the Tercentenary of the Publication of "Paradise Lost,"* ed. Amadeus Fiore (Pittsburgh: Duquesne Univ. Press, 1967); I quote from p. 132.

6 Herbert Marcuse, *Counter-Revolution and Revolt* (Boston: Beacon Press, 1972), p. 125.

7 The unidentified phrases are from *Of Reformation, Of Prelatical Episcopacy, The Reason of Church-Government,* and *An Apology for Smectymnuus.*

8 Christopher Hill quoting Henry Power in *The World Turned Upside Down: Radical Ideas During the English Revolution* (New York: Viking Press, 1972), p. 293.

9 See Eliot's essay on Blake, as well as "Tradition and the Individual Talent," in *The Sacred Wood* (London: Methuen, 1934) and Yeats's two essays on Blake, as well as "Poetry and Tradition," in *Essays and Introductions* (New York: Macmillan, 1961). Eliot's two essays on Milton may be found in *On Poetry and Poets* (New York: Farrar, Straus, and Cudahy, 1957).

10 *The Romantics on Milton,* p. 275.

11 I borrow the first phrase from Angus Fletcher, who borrows it from Ephim Fogel; the second phrase I borrow from Fletcher himself. See Angus Fletcher, *The Transcendental Masque: An Essay on Milton's "Comus"* (Ithaca: Cornell Univ. Press, 1971), pp. 132–33.

12 Ibid., p. 254.

13 Northrop Frye, *The Return of Eden: Five Essays on Milton's Epics* (Toronto: Univ. of Toronto Press, 1965), pp. 90–93.

14 Northrop Frye, "The Road of Excess," in *The Stubborn Structure: Essays on Criticism and Society* (Ithaca: Cornell Univ. Press, 1970), p. 160.

15 Mao Tse-Tung, *On Literature and Art* (Peking: Foreign Language Press, 1967), p. 12.

16 *Counter-Revolution and Revolt,* p. 111.

17 Two discussions of literary form are particularly useful here: see both Kenneth Burke, *Attitudes Toward History,* rev. ed. (1959; rpt. Boston:

Beacon Press, 1961), esp. pp. 34–91, and Northrop Frye, *Anatomy of Criticism: Four Essays* (Princeton: Princeton Univ. Press, 1957), esp. pp. 315–26. The problem with so many genre studies is the assumption that to describe a thing—to isolate its features, to define its conventions—is to say what a thing is. Description of surfaces is thus confused with definition of essences. The unrecognized difference between these two activities is analogous to that which distinguishes a photographer from a portrait artist, the one "describing" a physiognomy, the other "defining" a personality. The critic of genre needs to be less a "photographer" and more an "artist." Burke and Frye move in the right direction.

18 The phrase is Robert Gleckner's; see *The Piper and the Bard: A Study of William Blake* (Detroit: Wayne State Univ. Press, 1959), p. 66.

19 E. H. Gombrich, *Norm and Form: Studies in the Art of the Renaissance,* 2nd ed. (London and New York: Phaidon, 1971), p. 79. Gombrich has obviously affected my understanding of "form" as much as he has affected Rosalie Colie's. See her book, *The Resources of Kind: Genre-Theory in the Renaissance,* ed. Barbara K. Lewalski (Berkeley and Los Angeles: Univ. of California Press, 1973), which arrived too late to be taken into account in the course of revising this chapter but not so late that I cannot here acknowledge agreement between her conclusions and my own (see esp. pp. 119–22).

20 *The Transcendental Masque,* p. 143.

21 *Counter-Revolution and Revolt,* pp. 69–70.

22 Ibid., p. 101.

23 Joan Webber, "Milton's God," *ELH,* 40 (1973), 514–31.

24 Walter J. Ong, "Logic and the Epic Muse: Reflections on Noetic Structures in Milton's Milieu," in *Achievements of the Left Hand: Essays on the Prose of John Milton,* ed. Michael Lieb and John T. Shawcross (Amherst: Univ. of Massachusetts Press, 1974), pp. 239–68.

25 See Robert Sumner Jackson, "The Prophetic Vision," *Interpretation,* 16 (1962), 65–75.

26 *The Return of Eden,* p. 92.

27 Mao Tse-Tung, *On Literature and Art,* p. 30.

28 *How Sir Isaac Newton Helped Restore Law 'n Order* (Madison: Privately printed, 1972), p. xix.

29 See the important note by Michael Lloyd, "Justa Edouardo King," *Notes and Queries,* n.s. 5 (1958), 432–34.

30 *The Sacred Wood,* p. 140.

31 Ibid., pp. 142–43.

32 *Revaluation: Tradition and Development in English Poetry* (London: Chatto and Windus, 1936), p. 58.

33 Ibid., p. 8.

34 Ibid., p. 77.

35 Ibid., p. 113.

36 *Paradise Lost: Introduction* (Cambridge: Univ. Press, 1972), p. 28. Joan Webber provides a necessary corrective when she comments on the

subversive character of epic poetry: "in almost every instance," she says, "epic both praises and subverts" the values of its culture ("Milton's God," p. 515). Webber's understanding is surely right; but it would be a mistake to attribute it, unqualifiedly, to Milton; her understanding fairly represents what Milton thought an epic poem should be and not what he thought it, traditionally, had been.

37 E. M. W. Tillyard quoting Tasso in *The English Epic and Its Background* (1954; rpt. New York: Oxford Univ. Press, 1966), pp. 231–32n. See also Tasso's *Discourses on the Heroic Poem,* tr. Mariella Cavalchini and Irene Samuel (Oxford: Clarendon Press, 1973), pp. 77–78.

38 "Preface to *The Excursion,*" in *The Poetical Works of William Wordsworth,* ed. Ernest de Selincourt and Helen Darbishire, 5 vols. (Oxford: Clarendon Press, 1952–59), V, 2. Shelley is a principal member of this revolutionary tradition; for a fine discussion, see Stuart Curran, *Shelley's "Annus Mirabilis": The Maturing of an Epic Vision* (San Marino: Huntington Library, 1975).

39 "The Style and Genre of *Paradise Lost,*" in *New Essays on "Paradise Lost,"* ed. Thomas Kranidas (Berkeley and Los Angeles: Univ. of California Press, 1969), p. 25. The theorist whose view of epic most closely resembles Milton's is Tasso: "his vision of epic as the highest and most inclusive genre of poetry" finds its fullest embodiment in *Paradise Lost* (see Cavalchini and Samuel, tr., *Discourses on the Heroic Poem,* p. xxxi). Tasso invokes Homer and Vergil to exemplify the freedom of "the poet's art": Homer "did not select a single idiom or a single style, but wanted to use them all, and did combine them all together" (p. 191); so did Vergil, who "intermingled forms and styles," placing them in his poem so that "they are, as it were, the many steps of a theatre" (p. 192). For Tasso, then, as for Milton, epic is a "composite" form, "intermingl[ing] and temper[ing] all elements and qualities" (p. 205).

40 See "Discovery as Form in *Paradise Lost,*" in *New Essays on "Paradise Lost,"* pp. 1–14.

41 "The Apocalypse within *Paradise Lost,*" ibid., p. 176.

42 Richard Price, "A Discourse on the Love of Our Country," in *British Radicals and Reformers 1789–1832,* ed. Wilfried Keutsch, English Texts (Tübingen: Max Niemeyer, 1971), p. 11.

43 Ibid.

44 The phrase is Fletcher's; see *Milton's Transcendental Masque,* p. 135.

45 Mao Tse-Tung, *On Literature and Art,* p. 18.

46 I use this phrase reluctantly. The representatives of the aesthetic with which Blake identifies himself are much neglected by students of the eighteenth century and thus *will seem to be* part of an "underground" to modern students. In actuality, the works I point to were immediately available to a poet like Blake; and the ideas contained in those works were sufficiently disseminated so that Blake, even if he did not read them, would have certainly known their premises. For an exploration of this aesthetic—one that is complementary to my own—see David B.

Morris, *The Religious Sublime: Christian Poetry and Critical Tradition in Eighteenth-Century England* (Lexington: Univ. Press of Kentucky, 1972).

47 Blake's letter is dated 6 July 1803; see *The Letters of William Blake,* ed. Geoffrey Keynes (Cambridge, Mass.: Harvard Univ. Press, 1968), p. 69.

48 John Melton, *Astrologaster; or, The Figure-caster* (London: Printed for Edward Blackmore, 1620), sig. A^2.

49 I borrow the phrase from A. L. Morton, *The Matter of Britain: Essays in a Living Culture* (London: Lawrence and Wishart, 1966), p. 100.

50 *The Iliad, The Odyssey, and the Epic Tradition* (London and Melbourne: Macmillan, 1968), pp. 13–15.

51 "Tasso and Neoplatonism: The Growth of his Epic Theory," *Studies in the Renaissance,* 18 (1971), 110.

52 *The Prophets: Part II,* 2 vols. (New York: Harper and Row, 1971), II, 123–24.

53 *William Blake: A Reading of the Shorter Poems* (Seattle: Univ. of Washington Press, 1963), p. 15.

54 *A Blake Dictionary: The Ideas and Symbols of William Blake* (Providence: Brown Univ. Press, 1965), p. 18.

55 *The Burden of the Past and the English Poet* (Cambridge, Mass.: Harvard Univ. Press, 1970), p. 23.

56 Ibid., p. 77n.

57 John Hughes, "An Essay on Allegorical Poetry, & c.," in *The Works of Spenser,* 6 vols. (London: Jacob Tonson, 1715), I, xxix.

58 Eudo Mason quoting Henry Fuseli, in *The Mind of Henry Fuseli* (London: Routledge and Kegan Paul, 1951), p. 275.

59 *Mysteriously Meant: The Rediscovery of Pagan Symbolism and Allegorical Interpretation in the Renaissance* (Baltimore: Johns Hopkins Press, 1970), p. vii.

60 Ibid.

61 Ibid., pp. 17, 19.

62 Ibid., pp. 86, 116.

63 *The Romantics on Milton,* pp. 37, 96.

64 Allen, *Mysteriously Meant,* p. 47.

65 The relationship between creation and interpretation (as a Renaissance concept) is discussed by Allen, *Mysteriously Meant,* p. 282, and is the subject of the impressive book by S. K. Heninger, *Touches of Sweet Harmony: Pythagorean Cosmology and Renaissance Poetics* (San Marino: Huntington Library, 1974). The relationship between creation and interpretation (as a Romantic concept) is related to Blake by Northrop Frye, "The Road of Excess," in *The Stubborn Structure,* esp. pp. 160–61. For a discussion of this concept in relation to prophecy, see the comments by H. Wildberger in Claus Westermann's *Basic Forms of Prophetic Speech,* tr. Hugh Clayton White (Philadelphia: Westminster Press, 1967), p. 48. My own comments here are deeply indebted to Frye's.

66 "The Road of Excess," in *The Stubborn Structure,* p. 166. The same principle is evident in the way that Blake uses wash strokes as a device of punctuation. The device, employed in Copy A, is made emphatic in Copy D, where it arrests attention at the end of line groupings and where sometimes it turns attention to a word or phrase within a line.

67 I borrow the phrase from Eugene Vinaver's *The Rise of Romance* (New York and Oxford: Oxford Univ. Press, 1971), p. 71.

68 "The Road of Excess," in *The Stubborn Structure,* p. 167.

69 Ibid., p. 168.

70 Angus Fletcher, *The Prophetic Moment: An Essay on Spenser* (Chicago: Univ. of Chicago Press, 1971), p. 43.

71 "The Road of Excess," in *The Stubborn Structure,* p. 172. Thomas Vogler makes the same point, quite correctly, about Dante and, quite mistakenly, about Milton in *Preludes to Vision: The Epic Adventure in Blake, Wordsworth, Keats, and Hart Crane* (Berkeley and Los Angeles: Univ. of California Press, 1971), p. 8. Vogler's view doubtless derives from Tillyard's conception of "choric" quality developed in *The English Epic and Its Background,* esp, pp. 12–13, but is contradicted by Christopher Caudwell, *Romance and Realism: A Study of English Bourgeois Literature,* ed. Samuel Hynes (Princeton: Princeton Univ. Press, 1970), p. 43. Caudwell's views correspond with those advanced here.

72 See Robert M. Durling's excellent study, *The Figure of the Poet in the Renaissance Epic* (Cambridge, Mass.: Harvard Univ. Press, 1965), esp. pp. 211–37.

73 Irene Tayler, "Metamorphoses of a Favorite Cat," in *Blake's Visionary Forms Dramatic,* ed. David V. Erdman and John E. Grant (Princeton: Princeton Univ. Press, 1970), p. 303.

74 See *A Commentary upon the Divine Revelation of the Apostle and Evangelist John,* tr. Elias Arnold (Amsterdam: C. P., 1644), pp. 30–32 (of Preface).

75 The phrase is David Erdman's; see Preface in *Blake's Visionary Forms Dramatic,* p. viii. For a brilliant exposition on all that Blake's phrase implies, see Edward J. Rose, "Visionary Forms Dramatic: Grammatical and Iconographical Movement in Blake's Verse and Designs," *Criticism,* 8 (1966), 111–25.

76 Pareus, *Commentary upon the Divine Revelation,* p. 20 (of Preface).

77 "Adam on the Grass with Balsamum," *ELH,* 36 (1969), 178.

78 *Remarks on the Character and Writings of John Milton,* 2nd ed. (London: Printed for Edward Rainford, 1828), p. 17.

79 Ibid., p. 18.

80 I quote from Robert Martin Adams's rejoinder to Hartman's essay, "Contra Hartman: Possible and Impossible Structures of Miltonic Imagery," in *Seventeenth-Century Imagery: Essays on Uses of Figurative Language from Donne to Farquhar,* ed. Earl Miner (Berkeley and Los Angeles: Univ. of California Press, 1971), p. 130.

81 Hartman, "Adam on the Grass with Balsamum," p. 191.

82 *Lectures on the Sacred Poetry of the Hebrews,* 3rd ed. (London: Printed for Thomas Tegg, 1835), pp. 99, 113.

83 See Pareus, *Commentary upon the Divine Revelation,* p. 20 (of Preface).

84 Kathleen Williams, "Vision and Rhetoric: The Poet's Vision in *The Faerie Queene,*" *ELH,* 36 (1969), 132, 134.

85 Ibid., p. 144.

86 I borrow the phrase from T. J. B. Spencer; see *"Paradise Lost:* The Anti-Epic," in *Approaches to "Paradise Lost,"* ed. C. A. Patrides (London: Edward Arnold, 1968), p. 87.

87 *The Veil of Allegory: Some Notes Toward a Theory of Allegorical Rhetoric in the English Renaissance* (Chicago: Univ. of Chicago Press, 1969), pp. 209–10.

88 *The English Epic and Its Background,* p. 434.

89 Ibid., p. 445.

90 Ibid., p. 447.

91 For a fuller discussion of Milton's relationship with and attitude toward his audience, see my essay, " 'The Crown of Eloquence': The Figure of the Orator in Milton's Prose Works," in *Achievements of the Left Hand,* pp. 3–54.

92 Allen, *Mysteriously Meant,* p. 282.

93 *Orlando Furioso,* ed. John Harington (London: Printed for J. Parker, 1634), sigs. 4^r–[4^v].

94 *Godfrey of Boulogne: or The Recoverie of Jerusalem,* tr. Edward Fairfax (London: John Bill, 1624), p. [i].

95 John Diodati, *Pious Annotations upon the Holy Bible* (London: Printed for Nicolas Fussell, 1643), p. 99.

96 Allen, *Mysteriously Meant,* pp. 9, 86.

97 Ibid., p. 290.

98 Allen quoting from *Theatrum poetarum anglicanorum,* ibid., p. 290.

99 *The Early Lives of Milton,* p. 182.

100 Preface, *Orlando Furioso,* 2nd ed. (London: Printed for George Nicol, 1785), I, lx.

101 *The Prophetic Moment,* p. 37.

102 *Life of William Blake,* 2nd ed., 2 vols. (London: Macmillan, 1880), I, 78, 82.

103 C. N. Stavrou, "A Reassessment of *The Marriage of Heaven and Hell,*" *South Atlantic Quarterly,* 54 (1955), 381.

104 E. D. Hirsch, Jr., *Innocence and Experience: An Introduction to Blake* (New Haven: Yale Univ. Press, 1964), p. 5n.

105 Gleckner, *The Piper and the Bard,* p. 186.

106 The tradition of criticism that identifies *The Marriage of Heaven and Hell* as a satire derives from Northrop Frye, who describes the work as "the epilogue to the golden age of English satire" (*Fearful Symmetry: A Study of William Blake* [Princeton: Princeton Univ. Press, 1947], p. 201). This tradition crests in the splendid discussion by Harold Bloom, which specifies the genre of the work as "a Menippean satire" and points to Frye's discussion in *Anatomy of Criticism* for its context (*Blake's*

Apocalypse: A Study in Poetic Argument [Garden City, N.Y.: Double-day, 1963], esp. pp. 230–34). Yet accepting Frye's generic categories and descriptions, the reader is likely to find more points of correspondence between *The Marriage of Heaven and Hell* and Frye's third phase of satire—a phase in which the artist explores "all the possibilities of his form" by questioning its basic assumptions (p. 234), a phase that Frye identifies with the Book of Isaiah and that finds another Romantic example in Shelley's *A Satire Against Satire*. Edward J. Rose makes an important comment: "As a self-acknowledged and self-proclaimed writer of prophecy, *Blake knew that satire was inadequate by itself and must be bound down or informed by imagination or else it would inevitably be subject to reason*" ("Good-Bye to Orc and All That," *Blake Studies,* 4, ii [1972], 142). Moreover, Stuart Curran, in his valuable discussion of Shelley's attitude toward satire, lays out a ground of agreement between Shelley and Blake: Satire, says Curran, "can only be a portion of the 'uncreating word' "; it is "a fallen form, the defiant response of a Prometheus who hides Jupiter within his soul." And Curran concludes: "To conceive the paradise of the liberated Prometheus but to live as yet under the dominion of Jupiter is to share both and possess neither" (*Shelley's "Annus Mirabilis,"* forthcoming). Interested in the attainment, the possession, of paradise, Blake's *The Marriage of Heaven and Hell* spurns satire for prophecy, which, as an agent of vision, is the vehicle for creating a new heaven and a new earth.

107 Grant's penetrating conclusion comes as an editorial note to W. J. T. Mitchell's "Blake's Composite Art," in *Blake's Visionary Forms Dramatic*, p. 64.

108 *The Prophets,* I, ix.

109 Ibid., p. xii.

110 Ibid., p. xiii.

111 Ibid., p. 115.

112 *William Blake: A Reading of the Shorter Poems*, p. 295.

113 For a discussion of Blake's debt to the Book of Revelation, see the pilot study by William F. Halloran, "The French Revolution: Revelation's New Form," in *Blake's Visionary Forms Dramatic*, pp. 30–56; and see my own more recent essay, "Opening the Seals: Blake's Essays and the Milton Tradition," in *Blake's Sublime Allegory: Essays on "The Four Zoas," "Milton," and "Jerusalem,"* ed. Stuart Curran and Joseph Anthony Wittreich, Jr. (Madison: Univ. of Wisconsin Press, 1973), pp. 23–58.

114 *William Blake: A Reading of the Shorter Poems*, p. 292. I do not deny the presence of prophetic elements within Blake's *Songs*: two poems richly imbued with such elements are "The Little Girl Lost" and "The Little Girl Found."

115 Mary V. Jackson, "Prolific and Devourer: From Nonmythic to Mythic Statement in *The Marriage of Heaven and Hell* and *A Song of Liberty,*" *Journal of English and Germanic Philology*, 70 (1971), 207.

116 *Isaiah: A New Translation; with a Preliminary Dissertation, and Notes*

Critical, Philological, and Explanatory, 2nd ed. (London: J. Nichols, 1779), pp. 170–71 (of Notes).

117 See Tony Stoneburner, "Notes on Prophecy and Apocalypse in a Time of Anarchy and Revolution: A Trying Out," in *Literature in Revolution,* ed. George Abbott White and Charles Newman (New York: Holt, Rinehart, and Winston, 1972), pp. 246–82. Stoneburner invites testing "the utility of these notes on prophecy and apocalypse by bringing them self-consciously to a reading of such works as Blake's prophecies" (p. 265).

118 Hill, *The World Turned Upside Down,* p. 12.

119 Ibid., pp. 324–25.

120 Martin K. Nurmi, *Blake's "Marriage of Heaven and Hell": A Critical Study,* Kent State University Bulletin Research Series, 3 (Kent, Ohio: Kent State Univ. Press, 1957), p. 28.

121 *Isaiah: A New Translation,* p. li. Like the Apocalypse, Isaiah was understood to possess a sevenfold structure: its "seven divisions . . . are . . . seven independent 'Visions' " (see R. G. Moulton, *The Literary Study of the Bible,* rev. ed. [Boston, New York, and Chicago: D. C. Heath, 1899], p. 436).

122 Algernon Charles Swinburne, *William Blake: A Critical Study* (1868; rpt. New York: Benjamin Blom, 1967), p. 207.

123 D. J. Sloss and J. P. R. Wallis, *The Prophetic Writings of William Blake,* 2 vols. (Oxford: Clarendon Press, 1926), I, 346.

124 Stavrou, "A Reassessment of *The Marriage of Heaven and Hell,*" p. 382.

125 Clark Emery, *Blake's "The Marriage of Heaven and Hell,"* University of Miami Critical Studies, 1 (Coral Gables, Fla.: Univ. of Miami Press, 1963), p. 35.

126 Ibid., p. 35.

127 Bloom, *Blake's Apocalypse,* p. 74.

128 *Blake: Prophet Against Empire,* rev. ed. (Garden City, N.Y.: Doubleday, 1969), p. 174. More recently, Erdman has referred to "tyrannous Rintrah" in *The Marriage of Heaven and Hell;* see Erdman, with Tom Dargan and Marlene Deverell-Van Meter, "Reading the Illuminations of Blake's *Marriage of Heaven and Hell,*" in *William Blake: Essays in Honour of Sir Geoffrey Keynes,* ed. Morton D. Paley and Michael Phillips (Oxford: Clarendon Press, 1973), p. 171. Roaring is, of course, associated in the Old Testament with Moloch, but it is also identified there with the prophets. That Blake exploits the latter significance is suggested, first, by Blake's identification of Rintrah in *Milton* with the class of men known as the reprobate and, second, by the important line in *Jerusalem,* "Merlin was like thee Rintrah among the Giants of Albion" (93:13). See also Edward J. Rose, "Blake's Metaphorical States," *Blake Studies,* 4, i (1972), 21–27. Blake's point is not that Rintrah, a tyrant, is about to attack a civilization; but that Rintrah, a prophet, is about to assault its collective mind, not clouding it, but bringing illumination to it. It should be remembered, of course, that "roaring" is an

activity of the Mighty Angel of the Apocalypse, who, like Rintrah, associated with the clouds, represents the awakening of humanity into new life, roaring so that men will be "roused," so that, casting down Antichrist, they will "sleep no more." For these significances, see John Mayer, *Ecclestica Interpretatio* (London: Printed by John Haveland, 1627), p. 358; Thomas Taylor, *Christs Victorie over the Dragon* (London: Printed for R. Dawlman, 1633), p. 466; and Thomas Goodwin, *An Exposition of the Revelation,* in *The Works of Thomas Goodwin,* 12 vols. (Edinburgh: James Nichol, and London: James Nisbet, 1861–66), V, 12.

129 Heschel, *The Prophets,* II, 224.

130 Gustav Davidson, *A Dictionary of the Angels, Including the Fallen Angels* (New York: Free Press, and London: Collier-Macmillan, 1967), p. 246. Two Hebrew words help to gloss the names Blake assigns to his "prophet": Rimmon, meaning "roarer," and Rinnah, meaning "rage," "indignation," and "song."

131 *Isaiah: A New Translation,* p. lii.

132 *The Prophets,* II, 225.

133 *Milton,* in *Lives of the English Poets,* ed. George Birkbeck Hill, 3 vols. (Oxford: Clarendon Press, 1905), I, 154–56.

134 W. B. Yeats, Introduction in *Poetical Works of William Blake* (London: George Routledge, 1910), p. xxx.

135 Bloom, *Blake's Apocalypse,* p. 71.

136 Tr. John Whitehead, 6 vols. (New York: Swedenborg Foundation, 1931), I, 113.

137 See *Paradise Lost,* III. 111–34, 166–216; and *Annotations to Swedenborg,* in *Poetry and Prose,* pp. 590–601.

138 *Blake's "Marriage of Heaven and Hell,"* p. 59.

139 Blake's copy of Lavater is in the Henry E. Huntington Library: *Aphorisms on Man,* tr. Henry Fuseli (London: J. Johnson, 1788), p. 126 (no. 371).

140 "William Blake on the Unholy Alliance: Satanic Freedom and Godly Repression in Liberal Society," *The Wordsworth Circle,* 3 (1972), 213.

141 *Blake's Apocalypse,* p. 342.

142 Stanley E. Fish, "Reasons That Imply Themselves: Imagery, Argument, and the Reader in Milton's *Reason of Church Government,"* in *Seventeenth-Century Imagery,* p. 86.

143 Ibid., pp. 86–87.

144 Ibid., p. 87.

145 Ibid., p. 88.

146 Ibid., pp. 98–99.

147 Ibid., pp. 101–2.

148 Emery, *Blake's "The Marriage of Heaven and Hell,"* p. 43.

149 In the preceding discussion I have pointed to the conspicuous borrowings from Milton's prose works; in plate 19, there is an apparent allusion to *Paradise Regained.* Blake writes, "I by force suddenly caught him in

my arms, & flew westerly thro' the night," recalling the corresponding
moment in Milton's brief epic when Satan "catches up" Christ and bears
him "through the Air sublime" to "the glorious Temple" (IV. 541—50).
The flight through air has no biblical precedent in the Gospel accounts
of Christ's temptation in the wilderness.

150 *The Prophets,* II, 37—38.

151 For an illuminating discussion of this point, see Stuart Curran, "Blake
and the Gnostic Hyle: A Double Negative," *Blake Studies,* 4, ii (1972),
130—31.

152 See A. B. Chambers, "The Falls of Adam and Eve in *Paradise Lost,*" in
New Essays on "Paradise Lost," pp. 118—30, and also J. M. Evans,
"Paradise Lost" and the Genesis Tradition (Oxford: Clarendon Press,
1968), esp. pp. 219—92.

153 Blake's comment, as Denis de Rougement suggests, has been "curiously
vulgarized" with the result that this critic's subtle, in many ways
profound, interpretation seldom affects the way Blakeans read this
passage (see *The Devil's Share,* 2nd ed., Bollingen Series, 2 [New York:
Pantheon Books, 1945], pp. 131—34). I have presented my own arguments against the usual reading of *The Marriage of Heaven and Hell* as a
celebration of Satan in "The 'Satanism' of Blake and Shelley Recon-
sidered," *Studies in Philology,* 65 (1968), 816—33, and have summarized
these arguments in my introduction to *The Romantics on Milton,* pp.
3—32. I pause now only to observe that the usual understanding of
Blake's reading of *Paradise Lost* still obfuscates modern criticism, as is
evidenced by Jay Martin's review of John Collier's *Milton's "Paradise
Lost": Screenplay for Cinema of the Mind* (New York: Knopf, 1973).
According to Martin, who is not a Miltonist but who has been well-
schooled in the orthodoxies of Milton criticism, "William Blake *began*
the search for alternate heroes [in *Paradise Lost,* a search continued by
Collier] by suggesting quite in opposition to Milton's intentions Satan,
who at best is interesting in his ruin, was the central figure of the poem"
("Praise for the Blighted and Blasted," *New Republic* [June 23, 1973],
28). Martin is right to tie Romantic admiration of Milton's Satan to
Romantic antipathy for Milton's God; but to suggest that such antipathy
derives from "boredom" with "perfection" is nonsense: Milton's God is
problematical for Blake and later for Shelley not because he is perfect
but because, in his *imperfection,* he is prone to villainy.

154 *Paradise Lost,* ed. Thomas Newton, 9th ed., 2 vols. (London: J. F. and
C. Rivington, 1790), II, 446—47.

155 Blake's remarks here are elucidated and corroborated by two studies:
Edward Langton, *Satan: A Portrait* (London: Skeffington, 1946), and
Rivhah Schärf Kluger, *Satan in the Old Testament,* tr. Hildegard Nagel
(Evanston: Northwestern Univ. Press, 1967).

156 *William Blake: A Reading of the Shorter Poems,* p. 44.

157 Paul H. Casimer, "Blake's *Marriage of Heaven and Hell,*" *Contemporary
Review,* 183 (1953), 353.

158 Nurmi, *Blake's "Marriage of Heaven and Hell,"* p. 35.
159 *The Romantics on Milton,* p. 537.
160 Ibid.
161 *Antichrist in Seventeenth-Century England* (London: Oxford Univ. Press, 1971), p. 91.
162 Ibid., pp. 133–34, 157.
163 *Memoirs of Thomas Hollis,* comp. Francis Blackburne (London: Privately printed, 1780), pp. 621, 625.
164 London: Denew and Grant, 1786, pp. 7–8.
165 In *The World Turned Upside Down,* Christopher Hill makes the same point: "Milton was not of the devil's party without knowing it: part of him knew" (p. 326).
166 Again, Hill makes an important comment when he speaks of "the tension, the inner contradictions which produced Milton's poetry" (ibid., p. 327)—not all of it, Blake might argue, not *Paradise Regained,* but certainly poems like *Comus* and *Paradise Lost.*
167 Henry A. Beers, *Milton's Tercentenary* (New Haven: Yale Univ. Press, 1910), p. 37.
168 *A Defence of Poetry,* in *The Complete Works of Percy Bysshe Shelley,* ed. Roger Ingpen and Walter E. Peck, 10 vols. (London: Ernest Benn, 1927–30), VII, 116.
169 Channing, *Remarks on the Character and Writings of John Milton,* pp. 34–35.
170 *The Romantics on Milton,* p. 111.
171 Philip Neve, *Cursory Remarks on Some of the Ancient English Poets, Particularly Milton* (London: Privately printed, 1789), p. 146.
172 Hughes, *Ten Perspectives on Milton,* p. 275.
173 Anon., *A Collection of Prophetical Warnings of the Eternal Spirit* (London: Printed for B. Bragg, 1708), p. ix.
174 Donald A. Roberts's note to *Defensio Secunda,* in *Yale Milton,* IV, i, 555n.
175 "First and Last Romantics," *Studies in Romanticism,* 9 (1970), 231.

Epilogue: "FORWARD THRO' ETERNITY"

1 *A Father's Memoirs of His Child* (London: T. Bensley, 1806), p. xxx.
2 See *Blake and Milton* (London: George Allen and Unwin, 1935) and *Fearful Symmetry: A Study of William Blake* (Princeton: Princeton Univ. Press, 1947), esp. pp. 313–55.
3 "William Blake on the Unholy Alliance: Satanic Freedom and Godly Repression in Liberal Society," *The Wordsworth Circle,* 3 (1972), 212–22.
4 *The Anxiety of Influence: A Theory of Poetry* (New York: Oxford Univ. Press, 1973), esp. pp. 5–45. Several months after the appearance of Bloom's book Leslie Brisman's study was published (*Milton's Poetry of Choice and Its Romantic Heirs* [Ithaca: Cornell Univ. Press, 1973]).

Contrary to Bloom, Brisman argues that "Not plodding under an imposed burden of the past, Milton and the Romantics [Blake included] stand strong and choose a better way. . . . When the responding 'one' is a Romantic poet, Milton's influence takes its most seminal form" (pp. 1–2). For Brisman's study of Blake's poetry in relation to Milton's, see pp. 192–212 of *Milton's Poetry of Choice;* and see also the brief but exacting statement by Albert Cook, "Blake's *Milton,*" *Costerus,* 6 (1972), 27–33. Acknowledging that "Blake's *Milton* seems farther from Milton than most other Romantic epics," Cook observes that it is in actuality "closer to Milton than any," concluding that "Blake let Milton's revivified influence liberate him: he followed Milton rather than aping him, in rhythm as in theme" (pp. 27, 33). Blake's trafficking with Milton's poetry is interestingly studied by David Wagenknecht, *Blake's Night: William Blake and the Idea of Pastoral* (Cambridge, Mass.: Harvard Univ. Press, 1973); it is also the subject of an impressive dissertation by Thomas Minnick, "On Blake and Milton: An Essay in Literary Relationship" (Ohio State Univ., 1973).

5   *The Anxiety of Influence,* p. 13.

6   Ibid., p. 30.

7   Ibid., p. 29.

8   Ibid., p. 33.

9   In *The Imagination of the Resurrection: The Poetic Continuity of a Religious Motif in Donne, Blake, and Yeats* (Lewisburg: Bucknell Univ. Press, 1972), Kathryn R. Kremen observes, "I am uncertain . . . if this willful misinterpretation, due to one's anxiety about the paralyzing if not perhaps unmatchable greatness of one's predecessors, is the only or most desirable, kind of poetic influence." Kremen prefers "the example of Elijah's passing to Elisha his mantle of poetic inspiration" (p. 303n.)—an example that figures in Blake's *Milton* (24:71). For a more sophisticated discussion of this idea of poetic influence, see Brisman's *Milton's Poetry of Choice,* pp. 1–8, 192–212; and see, too, my review of Bloom's book in *Blake Studies,* 6, i (1973), 89–94.

10   *The Anxiety of Influence,* p. 39.

11   William Lilly, *Merlinus Anglicus Junior: The English Merlin Revived; or, A Mathematical Prediction . . . ,* 2nd ed. (London: Printed for T. V., 1644), sig. [A1^v].

12   William Perkins, *Lectures upon the Three First Chapters of the Revelation* (London: Printed for Cuthbert Burbie, 1604), p. 250.

13   "Of Prophecy," in *A Collection of Theological Tracts,* ed. Richard Watson, 6 vols. (London: J. Nichols, 1785), IV, 362.

14   The letter, addressed to Richard Eberhart, is quoted by Bloom in *The Anxiety of Influence,* p. 7.

15   *Complete Works of Ralph Waldo Emerson,* Centenary edition, 12 vols. (Boston: Houghton and Mifflin, 1903–21), IV, 42.

16   I take this phrase from a chapter title in Patrick Fairbairn's *Prophecy,*

Viewed in Respect to Its Distinctive Nature, Its Special Function, and Proper Interpretation (Edinburgh: T. and T. Clark, 1856), p. 177.

17   *Many-Minded Homer* (New York: Barnes and Noble, 1968), p. 178.

18   Fairbairn, *Prophecy*, p. 189.

19   Ibid., p. 187.

20   *The Anxiety of Influence*, p. 20.

21   The phrase is Emerson's; see *The Early Lectures of Ralph Waldo Emerson*, ed. Stephen E. Whicher and Robert E. Spiller, 3 vols. (Cambridge, Mass.: Harvard Univ. Press, 1959–72), I, 135. The relationship between apish imitation and false prophecy is spelled out by Smith, "Of Prophecy," in *A Collection of Theological Tracts*, IV, 304, and is a theme developed in Revelation commentary (see, e.g., Henry Bullinger, *A Hundred Sermons upon the Apocalypse of Jesu Christ* [London: John Daye, 1573], p. 68).

22   *Apocalypsis Apocalypseos; or the Revelation of St. John the Divine Unveiled* (London: Printed for J. Martyn and W. Kettilby, 1680), pp. 105–8.

23   Thomas Goodwin, *An Exposition of the Revelation* (1639), in *The Works of Thomas Goodwin*, 12 vols. (Edinburgh: James Nichol, 1861–66), V, 149.

24   Ibid., pp. 182, 192.

25   George Giffard, *Sermons upon the Whole Booke of the Revelation* (London: Printed by Richard Field and Felix Kingston, 1599), p. 197.

26   *Milton*, in *The Romantics on Milton: Formal Essays and Critical Asides*, ed. Joseph Anthony Wittreich, Jr. (Cleveland: Press of Case Western Reserve Univ., 1970), pp. 478–79 (my italics).

27   Ibid., p. 479.

28   *Life of William Blake, "Pictor Ignotus,"* 2 vols. (London: Macmillan, 1863), I, 155.

29   *Fearful Symmetry*, pp. 327–28.

30   "Notes for a Commentary on Milton," in *The Divine Vision: Studies in the Poetry and Art of William Blake*, ed. Vivian de Sola Pinto (London: Victor Gollancz, 1957), p. 102.

31   *The Theory of Epic Poetry in England 1650–1800*, University of California Publications, 15 (Berkeley and Los Angeles: Univ. of California Press, 1944), pp. 94, 127.

32   Quoted by Eudo C. Mason, *The Mind of Henry Fuseli* (London: Routledge and Kegan Paul, 1951), p. 347.

33   Ibid., p. 275.

34   " 'The Hem of Their Garments': The Bard's Song in *Milton*," in *Blake's Sublime Allegory: Essays on "The Four Zoas," "Milton," and "Jerusalem,"* ed. Stuart Curran and Joseph Anthony Wittreich, Jr. (Madison: Univ. of Wisconsin Press, 1973), p. 262.

35   See my essay, "Domes of Mental Pleasure: Blake's Epics and Hayley's Epic Theory," *Studies in Philology*, 69 (1971), 201–29, and Stuart

Curran's essay, "Blake and the Gnostic Hyle," *Blake Studies,* 4, ii (1972), 117–33. For a rejoinder to my views, see Judith Wardle, "Satan not having the Science of Wrath but only of Pity," *Studies in Romanticism,* 13 (1974), 147–54, whose "general impression"—the guiding light of her essay—is different not only from mine but from that of literary historians (e.g., H. T. Swedenberg), major poets and minor ones of the Romantic period (e.g., Coleridge and Southey) and from a number of Hayley's reviewers. Wardle rightly corrects my faulty citation of Hayley as a proponent of allegory in the Spenserian mode; yet her general impression and mine remain at odds, largely because she sees Hayley as, finally, a rather conservative aesthetician whose theoretical statements are embodied in his poetry. Hayley, I would argue, is a man divided against himself; his epic theory, it happens, does not agree with his own practice as a poet, and thus it is folly to quote Hayley's poetry as if it did.

36 London: Printed for J. Dodsley, 1782. All quotations from this edition are given in parentheses in the text.

37 Quoted by E. H. Gombrich, *Norm and Form: Studies in the Art of the Renaissance,* 2nd ed. (London and New York: Phaidon, 1971), p. 122.

38 An expurgated edition of Hayley's *Life* appeared in the first volume of *The Poetical Works of John Milton,* ed. William Hayley (London: J. and J. Boydell and G. Nicol, 1794). All quotations in this chapter are from *The Life of Milton* (1796), 2nd ed. with Introduction by Joseph Anthony Wittreich, Jr. (Gainesville, Fla.: Scholars' Facsimiles and Reprints, 1970).

39 "The Genesis and General Meaning of Blake's *Milton,*" *Modern Philology,* 25 (1927), 166.

40 Ibid., pp. 175, 217–18.

41 In the Preface to his *Life of Milton,* Hayley writes, "His [Dr. Johnson's] lives of the poets will probably give birth, in this or the next century, to a work of literary retaliation. Whenever a poet rises with as large a portion of spleen towards the critical writers of past ages, as Dr. Johnson indulged towards the poets in his poetical biography, the literature of England will be enriched with 'the Lives of the Critics' . . . " (p. xiv).

42 "The Genesis and General Meaning of Blake's *Milton,*" p. 173.

43 This is not to say, however, that Blake's attitude toward Milton is negative. Characteristically, the hero is flawed in order to encourage identification; but the accent in epic poetry always falls upon the hero's positive qualities.

44 This second plate of *Milton,* we should remember, is included only in Copies A and B.

45 *The Life of Milton,* p. xvii.

46 Ibid., p. 220.

47 Ibid., p. 230.

48 See ibid., pp. 233–80.

49 Ibid., p. 276.

50 Ibid., p. 277.

51 Ibid., p. 137.

52 The term is Brian Wilkie's; see *Romantic Poets and Epic Tradition* (Madison: Univ. of Wisconsin Press, 1965), esp. pp. 3–29.

53 Henry Fuseli makes a similar point: "When we consider the magnificent end of epic poetry, to write for all times and all races, to treat of what will always exist and always be understood, the puny laws of local decorum and fluctuating fashions, by which the omission or modification of certain habits and customs, natural and obsolete, is prescribed, cannot come into consideration. Such laws may bind the meaner race of writers" (quoted by Mason, *The Mind of Henry Fuseli,* p. 245).

54 In *On Blake's Illustrations to Dante,* Blake writes, "Homer is the Center of All I mean the Poetry of the Heathen Stolen & Perverted from the Bible not by Chance but by design" (p. 668).

55 *The Burden of the Past and the English Poet* (Cambridge, Mass.: Harvard Univ. Press, 1970), p. 128.

56 The judgment is fairly common in Blake criticism; the words are Mark Schorer's (*William Blake: The Politics of Vision* [New York: Henry Holt, 1945], p. 346).

57 For a brilliant discussion of this point, see Edward J. Rose, "Blake's *Milton:* The Poet as Poem," *Blake Studies,* 1, i (1968), 16–38. John T. Shawcross elucidates the symmetrical design of Milton's epic in "The Balanced Structure of *Paradise Lost,*" *Studies in Philology,* 62 (1965), 696–718.

58 I have used Copy D, reproduced for the Blake Trust by the Trianon Press (London, 1967) as the basis for this structural analysis. The removal of the second plate from Copies C and D of *Milton* makes the elaborate balancing of structural patterns quite conspicuous.

59 For example, the track for Milton's descent is described in Book I, but it is also the subject for an illustration in Book II (see plate 37 in the Trianon edition or plate 33 in *Poetry and Prose*). The appearance of the illustration in Book II has the effect of conflating Milton's descent and Ololon's, thereby reinforcing Blake's contention that "Events of Time start forth & are conceiv'd in such a Period/Within a moment: a Pulsation of the Artery" (29:2–3).

60 For a discussion of the circle image in Blake's verse, see Edward J. Rose, " 'Mental Forms Creating': 'Fourfold Vision' and the Poet as Prophet in Blake's Designs and Verse," *Journal of Aesthetics and Art Criticism,* 23 (1964), 173–83.

61 *Literary Remains,* ed. Henry Nelson Coleridge, 4 vols. (London: W. Pickering, 1836), II, 34–35.

62 *Norm and Form,* p. 78.

63 *The Metamorphoses of the Circle,* tr. Carley Dawson and Elliott Coleman (Baltimore: Johns Hopkins Press, 1966), esp. pp. 307–20.

64 "William Blake on the Unholy Alliance," p. 213.

65 Allen Grossman, "Milton's Sonnet 'On the Late Massacre in Piedmont':

A Note on the Vulnerability of Persons in a Revolutionary Situation," in *Literature in Revolution,* ed. George Abbott White and Charles Newman (New York: Holt, Rinehart, and Winston, 1972), p. 299. Nor would I argue that the idea is unique to Milton, for it is fundamental to *The Faerie Queene* and should, through Milton and Spenser, be traced to its source in commentary on the Book of Revelation, especially on its twelfth chapter.

66 Francis Ellington, *Christian Information Concerning These Last Times* (London: n.p., 1664), pp. 7–8.

67 Ibid., p. 9.

68 "The Mask and the Face: The Perception of Physiognomic Likeness in Life and in Art," in *Art, Perception, and Reality,* ed. Maurice Mandelbaum (Baltimore: Johns Hopkins Univ. Press, 1972), p. 40.

69 The lamp in Los's hand identifies him as a prophet, specifically linking him to John of Patmos, who was often portrayed as "a burning and shining lamp" and thus represented as the bearer of a lantern (see, e.g., W. Hindes's 1613 Preface to John Rainolds's *The Prophecy of Obadiah Opened and Applied* [Edinburgh: James Nichol, 1864], p. 1). The lantern is lighted ("shining") in accordance with the dictum: to have a lamp is not enough; one must have oil for it, he must have heavenly light, if his goal is to enter Jerusalem (see Ludowick Muggleton, *A True Interpretation of the Eleventh Chapter of St. John* [1662; rpt. London: E. Brown, 1833], p. 69). Moreover, as Isaac Newton observes, the lamp is an emblem for the teacher-prophet (see *Observations upon the Prophecies of Holy Writ, Particularly the Prophecies of Daniel, and the Apocalypse of St. John,* in *Opera,* 5 vols. [London: John Nichols, 1785], V, 469).

70 Morton D. Paley, *Energy and the Imagination: A Study of the Development of Blake's Thought* (Oxford: Clarendon Press, 1970), p. 249. The passages here cited from Blake's *Milton* tacitly invoke the Argument to Book I of *Paradise Lost,* specifically Milton's remark that Satan comforts the fallen angels by recalling *"an ancient Prophesie or report in Heaven"* of a new creation, "a new World" with new creatures. Here, in *Milton,* Blake boldly contrasts the poet's actions with those of both Satan and God in *Paradise Lost:* they are manaclers of creatures, whereas Milton is their deliverer.

71 Ibid., pp. 249–50.

72 See *Theogony,* esp. VIII. 453–506 and X. 617–735. Norman O. Brown, who has popularized Blake for the modern generation, has also provided an Introduction for Hesiod's *Theogony* (Indianapolis and New York: Bobbs-Merrill, 1953), which focuses on a set of themes important to Hesiod and also central to Blake's mythology. Zeus's triumph, as Brown explains, results from his decision not to repress his children (the various powers of human life) but to incorporate them. Zeus does not imprison Cronus (the first three letters inverted spell "Orc"), just as Milton does not abandon Orc; rather, each hero triumphs because he releases the

powers represented by the energies of human life: he "controls them, and finds a function for them. Thus the force and violence in the universe, which an earlier generation created and then tried to repress, finds a controlled outlet in the political organization of Zeus" (p. 24), and, we should add, in the new political order promised by Milton.

73 *Energy and the Imagination,* p. 242.

74 "Blake's *Jerusalem:* The Bard of Sensibility and the Form of Prophecy," in *The Ringers in the Tower: Studies in Romantic Tradition* (Chicago: Univ. of Chicago Press, 1971), pp. 65, 74, 75.

75 *Fearful Symmetry,* pp. 260–61.

76 Abraham Heschel, *The Prophets, Part II,* 2 vols. (New York: Harper and Row, 1971), II, 180.

77 Edward J. Rose, "Blake's Illustrations for *Paradise Lost, L'Allegro,* and *Il Penseroso:* A Thematic Reading," *Hartford Studies in Literature,* 2 (1970), 67.

This book was with the printer when Christopher Hill's "Milton the Radical" appeared (*Times Literary Supplement* [November 29, 1974], 1130–32). That essay adopts the same perspective from which much of my own book is written, and it is valuably supplemented by James M. Lewis's response to the editor (December 13, 1974), 1416. Hill's essay promises a book on Milton, forthcoming in 1975. Also arriving too late to take into account was Hugh M. Richmond's *The Christian Revolutionary: John Milton* (Berkeley and Los Angeles: Univ. of California Press, 1974). Like my own study, Richmond's urges a contextual approach to Milton's poetry; yet, failing to take into account much of the important criticism of our time (Northrop Frye, Angus Fletcher, and Christopher Hill, who have focused for Miltonists the subject that Richmond pursues, are not mentioned in his book), it contributes only marginally to what is certain to be an on-going dialogue in Milton studies.

Index

Abraham, 266

Achilles, 159

Adam, 41, 63, 68, 87; and Eve, 87, 110, 159, 194; temptations of, 292, 295

Adams, Hazard, xiii, xix, 174, 212

Adams, Robert Martin, 305

Addison, Joseph, 70, 72

Adlard, John, 268

aesthetics, 73; conservative, xvi; radical, xvi, 151–71; of eighteenth century, 71, 148, 303–4; revolution in, 176; Christian, 176

Aikin, John, 107, 109

Albion, 16, 18, 31, 35, 43, 47, 194, 256, 263, 266–67, 278; in his death sleep, 12, 28–31; sons of, 27, 29; awakening, 33; fallen, 48, 52, 66–67, 277, 278; Blake's evolving conception of, 55; hair of, 276

Albion Rose, 4, 48–69, 262, 277, 278; states of, 48, 54, 275, 276; inscription to, 50, 61; date of, 54–55, 275, 277, 280; as allegory, 56, 65, 277; as false apocalypse, 57; allusive quality of, 68, 69; political character of, 68, 69

Aldrich, Henry, 281

allegory, 33, 50, 56, 61, 88, 94–95, 176–77, 226, 235; kinds of, 172, 173–75, 179, 181, 183, 186–87, 314; Blake's definition of, 173–74; and vision, 175–76; and myth, 176

Allen, Don Cameron, 117, 176, 304

allusion, 73

America, 31, 52, 53, 64–65, 276, 277

Animadversions, 154, 166, 172, 203

Antichrist, 46, 227, 309

apocalypse, 14, 33, 35, 47, 57, 64, 68, 90, 95–96, 125, 162, 194, 197, 199, 203, 227, 247, 267, 287

Apollo, 49, 255

Apology for Smectymnuus, An, 155, 207–8, 213, 246, 301

apotheosis: tradition of, 35–38

apple. *See* symbolism

architecture. *See* symbolism

Areopagitica, 11, 25, 51, 154, 167, 202, 206, 242, 243, 257, 262

Ariosto, Ludovico, 179, 180, 184, 186, 248, 254

Aristotle, 51, 149, 179

Artis Logicae, 155

artists, 152–54, 156–57, 160–61. *See also* poets; prophet

Ascension, 261

ass. *See* symbolism

Assumption, 263

audience, xiv, 18, 150–51, 170, 178–79, 180, 181, 182–84, 185–86, 195, 198–99, 205, 206–7, 225, 306

Auguries of Innocence, 59

Babylon, 192–93

"back parts." *See* symbolism

Baker, C. H. Collins, 286, 292

baldness. *See* symbolism

Balestra, A., 271, 286, 288

baptism, 122–23, 124, 127, 132, 134, 135

Barry, James, 292

Barthes, Roland, 21

Bate, Walter Jackson, 175, 235

bat wings. *See* symbolism

bay. *See* symbolism

Bayle, Pierre, 268, 271–72

Bayly, Anselm, 175

Beelzebub, 215

Behrendt, Stephen, xix, 9, 263

Belial, 293

Bergson, Henri, 28

Bible, xvii, 161–62, 165, 167, 174, 176, 208–9, 228, 240, 247, 268, 315; tradition of, xiii; Apocrypha, 25, 26, 41–42; Luther's September, 99–100; design of, 162; as epic, 176; theology of, 190; Kitto, 291–92. *See also* illustration

—Exodus, 112, 247, 260–61, 262, 277

—Gospels, 121, 122–23, 124–25, 139, 142, 244, 263, 291, 296
—Job, 48, 67, 112, 134, 144, 209, 211, 247, 274; Blake's illustrations for, 58, 67, 68, 77–78, 79, 100, 132, 280
—Revelation, 10, 11, 16–17, 20, 24, 26, 31–32, 66, 95–96, 162, 164, 169–70, 176, 190, 194, 223, 242, 264, 268, 270–71, 274, 287; illustrations for, 14, 22, 100, 103; commentators on, 14, 46, 256, 257–58, 265, 313, 316; angels in, 16–17, 22, 32, 46, 227, 257–58, 264, 268, 309; as picture-prophecy, 20, 261; as handbook for prophets, 21; vision of the candlesticks in, 23; heroes of, 25; four horsemen in, 95; as radical document, 165; structure of, 168, 191, 193, 195, 308; as epic, 176; allegory in, 179; as tragedy, 181; dramatic form of, 181, 191; obscurity of, 187; in relation to earlier prophecy, 191; as medley of forms and styles, 191; patterns in, 191, 193; Blake's illustrations for, 191, 258, 263; time distances in, 196; imagery in, 227; Blake's study of, 227; two witnesses in, 227–28; seal prophecy in, 258; meaning of, 261; John's posture in, 261; warfare in, 297; Blake's debt to, 307
—various books of: Chronicles, 247; Corinthians, 78; Daniel, 264, 271; Deuteronomy, 31, 66, 143; Ephesians, 204–5; Ezekiel, 31–32, 247–48; Genesis, 112, 262; Hebrews, 23; Isaiah, 191–93, 307, 308; Jeremiah, 24, 65; Joel, 196; Judges, 273; Kings, 23; Malachi, 263; Psalms, 262; Samuel, 10, 11, 246, 262
Bicheno, James, 22, 258, 277–78
Bindman, David, 280
Binyon, Laurence, 56
Birch, Thomas, 70
Blair, Robert, 223
Blake, William: and tradition, xiii, xiv, xv, xvi, xvii, 3, 4–5, 69, 72–73, 101, 102, 103–29, 145, 152, 163, 222–23, 249; and the Bible, xiii, xvi; canon of, xiii, 76, 259; and his critics, xiv; and his audience, xiv; genius of, xiv, xvi, 4; influence of, xiv, xvii; as a revolutionary, xv, xvi, 66, 69; his Miltonic contexts,

xvi, xvii, xviii, 73, 224; as an iconoclast, xvi, 222–23; obscurity of, xvii, 13, 188, 283; his idea of "relevance," xviii; as a critic, xviii, 3, 73–74, 75–78, 79, 97, 103–4, 144–46, 148, 178, 186, 301; as an illustrator, 3, 71, 72, 74, 79, 85, 93–94, 97, 98–99, 145–46, 222, 259; originality of, 4; his knowledge of epic poetry, 5; his knowledge of the visual arts, 5; the ambiguity of his imagery, 9, 24–25, 27–28, 30–31, 33, 35, 254, 266; as a prophet, 10–11; as a Christian painter, 21; artistic principles of, 45, 49–50; and Samson, compared, 65; and William Hayley, 70, 235, 291; marginalia of, 76, 112, 128, 131, 134, 142, 143, 153, 173, 187, 204, 206, 213, 309; development of, 78; precision of, 82, 97, 272; as an engraver, 82, 102; his theory of accommodation, 181; as a visionary, 181; authorial intrusions of, 183; as an ironist, 215; as a creator of systems, 222, 224; his attitude toward precursors, 222–23; as a witness, 228; politics of, 228; uniting with Milton, 245; private mythology of, 246; his study of physiognomies, 254; letters by, 254, 287, 298, 304; as portrait artist, 256; qualities of, 273, 275; his sketches, 277; his wash strokes in colored prints, 305. *See also* Bible, Job, Revelation; Bunyan; Dante; Gray; Milton; and titles of individual works by Blake and by Milton
Bland, David, 101
Bloom, Harold, xvii, xix, 47, 72–73, 205, 218–19, 221–22, 225, 226, 228–29, 247–48, 264, 266, 272, 275, 282, 298, 306–7, 311–12
Blunt, Anthony, 49, 55, 56, 58, 68, 69, 283, 291
Boiardo, Matteo, 248
Botticelli, Sandro, 132
bow. *See* symbolism
Breasted, Barbara, 284
Brisman, Leslie, 124, 280, 311–12
Broadbent, J. B., 165, 286
Brothers, Richard, 11, 42
Brown, Norman O., 316
Browning, Robert, 222

Bullinger, Henry, 265
Bunyan, John: Blake's illustrations for, 78, 295
Burke, Edmund, 57
Burke, Kenneth, 301–2
Burney, Edward Francis, 60, 86, 255, 279, 285, 286
Burton, Henry, 265
Butler, Samuel, 229
Butlin, Martin, 92
Butts, Thomas, 65, 92–93, 172, 174, 175, 287
Byron, George Gordon, Lord, 260, 290

Calliope, 168
Calton, Sir Francis, 298
Cambridge University, 5, 35
Camoens, Luis de, 254
Campbell, Joseph, 130
Carey, Elizabeth Luther, 59, 257
Carlyle, Thomas, 264
caterpillar. *See* symbolism
Caudwell, Christopher, 305
cave. *See* symbolism
Channing, William Ellery, 136–38, 182, 298
Chantrey, Sir Francis, 293
chariot. *See* symbolism
Charles I, 36, 42, 259–60, 272
chastity, 37, 247
Chaucer, Geoffrey, 37, 174–75, 269, 293
Cheron, Louis, 7, 8, 60, 110, 254, 271, 288, 292
chrysalis. *See* symbolism
Cipriani, G. B., 44, 45, 253
circle. *See* symbolism
Clark, Ira, 296
Clark, Kenneth, 298
classics, 41, 240
cloud. *See* symbolism
Coban, 27
Coleridge, Samuel Taylor, 44, 94, 153, 238, 287, 290, 314
Colie, Rosalie L., 302
collar. *See* symbolism
Collier, John Payne, 310
Collins, William 44
comedy, 168
Comus, 9, 71, 120, 163, 164, 218, 235, 244; adaptations of, 44, 80–81, 86–87, 88, 271, 273; revisions of, 81, 83; ideology of, 84; illustrators of, 86, 87, 285; as drama, 86, 87–88; criticism of, 87–88; mythic pattern in, 88; moral allegory in, 88; as visionary poem, 88; as radical experiment, 168; contradictions in, 212, 217, 311
—Blake's designs for, 44, 76, 79, 80–88, 90, 93, 97, 101, 120, 145, 153; as commentary on *Milton,* 44
contraries, 78, 193, 199, 202–4, 237, 239
Conweena, 27
Cook, Albert, 312
cosmic paintings, 110–11, 293
couch. *See* symbolism
Covering Cherub, 27. *See also* Milton
Cowper, William, 44, 77, 95, 105, 290
creation, 162, 226, 263; poetic, 165–67, 178, 179, 180, 183; and interpretation, 178, 304
criticism, 76, 82, 97, 304. *See also* New Criticism
Cromwell, Oliver, 19
Cronus, 316
crosshatching. *See* symbolism
crown. *See* symbolism
crucifixion, 57, 58, 62–63, 67, 110, 112–13, 121–22, 123–24, 126–27, 132, 228, 244, 261, 286, 288, 292, 293, 295, 297–98
Curran, Stuart, xix, 307, 310
cycle paintings, 97–98

Daddi, Bernado, 293
Dalila. *See* Delilah
Dalton, John, 273
Damon, S. Foster, 73, 174, 256, 272, 281
dance. *See* symbolism
Dante, 33, 43, 71, 77, 168, 176, 178, 180, 194, 212–13, 217, 223, 234, 248, 249, 250, 305
—Blake's designs for, 93–94, 100, 273
Declaration of Independence, 50
De Doctrina Christiana, 136–37, 138, 296, 297–98
Defensio Secunda, 25, 162, 186, 187, 218, 242, 243
Defoe, Daniel, 281–82
Deism, 16
DeLaunay, Nicholas, 8

Delilah, 60, 275, 280

Dennis, John, 289

DeQuincey, Thomas, 229, 300

Descriptive Catalogue, A, 13, 35–36, 49, 69, 250, 283

Despair, 278

DeWilde, Samuel, 86, 285

Diana, 294

Dibdin, Charles, 214–15

Dibdin, Thomas, 70

Digby, George Wingfield, 49, 283

Dighton, Alexander, 86, 285

Diodati, Charles, 81

DiSalvo, Jackie, xix, 205, 221, 240–41, 274, 284

Divine Vision, 12, 15, 22, 25, 32, 37, 65, 112, 184

Doctrine and Discipline of Divorce, The, 144, 149, 166, 197, 204, 206, 242

Donne, John, 150, 164

door. *See* symbolism

dragon. *See* symbolism

drama, 169

Dryden, John, 271

Dürer, Albrecht, 103

Dunster, Charles, 105, 106, 109, 290, 294, 298

Durling, Robert M., 305

Dutton, T., 265

eagle. *See* symbolism

Eberhart, Richard, 312

elegy, 156, 168

Elijah, 26, 53, 196, 228, 257; and Elisha, 11, 228, 312

Eliot, T. S., xiii–xvi, 152, 163, 164, 224, 229, 301

Elisha. *See* Elijah

emblem books, 259

Emerson, Ralph Waldo, 224, 313

England, 15, 18, 42, 43, 46, 55, 61, 63, 66, 88, 230, 239, 247

Enitharmon, 16, 29, 269

Eno, 267

epic, 153, 156, 172, 176, 230, 233–36, 243, 249, 314; diffuse, 118, 119, 165, 234; brief, 118, 165, 168, 169, 234, 295; as an initiatory experience, 119–20; tradition of, 144, 168, 171, 173, 178–79, 224, 230, 233, 234, 241, 248–

49; structure of, 158–59, 235, 236; classical, 158–60, 165, 248, 297; Christian, 158–60, 165, 249; and cosmology, 159; and logic, 159; and prophecy, 159, 169–70, 176, 180, 181, 224–25; ideology of, 165, 298; as composite form, 167, 168–69, 303; mock, 168; Renaissance, 168, 172, 180, 303; Blake's manifesto, 171–72; literary, 177; oral, 177, 179; arrested movement in, 178–79; narrative in, 178–79; transformation of, 179; choric quality in, 185; obscurity of, 187; imitation in, 234; paradox of, 234; nationalism of, 234, 236, 243; revolutionary character of, 234, 303; rules of, 234, 315; characterization in, 235; role of women in, 235; machinery in, 235; psychological probing in, 235; mythology in, 236; conventions of, 236; themes in, 236; styles in, 303; as a theater, 303; and audience, 305; Romantic, 312. *See also* illustration; prophecy

Erdman, David V., xix, 30, 50, 53, 54, 55, 56, 60, 65, 68, 69, 99, 196, 258–59, 260, 266, 267, 270, 276, 277, 279, 287, 305, 308

Essick, Robert N., 38–39, 41, 56, 78–79, 260, 277, 288

Eternals, 28, 30

Euphrosyne, 86, 88

Europe, 53, 56, 59, 90, 173, 238, 276, 277

Evans, John, 255

Everlasting Gospel, The, 112, 142

Everlasting Gospel: tradition of, 125

experience, 83–84, 96

Ezekiel, 197

Faithorne, William, 6, 12, 253–54

Fall, 7–8, 109–10, 162

Feast of the Tabernacles, 244

feet. *See* symbolism

Fehl, Philipp, 298

Felpham, 5, 24, 228, 233, 291

Female Will, 60, 266

Ferguson, George, 263

Figgis, Darrell, 114, 283

Fish, Stanley E., xix, 169, 206–7

Fixler, Michael, 170

flames. *See* symbolism

Flaxman, John, 271, 286
Fletcher, Angus, xix, 153, 157, 171, 188, 189, 301, 303
Fogel, Ephim, 301
form, xv, 73, 150–51, 153, 156, 302; and content, 150; liturgical, 154–55; shattering of, 155; perversion of, 155–56; transformation of, 156, 157, 158; "total," 157; composite, 157, 158; "transcendental," 157–58; and style, 158; ideology of, 158; closed and open, 158; unities of, 160, 163; mechanical and organic, 236, 238; conventions of, 238. *See also* epic; genre; prophecy
Fourdrinier, Pierre, 281–82
Four Zoas, The, 24, 29, 31, 52, 53, 56, 59, 65, 78, 204, 245, 247, 259, 267, 299
Fox, Susan C., 299
freedom, 242
Freud, Sigmund, 199
Friedländer, Max J., 13, 77, 255
Frosch, Thomas, 21, 261, 266
Frye, Northrop, xix, 129, 153, 154, 160, 161, 171, 179, 221, 230, 260–61, 274, 284, 295, 298, 301–2, 304, 306–7
Fulgentius, F. P., 177
Fulke, William, 265
Fuseli, Henry, 70, 77, 86, 102, 136, 175, 269, 288, 304–5

garland. *See* symbolism
garments. *See* symbolism
Generation, 266
genius, 150–51
genre, 169, 235, 302
gesture. *See* symbolism
Giffard, George, 265
Gilchrist, Alexander, 49, 92, 114, 189, 229, 293
Gilgamesh Epic, The, 160, 165
Gillray, James, 95, 286
Giraud, Jane, 288
girdle. *See* symbolism
Gisborne, John, 290
Glad Day. See Albion Rose
Gleckner, Robert, xiii, 302
Gnostics, 210
God, 18, 67, 130, 155, 166, 167, 211, 241, 262; as law-giver, 45; as Urizenic

figure, 120; as poet, 165–66, 178, 180, 183; as architect, 166. *See also* Jehovah; Jesus Christ; poet; Urizen
gold. *See* symbolism
Gombrich, E. H., 9, 238, 242, 256, 267–68, 277, 302
Gordon Riots, 50
Grant, John E., xix, 31, 68, 189, 259, 261, 262, 268, 279, 280, 283, 287, 307
Gray, Thomas, 35, 44, 71, 223
—Blake's designs for, 5, 281
Grebnar, Paul, 262
Gutherie, William, 36
Gwendolen, 27

haemony. *See* symbolism
Hagstrum, Jean, xix, 27, 45, 103, 109, 287, 291, 293
hail. *See* symbolism
hair. *See* symbolism
hand. *See* symbolism
Hand, 27, 278
Handel, G. F., 283
Hanford, James Holly, 121
Harbison, Craig, 127
harp. *See* symbolism
Hartman, Geoffrey, 181, 182, 305
Harvey, William, 271
Hawkins, John, 271
Hayley, William, 5, 11, 40, 44, 51, 72, 105–6, 109, 117, 125, 128, 148, 175, 176, 229–30, 236, 238, 239, 241, 253, 254, 255, 290, 291, 294, 313–14; library of, 5, 12, 109, 291; *Life of Cowper,* 70; *Life of Milton,* 70, 231–33, 262, 272, 275, 281, 297, 298, 314; his idea of Milton, 229–36; *An Essay on Epic Poetry,* 230. *See also* Hyle
Hayman, Francis, 60, 86, 87, 279, 285
Haymo, Bishop, 269
head (severed). *See* symbolism
Head of Milton, 5–13, 253–54
Head of Spenser, 253
Hecate, 285
Hector, 159
Heninger, S. K., 304
Herbert, George, 150, 255
Heschel, Abraham, 173, 190, 199, 209
Hesiod, 246, 316
Hesperides, 83, 294

hieroglyphics, 21
Hill, Christopher, 214, 296, 301, 311, 317
History of Britain, 51
Hogarth, William, 95, 287
Hollis, Thomas, 40, 44, 51, 61, 70, 72, 214, 275, 279, 281, 297
Homer, 15, 59, 71, 98, 157, 165, 168, 173, 176, 177, 223, 233, 234, 240, 241, 248, 254, 257, 258, 271, 303, 315
Homeric poets, 224
Hoole, John, 188
horns. *See* symbolism
Howard, Donald R., 269
Hughes, John, 175
Hughes, Merritt Y., 96, 300
Hunter, William B., Jr., 297
Hyle, 27, 230
hymn, 167, 168

illustration: traditions of, 4, 22, 47–48, 77, 109, 111, 289; of eighteenth century, xvi, 76, 101, 282; relation to texts, 71, 81–82, 99, 145; and epic, 71–72, 112; as advertising, 72; and the poet, 72; and the publisher, 72; as criticism, 72, 75–76, 109, 145; techniques of, 78–103, rhetorical function of, 99; conventions of, 102; as the art of compromise, 102–3; subject matter of, 110; splendor of, 110; and the Bible, 111, 287, 291; of the nineteenth century, 282; and decoration, 288; different modes of, 293. *See also Milton*
Il Penseroso: L'Allegro and, 102, 134, 163, 235, 245, 283; illustration for, 285
—Blake's designs for, 78, 79, 93, 97, 262
imagination, 13, 25, 34, 69–70, 236, 238, 245. *See also* Jesus Christ
imitation, xiii, 4, 76, 165, 169, 173, 226, 240, 313
Incarnation, 41, 90, 131, 212
individuals. *See* states
influence: theories of, xviii, 3, 11, 72–73, 222, 223–29, 230, 248–50, 312; psychology of, 72–73, 224; opposing aspects of, 223. *See also* Blake; Milton
innocence, 83–84; higher, 84, 96
Ivins, William J., 256, 282
ivy. *See* symbolism

Jacob, 47
jealousy, 247
Jehovah, 47, 211–12. *See also* God; Satan
Jephthah, 247
Jerusalem, 11, 33, 37, 60, 65, 88, 125, 135, 142, 186, 192, 193, 196, 227, 228, 239, 242, 244, 247, 266. *See also* Milton
Jerusalem, xiv, 12, 29, 30, 35, 55, 59, 78, 125, 142, 163, 171, 173, 181, 199, 224, 236, 247, 249, 250, 259, 299, 308
—Blake's designs for, 60, 63, 244, 279, 316
Jesus Christ, 8, 12, 15, 23, 24, 27, 33, 46, 58, 62, 89, 94, 95, 97–98, 158, 170, 211, 226, 227, 240, 242, 244, 261, 263, 265, 291, 297, 299; as the morning star, 17, 223; transfiguration of, 25–27; in the wilderness, 41–42, 115, 127, 131–32, 291–92, 293, 295, 310; as a prophet, 62, 142, 197, 295; triumph of, 91–92; interpretation of his life, 130; as Urizenic figure, 135; as revolutionary, 141–42, 218; as allegorist, 177; and revelation, 223; as poet, 226; Gospel of, 227; as imagination, 245; and Orc, 276; portrayals of, 293. *See Paradise Regained*
Joachim of Fiore, 257, 261
John of Damascus, 266
John of Patmos, 14, 21, 25, 100, 176, 190, 197, 227, 271. *See also* Bible, Revelation
Johnson, Samuel, 40, 72, 107, 200, 231, 232
John the Baptist, 133, 135
Jonson, Ben, 164
Joseph, 89
Jung, C. G., 139
Jupiter, 307

Keats, John, 300
Keemer, M., 265
key. *See* symbolism
Keynes, Geoffrey, 49, 55, 60, 79, 114, 262, 270, 283, 287, 293, 295
King Edward the Third, 50
Knight, W. F. Jackson, 224
Kremer, Kathryn R., 266, 312

Kroeber, Karl, xix, 288
Kubrin, David, 160–61, 296

L'Allegro, 7, 283. *See also Il Penseroso*
Lamb, Charles, 82
lamp. *See* symbolism
Landor, Walter Savage, 300
Large Book of Designs, 55
lark. *See* symbolism
Last Harvest, 33
Last Judgment, 192–93, 261, 263, 270
Last Supper, 122, 127
laurel. *See* symbolism, of bay
Leavis, F. R., xiii–xv, xvii, 163–64
Lens, B., 281
Leonardo da Vinci, 276–77
Leutha, 28
Levites, 247
Lewalski, Barbara K., 118
Lilburne, John, 62
Lilly, William, 21, 42, 241, 273
linear net. *See* symbolism
linen. *See* symbolism
Linnell, John, 113, 293
Little Boy Lost, A, 91–92
Little Girl Found, The, 307
Little Girl Lost, The, 307
lion. *See* symbolism
London Chronicle, 214
Longinus, 175
Los, 12, 16, 19, 20, 27, 29, 32, 53, 196,
    232, 244, 245, 246, 269, 316
Los, The Song of, 55, 173
Loutherbourg, P. J. de, 292
Love, Christopher, 15
Lowell, Robert, xviii–xix
Lowth, Robert, Bishop of London, 175,
    183, 192, 195, 199
Lucian, 21
Luther, Martin, 99–100, 143
Luvah, 246
Lycidas, 9, 40, 162, 163, 164, 168, 235,
    245, 270
Lykaon, 159

MacKellar, Walter, 124, 133, 140
Malkin, Benjamin, 221
Manso, 6
mantle. *See* symbolism

Marcuse, Herbert, 155, 158, 284
Marilla, E. L., 297
Marlorate, Augustine, 265
Marriage of Heaven and Hell, The, xviii,
    23–24, 56, 171, 188–218, 229, 231,
    239–40, 264, 268, 269–70, 297; alle-
    gory of Printing House, 150–51; place
    of, in Blake's canon, 189; as prophecy,
    189–90, 191–99, 207, 208, 215–16,
    307; Blake's objectives in, 189–90,
    201–2, 203; as satire, 189–90, 306–7;
    composition of, 191; as composite form,
    191–92; contexts for, 191–99; reversal
    of Isaiah's prophecy in, 193; moral
    categories of, 193–94; structure of,
    194–95, 206–7; voices in, 195–96, 197,
    198, 212–14, 264; perspectives in, 195,
    197, 198, 215, 216–17; confusions in,
    196; dialectic in, 196, 199; as experi-
    mental work, 198; strategies of, 198–99,
    204–5, 206, 216; levels of interpretation
    in, 199; Milton and Swedenborg com-
    pared, 199–200; Milton in, 199–218,
    231; Swedenborg in, 200–201; ana-
    logues for its philosophy, 202–3; idea of
    "party" in, 203–4; proverbs of hell in,
    206; influences on, 206; sources for,
    206–7; radical unity of, 207; allusions
    in, 208; Devil's argument in, 208–9;
    plates 5 and 6, 208–12; political rhetoric
    of, 214; irony in, 215; meaning of, 250;
    borrowings from Milton in, 309–10;
    alleged Satanism of, 310
Marshall, William, 7, 285
Martin, Elias, 86
Martin, Jay, 310
Marvell, Andrew, 47, 273–74
Marx, Karl, 158
Mary, 89, 263
masque, 168, 234. *See also Comus*
Mayer, John, 265
Meadowcourt, Richard, 109, 289
Mede, Joseph, 261
Medea, 284–85
Medina, J. B., 281–82, 292
Medwin, Thomas, 290
Melancholy, 134, 285. *See also Il Pense-
    roso*
Merlin, 256, 308

Metz, Conrad, 86, 279
Michelangelo, 77
Milton, John: his critics, xiv, xv, xviii,
39–40, 41, 44, 81, 83, 86, 94–95, 145–
46, 148–49, 175, 182, 188, 232, 262,
272, 274, 297; influence of, xiv, xvii–
xviii, 18, 72–73, 208, 222–23, 229,
247–48, 312; as a revolutionary, xv,
xvii, 9, 14, 16, 33, 35, 36, 38, 41, 43–
44, 47, 48, 64, 71, 73–74, 89, 137, 146,
147, 149–50, 170–71, 194, 214, 215,
218, 222–23, 228, 231, 233–34, 260,
274, 279, 300–301, 316, 317; tradition
of, xvii, 4, 67, 69, 73, 172, 224, 243,
249, 272; his theology, xviii, 40, 77,
108, 210, 217, 241; and orthodoxy,
xviii, xix, 35, 112, 136, 137–38, 148,
151, 200–201, 210, 213, 217, 218, 232,
233; portraits of, 7, 39, 248, 253–54,
269, 279, 281; errors of, 9, 16–17, 20,
37, 38, 39–40, 43, 44, 232, 239, 243–
44, 258, 262, 270; self-portraits of, 10,
47, 242–43; as prophet, 10–11, 44, 63,
144, 177, 196, 218, 227, 250, 254–55,
261, 300; as pilgrim, 11–12, 28, 40; his
transfiguration, 13, 14, 26, 35, 36–38,
45, 271, 300; Blake's mythologizing of,
13, 35, 40, 47; as Christian agonist, 14;
as an awakener, 17, 18, 26, 31, 32, 34,
35, 41, 43, 45, 47, 119, 147–48, 218,
219, 239, 240, 246, 268; his power over
England, 18, 28; compared to Christ, 23,
25–27, 41–42; compared to Albion,
30–31; as defender of regicide, 36, 61,
244, 272; contradictions in his vision,
36, 151, 240–41; and the devil's party,
45–46, 213–14, 270, 311; compared to
Samson, 47–48, 61–62, 65, 241, 242,
273–74; genius of, 88, 233, 234; as
philosopher, 147, 149, 232, 300; as a
conservative poet, 149–50, 151; his
politics, 151, 228, 241, 260, 279; personality of, 151; canon of, 162–63, 171;
as allegorist and symbolist, 175–76,
179–80; and Spenser, compared, 179–
80; as visionary, 181; his theory of
accommodation, 181–82; authorial
intrusions of, 183, obscurity of, 186;
aesthetics of, 210, 230; and Dante,
compared, 212–13; and Swedenborg,

compared, 216; intellectual development
of, 217; as Covering Cherub, 218–19,
229, 231; as builder of Jerusalem, 227,
247; as a witness, 228; as an apocalyptic
angel, 257–58, 263. *See also* Blake;
Hayley; *Marriage of Heaven and Hell;
Milton*
—his works: prose, 35, 40, 41, 44, 70,
151, 162, 201, 233, 239, 240, 241, 243,
300, 309; editions of, 70–71, 102–3;
poetry, 151, 163, 167, 216, 233, 240,
300. *See also* titles of individual works
Milton, xviii, 55, 56, 57, 65, 77, 78, 85,
112, 120, 135, 171, 172, 188, 189, 193,
199, 204, 221, 226–27, 231, 236–50,
256, 269, 278, 312, 316; Bard's Song in,
10, 30–31, 35, 196, 237, 267; Milton in,
12, 19, 22–23, 45, 120, 231, 243; Milton's descent in, 16, 31, 37, 44, 119,
237, 315; perspectives in, 18, 19–20, 24,
28, 30, 34, 256, 264; copies of, 18–19,
43, 256, 258, 260, 267–68; relation of
designs to text, 19, 20–21; relation of
designs to the Book of Revelation,
20–21, 22; inscription on plate 50, 23,
264; mental warfare in, 25, 240; sequentiality in, 26, 267; mythology of, 35, 41,
112, 239, 243; epiphany in, 37; Preface
to, 39, 40–41, 232, 239–41, 272, 298,
314; as criticism, 43; as celebration, 43;
as prophecy, 43; analogues for, 44; and
Paradise Regained, compared, 119, 131,
299; the Bard as a witness, 227; Blake's
objectives in, 231–32; symmetry of,
236; theme of, 236; dark conceit in,
236, 237–39; structure of, 236–38,
245–47; Songs of Beulah in, 237; union
in, 237; repetition in, 237; Ololon's
descent in, 237, 269, 315; imagery in,
237–39, 241, 267; apocalypse in, 238;
as psychodrama, 239; relation to *Jerusalem,* 244–45, 283; donning of the sandal
in, 250; sexuality in, 256; date of, 260;
editions of, 260; possible epigraph for,
263; relation to *L'Allegro* and *Il Penseroso,* 299; Rintrah in, 308
—Blake's designs for, 13–48, 237, 256–57,
258–59, 267; pl. 1: 17–18, 19–20,
22–23, 27, 35, 36, 37, 38, 39, 41, 44,
256, 258, 261, 262, 263, 264, 268, 280,

281; pl. 2: 14, 17, 19, 35, 56; pl. 16: 17, 18, 19–20, 22–27, 28, 32, 35, 38, 42, 44, 48, 258, 259, 261, 262–64, 268, 280; pl. 17: 14, 17, 19, 35, 267; pl. 18: 10, 19, 38, 34–35, 45–48; pl. 19: 14, 19, 32, 34, 35, 259–60; pl. 30: 267; pl. 32: 14, 17, 19, 35, 223, 267; pl. 33: 270; pl. 37: 14, 17, 19, 35; pl. 42: 14, 17, 18, 27–33, 34, 35, 39, 42, 43, 44, 48, 256, 259, 266–67, 268–69, 315; pl. 45: 14, 19, 34, 35, 270–71; pl. 46: 14, 19, 35; pl. 50: 35, 241. *See also* Blake; *Comus*

Milton Encyclopedia, xix

Milton Gallery. *See* Fuseli

Miltonic poets, 224, 230

Minnich, Thomas, 312

Mirth, 134, 285. *See also L'Allegro*

mist. *See* symbolism

Mitchell, W. J. T., 49, 53, 98–99, 256, 258, 263, 266, 270, 275, 276

Moloch, 90, 91, 92, 308

Montaigne, Michel de, 231

More, Alexander, 214

More, Henry, 227, 261, 265, 299

Mortimer, John Hamilton, 60–61

Morton, A. L., xvii, 125, 304

Moseley, Humphrey, 7

Moses, 26, 47, 97–98, 105, 143, 177, 228, 239, 257, 260–61, 266

moth. *See* symbolism

movements. *See* symbolism

Muir, William, 260

Murrin, Michael, 184, 185

Nativity Ode, 40, 79, 80, 88–92, 93, 145, 163, 167, 235

Nebuchadnezzar, 193, 203

Nelson, Horatio, 35, 68, 69

Nelson Guiding Leviathan, 68, 280

Neptune, 285

Neve, Philip, 40

New Criticism, xiv, 163–65

Newton, Isaac, 5, 64, 271, 277–78, 316

Newton, Thomas, 72, 104, 105, 109, 210–11, 289

Nietzsche, Friedrich, 161

nightingale. *See* symbolism

nudity. *See* symbolism

Nurmi, Martin, 202

oak. *See* symbolism

ode, 167, 234. *See also Nativity Ode*

Of Prelatical Episcopacy, 301

Of Reformation, 144, 301

Ololon, 14, 19, 24, 28, 29, 34, 37, 232, 237, 246, 247, 266, 269, 270–71, 315. *See also Milton*

Ong, Walter J., 158–59

On Homer's Poetry, 177

Opie, John, 102, 288

oration, 168, 249

orator, 10, 243, 247–48, 255

Orc, 51, 52, 66, 245–46, 316–17; cycle of, 53, 54, 276; state of, 53, 56–57; as revolutionary energy, 245, 246; as Luvah, 246; redemption of, 246, 247; and Christ, 276; and Urizen, 276

Orpheus, 10, 245

Our End is Come, 50

Ovid, 177

ox. *See* symbolism

Oxenden, Henry, 299

Palamabron, 227, 232

Paley, Morton D., 24, 25, 68, 245, 246, 264, 267, 280

palm. *See* symbolism

Palmer, Samuel, 40, 70

Pan, 8, 255

Panofsky, Erwin, 126

Paradise Lost, 9, 18, 38, 40, 43, 57, 87, 102, 104, 106, 107, 112, 117, 126, 127, 130, 133, 140, 144, 162, 164, 165, 168, 169, 177, 181, 191, 205, 210, 213–14, 215, 218, 233, 235, 241, 243, 244, 247, 249, 271, 292, 309, 310, 316; Satan in, 15, 59, 210, 213, 226, 281, 310, 316; prologues to, 47, 226, 239, 248, 271; Sin in, 59; contradictions in, 81, 212, 217, 240–41, 311; theology of, 93–94, 144, 170, 201; Christocentric character of, 94, 97, 273; hero of, 94, 310; allegory in, 94–95, 226, 297; expulsion scene in, 95–97, 287; fortunate fall in, 96–97; suppression of, 133, 298; as composite form, 167–68, 169–70; as epic-prophecy, 169–70, 185, 303; structure of, 169–70, 315; obscurity of, 170; inversion of styles in, 170; as revolutionary epic, 185, 233, 297, 298; rout-

ing of rebel angels in, 211; Christ in,
211, 263; God in, 226, 310, 316; Book
VI, 233, 239, 241, 297, 298; Adam's
education in, 239; Preface to, 240, 249;
and the *Odyssey,* 248; illustrations for,
288; and the Crucifixion, 292, 297–98
—Blake's designs for, 76, 79, 80, 85,
92–97, 111, 114, 145, 238–39, 278,
286, 287, 294
Paradise Regained, 35, 38, 40, 47, 62, 71,
74, 76, 78, 79, 112, 122, 129–44, 151
162, 163, 164, 168, 169, 185, 201, 205,
208, 213, 215, 217, 218, 233, 235, 240,
243, 247, 249, 295, 309–10, 311; denunciation of the classics in, 41, 240;
critical history of, 104–9, 116, 129,
289–90; compared to *Paradise Lost,*
104, 106, 107, 117–18, 129, 290, 294;
theology of, 104, 107, 121–22, 127–28,
273, 289; integrity of, 105–6, 117, 290;
failure of, 107–8; illustrations for, 108,
109–13, 118, 288, 291–92; hero in,
108, 120, 129; and the Bible, 112,
121–22, 123, 296; and the Book of Job,
112, 135, 144, 163; radicalism of, 112,
296, 297, 298; and orthodoxy, 116–17,
125–26, 128, 136, 298; Satan in, 117;
Christ in, 117–18; typology in, 118;
generic characteristics of, 118–19;
descents in, 119–20; epic conventions
in, 119–20; interiority of, 120–21,
130–31; epiphany in, 120–21, 128, 140;
literary analogues for, 122; prologues to,
122, 139; and the *Aeneid,* 125; mythology of, 129, 139–40, 296, 299; as
drama, 144; as modern heroic poem,
144; and *Samson Agonistes,* 290; temptations in, 291–94, 295; strategies in,
295–96; identity motif in, 296; as
mimesis of universal action, 296; and the
Crucifixion, 297–98
—Blake's designs for, 12, 70, 76, 78, 93,
97, 101, 110, 112–15, 116, 118, 120–
21, 129–44, 283, 292, 293–95
Pareus, David, 181
Parker, William Riley, 298
Passion, The, 40, 163
pastoral, 7, 8, 153, 156, 168, 234
Patrick, J. Max, xix
Patrides, C. A., xix, 126, 296, 298

Patterson, Annabel, 173
Paulson, Ronald, 284
Peckham, Morse, 109, 116
Perkins, William, 62, 261, 265
perspectivism, 266. *See also Marriage of
Heaven and Hell; Milton*
Petrarch, Francesco, 230
Petronius, 69–70
Phillips, Edward, 147, 187
Phillips, Michael, 63, 64, 273–74, 289
Piazetta, G. B., 286
Pierce, Frederick, 231–32
Pigne, Nicholas, 7, 110, 254, 285
pillars. *See* symbolism
pipes. *See* symbolism
Pitt, William, 35, 68, 69
Pitt Guiding Behemoth, 280
Poems of Mr. John Milton, 7
Poetical Sketches, 171, 280
poetry: poet's involvement with, 150–51;
and tradition, 152, 224, 240; history of,
158; nativity, 167–68; dream-vision,
168. *See also* prophecy
poets, 172–73, 213; pantheon of, 36, 43;
as amanuenses, 172–73; Orphic, 183–
84; as creators and interpreters, 186; as
poems, 236. *See also* creation; Homeric
poets; Miltonic poets; poetry; prophet
Pointon, Marcia, 34, 35, 60, 86, 114, 279,
285, 286
pomegranate. *See* symbolism
Pope, Alexander, 163
Pope, Elizabeth Marie, 121, 295
portraiture, 9, 12–13, 34, 35, 242–43,
255–56. *See also* Blake; Milton
Potter, J., 265
Poulet, Georges, 238
Pound, Ezra, 224
Powell, Mary, 81
Power, Henry, 301
Praz, Mario, 255
Prolusions, 185
Prometheus, 14, 31, 268, 307
prophecy, 7, 8, 10, 27, 34–35, 38, 65, 66,
90, 159, 172, 199–200, 224–25, 241,
245, 247, 265, 268, 313; tradition of,
11, 42–43, 224, 257, 261, 264–65, 268;
commentators on, 18; language of, 20,
258, 261, 277–78; pictorial, 20–22, 99,
241, 261, 280; of seventeenth century,

21; of Virgin-King, 42–43; of Eagle, 42–43; of Dead-Man, 42–43; form of, 150–51, 169–70, 190; structure of, 168, 169, 190–91, 247; as drama, 170, 183–84; plotlessness of, 179; obscurity of, 188; clarity of, 189; and apocalypse, 192, 193, 308; hallmarks of, 195, 250; voices of, 197; as new revelation, 225; interconnectedness of, 225; spirit of, 226–27; as allegory, 245; subversive character of, 258; themes of, 264; muse of, 264; as creation and criticism, 304. *See also* Bible, Revelation

prophet, 9, 12, 31, 35, 150–51, 170, 177, 178, 182, 197, 205, 213, 223, 228, 241, 247, 257; and sonship, 11, 18, 150, 225; as a revolutionary, 42; true and false, 42, 66, 199, 201, 207–8, 216, 223, 226; as a visionary, 151; task of, 190; as creator and interpreter, 225, 226; the making of, 243; company of, 246–47; emblems of, 254, 255. *See also* Bible, Revelation; Blake; Milton

Pro Populo Anglicano Defensio, 10, 25, 45, 51

Pro Se Defensio, 242

Public Address, 148

pyramid. *See* symbolism

rain. *See* symbolism

rainbow. *See* symbolism

Raine, Kathleen, xiv, xv, 49, 275

Rainolds, John, 10, 271

Rajan, Balachandra, 280

Reason of Church-Government, The, 52, 134, 141, 144, 149, 154, 165, 166, 172, 202, 203, 206–7, 218, 241–42, 301

redemption, 23, 41, 46, 47, 65, 109–10, 125, 244, 249, 262, 263

Reeves, Marjorie, 257

regeneration, 30, 32–33, 48, 245

resurrection, 27, 31, 41, 62–63, 84, 110, 227–28, 244, 261, 263, 297, 299

revolution, xvii, 48, 57–58, 160, 171–88, 194, 197, 284

Revolution, American, 50

Revolution, French, 57, 191

Revolution, Puritan, 40, 46, 47, 300

Richardson, Jonathan, Sr., 8, 254

Riches, T. H., 113

Richmond, Hugh M., 317

Rickword, Edgell, 300

Rieger, James, 230

Rigaud, Stephen, 86, 285

Rimmon, 197, 309

Rinnah, 309

Rintrah, 194, 195, 196–97, 198, 205, 227, 232, 308–9. *See also Marriage of Heaven and Hell; Milton*

roaring. *See* symbolism

Roberts, Donald A., 311

Roberts, J., 86

Robinson, Henry Crabb, 40, 70, 177, 280–81

rock. *See* symbolism

romance, 168, 178, 179

Rome, 159

Romney, George, 34, 296, 271, 285

root. *See* symbolism

Rose, Edward J., xix, 53, 60, 102, 112, 272, 273, 274, 305, 307

Rosenblum, Robert, 45

Ross, Alexander, 10, 255

Rossetti, William Michael, 113–14, 253

Rougement, Denis de, 310

Runciman, Alexander, 285

Rust, George, 126

St. Paul, 193–94

Salmasius, 44, 45, 214

Samson, 45, 46–47, 57–58, 60, 66, 241, 242, 273–74, 275, 278; as hero, 47, 51; as revolutionary, 47–48, 274, 279; as Orc figure, 51, 52, 66; meanings of his story, 52; as liberator, 52, 61; Blake's portrayals of, 52, 275–76; and Christ, compared, 62–63; and Job, compared, 67; and Pharaoh, 277; in *Samson Agonistes,* 278; in Old Testament, 278; Milton's attitude toward, 279; Blake's attitude toward, 279; in Revelation commentary, 280. *See also* Blake; Milton; *Samson; Samson Agonistes*

Samson, 63, 64, 275, 280

Samson Agonistes, 4, 47–48, 50–51, 52, 57–58, 64, 140, 162, 168, 274, 278; as drama of regeneration, 50, 61, 164; as tragedy, 50–51, 63, 64, 162, 164–65; as historical allegory, 51, 61, 275; as autobiographical poem, 51, 61, 275; criticism of, 51, 62, 63, 289; in relation to *Paradise Regained,* 51, 62, 140; date of, 51, 62, 275; illustrators of, 60–61, 279; Chorus in, 65; as false apocalypse, 162–63; composition of, 164; its literary context, 164; its biblical context, 164; revisionist interpretation of, 275

Samuel, Irene, xix, 52, 275, 296

sand. *See* symbolism

sandals. *See* symbolism

Sandler, Florence, 14

Sandys, George, 91

Satan, 16, 29, 46, 47, 52, 60, 67, 68, 69, 87, 92, 94–95, 130, 201, 211, 269, 278, 281, 293, 299, 310; spectre of, 28–29; state of, 57, 278; attributes of, 118; as fallen prophet, 176; as God's ape, 226; history of, 281–82

Satan in His Original Glory, 278

Satanism, 6, 310. *See also Marriage of Heaven and Hell*

Satanist controversy, 282

satire, 306–7. *See also Marriage of Heaven and Hell*

Saurat, Denis, 221, 297

Schiller, Gertrud, 26

Schorer, Mark, 315

Schultz, Howard, 129, 298

Sealts, Merton, xix

self-annihilation, 12, 20, 23, 58, 63, 66, 67, 119, 244–45, 246, 247, 263, 265

selfhood, 22, 65, 67, 131, 247, 263, 265, 266

self-love, 15, 273, 278

sepulchral figures. *See* symbolism

serpent. *See* symbolism

Seven Angels of the Presence. *See* symbolism

Seven Eyes of God. *See* symbolism

Seward, Mr., 77

sexuality, 81, 83, 256

Shakespeare, William, xiv, 15, 50, 59, 103, 157, 164, 213, 222, 240, 257, 264

Shawcross, John T., 168, 169, 273, 284, 315

Shelley, Percy Bysshe, xiii, xiv, xv, 73, 128, 147, 164, 167, 169, 212–13, 217, 222, 290, 300, 303, 307, 310

Shelley, S., 86

Shipton, Mother, 42

Sidney, Sir Philip, 168

Simmons, Robert, 53

Sistine Chapel, 97–98, 132

Skinner, Charles M., 299

slavery, 151, 162, 222, 234, 277

sleet. *See* symbolism

Smirke, Robert, 86, 285

Smith, John, 11, 223, 313

smoke. *See* symbolism

Songs of Innocence and of Experience, 10, 91–92, 134, 191, 307

sonnet, 168

Sonnet 16, 19–20

Sonnet 23, 269

Sophocles, 249

Southey, Robert, 314

spectre, 278

Spencer, T. J. B., 306

Spenser, Edmund, 153, 157, 164, 168, 175, 176, 177, 178–80, 186, 222, 253, 254, 269, 293, 316

Stahl, Harvey, 258

star. *See* symbolism

states: and individuals, 29, 30, 237, 266

Steadman, John M., xix, 36

Stevens, Wallace, 224

Stoneburner, Tony, 308

Stothard, Thomas, 60, 275–76, 279

sun. *See* symbolism

Svendsen, Kester, 96

Swedenberg, H. T., 230, 314

Swedenborg, Emanuel, 12, 15, 16, 23, 24, 25, 26, 32, 48, 191, 193, 194, 196, 198, 200–201, 205, 255, 258, 262, 264

symbolism: of harp, 5, 6, 8, 10–11, 35, 246, 255, 271; of apple, 6, 7–8; of serpent, 6, 7–8, 9, 56–57, 87, 95, 294; of bay (laurel), 6, 8, 9, 254, 255; of pipes, 6, 8, 10, 11, 255; of palm, 6, 8, 10, 11–12, 141–43, 255, 299; of oak, 6, 8, 12, 141–43, 254; of collar, 6, 9–10, 255; of garments, 6, 11, 13, 17–18, 22–27, 36, 39, 42, 135–36, 228, 256, 259, 261, 262–63, 264–65; of hair, 6, 20, 48, 52, 55, 59, 256, 262, 274, 276, 278; of flames, 8, 13, 18, 20, 22, 36; of pomegranate, 8, 197; of trumpet, 8, 267; of mantle, 11, 27, 35; of lamp, 11, 316; of clouds, 13, 17–18, 19–20, 22, 24, 27, 36–37, 55, 56, 57, 64, 87, 258,

261, 263, 264, 277–78, 295, 309; of
nudity, 13, 36, 256, 298; of star, 13–18,
223, 256, 264, 271; of eagle, 14, 17, 18,
29, 30–33, 35, 42, 43, 150–51, 268–69;
of comet, 14–15, 19, 59; of wormwood,
15; of feet, 17; of hand, 17, 18, 113,
256, 264, 278, 280; of gesture, 17, 18,
113, 256, 264, 280; of rainbow, 17, 30,
85; of sun, 18, 26–27, 55, 85, 263–64,
265, 266, 278; of halo, 18, 27, 263,
295; of smoke, 20, 22, 262; of crosshatching, 20, 24, 38–39, 41, 56; of
girdle, 23, 27, 263; of linen, 24, 264; of
couch, 28–30; of Seven Angels of the
Presence, 29, 226–27; of rock, 30; of
linear net, 30, 38–39; of gold, 30, 262–
63; of vine, 32; of sandals, 43, 250, 265;
of moth, 49, 54, 55, 56–57, 59–60, 64,
278; of chrysalis, 49, 56–57, 64; of bat
wings, 55, 56–57, 59, 60, 67, 270, 278,
279; of caterpillar, 56; of rain, 56, 57,
277–78; of worm, 56–57, 60; of dance,
57–58; of sand, 64–65; of pillars, 67; of
dragon, 83; of key, 83; of haemony, 83;
of root, 83; of mist, 85, 87, 262; of ox,
89; of ass, 89; of thorns, 95, 96–97; of
thunderbolts, 95, 133; of movements,
97; of crown, 123–24, 294; of vegetation, 142; of architecture, 143; of cave,
150; of lion, 150–51; of roaring, 196–
97, 308–9; of chariot, 197; of Seven
Eyes of God, 227; of nightingale, 237;
of lark, 237, 268; of circle, 237–39,
315; of bow, 242; of door, 244–45; of
horns, 246; of timbrels, 246; of garland,
253, 271; of ivy, 254; of severed head,
259–60; of "back parts," 261; of
sepulchral figures, 267; of pyramid, 269;
of baldness, 274; of sleet, 277; of hail,
277–78
Symmons, Charles, 107
Symons, Arthur, xiii

Tannenbaum, Leslie, xix, 259, 269
Tasso, Torquato, 71–72, 111, 166, 167,
173, 180, 186, 290, 303
Tayler, Edward, xix
Tayler, Irene, 9, 44, 80, 81, 82, 84, 85,
87, 98, 253, 281, 284
Taylor, C., 285

Taylor, Clyde, 282
Taylor, Thomas, 254, 271, 273
Taylor, Thomas, Platonist, 175
temptations: tradition of, 294, 295. *See
also Paradise Regained*
Tetrachordon, 210
Tharmas, 59, 246
Theseus, 213
Thomson, James, 257
thorns. *See* symbolism
Thorpe, James, 101
Three Ages of the World, 125
Three Classes of Men, 196, 197, 205, 308
Thrupp, Frederick, 299
thunderbolts. *See* symbolism
Tillyard, E. M. W., 185, 305
timbrels. *See* symbolism
Tiriel, 78
Todd, Henry John, 70, 82–83, 106–7,
109, 290
Toland, John, 133, 188
Tolley, Michael J., 90, 266, 267, 268, 270,
276
Tonson, Jacob, 8
tradition, 150–51, 157, 254, 260. *See also*
poetry; prophecy
tragedy, 156, 165, 168, 234
Trapp, J. B., 109
trumpet. *See* symbolism
Trusler, John, 188
Truswell, Mr., 42, 62
typology, 109–10, 111–13, 118, 145,
292, 295, 297

Urizen, 24, 28, 38, 45, 46, 47, 48, 53, 56,
60, 100, 135, 143, 196, 242, 246, 247,
258, 259–60, 262, 270, 276, 277
Urizen, The Book of, 53, 135
Uwins, Thomas, 286

Vala. See The Four Zoas
vegetation. *See* symbolism
Veneziano, Paolo, 293
Vergil, 7, 43, 71, 98, 125, 157, 159, 165,
168, 176, 177, 223, 233, 234, 241, 248,
249, 258, 269, 271, 303
versification, 247
Vertue, George, 6, 254
Vinaver, Eugene, 305
vine. *See* symbolism

virginity, 247. *See also* chastity
Vision of the Last Judgment, A, 49–50,
    98, 174, 187, 256, 263, 266
Visions of the Daughters of Albion, 31
Vogler, Thomas, 305
vortex, 26, 29

Wagenknecht, David, 312
Warburton, William, 104–5, 119–20, 289
Wardle, Judith, 314
warfare, 27, 46, 58, 64, 66, 136, 240–41,
    298. *See also Milton; Paradise Lost*
Wark, Robert R., 253–54
Warner, Janet, 30, 58, 60, 266, 276, 278,
    280
Warton, Joseph, 103
Warton, Thomas, 70, 91, 103
Wasserman, Earl R., xiii, xiv, 73
Webber, Joan, xix, 158, 302–3
Weitzmann, Kurt, 81, 82, 99, 102
Wells, William, 253
Wesley, John, 227
West, Mr., 280
West, Mrs., 67
West, Robert, 149
Westall, Richard, 34, 60, 86, 90–91, 269,
    279, 285, 286

White, T. Holt, 262
Whitefield, George, 227
Whitehead, Alfred North, 149
Whitman, Walt, 222
Whittick, Arnold, 11
Wicksteed, Joseph, 148
Wildberger, H., 304
Wilkes, John, 279
Wilkie, Brian, 315
Williams, Kathleen, xx, 183–84
Wills, James T., 294–95
Wilson, Mona, 277, 283, 287
Wordsworth, William, 44, 166–67, 217,
    289
worm. *See* symbolism
wormwood. *See* symbolism
Wright, Joseph, 86
Wright, Thomas, 283

Yeats, William Butler, xiv, xv–xvi, 152,
    157, 200, 222, 301
Young, Edward, 55, 71, 223

Zerubbabel, 228
Zeus, 246, 268, 316–17
Zoas, 30, 246, 287

DESIGNED BY EDGAR J. FRANK
COMPOSED BY THE COMPOSING ROOM, GRAND RAPIDS, MICHIGAN
MANUFACTURED BY THOMSON-SHORE, INC., DEXTER, MICHIGAN
TEXT IS SET IN ALDINE ROMAN, DISPLAY LINES IN CASLON AND ENGLISH

Library of Congress Cataloging in Publication Data

Wittreich, Joseph Anthony.
Angel of Apocalypse.

Includes bibliographical references and index.
1. Blake, William, 1757-1827—Criticism and interpretation.
2. Milton, John, 1608-1674—Influence—Blake.
3. Milton, John, 1608-1674—Iconography. I. Title.
PR4147.W53   821'.7   74-27316
ISBN 0-299-06800-5